DIST

"Journeys are integral to all our lives. They present testing challenges, moments of exquisite reward and insight, and times when you are racked by self-doubt and problems.

Battling it out involves confronting fears, making yourself vulnerable, aiming for something worthy and clinging onto self-belief and passion even when it seems that everything is stacked against you.

In the end a journey invariably offers us a chance to learn and grow and reach out for our dreams. I am still amazed at how things seem to work out in the most unlikely ways; it's as if you just have to be willing to give it a go. There is always something new to be discovered, something waiting to surprise us around the next corner."

Tim Cope
Australian Geographic Adventurer of the Year 2006

To Dom,
With my best

Copyright © Sam H. N. Manicom 2008

Sam Manicom has asserted his right to be identified as the Author of this work in accordance with the Copyright, Designs and Patents Act 1988.

A CIP catalogue record for this title is available from the British Library.

ISBN 978-0-9556573-2-0

Edited by Paul Blezard
Cover design by Fil Schiannini
Page layout by Fil Schiannini
Proof read by Nikki Madan-Schiannini
Photos by Sam Manicom and Birgit Schuenemann
Line art by Sam Manicom and Jez Cooper
Published by Sam Manicom
Although every effort has been made to trace the present copyright holders, we apologise in advance for any unintentional omission or neglect and will be pleased to insert appropriate acknowledgement to individuals in any subsequent edition of this publication.

Distant Suns Reviews

"Drama, action, passion, disaster, and the pure adrenaline buzz of overlanding are all here in Sam Manicom's vibrant third book. He has a gift to describe people and places"

Overland Magazine

"He writes engagingly, and in the classic style of the travel writer, with a marked ability to draw out the salient features of a scene and place them centre-stage."

Visor Down

"Distant Suns doesn't just document the journey, Sam also describes cultural differences, traditions and lifestyles of the various countries they cross, whilst painting a vivid picture of the terrain they cross... A really great read that'll doubtless give you itchy feet..."

TBM - Trail Bike Magazine

"The book is a fascinating glimpse into people, places and ways of life that are changing and adapting to our modern world. ... Few travel writers can conjure up sights and smells so provocatively as Sam."

Daily Record - Scotland

"Author Manicom and his companion are the real thing..."

RiDE Magazine

"It's been a pleasure to read as it makes me feel as if I'm there seeing the people and landscape that Sam describes. He has a gift for painting pictures with words, which is rare amongst long-distance riders... In summary, a damn good read, not to be missed."

BMW Club Journal

"Once again, a superbly entertaining piece of travel writing..."

BM Riders

"This is a great story which reads with the ease of a novel. Distant Suns has it all: love, good guys, bad guys, beauty, danger, history, geography and last but not least-bikes! Distant Suns is a fast, easy and thoroughly enjoyable read."...

webbikeworld

"So is it any good? Had Sam peaked with his last two books? Not a chance. In fact it's better. I didn't have to but I pretty much read it straight through from start to finish."

Honda Trail Riders

"Distant Suns could easily be Manicom's best book yet! I was riveted right from the very beginning and enjoyed every minute. Unlike his previous books, Sam travels with a companion, Birgit, who we met during the course of his previous book 'Under Asian Skies'. Birgit caught my attention right away with her incredible initiative and capability with her bike..."

canyonchasers.com

Foreword

Drama, action, passion, disaster, and the pure adrenaline buzz of overlanding are all here in Sam Manicom's third adventure motorcycle travel book.

Sam originally intended to spend a year riding the length of Africa but this evolved into an eight year, 200,000 mile journey around the world. His books *Into Africa* and *Under Asian Skies* covered his first four years of phenomenal travelling experiences; powerful enough to make him want to keep on exploring, despite disasters that would have seen many people pack up and head for home. The fact that he's still in one piece is a testament to his approach to life.

Distant Suns takes you on a three year voyage of discovery through Southern Africa and South America. This time Sam rides and shares the adventures with someone special, the brave and indefatigable Birgit. The two of them have an endless fascination with the world and though their life experience is very different, they compliment each other perfectly and the adventures just keep on happening.

This was a time before most travellers had even heard of global positioning satellites or "SatNav". A good map made the difference between a fun, successful journey, and a nightmare of dead ends to nowhere.

It was a time before emails had become the norm, when remote towns had no internet cafés and when telephone systems were totally unreliable in many Third World countries. Businesses had to rely on the antiquated telex, unreliable faxes, or CB radio to keep in touch. If you wanted to make a call you'd have to go to the telephone exchange in the city, book a call and wait until a cubicle became free. Then you prayed that the connection was still there... A lot of calls never got through at all.

This was the spring of 1996. It's really not so long ago, but times were changing. You could no longer go to sleep listening to native drums passing messages between villages and mobile phones were the coming thing. In fact by 1998 mobile phones had become such a status symbol in Chile, that over one third of those apparently in 'use' were really dummies. It was cool to be seen with one, to appear to be connected. The mobile was the poor man's Porsche.

Sam's richly evocative writing opens up a world where people travel their own fragile, unsupported paths and his acute and quirky observations transport you to their universe. His descriptions illuminate the darker times like shafts of sunlight, and suck you right into the scene. *Distant Suns* will grab you, enthral you, shock you, make you laugh, and might just spit you out as a convert to the dream of overlanding by motorcycle. Promise.

Paul Blezard
Editor

Contents

*'May the sun shine all day long, everything go right and nothing wrong.
May those you love bring love back to you, and may all the wishes you
wish come true!'*

Irish blessing for travellers

Acknowledgements		p7
Authors Note		p10
Chapter 1	A fast woman	p12
Chapter 2	Death of a hermit	p27
Chapter 3	Did I kill it?	p58
Chapter 4	When the world holds its breath	p76
Chapter 5	Marco Polo	p100
Chapter 6	Land of silver	p106
Chapter 7	An angry wind	p124
Chapter 8	Olga the shot putter	p148
Chapter 9	Two formidable women	p174
Chapter 10	The 'longest motorable road' in a small world	p184
Chapter 11	Valley of the moon	p205
Chapter 12	A living epic	p212
Chapter 13	A dream and the unknown	p235
Chapter 14	Hotel Casanova	p256
Chapter 15	Chaos and loving it	p276
Chapter 16	The gauchos are in town!	p303
Chapter 17	Ice-cold Balboa	p331
Chapter 18	A hard day's night	p339
3D Jigsaw Puzzle		p352
Adventue Travel Listing		p360

Acknowledgements

'Success is not the key to happiness. Happiness is the key to success.
If you love what you are doing, you will be successful.'

Albert Schweitzer

The first person I need to thank is, without doubt, my partner Birgit. There were times when she must have wondered what on earth she was doing in the desert or the mountains, riding a motorcycle, with me. Travelling with me required the ability to think positively and very optimistically.

Birgit stopped me from turning into a travelling hermit and together we shared some of the most beautiful sights in the world. My journey was a far richer thing as a result of our travelling together – she assures me that she had a pretty good time too!

She is one of the most resourceful and courageous people I have ever met, and she writes a really full diary. *Distant Suns* is based on her diaries.

Without her this book would never have been written – it's not often that your partner will come home saying, "I've jacked in the day job and I'm going to write another book."

Paul Blezard has very kindly edited *Distant Suns* and has made the difference by being precise, pedantic and extremely encouraging. He is one of the most critical people I know, in the nicest possible way, and without his ability to combine that with his endless positive enthusiasm, this book would have been a far lesser thing.

I'm delighted that Fil Schiannini has been on hand to work his magic with the book cover, layout and proof reading of the manuscript. His skills are something that we readers of books just take for granted when it's done well, but when it's not…

I also need to thank Nikki Madan-Schiannini for doing the final proof read for me. Not a lot gets past her eagle eyes! I'd be lost without friends such as these – thanks guys!

I must thank all the doctors, nurses and physiotherapists I met along the way, but you'll need to read on to find out why!

I'd like to thank my parents for bringing me up with my eyes wide open to the possibilities of the world, and for giving me an education that would allow me to get out into it. A big thanks also goes to my sister Rachel and her husband Graham, who helped by storing equipment and sending it out to us whenever we needed it.

Thank you also to Bob Porecha who used his great knowledge of BMW bikes to diagnose problems for us over the phone when we got into trouble with the bikes. He also then kindly organised spare parts to be sent out to us. Some of our adventures could have been dire without him.

When an author decides to go down the self-publishing track there is a very good chance that he/she will fall flat on their face. It's a tricky trail to ride and the time and financial investment are significant – that's why there are big publishing firms who do the above tasks, and the marketing and promotional work. Financial backing, experts, experience and connections make all the difference. I have full respect for them, but ever since I was told that my first book was liked but wouldn't sell because I'm 'not a media personality' I've been even more determined to make my books succeed. The people who have agreed to advertise in *Distant Suns* are all people who believe in helping to make adventure come alive, and in my books. They have helped me to cover some of the costs of publishing and promoting the book. I'm very grateful.

A note of thanks here too, to the people I have quoted in *Distant Suns*. Your words have helped to open up the world of travel. Paul Theroux's writing in particular has been inspiring people since the late sixties.

I also wish to thank the people, publications and organisations that have published reviews of *Into Africa* and *Under Asian Skies*. I very much value the time and the space you have given me. I am really glad that your attitude towards me when I've been knocking at your door has been encouraging. Thank you.

We were extremely fortunate to be partly sponsored by Avon Tyres, DHL, Hein Gericke, Balino, Cadec and Lindeman Engineering.

The trip was a finer thing because of their help, and in particular, the way in which they helped us. The key issue was that they expected us to repay their sponsorship with advertising, but did not put any time pressures on us. We have managed to ride away from our adventure having done just that, without deadening, altering negatively or making mercenary, any part of the journey. Thank you guys – your kit and your assistance were great.

Finally, I would like to thank all the people we met out on the road. I've changed some of your names, either to protect you or because I have no wish to embarrass you. Thank you for opening your homes to us, for sharing your lives with us, for sharing your adventures with us and for putting up with my lousy Spanish!

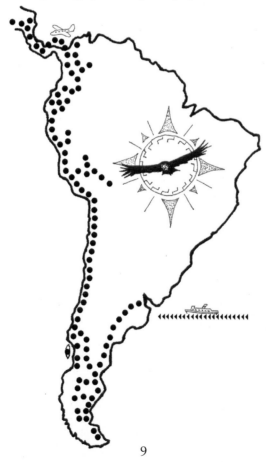

Authors note

Suddenly I was in a position where there really was nothing to stop me setting out to have adventures on a motorcycle, but I did try to find excuses not to go; after all, the dream to ride the length of Africa wasn't ordinary, even if I was. One day, when I was thinking about where my life was going and what I was doing with it, I had an inspirational thought. I suddenly realised that if I put my mind to it I could actually do anything I wanted. At that moment this was an awesome feeling. It was time to do something completely different. There really wasn't a reason why I shouldn't.

About two thirds of the way down amazing Africa I realised that in spite of the ridiculous number of times I fell off the bike (no surprise as I'd only been riding a bike for three months by the time I'd reached the Sahara), and regardless of being arrested three times, in jail once, shot at twice, nearly having died from malaria, and a seventeen-bone fracture prang in the desert in Namibia, I was thoroughly enjoying adventuring on a motorcycle. The freedom the bike gave me was phenomenal and the adventures she got me into never stopped rolling. I was loving it, and I wanted more! Could I keep going? Was there any good reason to stop?

I could and there wasn't, and after the next three years adventuring across the Antipodes, Asia and the Middle East, I was even hungrier for more. South America was the new dream, and when I realised that I could scrape enough money together to keep going, the adventure continued to roll. When my guardian angel was there for us, the journey was a combination of laughter, adrenaline burning fun and pure awe.

I see myself as a pretty ordinary bloke and when I set off to travel I'd no intention to write a book, or even books. I was out to have an adventure. I wanted to see some of our world, and I couldn't think of a better way to do it than on a bike. When I sat down to write my first book, *Into Africa*, it all felt a bit of a cheek. I wasn't sure what made me think I should try this new type of adventure, but the itch to tell the story came from people I've met over the past years. Many said to me, 'You're incredibly lucky to have been able to travel the world, I wish I could'. At first when people said that I blindly thought, 'if I can so can you'. I believed that people generally have the ability to make their lives head in the direction they wish; I couldn't have been more wrong.

I learnt from the people I met on the road that we don't all have the ability to make dreams a reality. However, we can make high points happen and we should value them for what they are. We can also taste and develop our dreams through the adventures of others. Where would we all be without dreams?

Distant Suns is written for those of you fortunate enough to know that you can go out and live the dream. Value that, and just do it; go and travel – you'll never regret it.

This book is also written for those who love the sound of travel but are quite happy with adventure from the pages. We also love to be able to escape into a world of adventure and foreign lands from the comfort of our armchairs at the end of a working day. I hope you will enjoy the stunning, the beautiful, and the surprises.

Distant Suns is very much written for those of you who are tied down by responsibilities. The reality is that there are many who may never get the chance to travel a long road, but don't stop dreaming. You never know what opportunities tomorrow will bring. In the mean time I hope that you will enjoy travelling with us through some of this amazing world.

I want to end my note by thanking you the reader. Without the

  feedback that you have written in to us about my first books, I would not have had the courage to write this one. I've quite an amazing feeling as I'm typing that. Just three years ago, as I published *Into Africa* and was wondering if I was about to fall flat on my face, I'd no idea that I would be publishing a third book now. You have allowed me to share the fun. Thank you.

Chapter 1

'A fast woman'

*'Life is not a journey to the grave with the intention of arriving safely in a
pretty and well-preserved body, but rather to skid in broadside, thoroughly
used up and proclaiming "Wow what a ride!"*

Bill McKenna

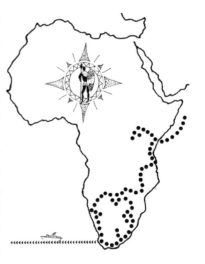

We reached the last section of the tarmac just as the sun dipped blood-red below the silhouetted line of densely packed palm forest. As it did so, the sky started its rapid change from flaming orange into a deep midnight blue.

This far south from the city of Mombassa, the sky was clear and quite unadulterated by man-made light. The lack of city pollution and wood-smoke from cooking fires meant that everything around us was sharp-edged. The clear midnight blue was only broken by spangles of brilliantly white stars.

But the dirt road in front of us disappeared into the dangerously dark shadows under the trees. There was just enough light left in the sky to be able to see that within a few metres, the gravel changed into patches of soft sand and rutted potholes. The cicadas were in full song in a warm slightly dank air that was scented with just a hint of tangy sea breeze. Beneath me, my bike engine ticked over calmly as it waited patiently to be told what to do next.

This was the first time that I would have ridden a dirt road in the dark for nearly four years, and back then I'd vowed never to attempt it again. Motorcycle headlights may be sufficient for road usage but are pathetically useless for dealing with horribly unpredictable backcountry tracks.

Birgit fidgeted nervously on her bike beside me. This was the first time she'd ridden at night, it was her first day of riding in Africa and the dirt track in front of us would be the first she had ever ridden.

In a way I was glad that it was dark. I could see enough of the track to be able to tell that it was going to be one of the worst I'd ever been on – perhaps it was better that Birgit couldn't see how bad it was. But she could see enough to know that what was coming next was not what she had hoped for on her first day in Africa. We should have changed our plans at that moment, but it had been a long, action-packed day and we had allowed ourselves to become too tired and too wired with the joy of being free, to be able to make sensible decisions. Our minds were set on pitching camp under palm trees on a white sandy beach, and to waking up in the morning to a view of warm turquoise sea.

We'd arrived in Kenya just a week earlier. We'd flown into Nairobi on a Kuwait Airlines plane and had had the wonderful experience of sitting next to an Arab dressed in full robes. The man oozed regal power – I wondered who he was. A sheik perhaps? We'd chatted briefly. He was a businessman, in oil of course, and as the flight had come towards its end, he'd leant over and given us a bottle of Chivas Regal. "Enjoy this," he'd said. "I hope you have many wonderful adventures."

This was totally unexpected and Birgit and I rummaged around to try to find something to give him in return. All we could manage was a rather rumpled bag of boiled sweets. Though there was no comparison in the value of the gifts, he seemed pleased that we had reciprocated. He gave us a brief smile and a small nod of his robed head before turning away from us, his mind obviously on what would come next in his life.

From Nairobi we'd caught a bus down to the port of Mombassa. We'd arranged for our bikes to be shipped there. Neither of us had been to the city before and we had no idea where the docks were. Nor did we know exactly what hoops we would have to jump through to get our bikes out of customs.

The beginning of this voyage of discovery was the attempt to find somewhere to stay that had off road parking for our two bikes,

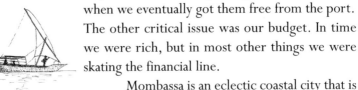

when we eventually got them free from the port. The other critical issue was our budget. In time we were rich, but in most other things we were skating the financial line.

Mombassa is an eclectic coastal city that is almost a microcosmic, living history lesson. In its time it has been controlled by many cultures and each has left its mark on both the buildings and the people. Broad black-faced Bantu people mix with Asian-featured men and women, and with those who are obviously descendants of those white-skinned nations who have filled their moment in the city's history. Elderly British colonial-era houses, shops and factories stand next to Arab mosques and markets. A rugged castle with thick, stone walls looks out along the palm tree-lined coast. It looks down across the old docks where dhows set their triangular sails as they ease away from the jetties on voyages as far away as Arabia, but more often to go fishing or to trade up and down the coastline.

The air is so full of scents that it's worth taking the time to just sit and breathe it in. Spices, roasting goat meat, maize cobs cooking on braziers, baking bread, the sea, fresh fish, roasting red-skinned peanuts, and coconut oil all mingle with the heavy scents of petrol and diesel engines in an atmosphere that's also filled with full-on African city noises.

Trucks, buses and taxis battle their way through frequently potholed streets that are lined with stalls or crowded with the pushing rush of humanity – which pushes and rushes at a particularly African speed. The language of the coast is Swahili – an audible sign of the city's history. It's made up of snippets of each of those former controlling cultures. 'Hakuna matata' means 'No worries' and that describes the pace at which those on foot move through the streets. In spite of the sea breeze that does manage to sneak through the old city into the new, it's too hot for anything to move at any great speed. Above the roar of ancient buses and trucks, the sounds of horns bounce off the walls to briefly dominate before being lost in the mash of life on the street.

In the midst of all of this, the only hotel we could find with any vacancies that didn't involve payment with arms or legs, was perched on top of a row of shops. It didn't have any off road parking. We'd stared enviously at the 5 star tourist hotels with their wide sweeping drives and smartly-clad security men, but had been glad to have found anywhere at all.

The first question to ask after, "Any space?" and "How much?", is "Do you have showers?" Being a little cynical and having stayed in places where the best you get is a trickle of water at odd times of day, I wanted to see the showers. They were stunning. Everything gleamed. I should have smelt a rat, but we soon learned a lesson. When we had settled in and unpacked, Birgit headed off for a shower, only to find that there wasn't any water!

We had asked to see the showers, but foolishly failed to check that they actually worked! But, it's amazing how clean you can get with a bucket of water and a scoop, and the bonus of the hotel was that it had a flat roof – we could go up there to hang clothes to dry, and to cook.

Cooking the bulk of our food for ourselves worked really well. We loved hitting the markets to bargain for food and I'd discovered a side to Birgit that I didn't know was there. She would make an excellent poker player and she always had the market 'mamas' wondering just how far they could go with trying to get us to pay 'tourist price' for things. We played a double act, with me throwing into the bargaining the twenty odd phrases of Swahili I'd picked up on my first journey through Africa, and with Birgit playing the tough guy: "Don't take me for a fool, I'm not paying that much!". We came away with some absolute bargains, though I'm sure we still paid more than the locals would have done.

If you enjoy fresh food and spices, Mombassa is the home of taste bud delight. We breakfasted every day on papaya. They were so ready to eat, sweet and juicy, that once started you just had to finish these great pink-fleshed yellow-skinned torpedoes. The stew that gets served with the staple stodge of boiled or steamed maize meal tended to be rich with subtle hints of exotic spices. The corn-on-the-cobs that men would grill over braziers by the roadside were always offered with a slice of lime, and a brown paper twist of a tangy paprika-red spice mixture that really got the taste buds zinging. There were mandazi, and samosas, and goat curry, and so the list goes on. For an African city, Mombassa was pleasant to spend time in, and that was just as well because it took us a whole week to negotiate our bikes out of the harbour.

It wasn't a disastrous chore though. It was a manageable and delightful time, during which we met some great characters, and had some of our subconscious superiority astounded out of us.

The main port is one of the biggest on the east coast of Africa, and as such it's the start of many things. Imports bound for the whole of Kenya and Uganda begin their journeys through Africa here. The port is massive and it's run on red tape, in the true sense of the phrase. The red tape is left over from colonial days and the systems still functioned amazingly well. Tidy offices were lined with great red bound tomes and ledgers – computers were in the first weeks of being introduced. Utilitarian and very battered but still completely functional furniture filled the floor spaces. The flooring itself was inevitably a cracked and peeling lino, but so clean that if someone told you that you had to eat your food off it, you'd feel able to risk it. Giant derricks lined the wharfs, and port trucks, vans and buses scuttled their way busily around.

Another thing that's left over from colonial days is the name of the country itself, but Kenya was a mistake! The story is told that two early explorers of the region were being shown around the area beneath Mount Kenya, which is Africa's second highest peak. They asked their guide what it was called and their guide, who was carrying a gourd, thought that the explorers meant to ask the local word for a gourd. He replied, "This is called Kii-nyaa." I wondered how many other things had been lost in translation and cultural difference along the way....

Our adventure began at the gates of the port. We'd taken a short ride in a matatu (local mini bus) from the city centre down to the port. The matatu stopped right outside the port and we approached the gates to join an orderly file of people who were moving purposefully forward, but with good manners. We'd already arranged the paperwork we'd need to get into the port with the kind assistance of one of the shipping agents. He hadn't seemed fazed by the fact that all we wanted was his advice, and wanted to clear the bikes ourselves. I just hoped that it wasn't going to take us anything like as long as the six weeks I'd been stuck doing this same thing in Madras.

Our passes worked a treat, our passports were examined and our shipping documents were inspected. Once we'd established that we had a right and a reason to be there, the guards were quite happy to point out where we had to go. If you don't have a port authority car or van to use, then the port bus is vital. The docks are so big it would take an age to walk from one side to the other, and trying to do business would have been a very time-consuming chore – well, more time-consuming than we knew it was going to be anyway. The port is made up of miles of jetty, where ships with flags from all over the world were moored. Some were tired old rust-buckets that looked as if they had no right to be afloat, but some were gleaming and monstrous container ships whose crisp black and white hulls, and tidy, multi-storey, multi-coloured stacks of containers added another air of order to the surprisingly tidy docks.

For some reason I'd expected the port to be like an overgrown African town. But no, rubbish didn't blow from every corner, the barbed wire didn't look as if its purpose was to dry carrier bags and people moved through the wide areas between the warehouses as if they had a job that had to be got on with as quickly as possible.

To our surprise, the bus was boarded by people who'd stood calmly in a queue. On board the bus, men even stood up to let women sit down if there were no vacant seats. This was a total contrast to the tense moments of scrum that were involved with getting into a matatu in the city. It was almost as if we'd stepped into a different world.

A man near us struck up a conversation. "Which area are you looking for? Do you know where to go?" What a great start, and this was to be the way of the coming days, but we did move slowly through the red tape.

Getting the right forms was the first task, and then making sure that we'd correctly filled in the only copies we'd been given was the next. By day five we knew we were getting close. We had to be. It was a Friday and we were faced with the port offices being closed over the weekend, and the Monday was a holiday.

What was now giving us some real pressure to get moving was that we'd discovered that if we didn't get the bikes released within the five days then we'd have to start some sections of the work again. The bikes would have been moved to a different warehouse and the port would start to charge us storage. The final push was on, and now we were wading through the red tape mire with frustration at how long it took for each piece of the bureaucratic jigsaw puzzle to fall into place. At last we had the final customs papers completed and we rushed over to the customs offices, those papers in hand.

In the office stood a long, chest-high counter, behind which the customs officers sheltered from the mass of paper-waving, pleading agents. These agents seemed to be uniformly dressed in smartly pressed black trousers and short-sleeved white shirts. Some had ties on, but most were open-necked in the heat. Above this frantic and sweaty scene, overhead fans whopped lazily, pushing one scoop of heavily laden air from one place to the next. None of the windows were open and everyone had beads of sweat dripping down their faces. I could feel the instant spread of sweat rings under my arms as soon as we walked in. Swedish saunas had nothing on this place, but the air around the average Swede just had to be sweeter than this!

It dawned on us at that moment that we were highly unlikely to get the bikes in time. There was no way to queue-jump – there wasn't a queue, and anyway, that wouldn't have felt fair. We were on an adventure; these people were doing all they could to make a living. But with everyone else trying to push their way to the front, I thought, "Why not us too?" It was almost as if everyone was involved in a giant rugby scrum in which everybody was being almost totally gentlemanly. The manners didn't go so far as each person saying, "After you, I insist", but elbows and size were used politely and without aggression. I'd never seen anything like it, and when one of the customs officers looked up and saw us there, his expression betrayed that he'd never seen anything like us!

In the midst of this mass of heaving people, Birgit and I had our leather jackets, our helmets and the wedges of paperwork that we'd been collecting. I think that this sight piqued the customs officer's interest and he indicated to us to come over to his section of the counter.

The funny thing was that being white seemed to make not a jot of difference to anyone. Outside of the port, in one way or another, it always did. But in this room in particular, I had the feeling that if we'd been green, then we might have attracted some attention and that in fact, the only reason the customs officer was interested was that we looked like a couple of complete prats standing there sweating with all the bike gear.

"Why are you here?" he asked. Sensing that this was a window of opportunity that would not come again, I quickly leapt into a rapid-fire summary of our adventure, concluding that we just wanted the final stamp on our papers so we could get the bikes out before the weekend, and that if he could only do that then we'd get out of his way, and the other men could deal with their important business, but what a pain it would be if he couldn't help us, so could he, please?

I wasn't exactly begging, (one does have some pride after all), but I could see the clock on the wall ticking round ever faster, or so it seemed. The bikes were still locked in their wooden crate, and to save costs on shipping, we'd taken them partly to bits. We'd have to rebuild them before we could head for the gates. This was not going to be a quick job!

The customs officer, who was a tall, broad-shouldered man with a bullet-shaped shaven head, wore an immaculate white shirt with gold bars on his epaulets. He had a strong, handsome and slightly arrogant face, and was the only one in the room that didn't seem to be sweating. He cast a sceptical eye over our paperwork. He pushed back his chair and twisted towards us. "Why is this paperwork not typed?" He asked in a slightly indignant tone. "Um, we don't have a typewriter sir," I responded, "and we are doing all this work ourselves to save money."

The words sounded daft as soon as they popped out of my mouth. Here we were, two western tourists, with big motorcycles, trying to clear them from customs and trying to save money?! Quick as anything he bounced back with a comment that had all business stopped for a few moments, and resulted in good-natured laughter ringing around the room, at our expense.

"So," he said, "you are trying to save money by not having these forms typed eh? Would you like us to have a whip round for you?"

When the laughter had subsided, he was obviously pleased at his witty ability; he rubber-stamped the documents with a flourish and bade us get on with it. "You just have time if you hurry. Good luck with your adventure" and his tone was quite sincere when he said that.

Down on the docks we waited for the next bus to come, hopping from one foot to the other. The bus came and for once we were impatient with the safe and secure driving style. We needed matatu-style movement. Though it probably only took ten minutes, the ride seemed endless but at last we were outside the warehouse. A team of white ghosts greeted us. The men had been loading sacks of white flour onto a train and were covered from head to toe in the stuff. The only bits of black showing were their pupils, their lips where they had been licking them and the ends of their noses where they had been blowing them in an attempt to get rid of the clog of flour that must have been collecting up their nostrils. Not a single one of them had been issued with a facemask. I hated to think what their lungs must have looked like.

Inside the cool gloom of the warehouse we joined another queue, but this one was thankfully short and we were expected. The customs officer had kindly taken it upon himself to phone to warn the warehouse manager that we were on the way. Within minutes of arriving, the manager had arranged for a giant forklift to deposit our crate in the shaft of light that came in through the giant doors. We soon had an audience.

Men hang around the warehouses looking for work – they all seemed to be somehow licensed to be there and all looked hopefully towards us. Though we had no work for them to do, the wood from the crate would be going free, and that would be worth a good-sized meal or two for whoever was high enough up the porter hierarchy to be the one to snag it. We were loaned a hammer and a crow bar, and got straight to the task of taking the crate to bits. It was a right royal chore. The thing had been built by people who really cared that our bikes made it safely. Under the time pressure, the skill with which it had been built was irritating but the bikes might never have made it intact without that skill.

By fluke, Birgit's bike was the one that was on the side of the crate to come open first. When she had said, all that time ago in Asia, "Yes I'll come with you to South America, but I want to ride my own bike," I'd said, "OK, but you'll have to maintain it".

She'd taken this comment to heart and had bought a beaten-up old BMW R60/5. With a friend she had ripped the bike to bits, and had rebuilt it, twice. She'd become a really good mechanic and in some areas was far better than I was, even after my four and a bit years on the road. Now, as her bike was to the front, Birgit pulled out her tools and got on with the task of putting it back together.

The crowd of labourers was now about thirty strong and they looked on in stunned silence as a girl got to work doing a man's job. What made it more confusing for them was that I, as the man, was hanging around, seemingly as a spare part. In actual fact, of course, I was just respecting Birgit for her ability and knew that she'd ask if she needed help. I was also shooting an occasional glowering look at the men as best I could. This was an unspoken, "Stay back and keep your hands off our tools and kit" type of stare. It would have been too easy for something to go missing if we both got our heads down and were focusing on bike mechanics.

The porters' eyes flicked from Birgit with confusion, to me with a mixture of contempt (how could I let a woman do a man's job?) and admiration (Good grief, he's even trained his woman to do this for him. He must be a king!)

I stood watching all this and wondered where we would be going with the situation. Then I couldn't resist it any longer. Time to stir things up! At just the moment when all eyes had flicked to me, I announced, "Oh yes, she is the mechanic you know, I do the cooking."

There was a stunned silence; the men looked at each other and then one of them clicked and within seconds laughter pealed out and literally, tears were rolling down faces. In that instant, the slight undercurrent of tension disappeared. Humour had broken away many of the barriers between us. A couple of the men leapt forward to give a hand with lifting Birgit's bike and then I could get to work on mine. Now the men were casting appreciative glances towards Birgit, and honour-satisfied looks towards me.

Outside, the sun had dipped near the equator and there was only an hour of daylight left. With thirty minutes to go before the port gates closed we piled the last of our stuff aboard, pulled on our helmets, said goodbye to the men, including the white ghosts who'd stayed for the fun, and roared straight to the gates. There, a bored guard lazily looked over our papers, smiled and said, "Asante sana. Kwaheri." (Thank you very much and goodbye). That was it – we'd done it. The bikes were ours and we were free. Africa lay before us.

We had the slight problem that during the course of the previous week we'd still not been able to find an affordable hotel with off road parking. The nearest place was a camping site at Tiwi beach, south of Mombassa. To get there we had to scurry in rush hour traffic from one side of the city to the other, queue up for and get on a ferry across the river that skirts the city, and then ride hell-for-leather to try to get camped before the sun set. The notion of achieving all that was pure optimism.

Flame trees and market stalls lined the long concrete slope down to the ferry gates. A queue of hundreds of people, many pushing loaded bicycles and some pulling livestock behind them, stood patiently, but not in line, waiting for the ferry to crash its steel gates onto the rough and stained concrete surface of the slope. The multi-coloured crowd was split only by a long line of cars, trucks and mini buses.

The concrete was stained with a hundred different things which collected together to tell the story of life on the jetty. Oil splatters mingled with blackened lines of burnt rubber and exhaust fumes, which led straight down to the water's edge. Orange coloured splatters told of where people had discarded mango pips, to be squashed underfoot and tyre. A mass of curved, black, intermingling stains, looking like some sort of horror movie modern art, told of where someone at some time had decided to burn a load of rubber tyres. Dog shit had stained, as you would expect it to, in the colours you would expect it to, and where goats were tied up, their urine had yellowed the concrete into random runs of sepia. Spitting is a thing that many men in Africa do and the concrete was marked with decades of splatters of all sorts of colours, depending on what the spitter had been chewing or trying to get rid of at the time. At some time someone had dropped a tin of blue paint and this had been spread enthusiastically from the original point of impact. Footprints showing feet shod with flip-flops, heeled shoes and plain bare feet had obviously done this work, and what they had not managed to spread, vehicle tyres had finished off in a Morse code of dots and dashes down the concrete.

Engines revved as the ferry approached. People pushed forward, and as soon as the rush of vehicles and people getting off the ferry had cleared the slope, everyone surged towards the boat. Me first, every man, woman and child for themselves!

We were literally buffeted by the hustle and bustle as we headed down the ramp, only just making it aboard. I wondered what it would be like if the ferry decided to sink. It didn't look as if it were long for this world. In fact I suspected that it was well past its 'use by' date, but in typical African fashion, by hook or by crook, it was kept going. A great many lives would have been made infinitely harder without it.

The ferry gates crashed to the ramp on the other side, and there was an instant swirl of activity, but this time the air of urgency had gone. The vital crossing had been made and now people could head for home at a more comfortable speed. Not us. For starters, we didn't know exactly where home was and we'd no idea what we would have to deal with to get there. What we did know was that we had better get a scoot on, and after being cooped up in the crate, the bikes seemed really happy about that.

We quickly left behind the riverside village with its rutted curbs, fruit stalls, mangy dogs, scrawny goats that were acting as waste removal beasts, houses that looked as if they'd all been painted once, and the matatu stop where the mini buses circled like predatory sharks.

The asphalt that stretched in front of us was smooth and there wasn't a pothole in sight. The traffic was almost nonexistent and the only manoeuvring we had to do was to swerve around the odd cyclist.

Beside us to our right, the sun was a superb flaming eyeball-aching orange, and the sky around it was a hundred shades of red through to a yellow-tinged blue. Each time I glanced at the sun, it had fallen further. I wondered how Birgit was feeling. I knew Africa a little, but this past week had been all new for her, and the battling with the port had been an additional pressure. She must have been feeling really tired. We also had not eaten or drunk enough as we had pelted through the day. That was stupid and no doubt contributed to what happened next.

We dipped the bikes off the raggedy edge of the asphalt and down into the dust. Behind the visor of her helmet, I could imagine a stoic expression, tinged with a dash of fear. I certainly was afraid, but as I was the more experienced rider I had to go first. We'd elected to do this for the first few months. That way Birgit would be able to learn from how I rode the bike. I'd learnt a lot by doing this behind my friends Mike and Sally on my first trip to Africa.

The back wheel of my bike skittered in some loose sand and the front wheel dropped down into a pothole, whose depth I'd only been able to guess at. This time I'd got it right. Birgit sat close behind me on her bike.

I eased on up to twenty miles per hour and began the rollercoaster slalom through the bush. My headlight was picking up boulders, potholes, soft looking ruts and patches of corrugations. With a loaded up bike these sort of obstacles were a challenge at any time, but in the dark I couldn't tell just how high

24

the boulders stuck up. Nor could I tell how deep the potholes were, and what scared me more was that I couldn't tell in advance whether the ridges were soft, pretty soft or dangerously soft. I looked in my mirror.

Birgit was there, tucked in just to my right. But she was too close for comfort, so I opened the throttle a bit. She stayed with me so I opened the throttle a little more. I was now scared that if I fell off, she'd ride right over me!

I went faster, crashing through holes, leaping over boulders and squidging my way through the sand. I looked quickly in my mirror again. Birgit was still there. I went faster still and as I did so I started to admire her skill.

Her first dirt road and she was dealing with it like a person who had years of experience, not a complete novice. But now she was going so fast, I was at the limit of my ability and I was really worrying about what would happen if I fell off. The track took a very sandy twist through the bush and my bike wiggled like the backside of a belly dancer; I battled to stay on. There in my mirrors was Birgit looking, as far as I could tell, completely calm and in control.

We crashed through a series of potholes, with my bike bottoming out each time. This was now really dangerous, but I daren't stop. If I did Birgit would hammer straight into me. There was no way to pull off the road. I could only keep going and hang on for dear life. Suddenly the surface changed to hard, sun-baked earth and with a gap in the trees there was enough light from the moon for me to see where I could pull over. We'd arrived. I stood still for a moment, sweat pouring off me and my heart racing furiously. I climbed weak-kneed off my bike and headed over to Birgit where she'd stopped dead in the middle of the road, unable to move.

"You're amazing!" I shouted at her. "What a fantastic ride! You were superb! This is brilliant. How do you feel?"

She lifted her visor and turned towards me to say, "Did you have to go so fast, that was horrible, my lights are awful, I was so afraid of losing you! I could hardly keep up!"

We rode the last few metres down to the campsite and under a palm tree of giant proportions; we made camp, feeling shattered but rather pleased with ourselves.

When it was time to leave, days later, Birgit rode five metres and promptly fell off. It was daylight and we could both see just how bad the road was. The two hundred and ten kilos of bike, with its oils and fuel, ten kilos of spare tyres, plus thirty kilos of luggage had suddenly felt phenomenally heavy. But with no other way to get her bike back to the tarmac, she had to ride it, and did so. Slowly, but determined not to be beaten.

Chapter 2

Death of a hermit

'The physical aspect of travel is, for me, the least interesting; what really draws me is the prospect of stepping out of the daylight of everything I know, into the shadows of what I don't know.'

Pico Iyer

Tiwi beach had been a marvellous spot to unwind from this entry into Africa. The white sandy beach stretched out along that turquoise sea we'd craved, and the brilliantly coloured fish trapped inside the reef provided us with endless entertainment. So did the beach touts. These young bucks were out to make money by selling carvings and kikoys (Kenyan Sarongs) to the tourists in the other beach resorts. Our campsite was definitely at the bottom of the scale and nestled as it was between high-class hotels, I wondered how long it would last. Perhaps we were seeing it in dying days – in African terms, the land must have been worth a fortune. But the touts left us alone once they had got used to us and realised that we were budget travellers, on bikes and therefore had no space to carry anything. For us they were a laugh and always good for a chat. Not for the other tourists though, and I began to pity the gauntlet they had to run every time they wanted to take a stroll along what should have been an idyllic beach.

It was also work time on the beach for us. The bikes had been crated and shipped thousands of kilometres from Europe. They'd been shoved back together under pressure and then been subjected to the rougher side of Africa. They needed a thorough checking over. We'd maintained and serviced them to the highest possible standard before putting them in their crate. And in fact, this was one of the reasons that Birgit hadn't practised riding her bike off road before we left Europe.

A private BMW mechanic in Konstanz on the Swiss border with Germany, near where she'd been working, had sold her the bike. He agreed to work with her to rebuild it to a high enough standard to deal with our trip. I was working up in north Germany at the time but the mechanic seemed to be 'kosher'. He had an OK reputation locally and he'd done a bit of work on my bike when I'd arrived in Germany from Asia. (My bike is a class machine by the way. She waited until she was back in the land of her birth before breaking her drive shaft, just a short distance from the man who could fix BMWs.)

With the positive evidence of the repair done on my bike, and conscious that there was no better way for Birgit to learn about her bike than to strip and rebuild it with expert guidance, the bike was bought and the rebuild began.

Unfortunately the mechanic turned out to be a scoundrel. With me not there, he took complete advantage of Birgit. He put broken and barely functioning parts onto the bike and charged her a relatively large amount for the privilege. When she eventually got it to the north of Germany where her parents live, the bike had broken down and been declared unsafe.

Birgit turned to Klabbie who was a friend of a friend and a police motorcyclist who liked to service and restore bikes in his spare time. With hindsight we should have hunted him out and asked him to do the work in the first place. I'd just been stunned that the mechanic in Konstanz had been so much of a rogue that he'd been prepared to put Birgit's life at risk. Typically, she looked on the positive side of this potentially dangerous experience: "Well, having worked on the bike twice now, I know so much more about it."

The sense of freedom that a motorcycle gives was something that I was well aware of and thoroughly enjoyed by this time. I was, quite simply, an addict. Touring through the world on two motorised wheels was exactly what I wanted to be doing, but I recognised the feelings that Birgit was having. She was just at the start of the learning curve that every motorcyclist has to ride before gaining confidence, but her African training ground was full of the unexpected. The following months would be hard, but the next few days riding away from Tiwi were stunningly difficult.

28

She's a very independent character and it was this in part that had made her want to have her own bike. There was nothing wrong with being a pillion, but now she'd heard about the accidents I'd had over the years through Africa and Asia…

Because of the difference in our levels of experience, she'd agreed that following me was the best thing to do, though instinctively she's happier when she is in control of her destiny – as far as one can be that is. It made sense, but I hadn't realised how much of a drag she was going to be. Where once I'd been able to float along at my own pace, now I had to be doing the thinking for two people, and I found it incredibly hard. I surprised myself with the selfish thoughts I was capable of.

I itched to play my own version of 'space invaders' with the potholes but where the ridges or heat heaves in the asphalt were normally an enjoyable challenge, riding with Birgit they became uncomfortable annoying obstacles.

It set my mind thinking about when I'd first got to Africa and had linked up to ride with Mike and Sally, an English couple I'd met on the ferry from Piraeus in Greece to Alexandria in Egypt. I'd been so busy coping with riding the bike and surviving each moment that it had never occurred to me that I must have been very frustrating for Mike to be riding with. Now that the boot was on the other foot, I made a mental note to ask him about it next time I saw him. But these thoughts put things firmly in perspective for me. If Mike could be so patient with a complete stranger, then good grief! – I should get my act together and stop my mental whinging!

Birgit had two problems which nearly killed her over the next couple of days. She'd not packed her bike carefully enough when we'd left the beach and one of her aluminium panniers was considerably heavier than the other. This meant that not only were the roads trying to throw her off balance, but gravity was playing a constant game with her too. The other problem she had, besides her inexperience, was that we'd only recently realised that her bike, an R65 650cc twin, had a short frame and this made it react the same way that a short wheelbase

Land Rover would. A long wheelbase Land Rover would absorb the bumps to a significant extent – a shortie would telegraph just about everything to its passengers, with real discomfort. In the same way, Birgit's bike uncomfortably skipped over bumps instead of soaking them up in the way that my 798cc R80GS did. It didn't seem to matter how slowly I rode or what route I took in front, she could never make her bike do quite the same thing.

We were heading inland towards Nairobi and I'd been watching her in my mirrors. Where she should have been enjoying the wild animals that were watching us with bewilderment from the Tsavo National Park, she was riding rigid with tension and fear.

Suddenly, her bike leapt wildly over a set of heat heaves and she was instantly heading straight for the scrub-covered verge! There was a ditch there too – I'd just been looking at how deep it was. I could see her grabbing her brakes with every bit of strength she had and I could see how her eyes were wide with fear. The bike was skipping madly and I was sure she was about to come a cropper, big time.

But no, with surprising strength and huge willpower she managed to pull her bike to a halt, just short of the ditch. When I got

to her she was sitting on the bike shaking with the after effects of effort and fear. She said, "I can't do this!" and tears rolled down her face. They weren't tears of fear, they were tears of frustration that she'd even thought, 'I can't do this'.

We spent the next half hour completely re-packing her bike. Both of us were using army surplus knap sacks as throw-over tank panniers and by moving some of the heavier objects out of her aluminium rear boxes into those, we managed to balance the weight out a bit. Part of the problem was that as the fuel level dropped in her 26-litre tank the front end became less stable. I wasn't suffering that effect at all since with my 43-litre tank and longer wheelbase my bike was still well balanced.

We made the decision that Birgit should ride in front. It wasn't making any difference to her that I had been riding slowly and carefully.

The combination of her inexperience and less stable, smaller bike meant that she was struggling to match even my most considerate riding. And I had been spending a dangerous amount of time looking in my mirrors checking that she was OK.

Our revised riding order was an immediate success. She was able to ride exactly as she wanted to, or how her bike dictated she had to. This made her feel as if she was as much in control as possible. She relaxed, and I could even imagine her grinning behind her visor.

As for me, well I was back in the slot that I had always ridden in when I'd been riding with another biker. I'd always preferred 'tail end Charlie' as from there I could see everything that was going on, and react accordingly. It was a total relief not to be spending so much time looking in my mirrors and I suddenly realised that if was I going to be able to give Birgit any help at all with her learning curve, then I was now far better placed to be able to see things that she could do in a safer or more effective way.

Sometimes I'm incredibly dense. If I wasn't I'd have worked all this out before. The next thing to learn was how to pass on advice and tips without making her feel as if I was constantly assessing and criticizing her.

One of the things I really love about motorcycle adventuring is the thinking time that being on a bike gives you, when you aren't battling with the hazards of the roads in foreign lands that is. I reflected that this had been a pivotal moment in the riding that we were planning to do together and I wondered how many more there were going to be over the next few years.

In one way, riding on my own for so long had actually been a personality-damaging thing to do. It wasn't until I was riding or spending real time with other people for more than a few days that I realised how selfish the life of a lone traveller can be. There are stunning differences between solo and duo travel. I'd tried both and appreciated both styles, in part for the fact that they gave very different aspects of travel the chance to come to the fore.

On my own, I could go wherever I wanted, whenever I wanted. I could choose which roads to ride and where to stop. If I wanted to talk to someone, I could or conversely, be completely anti-social. If I wanted to stay somewhere for more or less time it was entirely up to me to make the decision. In fact, when solo travelling, it's sometimes very easy not to make any decisions at all, but to let life and situations and instincts make them for you.

There are other upsides too. I always find that I seem to be more approachable when I'm on my own. People come and talk to me rather than me having to hunt them out. I've made some great friends along the way and had some amazing adventures because of this. Of course, it never hurt that being on a bike made for a wonderful conversation-starting topic. I feared that the vast majority of these wonderful things would be lost when Birgit and I decided to travel together. Perhaps that wasn't such a bad thing. It can't be healthy being a travelling hermit, can it?

But solo travel has its down sides too. It can be really lonely. It can mean that you and your belongings are more vulnerable. And I was often conscious that something important in life was missing – something that is quite natural for the vast majority of us – sharing, tenderness, warmth, and a joy that you only find when you are with someone that you really care about.

There had been many times when I would have loved to be able to share a special situation with someone. There can be a sort of glow about something amazing when you can experience it with someone you're 'in tune' with. Sunsets, phenomenal views, and those wacky funny moments that seem to happen all the time when you're on the road, are just a few of the moments that should be shared.

There were also more than a few occasions in my 'solo' past when it would have been very nice to have someone around to help me pick my bike up when I'd dropped it, yet again!

Now more at peace with each other, and with how we were riding, we continued on. Strangely, even though this road is the main route between Mombassa's port and the capital, Nairobi, which is a hub for Kenya, the road wasn't busy. For much of the way it takes you on a gentle roll across a great plain where the only breaks are small hillocks or rain-gouged gullies. In the dry season the land is wind-blasted and sun-scorched into a never-ending mustard and beige carpet. This carpet stretches far to the north and on up into Somalia and Ethiopia. It covers vast tracts of land right through towards the west and the Kenyan Highlands, and then up towards the border with southern Sudan. It's only the effects of the highlands and the Great Rift Valley that break up this magnificent and arid rolling land.

An awful lot happens along the roadside, when you look closely. It would be so easy just to focus on where the next heat heave or pothole was, and to miss the life that happens with the strange mix of vibrancy and slow movement that is typical of many parts of Africa.

The roadside is broken sporadically by a tarmac road, and more frequently a dirt track, which head off out into the bush. Some of the tracks disappear as dots on the horizon, from where, unseen from the Nairobi road, they continue into the depths of the bush. The land they head for is dry and frequently desert-like and is home to small clusters of people who scratch out a living under harsh conditions. It's a subsistence existence and can easily be compared to the Middle Ages in Europe.

This land even has its own gangs of bandits (shiftas) who roam like vicious and spoilt hungry children under the control of robber barons. These men are based in the bush up near the borders with Ethiopia and Somalia, lands where an AK47 is easy to get hold of and where children are taught to kill with them, by those in search of power and wealth.

Also tucked away in these areas are enclosed villages of the dispossessed. They were supposed to be temporary shelters for refugees, but the wars in Ethiopia and now Somalia went on for so long that there's a whole adult generation that knows no other life than this. It must be a harsh way to live, but better than returning to their homelands, with things the way they are, particularly in Somalia.

As we rode the adventurous asphalt of the main road, I wondered just how many dispossessed people there were living throughout this continent. I wondered what it would take for the need for flight to stop. I wondered if a solution would ever be practicable or whether it made more sense to accept that 'This is Africa' and that not a lot was going to change it. I quietly hoped for a solution, but couldn't fathom what that might be.

I'm not a great fan of cities. Normally, the only reason I go to them is when I have no choice, or there is something fascinating that I want to see. Capital cities can be the worst, but of course they are inevitably where you have to get your visas. By the time we got to Nairobi, Birgit had had enough of riding for a while and she was keen to see the city – I'd told her enough tales about it to pique her interest.

For me, Nairobi is the perfect example of an African city. It has all the warts yet also has space for surprising beauty. It's as vibrant as it is harshly brash. It's steeped in history both past, and in the making. It's also corrupt and some of the warts are pure poverty. If you want adventure, this city has it – even if the adventure is just making it from one side of the road to the other.

It has danger, and I don't mean the traffic. There are 'no go' areas for anyone who doesn't know their way around really well. In fact just skirting one of these areas can raise the hair on the back of your neck, so tangible is the change in atmosphere. If you want your pockets to be picked then there is no better place to go than Nairobi, or 'Nairobbery' as many travellers and locals alike call it.

I'd loved all this on my first visit. There's an energy to the city that I have never found anywhere else and it's an amazing place to explore. The key is to make enough time to do it. There are so many nooks and crannies that you can rush past, never knowing they were there.

Some of my favourite 'nooks' are the second hand shops. From the outside, most of them look totally unappealing, but as soon as you step inside you know that you have walked into something that is rather like a cross between a dusty Aladdin's cave, and a world of history. There are items on sale that have found their way there from the earliest colonial times, right on through to the present.

Sometimes I wished that an item could speak. How many heads had that 1930s leather motorcycle crash helmet sat on, and how many miles through Africa had it seen? That old leather-flying jacket – something a Kenyan airman had brought home from the Second World War? The Victorian dolls' house that stood sad and dustily unloved in the corner. Had it once been loved? How many children had played with it? How many dreams and fantasies had come to life within its walls? And the old-fashioned iron that was stopping open the door of the shop – when had it last seen action against creases?

But these were just the western things. Inevitably, buried away, there would be carvings or statues that quite simply looked old. They didn't have the mass-produced feel of modern street carvings, and they were cheap in comparison. I found a wooden head and shoulders bust of a man with a proud, strong face whose stare would have been arrogant had it not been for the laughter lines that had been so carefully and skilfully carved in. He looked as if he was fighting not to burst into uncontrollable laughter; the type of man you'd love to have as your grandfather. He'd teach you pride, but balance that with humour.

I was keen to take Birgit to stay at Mama Roche's. I'd stayed in this rough and ready campsite on the edge of the city on my way down the first time, and it had lived strong in my memories as being a great place to stay. I knew the risk though. Things and places change – sometimes for the worse, and I knew that Mama's might be a place that I really shouldn't return to.

This pirate of an old lady with her wild sense of humour, her enormous heart and a skin that she liked to pretend was rhinoceros thick, was someone that I'd grown to really care for over the weeks I'd stayed there before. I'd sent her a couple of postcards years before but

I'd never had a reply, not that I really expected one since she was always going to be busy with the next bunch of people she had to stay, the city council, the police, her next bottle of vodka...and so on.

We rolled through the tall, barbed-wire-topped metal gates. My first thoughts as I looked through the rag-tag flower gardens at the old stilted wooden house with its verandas were, "Hmm, place hasn't changed much – could do with a spot of paint – looks busy – I wonder if Mama is around?"

At that very moment she came striding through the garden towards us with a gait that I always thought was a sort of cross between 'penguin' and 'ship in full sail'. As I slipped my helmet off she stopped, looked at me with her piercing eyes and said in her strong Polish accent, "I know you. You da boy dat had da big accident in Namibia – I hear about dis. You come back. Good. You come here say hello to Mama!"

When Mama gives an order like that you don't disobey, not that you'd want to, and she seemed pleased as punch to see me. When I introduced Birgit, Mama gave her a good looking over, clucked approval and that was that, we were home – at least, that's how Mama's always felt.

When Birgit had said to me that she'd come with me to South America, but that she wanted her own bike, she'd also tagged on, "And I want to go to Africa first". I didn't mind a jot – in spite of the fact that you can be disappointed when you return somewhere that has been happy. For me the whole idea was a major bonus. I hadn't expected to go back to Africa, and I'd had an amazing time in spite of being arrested three times, thrown in jail once and suffering a major accident that gave me seventeen bone fractures. I was quite happy for more – well, not the rough bits – but the times in between had been amazing. There were lots of things I hadn't been able to see the first time around, and now potentially I could, and I could share them with Birgit.

There were places I'd loved, and people I'd made friends with who were going to be great to get back to. I was confident that things would work out because I felt I had the right attitude: things do change and sometimes very much for the worse. I was happy to accept that this was the case and challenged by the thought of trying to find out why a place might have changed for the worst. It's one of the things that intrigues me about travel – the question why? Perhaps naively, I felt sure that with this attitude I was going to have an excellent ride across this stunning continent again. The excitement came from the thought that many places would have either remained the same in a sort of time warp, or would have changed for the better. All three possibilities sounded good to me.

Nairobi's changes were not what I'd hoped for. The slums were bigger and looked more desperate. The countryside was no longer supporting the mass of people and more and more were coming to the city in search of survival. There were far more young men hanging around in the streets during the daytime and we were told that the majority were unemployed. There was an undercurrent of sadness and aggression that I'd not been so aware of in 1992.

Some of the city's open areas had been built on and that surprised me; I'd thought that they were publicly owned lands and therefore would stay as parks. In contrast to the increase in poor people, there also seemed to be more people driving about in flashy BMWs and Mercedes. These people almost dripped wealth and they either ignored the struggling poor around them, or they looked down their noses at them as if they were something they shouldn't soil their handmade shoes on. It seemed that during the years I'd been away, the wealth gap had got wider. Now there was a very obvious and ostentatious elite.

We heard tales of mass arrests of people protesting against the government – corruption apparently had reached new heights. We heard tales of wrongful arrest and of old laws being brought back into use to try to stop the democratic process in the country – you had to get a special licence from the government if you wanted to hold a meeting of more than nine people. We also heard about mysterious car 'accidents' that had happened to more vocal advocates of full democracy.

President Moi, who took over from the first president Jomo Kenyatta, had turned Kenya into a one party state. The KANU party had become a hated name for many. It also seemed that, to maintain power, President Moi and his cronies had been using tribal groups as a way of crushing opponents, and rewarding those loyal to him. Apparently, the Kikuyus, the Luhyas, Maasais, Sabaots, Kisiis and the Luos were the most affected by this.

From what I could understand, the source of the situation stemmed back to such things as the cultural changes that colonialism brought about, the lack of understanding by many in Kenya of how democracy should work, and the historical respect that is shown to powerful men in Africa. But this recipe for disaster has far more ingredients than just those three and the mix was enough to result in corruption even amongst the judiciary. There were even rumours of government torture chambers right in Nairobi. No wonder there was an edge to the air.

Yet even in this atmosphere, African humour was visible and enthusiastic but I had a nasty tingle in the back of my mind that said even this had changed. Once I'd thought that the almost slapstick sense of humour was light, uncomplicated and refreshing. Now I wondered if there was just a tinge of desperation about it. Yet when something funny happened the laughter seemed to transcend any differences, and everyone would join in regardless of their status or wealth; apart from the elites – such things appeared to be beneath their dignity.

I just hoped for the people of Kenya that things would change for the better, and do so rapidly. But I knew that while President Moi and KANU were in charge this was not going to happen, and I suspected that the situation could get even worse. I was sad for this amazing country and its friendly people.

Africa is always full of surprises and one of these was going to be Uganda. Winston Churchill once called Uganda the 'Pearl of Africa' and he was right. It's a beautiful and mostly fertile country. As we rode on west across Kenya, I itched to get back there. The country had been under the Presidency of Yoweri Museveni for nearly ten years by this time and when I'd been in Uganda the last time he was being feted as a saviour. They certainly needed one after Idi Amin had terrorised and ruined the country.

I also hoped that we could link up with our old friend Heather and her husband Pastor Chris. Kampala, the capital, had changed – in fact I was stunned by how much it had done so. Gone were the pitted bullet marks which had previously decorated the outside of buildings, like some sort of cancerous rash. They had been a random testament to the power and greed of mankind. Gone were the long sections of massively potholed roads that must have kept the shock absorber suppliers very busy. It actually felt quite strange not to have to dodge potholes any more – children trying to cross the road and the aimless dogs and goats now ran far less risk of being hit by vehicles lurching erratically as they swerved to avoid the gaping holes of yore. Then again, with the improvement in the road surfaces, the speed at which people were driving had dramatically increased.

The city authorities had added 'Speed Kills' warning signs to those about AIDS. Yet that was actually a ray of sunshine. Uganda still held the record for the greatest decrease in Africa, by far, in the rate of AIDS infection. It was still dropping dramatically and when I talked to some young guys about it they seemed indignant that anyone would think that they would have sex without using a condom. In the background, one of the more evangelical, American-supported churches was banging on about how condoms were against God's will. I wondered at the stupidity and callousness of those people.

When we were out for a drive one day, Chris took us down 'coffin street'. It's strange to ride a street like this, where the vendors manage to combine a respectful expression with one which says "I wonder if he is about to die and give me some business?" This was one of the busiest streets in town and you could get an amazing selection of coffins. They ranged from basic cardboard to gleaming polished wooden monsters that looked big enough to house a small family, and probably cost about the same as that small family needed to feed themselves for a year!

But when I commented on this, Chris started to laugh. Birgit looked shocked, until it dawned on us that this was just his defence mechanism. Most people knew of someone who had died recently, but as a pastor, Chris was subjected to the results of this horrifying wasting disease every single day.

Around the coffin vendors, life swirled on in a very matter of fact sort of way. No one, except us, gave the scene a second glance. The street of death had just become part of the wallpaper. The street was a shortcut through to another part of the city where life and survival were being celebrated. What was strange was that this didn't make the people callous – not at all. Apparently, just resigned to the fact that life is followed by death. Perhaps Europe was like this at the time of the Black Death, or the Plague.

But, there was enough enjoyment of life in these times that most people seemed to have taken on board the fact that though there was no cure for aids, and the medicine to slow the effects of it down were out of the reach of most of the everyday people. Condoms worked and it wasn't unmanly to use them.

That was the issue for many of the African cultures. When people got over that point, and there was a readily available supply of free or cheap condoms, then surely the problem would diminish in size? Perhaps, in spite of what the Ugandans had proved, I was being naively optimistic.

Heather and Chris wanted to take us to Chris's village, way up in the north of Uganda. Times had calmed sufficiently for this to happen, though there was still a risk.

The bunch of so-called freedom fighters, the Lord's Resistance Army, were in fact no more than a bunch of men who had started off with an ideal but had got lost – so lost that they seemed to have forgotten the point of their exercise, particularly once they realised that there was power and a living to be made at the point of a gun. Guns were readily available as a result of the wars in the region and raids on villages still happened. Many of them were to rob and to take children to become boy soldiers or to become whores for the soldiers. It seemed quite perverse that a group that had started off wanting to have Uganda governed by strict Christian rules could turn into the callous monsters that they had become. It was a sad and painful reflection on the harsher side of human nature.

Chris had recently become head of the village and in spite of the fact that he lived and worked so far away in Kampala, he and Heather visited often. They were in the process of building a home for themselves in the village.

The village was a few kilometres away from the main road, and a kilometre and a half away from the river, which was the water source – they had no running water. The houses weren't houses as we know them but were mud-walled huts with thick straw roofs. They were placed in a rough sort of circle around a tree and the fireplace.

One was the cooking hut and the others were where people lived. Oh, and there was one other building: a church. And this was one of the nicest churches I'd ever been in. Like the huts, the roof was straw and the floor a beaten reddish-coloured earth, but the walls were only about a metre high, so when you were inside in a service you could see right out into the fields. It was as if being in church did not mean that you had to be separated from real life; it was all around you. You could feel the breeze of the fields and you could smell the scents of the African bush on that breeze. I was conscious of the damp earthy smell that is so typically African, the scent of millet that had recently been harvested, the delicious smells of a chicken that was being boiled in the cooking hut, the faint scent of some wonderful flower which I couldn't see, and the acrid tang of goat.

The service was translated sentence by sentence for us, with great patience from the rest of the congregation. It was as if they had all the time in the world and they didn't want us to feel left out or to miss out on anything. The usual collection was taken, but in a very unusual way, for us.

Money is scarce in villages such as this. Farming is pretty much on a subsistence level and anything that is grown and is left over, is

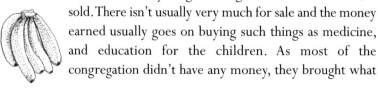

sold. There isn't usually very much for sale and the money earned usually goes on buying such things as medicine, and education for the children. As most of the congregation didn't have any money, they brought what they had grown or reared. A chicken, some rice, some maize, some bananas and so on. These things were either given to families that were struggling – perhaps there was illness and the crops couldn't be tended – or they were sold at market to buy things to improve the church and the lives of the villagers. I wondered how the minister would react if I were to try to put a goat in the collection box in a church in the UK.

As we were guests in the village, and guests of Heather and Chris at that, we were not allowed to do a thing. I was happy with that. It gave me a chance to watch what was going on, talk sign language with the men and to go nuts with my camera. But Birgit had other ideas, and after much persuasion she got the ladies to allow her to go with them to the river to get water. The walk is a good 2 kilometres through the bush along a well-beaten path that wound its way around the occasional tree, a termite mound, a clump of grass or a bush or two. The pace was gentle and the women seemed to treat the expedition as a bit of a laugh, or perhaps it was more that they were amused by Birgit wanting to help – after all, she was a white woman!

Birgit had two problems. The first was that she simply didn't have a lifetime of neck muscles developed to deal with carrying heavy weights on her head, nor the training the local girls get from a very early age. The women were elegantly carrying bright yellow, battered old 25 litre plastic jerry cans on their heads, and weren't using their hands to keep them there.

That was the other thing that had the women in fits of laughter. They used a twist of cloth as a cushion under their jerry cans. Birgit's hair was far too smooth to stop the cushion and jerry can from tumbling to the ground every few metres, without being firmly held. However, they obviously admired her perseverance and once the usual slapstick humour had been got out of the way (and yes, she did look funny), the women visibly appreciated her for being so determined. I later lifted one of the jerry cans, when no one was looking I might add, and it lasted about 3 seconds on my head!

Birgit really endeared herself to the women when they got back to the cooking hut. Now this hut must have been appalling to work in.

Like the others, it was made of mud and straw, but there was almost no light and the hut seemed permanently filled with smoke. The main fire outside was for cooking big things, but everything else was done in the hut. Rice and maize meal or steamed green bananas called matoke are the main staples. Sometimes millet is also ground up to make what looks like a brown speckled mash potato. But rice has to be dealt with in a special way.

It's normally locally grown and all the processing is done on the ground. It's cut and dried, then threshed and winnowed to get rid of the husks. The trouble is that while all this is going on, on the ground, small stones tend to add themselves to the processed rice and it seems that nine times out of ten, the stones that make it through are white or clear. You'll be able to imagine how hard they are to pick out. But that's what they have to do and Birgit joined the women as they sat on rush mats with little piles of rice in front of them. They carefully spread the rice out, little by little, over the mat, picking out the stones as they went. Sadly, they aren't always one hundred percent successful so whenever you eat rice it's really important not to bite down too hard. That was a lesson I nearly learned the hard way.

There's that nasty moment when, inevitably just too late, your brain is screaming, 'don't bite down any harder!' You are either lucky, or you aren't. A cracked tooth could be a real nuisance to have to sort out in the middle of the bush.

I was impressed with how everything was done with such good humour and with everyone helping everyone else. All knew their jobs, and it seemed as if the men were well aware that their inevitably ham-fisted attempts at cookery just meant that they were in the way. So they retired to the shade or the fireplace to discuss local politics, the fighting, education for the children, what they'd seen in town and so on. My natural place seemed to be with the men so, though I couldn't understand the conversations, I sat to watch the body language and facial expressions. I think I managed to smile or look suitably grave at the right moments, and I think that it was appreciated that I was listening and respecting them enough to be involved – I could have been a standoffish white man and gone and read a book instead.

We managed to perplex the villagers the next morning. We were already used to staying in places where water was at a premium and where you were expected to stand in a big plastic washing up bowl to have a wash. The idea being that you have your bucket of water, which was sometimes warm, and you used a scoop and your flannel to wash with. The water that collected in the bowl would do your feet last of all and then the water could go on the garden.

So, when the villagers bought us this set up, we quite naturally got on with the job, but didn't need as much water as they gave us. Remember that this water had to be carried from the river and then heated on the open fire. We'd not asked for hot water, but the villagers wanted to give us every luxury they could manage. They were like that, but we upset them because we didn't use all the water. Chris told us later that he'd had a mini delegation asking if perhaps there was something wrong with the water, not hot enough? Or, perhaps, it was that we didn't know how to wash properly?!

Catching lunch in the village involved something that was totally unfair for chickens. Villages always seemed to have half a dozen or so scrawny chickens clucking around. Bearing in mind that they had to fend for themselves and feed themselves with whatever they could find, they always looked healthy and some had magnificent plumages. The villagers didn't eat meat very often so it was a real treat when the plan was set to kill a chicken for dinner, or rather, a cockerel. The bird had been strutting his stuff around the village, apparently unaware that its days were numbered. It had woken me far too early that morning so as far as I was concerned, it had been allowed to live for far too long. But this bird looked like a thoroughbred and I wasn't sure how anyone was going to be nimble enough to nab it.

One of the small boys chased the cock through the village – the cock knew something was up so was shrieking in an indignant and outraged tone. Despite being chased, it knew it was king of the village. It kept looking over its shoulder, not in fear but with an insolent sort of 'you can't catch me' type of stare. Yeah well, when boy number one got knackered from leaping over tables, round chairs, through huts, down the maize field, through the banana trees and back through to the main fireplace, his older brother took over.

The baton had been passed and with brother three, I started to admire the cockerel's stamina, though it had finally stopped looking quite so sure of itself. It no longer bothered to look over its shoulder as it ran – it was on borrowed time. Finally nabbed, the thing looked too knackered to care what happened next, the boys looked proud and everyone else looked hungry. Fortunately they didn't prolong the situation and within a couple of moments the cockerel was despatched. But it got its own back on us at dinner.

All that long distance runner sinew was as tough as old boots – it tasted good though. To my disgust in the morning, son of long distance runner woke me up at the crack of dawn with a rather triumphant 'cock-a-doodle-doo', which said, "I saw you catch the old man, you won't grab me the same way; I'll make you too tired to chase me!"

We'd allowed ourselves nine months, more or less, to make it down to Cape Town, so we had plenty of time to explore. We cruised a lot of Uganda, with Birgit becoming a better and happier rider every day. She still chuntered about missing her bicycle though. When we'd met she'd been spending six months riding her bicycle through New Zealand and I'd reckoned that anyone who was nuts enough to ride a bicycle up and down all those mountains was probably nuts enough to travel with me.

Fortunately I'd been able to persuade her that a bicycle with an engine was a far better deal than one without. She still wasn't convinced, but was just beginning to enjoy being in control and to appreciate the freedom that being on a motorcycle gave her.

We camped in some amazing spots, by mountains and by lakes. We rode through the stunning scenery of the south of Uganda, which many people call 'Little Nepal' because of all the terraced hillsides and the corrugated roofs of the buildings. We went out to look at the island on Lake Bunyonyi where I'd worked on the aid agency project – years later the work still seemed to be going on. I supposed that it was a case of having enough funds to get on with the work of renovating the buildings.

We slept in the haunted forest – haunted by the people that Idi Amin made disappear into mass graves somewhere in that particular forest. The shadows certainly had something eerie about them and to my sensitised imagination, the breeze whispered strange voices as it worked its way through the trees. That night, as we cooked our dinner within the glow of light that our petrol stove cast, I had the feeling that hundreds of pairs of sad eyes were watching us from the surrounding darkness, but in reality no one was there.

We earned a crust by doing some painting and decorating for an aid agency and we earned ourselves some empty seats on a floatplane flight leaving from Lake Victoria. The work was to give the plane a good scrub – from wings to floats.

We ate dinners with ex-pats, all of whom seemed to have amazing life stories. I wondered what it was that had put all of the characters around these tables at this moment in time. Some of the pilots from Mission Aviation Fellowship and I plotted the idea of doing a speed motorcycle run the length of the continent to raise money for charity. We reckoned that, with our combined experience, if everything went reasonably smoothly, we could do the ride in 30 days. Of course the chance of anything working out as it should was pretty remote, but it was a great idea and over a few beers the idea was the source of a stream of anecdotes that had us either enthralled or laughing.

We could easily have stayed – the life seemed to suit us, though of course we knew that it would be very different if we were having to earn our living in an environment where the phones were unreliable, electricity erratic, bribery and corruption bubbling away in the background, and where we would have to live in our own personal barbed wire ghetto – the only way to be able to sleep easily at night. Even in Kampala there were still shootings and if things weren't nailed down, and guarded, then they'd go missing. Of course you could still try the thieves' market the next day and we were told it was still more than likely that you'd be able to buy your belongings back.

Birgit was enthralled by the Rift Valley as we headed back through Kenya, and she loved the sight of Mt Kilimanjaro. This really is a beautiful mountain. It stands proud and rather magnificent above the mustards and sages of the plain. It's almost regal with its snowy white top and the purple shroud which hangs as a trick of the light around the upper slopes. I was delighted to find that the road I'd ridden around its base four years before was no longer a rain-washed very muddy track, but was clean new tarmac.

I felt I'd proved my point about dirt roads. I could do them and I enjoyed finishing them, but at times I just wanted to be in the position where I could pick whether I rode them or not. Birgit was still nervous of them, though by now she'd realised that her lack of height could act as a paradoxical 'plus' on the dirt. At only five foot one, she could barely get a single toe on the ground, so was less tempted to take a steadying 'dab' than a taller person would have been. She just had to 'go for it' and sink or swim. "You've just got to keep going" she'd said.

She was right. The rules of off road riding are as follows: pick your point well in advance, and keep your eyes on that marker, until you are ready to focus on the next; relax and let your brain, body and bike work instinctively together so that they just deal automatically with the immediate problems, while you are planning ahead. That way you can cruise through even the really hard stuff. Of course the word 'cruise' is relative but the point is that you fall off a hell of a lot less with this system, and because you aren't last-minute crisis-managing all the time, you have far more fun.

We were heading for the island of Zanzibar. On my first African bike trip I couldn't afford to go over, and I'd regretted that ever since. Every time someone asked if I'd been, or told stories of their visits, I knew that this was a place that I really should try to get to. We decided that as we'd been on the move for several months by now, we had earned a bit of rest and relaxation. We were dying to see what this island would be like. We'd enjoyed Mombassa, in part because of the mix of cultures, but we'd read that Zanzibar was even more of a melting pot. It's thought to be the birthplace of the language of Swahili, or Kiswahili. This hybrid language is a key result of this melting pot and has made for easy communication as far north as Ethiopia, as far west as the Congo and as far south as Mozambique.

Zanzibar's nickname is the 'Spice Island'. The Arabs, when they'd had control, had planted great plantations of pepper, nutmeg and cloves.

 We'd never seen these growing before so that thought was a real draw. The island was also famous for its fruit. There were fruit shaped like stars, fruit that had all of the tastes of a fruit salad in one bite, and another that was supposed to taste like Cornish vanilla ice cream. The island is also famous as being the birthplace of Queen's lead singer, Freddie Mercury.

It also didn't hurt that I'd seen a postcard of one of the beaches. The sand was white but just a shade towards cream; the sea was the clearest turquoise I'd ever seen and the photograph had one of those classic palm trees that seems to defy gravity by growing sideways just above the sand before heading skywards to sprout its fronds. The Perhentian islands in Malaysia and Gilli Trawangan in Indonesia had given me a taste for such beaches. Diversions such as this, I decided, were some of the real bonuses of slow, long distance travel.

We were still pretty much governed only by budget, length of visa and the weather patterns. We were doing OK with our budget, and somehow had even managed to save a little. We'd only been in Tanzania for a couple of weeks so still had two and a half months left on our visas, and the weather? We couldn't have timed it better. We'll just go for a week we'd thought....

How do you spend three weeks on a tropical island and still want more? It's too easy. There's so much to see – particularly on Zanzibar. The cultural mix is excellent and over the generations a race of dark-honey-skinned people seems to have evolved. They are a mix of Christian, Moslem and Animist. In the main they seemed to rub along quite well together. After Asia, it was nice to hear the muezzin calling people to prayer again. The Moslem girls and women looked elegant in their robes and scarves. The spice plantations were fascinating and a real education. And the fruit that tasted like ice cream existed. Jack Fruit was delicious. Fresh fruit grew in abundance and we feasted on it.

Stone Town, the old part of Zanzibar Town, is a place that's full of tall old buildings and alleyways that twist and turn their way across it. At ground level, groups of men or children sit and play games or chat. Stalls set into the rough rendered stone walls sell a little of everything – always dust-covered and frequently out of date, but still available.

The gem for us though was the night-time fish market on the edge of Stone Town. The streets are so ill-lit that some would consider them dark and dangerous, but for us the pale light cast a romantic air over the streets and set the mood for the walk down to the waterfront. Here, the local fishermen have set up their stalls and the fish market is a place for promenading, as well as buying fresh fish.

All the seafood that's being cooked and sold is virtually straight out of the sea. Tuna, octopus, squid, some sort of mullet and an endless number of types of fish the like of which I'd never seen before. Alongside these stalls, which are floating delicious scents out into the night air, are the sellers of freshly squeezed fruit juices, of piping hot mandazi doughnuts, kebabs of goat meat and also those who cater for fizzy drink addicts.

In amongst these stalls are sellers of home-crafted jewellery and hand-woven cloth. Bicycle bells ring, ships out in the bay hoot their horns, the vendors calls ring out 'come and buy' in Swahili and there seems to be laughter everywhere. The mood is totally infectious and it seemed to be the same every night. It didn't matter that each night would have a new collection of people exploring the market's delights, the mood seemed to float from one night to the next as if there had never been a day in between.

Cities are still cities and we wanted to find a beach. But we wanted a beach that didn't have any resorts backing onto it. We'd heard that the north was relatively undeveloped, so that's the way we headed. We'd saved costs by not bringing the bikes over to the island, but it was also a conscious decision that by not having the bikes with us we'd be able to use public transport to get around. A good choice, and there were two main options. The usual matatu mini buses or some works of art on six wheels.

The cabs and chassis of these buses were elderly and clearly much-loved Bedfords. The seating compartments were where the real artistry was though. They were made by the island's boat builders using boat techniques. This meant that you could ride in a beautifully varnished and polished wooden boat on wheels that wasn't a boat at all. It was a totally separate thing, quite unique.

The nearest village to the beach was a couple of kilometres away, so we stocked up on knarly potatoes which had probably been grown in a field of rocks, bananas, and some onions that looked as if their growth had been stunted, and set out on the rocky path. As we walked my mind worked out a route for riding the path on my bike. I seemed now to do this in an unconscious sort of way whenever I came across anything that was even remotely rideable. This path would have been hard though, and I wondered how my bike's tyres would have stood up to the very sharp-edged rocks and stones.

Just down the beach from some palm tree cabins stood a grove of sandalwood trees, and under them seemed to be as perfect a camping spot as we were likely to find. It was far enough up the brilliantly white sand that only a fairly strong storm would bother us, and the shade would be great to have. There was also something rather special about the scent of the sandalwood that surrounded us. The only other times I'd smelt it was from the carved wooden boxes in the markets in India, the joss sticks in Malaysia and India, and the talcum powder that I always seemed to be given at Christmas when I was a teenager.

There'd been enough time between the last of these presents and this beach for me to appreciate the subtle scent. That night, a wide-eyed, fuzzy grey bush baby looked down at us from the tops of the trees. They are magical little creatures and very cute to have as neighbours.

The next days were so idyllic that our week seemed to disappear without us realising. We swam in turquoise water that was so warm it only just cooled the heat of the sun off our skins. We walked the long beach, going from remote village to remote village. We talked with the fishermen with their long wooden fishing canoes. We watched coastal trading dhows cruise past. Birgit learnt how to make fishing baskets, and impressed the fishermen with how quickly she caught on to the technique.

We barbecued freshly caught tuna over a fire made of sandalwood twigs and a grill made from a length of wire that had somehow been washed up onto the beach. Woven, this made a perfect mesh to support the fish above the glowing embers. Water came from the village up the beach and the daily walk to get it taught me that Birgit is fascinated by everything, and also a collectomaniac. She spent so much time trawling the waterline for shells, strangely shaped driftwood and seeds that she ended up with a very brown back, and a still-pale front!

Eventually it was time to move on. Nothing really said to us, "You have to go", it was more that suddenly it felt like the right thing to do. Back on the mainland the bikes were still safe at the Silver Sands hotel where we'd left them, and after a night camping next to a rowdy overland truck full of people who were cheerfully exploring Africa with a great view, we set off for Dar es Salam and then towards Mbeya.

I was nervous at this thought. This was where I'd had the awful accident when Mr Sanga had stepped out in front of me. In an appalling disaster his leg had been chopped off below the knee. It was where I'd been thrown in prison, and narrowly escaped being raped. Being back in the vicinity had revived the ghost of that nightmarish situation which had stayed with me for the past four years.

I knew that I had to make a choice. I could go and seek out Mr Sanga to see how he was doing and I could do the same with Captain Joseph who had pretty much saved my skin by translating for me every day, and who had even put his farm up as bail surety for me.

The Alternative was for me to just keep my head down and be the travelling visitor to the town that I'd not been able to be the last time. There were still plenty of kilometres remaining in which to think about it.

The Mikumi National park held a great surprise for us. The main road runs straight through the park and on my last trip through I'd not

 seen any wild life at all. But this time for some reason the animals were quite happy to be almost at the roadside. The first moment we knew that we were going to be lucky was when, just after a red and white roadside triangle warning of elephants, a tree began to shake violently. There below it was the rounded grey back of a fully-grown elephant, and on closer inspection, a much younger elephant was tugging shoots off the branches that the bigger elephant was pulling down for it. Moments later we saw gazelle, and then wart hogs, and then giraffe. It felt as if Africa had just given us one of the most special gifts it could.

The road was as good as I remembered it and even the heavy trucks and buses hadn't managed to chew the surface up. We cruised on. The weird and wonderfully shaped baobab trees floated past us on both sides, and small red-earthed villages sat by the roadside – there seemed to be an air of prosperity about the mud brick and wattle-and-daub huts. Then we were there – Mbaya.

It looked completely different. To my surprise I didn't remember a thing. So much had changed in four years that I almost didn't recognise the point where the accident had happened. But to my amazement the metre long angle iron post that had severed Mr Sanga's leg, still stuck out of the ground.

I decided that the depth of the changes was a pretty strong indication that I should let the situation rest. I wouldn't hunt the two men out. I had no right to go back, fleetingly, into their world. I could only cause upset.

So, I saw a different side of the town. No longer did I imagine that all the people were looking at me accusingly. This time no one seemed the slightest bit interested and that was a major relief. This new anonymity left us free to explore and to do the things that travellers do.

We found the market at the end of a lane whose rust-coloured surface was dusty and rutted. All the buildings were built up from the road as if the street had the chance of becoming a mini river at the height of the rainy season. Concrete steps jutted out into the dust and I nearly fell over a couple of them as I rubber-necked the surroundings. The market was a mix of those who had established a right to their plot and who had, over the years, built themselves ramshackle stalls out of branches and rags. These stalls at least kept their wares out of the dust that all others hawked from and spat into.

In spite of that, I preferred to shop from the ladies on the ground. They all had their wares spread out on brightly coloured kikoys, and the clashes of colours drew us like bees to flowers. There's something rather spectacular about mangos, guavas, bananas and papayas which are giants in comparison to the anaemic-looking, under-ripe, specimens we get in England. And when they are displayed on the vivid kikoys, the still life is something that an artist would itch to paint, but the resulting picture was another that no one would believe was real.

The Poste Restante in the town was as they all seem to be. It's a system that post offices across the world use to allow post to be received and held, for those who do not have a permanent mailing address in the area. Until the advent of email and worldwide internet cafés, for travellers it was the only affordable way of communicating with family and friends.

But I like queuing for my mail as it's always a good people watching opportunity. As you have a right to be there, and everyone knows that you'll be there for a while, staring at people is expected. Under the circumstances, staring ceases to be an invasive matter of pure bad manners. Everyone becomes fair game. You yourself are the target of stares that seem to be of far greater intensity than out on the street. But as the other people don't mind the scrutiny, it's easy for you not to mind either.

There's also a build-up of anticipation that can climax in a major disappointment. In fact the risk of disappointment is so great that I would never put money on getting any mail. All sorts of things can go wrong. Some of them are your own fault. You may have mis-timed your arrival, and your mail, kept only for a set period of time, may well have been 'returned to sender'. This was always an issue, as you never knew from one post office to the next what the holding time would be.

Mail could have been addressed incorrectly and never made it to the post office you are in. The sender's handwriting could be a problem, and in some countries the surname has to go first on the envelope, but you never knew this until you were in that country. I would always ask for both Manicom and Sam to be checked, just in case I'd turned into a Mr Sam overnight. There was also the chance that the postman was too lazy to get it right and sadly it was a fact that interesting-looking mail could sometimes go 'missing'. All of this meant that if you did get mail, you knew that you were privileged. The delight of getting a letter from home was enhanced by the fact that it had 'run the gauntlet' and had made it all the way to you. It was a survivor and worthy of respect.

Sometimes I would sit for quite a long time, inspecting the envelope, before I opened it. What does the postmark say? Do I recognise the writing, and does it smell of anything? Is there anything inside other than paper? Will it be good news or bad? If it was from my family or a friend I always started to read with a picture of the sender's face in my mind.

Poste Restante gave me more appreciation for the postal service too — something I took totally for granted at home. It made me think of days gone by when it could take years for mail to make it through. I also thought back to the times of carrier pigeons and horseback messengers. Times had moved on and as the post office in Stone Town had said:

'The Postal System Alone Can Do'

'The need to communicate across national frontiers — despite the march of time and the development of telecommunications has remained constant to this very day. The expansion of the world's postal systems represented by 170 nations of the UPI, staggers the imagination. For even our latest technology and instant delivery services cannot do what the postal system alone can do: Get the mail through, anywhere on earth, at very small costs.'

The advent of email of course was dramatically changing all of this, but I suspect that I will still always use Poste Restante, for as long as it exists. I was sure that the set of emotions attached to receiving a letter would be far greater than any that could be attached to an email. It was also the fact that a letter had affected many lives, in small ways, along the way and the time it had taken to get to me simply enhanced the sensation of being distant, of being a long way from home.

Changing money at the bank could also be an adventure. In more out of the way places sometimes it was even a case of telling the bank teller what to do. We were using the banks more than I had on the way down the first time. It was another point of change. The black market in the countries we'd been in so far no longer thrived. It made travelling more expensive for us when we weren't getting the bonus value for our US dollars, but we could both appreciate that a black money market is yet another indication of a country struggling. It was quite satisfying to be in countries that seemed to be getting their act together well enough that the black markets couldn't survive. I suspected that the only illegal money markets now had more to do with money laundering than with common sense survival in hard times.

Birgit managed to make a bank teller's day in Mbeya. Although it was the last town of significance before the border with Malawi, we still needed some more Tanzanian Shillings. She cashed a traveller's cheque and when she had done so she had a slightly bemused expression on her face. Outside the bank we found a quiet corner, because she wanted to double check what had happened inside.

The teller, in a disastrous error, had counted out over $50 more cash than he should have. We couldn't understand how he could have managed to do this. It would have been discovered at the end of the day, and the teller would almost certainly have been sacked, or forced to pay the money back himself. It would have been a ridiculous amount for a local person to find. The expression of sheer relief on the teller's face, when Birgs handed the money back, was a picture that will stay with me forever.

On our slim budget it would have been quite luxurious for us to be able to have a mini beer fest and a good feed in a posh restaurant, or a couple of nights in a hotel that had clean sheets and a shower that wasn't rimmed with weeks of grime. But, the sense of having done the right thing had far more value at that moment. In later times I wondered if my superstition that what goes around comes around was true, and if by being honourable we had weighted the scales on our side for the next 'situation' that must be down the road for us somewhere.

The border crossing into Malawi hadn't changed a bit, but I had. I now had long hair and after the decades President Hastings Banda had been in power he'd left a legacy. He'd hated anyone who looked even remotely like a hippy. The last time I'd been through this border a Norwegian had had his mane sheared with a pair of scissors that were so blunt that the poor bloke winced with the pain of each hack the immigration officer made. The posters about long hair were still on the walls and the scissors on the table looked suspiciously like the ones that the Norwegian guy had been shorn with.

Hastings Banda was the president of Malawi from 1966 to 1994. A son of poor farmers, he nevertheless qualified as a doctor in the United States, and then all over again in Edinburgh. After World War II, Banda worked as a General Practitioner in London, but he returned to his homeland of Nyasaland in 1958, to campaign against the federation of Nyasaland with Southern and Northern Rhodesia (now Zimbabwe and Zambia). In 1961 Banda's Malawi Congress party won a massive election victory and in 1964 Nyasaland became independent, as Malawi.

A few years later he made himself president for life! His official title was 'His Excellency the Life President of the Republic of Malawi, Ngwazi Dr Hastings Kamuzu Banda.' (The title Ngwazi means 'great lion' in Chicheua.) The country went through a period of transition, growth and stability but, increasingly autocratic, Banda's opponents were routinely jailed and some killed, while he lived in the lap of luxury. Like many African "Big Men" in the post-independence era, Hastings Banda seemed to overdose on power and he developed an inordinately large dose of vanity. He loved to have his photo taken, and during his thirty year presidency he had seventy-four different bank notes produced with his picture on them. This record was only beaten by Zaire's tyrannical president Mobutu.

The west acted against Banda's despotic rule and in 1992 they suspended aid, which led to anti-government rioting. That forced him to abandon one-party rule and in democratic elections held in 1994, to great celebration, he was defeated by Bakili Muluzi. Banda eventually died in South Africa, aged somewhere between 99 and 101!

This short time after those '94 elections, many of Banda's rules were still in place and I wondered how I was going to fare. I'd put my ponytail in a tight band and had stuck it down the inside of my bike jacket. With the collar of the jacket up it could hardly be seen. I hoped that, with a bit of judicious positioning, I might escape the chop. It was horribly hot inside the jacket though. The crossing and the paperwork seemed to take an age. The officials seemed to be having bad hair days and were being picky about anything and everything. So much so that I even considered just getting it out and chopping it off in front of them, but I still wanted to see if I could get away with it.

The customs officers' faces sweated in the concrete-and-tin-enhanced heat. The immigration officers sweated over the passports and behind them even the 'Wanted' posters seemed to show men that were sweating. Questioning eyes followed us everywhere, and I worked hard at keeping my face towards the officials and my back towards the safety of the closest wall.

Eventually it was done and with a sudden smile that broke the apparent tension in the room, we were told, "Welcome to Malawi. I hope you are having a fine stay." Just a few kilometres into Malawi, things started to go wrong.

Chapter 3

Did I kill it?

'No matter our intended design or schedule, chance is our ever-present travel partner in discovery. Fate and destiny orchestrate our journey, map out our path. Fortune and luck plot our course, serve as our compass.'

Steve Zikman

Birgit's riding style changed from relaxed slalom to decidedly odd, and before long she pulled over looking both despondent and worried. I wondered if she'd somehow managed to hurt herself on the potholes we'd been riding but no, it was her bike. Henry, as he is called, had a problem. Henry was short for 'Sir Henry the Hybrid', after the parts from seven different bikes that had gone into getting him fit for Africa, and the fact that once ready he looked rather like an old gentleman wearing a monocle.

What had started off as a bit of a squeal from the back wheel had turned into a screech, but then had disappeared. The noise had played games with her for the past kilometre. One moment it was there and the next it was gone. It was almost as if a small stone had got stuck somewhere and then was working itself loose – that was a noise we were both familiar with by now. But then a new squeal turned into a loud screech, and then a howl of tortured metal.

For long sections the scrub had come right up to the roadside and African drivers would cheerfully bat anything smaller than they were out of the way. It wasn't malevolence, more a case of "I'm bigger than you, on important business, just "GET OUT OF THE WAY!" So we thanked our lucky stars that there was somewhere safe to pull over to inspect the bike. But when we stripped off the luggage there was no visible sign of damage.

The bad news was that we couldn't get the back wheel out. The spindle seemed to be stuck solid – even hitting it with our outsized tyre levers wouldn't budge it. We had no choice but to ride on, ever more carefully, both of us worrying about the damage that must be happening. We rode along wondering whether the problem was something we were going to be able to fix. Malawi isn't a place famed for its motorcycle mechanics, let alone BMW mechanics, so if we couldn't fix it, then we were about to take an unscheduled break from the road.

We finally made it down to Nkata Bay on Lake Malawi. I'd stayed there before, knew where the campsite was and that there was enough of an infrastructure for us to be able to sort the bike out, with a bit of luck. I also knew that there were few better places to be stuck, if it couldn't be avoided.

Another change had occurred though. The beach, once a deserted place for fishermen and travellers with their own vehicles, now sported  a bar and a hostel that was a good step up from the sort of places we would normally stay in. But my old spot under the trees was still there and the local kids were just as enthusiastic to run errands for us. I shouldn't have been surprised at the building though. It was a great location and tourism was developing fast in this peaceful and beautiful country. At least the buildings had been done in the local style and blended in sympathetically with the surroundings.

Sir Henry was a problem. After another hour of pushing and pulling we were no closer to getting the wheel out – time to resort to a sledgehammer. We borrowed one and tentatively started to bash at the bike. Nothing shifted, but an audience gathered. After fifteen minutes of firm tapping we knew that the wheel spindle wasn't going to come out of the casing without a hard whack.

It seemed sacrilegious to do it. After all the nurturing and TLC that we usually lavished on the bikes, hitting one of them with a sledgehammer seemed totally out of order. But it worked, and with a change from steely resistance to a rushing release the spindle finally shifted, but with part of the wheel apparently stuck to it.

Several more serious whacks had the spindle completely out and we could then see what the problem was. Somehow the back wheel bearing had seized and heat-welded itself to the spindle. "Not a problem", we thought. We had a spare bearing and in any case, even if we hadn't, a replacement bearing of some sort wasn't likely to be too hard to track down. The real problem came from the fact that riding the bike with the seized bearing had meant that its casing had been moving in the wheel housing. This movement, combined with all the sand and dust that had been swirling around it, had ground away the housing to the extent that the new bearing 'swam' in the slot. It was totally useless – time for an excellent Malawi Carlsberg beer, and a rethink.

Could we put a sleeve into the wheel bearing housing? Yes, probably, as a temporary repair, but we'd no idea if the job could be done well enough to be sure that the bike would be safe to ride. The roads were sufficiently punishing to make this consideration even more of an issue than normal. Henry is shaft drive and such an old bike that we didn't think we'd be able to find a spare wheel stashed away in the back of someone's workshop. It wasn't entirely implausible though; many African police forces used BMWs and that meant both knowledge and parts were quite likely to be available. But there was no rear wheel to be had for an R60/5 BMW in Malawi.

We phoned our friend Bob Porecha in London. Bob ran a small private BMW garage in Sydenham and to my mind was one of the BMW mechanical greats. His knowledge and experience were tremendous and we trusted his advice implicitly. "What do you think Bob? Can you get a replacement wheel sent out for us? And if you can, could you put a new bearing in please."

"I can get one I'm sure," said Bob. "And I can fit a sealed bearing for you. That should save you having this problem in the future." Excellent and simple – how good it is to have friends who want to help, and how good it was that DHL could deliver the wheel almost to our door. All we needed to do was to sit back and enjoy Nkata Bay for a week or so. Neither of us was worried about doing that – we both knew that this unplanned situation would create a new adventure.

That afternoon we moved to a new campsite closer to the town and there, just as a thunderstorm began to hit the shore, we bumped into a couple of friends we'd last seen on Zanzibar. It pounded across Lake Malawi, throwing up waves that crashed on the few shoreline rocks.

The fishermen scurried around in the driving rain to pull their heavy log canoes further up the beach.

Far out on the lake, with a purple, indigo and charcoal grey backdrop, a canoe, packed with a line of people holding umbrellas, stood out as a splash of multi-coloured vibrancy in one of the last remaining rays of sunlight. In an instant, the light had passed on and the brilliant reds, yellows and greens of the umbrellas dulled into a vague, rain-drenched shadow on the lake. I wondered if the canoe would make it to safety before the storm really hit.

Around us the palm trees rustled furiously, tin roofs rattled, donkeys pinned back their ears and brayed – all combining into some sort of weird background percussion. A sort of warm-up for the crackling thunder that accompanied the giant multi-pronged flashes of lightning that started to hammer at the lake and at the land behind us. There were only seconds between the flashes and the bangs and the two coincided as the storm arrived overhead.

The rain came down in stair rods, shredding the palm leaves as it powered through the trees. Every few seconds the world was lit up as if an enormous flashgun had gone off. I wondered how much power there was in each of the blasts of light and sound and tried to recall what one is supposed to do when caught in a thunderstorm. I couldn't remember, but common sense said that we should be OK. The straw-roofed shelter over our tent shouldn't attract the lightning and the bikes were a good five metres away from us. If we were hit, it was going to be pure bad luck. We sat watching the magnificence of the storm and as we did so I knew we'd done the right thing by moving from our last camping spot. We'd have been flooded out by the waves there and the view of the storm would have been nothing like as spectacular!

By morning the storm had gone and in its wake had left a slightly stunned air in which everything was cleaner than it had probably been for months, but there was also quite a bit of damage. The town had been spared any lightning strikes, but most of the sun shelters had come tumbling down. Thanks to quick repair work there was little sign of the storm's passage by late morning, except that the shredded leaves of the palm trees sounded quite different in the breeze.

Watching Birgit over the next few days, she seemed to be suffering from 'motorcycle withdrawal'. It was a sign of just how comfortable she had become with her bike and of how much she appreciated the freedom that a bike gives you, now that hers was in bits. Right now, Henry was just a painful reminder that, after months of freedom and being mostly in control of her destiny, she was anchored to the spot and reliant on others. There were so many things that other people had to get right before she could get her new wheel, and there was always the nagging doubt that, for some reason, it wouldn't fit.

Normally Birgit was a happy-go-lucky person who could take knocks in her stride. Now she was distracted and fidgety, needing to find new things to do all the time to keep her mind off the wheel. She learnt to paddle a dugout canoe, much to the encouraging amusement of the fishermen. She got stuck in to bargaining with the locals for their woodcarvings. She practised her juggling skills and the village was explored from top to bottom, a dozen times. I was glad when DHL let us know that the wheel had arrived and that we could go to pick it up from the next town. Hanging around on a beach was exhausting!

Dealing with DHL was a pleasure. We were well treated by them and they were incredibly efficient. The wheel arrived safely and undamaged. And not only that, they brought it into the country on the back of Henry's carnet. This meant that we didn't have to pay any import taxes – it entered the country as a temporary import too. We'd asked Bob to put a low value on the wheel just in case this ploy wasn't successful, but it was a darned sight easier without having to go through the import duty hassle. In fact, this was a lesson well learnt. If we'd asked Bob to post us the wheel, it would have taken longer, would have been far more likely to have got 'lost' and we would have had to travel to its point of entry into Malawi to process it through customs. What a pain that would have been.

The new wheel went in with a slip of grease and a tap. Birgit's face shone – she had her freedom back. Surviving this sort of treatment was actually a testament to BMW's engineering, and to the skill with which Birgit and Klabbie had put Henry back together. The bike had already covered a lot of miles and the roads had mostly been far from smooth. What had happened had been unfortunate and had cost a bob or two, but in the end the unexpected delay had allowed us to learn new things and had given us some happy little adventures.

We stopped off in Monkey Bay, in the capital city Lilongwe, and then headed for the Zomba plateau. We were in 'cruise mode' and the countryside eased by us each day.

The roads were better than many and the locals colourful. It actually got cold in the lush green hills as we headed up over the plateau and down towards Mozambique. When I'd last ridden this way in 1992 there had been a real flare-up within Mozambique and it hadn't been possible to ride through, not even in armed convoys through the infamous Tete corridor. I'd had to go round through Zambia to get into Zimbabwe, which wasn't a chore, but it wasn't Mozambique!

After independence from Portugal in 1975 the new socialist FRELIMO government (Frente de Libertação de Moçambique) had found itself in a civil war with RENAMO (Resistência Nacional Moçambicana), who were sponsored by the governments of Rhodesia (as Zimbabwe used to be called), and South Africa. Economic collapse marked the first decade of independence; an estimated one million people died in the war, 1.7 million escaped to surrounding countries and several million more were displaced internally.

Now things were calm and with the help of a local businessman, who was also making the journey through the Tete corridor, we had a pretty smooth passage. Roberto was a flamboyant character and the archetypal 'wheeler-dealer'.

He was fat, dressed in beige and cream-coloured clothes, and had a giant red polka-dot handkerchief with which he was constantly mopping his brow. His hair was slightly long and greased back with some sort of scented hair lotion. His armpits were drenched in sweat and the back of his shirt was a solid dark, wet stain where he'd been sitting on his car seat. The backs of his thighs were equally stained and as he waddled rapidly from official to official, his trousers seemed to squeak from the compressed movement of damp fabric between his chunky legs. He treated all the officials as if they were members of his family, hugging each and every one, but he did so with a respect that showed that he knew just how far he could go. Either that or he had worked out that border officials and soldiers at checkpoints don't particularly enjoy being recipients of sweaty hugs and would do all they could to get him on his way, and out of theirs. Whatever, it worked and we seemed to be swept along in his large slipstream as he bounded around the border and checkpoints with far more energy than a man of his size should have had. I have no doubt that we escaped numerous demands to pay considerable amounts of 'dash' (bribe money) to the officials thanks to Roberto and his 'sweaty cuddle system'.

The steel girder bridge over the Zambezi River crawled with olive-green clad soldiers. Sandbagged machine-gun emplacements guarded the approaches. The town of Tete looked beaten-up, old and tired. Water and lichen-stained concrete walls held up patched and rusty corrugated iron roofs. There weren't any children at play in the streets. Skeletal dogs slunk from shady patch to rubbish tip to shady patch.

The people looked nervy and not a soul watched us ride through. It was almost as if it was dangerous to watch what anyone else was up to. Normally we'd be better than TV, or even a night of story-telling around the village fire. But here, we were visibly ignored. The only people who stared were the soldiers, all of whom looked as if they thought life was cheap. The mood was catching. We rode on through, trying hard not to catch anyone else's eye, and eased away as quickly as we could from the town and its streets full of broken tarmac.

The corridor wasn't particularly remarkable and if it wasn't for the violent history that surrounded the road, it would have felt as if we

were out for a Sunday afternoon ride in the countryside. Some of the surface was muddy and rutted, quite possibly where a vehicle had been blown up, or perhaps as a result of poor quality road building and the weather.

Some of the trees along the roadside were shattered and blackened. Lightning strikes or gunfire?, we wondered. Occasionally there would be the rusting skeleton of a 4x4 or a truck, over which 'morning glory' vines had already wrapped their tendrils and deep purple flower trumpets were helping to return the iron into the ground. There was nothing to say whether they had simply expired there, or whether they were victims of a violent end. Sporadic baobab trees stood solid, and mysteriously, just back into the bush. These great trees looked as if nothing would or could touch them. They always reminded me of wise old men who had seen everything, and I wished that they could speak of what they had seen in their lifetimes. Some can live for over 400 years, which is roughly how long Mozambique was a Portuguese colony.

Tall elephant grass swayed along much of the roadside and we hardly saw a soul. Normally we'd see men wheeling black, 'sit-up-and-beg' Chinese bicycles, loaded high with bundles of goods or with bunches of fruit. We'd see barefoot boys dressed in shorts and raggedy shirts herding goats or cattle. And we'd see women walking elegantly with bundles of firewood almost as big as they were on their heads. But it was almost as if the road had been so dangerous for so long that people had found other ways through the area, and even though peace was supposed to be there, the habit of taking the alternative route was a hard one to break. Except for the occasional vehicle, the area was deserted, and we didn't see any wildlife at all, not even a bird. I wondered if the landmines that were supposed to litter the roadsides and the bush surrounding the road had something to do with the lack of larger wildlife. We'd been warned not to step off the road if we needed to go to the loo.

All too soon, Roberto was stopping his car and wishing us 'happy travels' in his Portuguese-accented English. His long-suffering vehicle had a permanent sag on the side he sat and the suspension groaned every time he sat in it.

Twenty minutes later we were at the Nyamapanda crossing point into Zimbabwe. It was getting late and we knew that we shouldn't try to free-camp anywhere near the border. Smugglers abound, and the area was still sensitive. I dislike crossing borders at the end of a day. You're always tired and so are the officials and after the traumatic night-time ride on the dirt road to the beach in Kenya, I didn't relish riding in the dark again. I knew that Birgit was getting tense with the thought of it – her riding style had become stiff and urgent as she was pushing on harder than she normally did.

There was already a darkening tinge to the sky by the time we made it to the first official's desk. In true African style, nothing was hurried. It was our fault for being there late and the official had no idea that we were more impatient than we would normally be. Birgit was hopping from one foot to the other and was becoming increasingly edgy. Until this time I'd done all the border crossing paperwork, and the negotiations. After all, I'd been there before and I knew what was needed. Birgit had been happy to let me get on with it. This allowed her to concentrate on riding her bike, and on the sights of the alien lands that surrounded us. Not this time though. In her eagerness to get off the road and parked up before it got too dark, she was with me and enthusiastically wanting to make things happen.

The crunch came when Birgit refused to give some of her credit card details to the customs officers. An argument ensued, with the officer in front of us getting quite annoyed with her. So much so that after she had dug her heels in, he leant across his counter and looking down at her said, "The government of Zimbabwe doesn't just drag us off the street and stick us in a uniform you know!"

He didn't like the fact that we didn't trust him and that Birgit was letting it show. It was a rock and a hard place – one of those moments when you just have to go with your instinct. Mine now said he was 'kosher' and though the rule seemed quite strange and open to potential abuse, we should give over the details and get on with it. Birgit was adamant – it was too much of a risk. The official leant over again, exasperated. At any moment he could turn away from us, bored and disinterested, or with his nose firmly out of joint. Either would be dangerous, frustrating and probably expensive for us. Looking down at Birgit, he said, "Well, just go back to Mozambique then."

It was tempting to say, "Stuff it", and see what would happen. But then commonsense kicked in. We only had transit visas for Mozambique and by this time the offices on the other side of the border were about to close too. With fingers crossed we handed over our details. Our carnets and passports were stamped and three minutes later we were back with the bikes looking down a road that no longer had any sun on it, just long dark shadows.

It was only then that I realised just how bad Birgit's headlight was. It was absolutely pathetic – no wonder she had been so afraid of losing me on the dirt road in Kenya. She'd been riding the dirt track using my dancing headlight beam to see where she was going! Now, in the dark of the border road, she was in trouble. We slowed to 50kph and as we did so it was easy to see that my light was at least three times more effective than hers.

We stopped to make a plan – the evening sky was moonless. Free-camping was still out of the question and the only villages were small and very scruffy affairs that looked as if they were there only to service the long distance truck drivers' needs. In the gloom, every character around the ramshackle collection of huts looked dubious. The flickering light of paraffin lamps lit the people, throwing dark, dangerous shadows where the yellow glow didn't reach.

We decided to carry on with me riding beside her but even that was precarious going. It was 5pm and at Birgit's speed we had six hours of riding to do in the dark. It's amazing what sort of daft decisions you can make when you are tired, in an alien land, and are allowing your imagination to run wild.

People say that you have to go through the hard times to be able to really appreciate the good times. I suppose there is some sense in that, but when you are in the middle of a hard time, the thought sounds crass! What we did appreciate was that the road was really good tarmac and the fact that there was so little going on meant that traffic was minimal. We didn't even have to contend with the erratic behaviour of goats and dogs. We also thoroughly appreciated the streetlights that suddenly lit our way as we got to the edge of Zimbabwe's capital, Harare. The welcome we got from other campers when we rolled up at the backpackers' hostel we'd chosen, made us feel that we'd achieved something special – even if it was just a ride in the dark on a good road.

Jo and Pete were at the hostel when we arrived. Pete was suffering from malaria and looked more like a skinny Ghandi than a backpacker from the UK. However, he was a biker and that meant when he heard our engines come out of the gloomy orange sodium lights outside the hostel, he dragged himself from his sick tent to say hello. His partner Jo was a bubbly, friendly person and was just what we needed at the end of such a day. We liked the two of them instantly and over the following days built up a lasting friendship.

Birgit and I spent the next month exploring Zimbabwe. What a wonderful country it was, at the time. The people were amazingly friendly. No one looked as if they were starving. The fields had crops growing, buildings had paint on, the roads were in brilliant condition, and the scenery was varied and stunning.

Now, looking back, there were a few niggling signs that the country was slipping downhill. But there were no obvious indications that Zimbabwe's former 'freedom fighter' and democratically elected president, Robert Mugabe, had become a despotic ruler who lined his own pockets and ruled ruthlessly by fear.

It was easy to be there as a traveller and be so wrapped up in everyday things that despite all the exploring we were doing and questions we were asking, we did little more than ride across the surface of the country in awe. We had no idea that over the next ten years almost a quarter of the population would flee the country, driven mostly by fear or hunger. Life expectancy for women would fall dramatically to just 34 years of age, the lowest anywhere in the world, according to the UN. For men it would fall to just 37.

The locals we spent time with kept their problems to themselves – Africans can be proud that way. We saw no beggars anywhere and the Zimbabwe of the time remains in my memory as a land where people smiled a lot, and made us very welcome. Our border and everyday living problems were not unduly troubling – they were just challenges that we were well equipped to deal with.

It would have been easy to stay longer, but after our time exploring we felt we ought to get down into South Africa. We knew that it wasn't going to be easy to arrange a sea passage across to South America and wanted to do some research before heading up into Namibia and Botswana.

We dropped down to South Africa's capital, Pretoria, to see the famous jacaranda trees in full flower. Their blossom transforms the city into a vibrant and beautiful vision of brilliant mauve-blue. Then we cut across to the lush and very fertile mountains of Swaziland before heading down into the port city of Durban.

Durban didn't look as if it had changed much in four years, except that there were less white people around and the streets were more 'African' than they had been, with impromptu street markets and stalls dotting the sides of many of the roads. In the past these roadsides had been just clean gutters and drains. After a few days checking things out, there was no doubt that Durban, as one of the biggest ports in Africa, was the place to look for a ship to either Argentina or Brazil.

Armed with that knowledge, we carried on south. We wanted to see some of the Transkei, one of the ten former homelands, or Bantustans, which were originally created in colonial times, but made progressively more separate by the apartheid regime of the National party as it attempted to disenfranchise black South Africans in the 1970s by declaring them citizens of separate countries inside South Africa's borders.

Transkei was the first homeland to be given 'independence' by the South African government, but no other nation recognised it as such. After the end of apartheid and Nelson Mandela's tumultuous election as president in 1994, Transkei officially became part of South Africa again, which was fitting since it's where Mandela was born.

The Transkei is made up of rolling hillsides and is, in parts, surprisingly fertile. I had liked it when I'd been there before but was sad to hear all the warning stories that were floating around now. The capital city Umtata was supposed to have a worse level of gun crime than Johannesburg. Mugging and robbery were supposed to be common, and most South Africans we met would rather drive hundreds of miles inland to skirt through the mountain kingdom of Lesotho, than risk driving through the Transkei. At first I wasn't sure what to think but we decided that, if we watched our 'Ps and Qs' and used common sense, we'd be OK.

We were, but there was danger from two completely unexpected directions. The locals were great. They were friendly and acknowledged us with smiles and waves or else just got on with their daily business as if we weren't there. That suited us fine and as the fear factor began to slip away we started to enjoy riding the rolling hillsides.

All of a sudden a sleek, tan-coloured blob streaked out from the scrubby tan- coloured roadside grasses! Birgit's bike leapt madly up into the air before coming back to hit the ground with a violent wobble that had me thinking, "She isn't going to make it out of this in one piece!"

As I rode past the point of impact I could see that she'd hit a large dog. This dog was now lying stunned by the roadside and if I'd not known it was there I wouldn't have seen it. It was perfectly camouflaged.

Birgit managed to stay on the bike. Her face was red and she was completely unsteady. "It just ran out in front of me", she said. "I couldn't miss it. I wasn't going fast was I? Did I kill it?" I helped her off her bike and leaving her to squat, completely shocked, I headed back to the dog which had now rather pathetically raised its head up from the grass. I wondered what on earth to do.

Could I kill this dog? It must be in misery. Henry was a heavy bike and Birgit must have ridden straight over it. Surely its back was broken. I couldn't kill it with my bare hands. Could I do it with my Swiss army knife? I doubted it. I looked around for a large rock – there wasn't one to be seen anywhere. I was torn between finding something to finish it off with and getting back to Birgit to make sure she was OK. I chose the latter, in part because I was worried, but also, I'm ashamed to say, because it allowed me some delay. I would return to perform the 'coup de grâce' with my penknife shortly.

I got back to Birgit and again she asked "Is it dead, did I kill it? I told her it wasn't dead but not that I was going to have to go back and put it out of its misery. I wasn't sure how she would cope with that thought, shocked state or not.

At that moment the dog got up, shook itself, and shooting us a look of pure contempt, turned and headed off into the grasslands. It didn't even limp. To this day I am mystified by its apparent lack of injury. At that moment a look of pure relief flooded across Birgit's face.

That night we camped on the grassy bank outside a backpackers' hostel in a small town called Coffee Bay. It's right on the so-called Wild Coast. It looked wonderfully cosy inside the hostel but it was significantly cheaper to camp, and anyway, there's always something nice about being outside. That night though, I wasn't so sure.

The temperature dropped like a stone. It got really cold, very fast. The air started to feel quite heavy and there was a sense of menace to it. In the village, the goats, donkeys and chickens started to kick up a row. Something bad was coming, but we'd no idea what.

Out at sea the wind had suddenly got up and as it did so the waters in the bay began to churn. Large white-crested waves started streaming in and smashing against the shore, throwing great plumes of spray into the air. If I'd been a surfer I might have been quite excited by the sight, but all I felt was a sense of dread. The wind was getting stronger. The tents around ours started to flap violently. The spray was rising ever higher into the air, and leaves and twigs from the trees down by the bay were coming past us at such a rate that it began to dawn on us that this situation was potentially dangerous.

One of the sights to see is called the 'Hole in the Wall'. It's a freestanding plinth of rock through which the waves have worn a giant hole. This rock was usually visible for kilometres. Now we couldn't see a thing through the spray and driving rain. I'd never really understood what 'driving rain' meant until then. The wind was blowing a torrent of enormous raindrops almost horizontally at us. The other campers retreated inside.

Birgs and I stayed where we were. Luckily we'd put our tent tail-first into the wind. We now instinctively looked for the direction that the worst weather might come from, and tailed the tent into that direction. It was working well. Around us other tents began to buckle and collapse. Their owners came rushing out to try to take them down but none of them succeeded. Moments later, freed of some of their guy lines and tent pegs, the tents took off up the hill. It was like watching a few seconds of a paragliding movie running backwards, and speeded up.

Our tent was still doing well though. When we were in Durban we'd been sponsored with this tent at cost price by a South African firm called Cadec. The 3- person tent, a Sunseeker, had been designed to be used on Everest expeditions. It was heavy, at least two kilos heavier than we'd have liked, but it had a great amount of living space and the special design was standing up well to this Indian Ocean storm. We could certainly see why it was called the Wild Coast, and why so many ships had been wrecked upon it.

When the wind got stronger still, we had to make a choice. On the slope it was possible to lean over into the wind and for the wind to support my bodyweight. In fact the wind was so powerful it wanted to flip me right over backwards! We weren't sure how much more of this storm our tent could take.

Should we risk trying to take it down, or should we lie down in it and use our bodyweight as an anchor? We chose the latter and to our surprise there was an icy river flowing under the tent. It was like lying on a waterbed that had been filled with glacier run-off, but amazingly, the inside of the tent stayed dry.

Outside, the wind howled and that was all we could hear. We lay there 'discussing', at the top of our voices, what the chances were that our tent would take off and do a paraglider impersonation of its own. If it did that with us still in it, bones would certainly be broken. We finally decided to make a dash for the hostel. Inside, everyone was watching the storm through the big picture window and a log fire was blazing.

I hadn't realised until that moment just how cold I'd got. Birgit was shivering too, and she has a far better tolerance for cold than I do. Outside on the slope, our tent continued to shiver violently in the wind. I rather felt I'd deserted it. It had fast become a friend – a status we awarded to kit that had proved itself and without which life would be far worse. It had earned that accolade in a few short weeks and now it looked as if we were going to lose it.

With nothing left to do, and the storm still raging, we lay down to sleep. Eventually, as dawn rose, the storm began to ease a little. Some of us went out to see what was going on. It was still a battle to walk anywhere and to my complete amazement our tent was still there, clinging to the slope. In the town, roofs had been ripped off, trees had been torn out by the roots and a couple of cars had been blown over. The mini supermarket sign had been ripped away from the wall and was embedded in the wall of the house on the other side of the street, just by a window. Inches to the right and…

One of the locals shouted to us over the noise of the wind and flapping corrugated roofing iron, "This house lost its roof because of a broken window." At first I thought I'd heard him wrong and that I'd only caught some of his words in the wind. But I'd heard him correctly.

A big house just down the street had had a window broken by some flying debris, and as soon as that window had broken it had become a point for the wind to get in. The pressure had built up so strongly inside the room that it had popped the roof off. I'd never heard of such a thing before but could easily see how it could happen. Once again we'd been very lucky. Down in the bay below, the whole beach had disappeared. Just a few craggy rocks and a few mangled trees remained.

When the sun came back out we headed down along the beautiful but very touristy Garden Route, and on into Cape Town. It was important to us to make a loop down that way because if we shipped out from Durban, Birgit might otherwise never get the chance to see the southernmost tip of Africa, and I wanted to link up with my friends Lee and Toni, and my cousins Rod and Claire.

Pulling into Cape Town's Backpack Hostel was another homecoming. After breaking bones in seventeen places in Namibia in 1992 I'd had to stay at the hostel so long that it really had felt like home. That was largely due to the amazingly warm and kind people who staffed the hostel. To my delight most of them were still there and everyone took to Birgit straight away. The hostel had changed though. It was no longer a place for budget travellers to stay, but more for those with a little more money in their pockets. The rent was a bit steep for us and we felt a little awkward about the thought of moving on to a cheaper hostel. It almost felt disloyal. But Lee must have been a mind reader – I'm sure that we kept our concerns to ourselves. But then again, Lee was a good mate and an experienced traveller.

She'd been asked to house-sit a local millionaire's property while he was away; would we do it? It was much more convenient for her to be able to carry on living in her own house, she said. We leapt at the chance! It was one of those rare moments when the road throws up something quite bizarre. It felt wonderfully perverse for us to be living in a millionaire's house that looked down over an expanse of pale yellow sand. It had enormous patio windows, through which we were able to watch stunning and flamboyant southern cape sunsets.

Cape Town is yet another of Africa's 'very easy to get stuck in' places. The weeks whizzed by happily. I checked out old haunts with Birgit and we explored new places together, but eventually we knew that we should be on the move. Birgit had got it into her head that she wanted to go to the southernmost point of South America. I wasn't so sure. I don't enjoy the cold very much and after my ride back to Europe through Iran and Turkey in the middle of winter, I knew that it could be decidedly dangerous as well as damned uncomfortable.

If we were going to do it, then we had to be there in the two to three month 'weather window' in the middle of the summer. Outside of this period, from mid-October to late January, the road could be covered in snow. I was determined never to ride on snow again, if I could possibly avoid it. It was now late May, so the clock was ticking. We still wanted to get up into Namibia and Botswana, and we had no idea how long it would take us to get a ship across the southern Atlantic.

In spite of this, we headed north with confidence. We felt sure that we could organise what we needed, and see everything we wanted to see. The next six weeks passed in an orgy of riding some of the most fantastic roads in Africa. The canyons, the dunes and the coastline of Namibia enthralled us. And to top it all we linked up with a couple of friends we'd made in Malawi.

Carlo was an Italian who was riding a BMW R100GS BMW called 'Stewpot' (we never did find out why). To look at he was the sort of bloke that would have girls going weak at the knees. He was tall and lean with a roguish smile and twinkling eyes set into a rugged, lived-in face. He too was on a mega trip and had come across to Africa from an extended ride through the Americas. We picked his brains mercilessly, and it seemed that the Americas held some great adventures in store for us.

Our other new friend was a Dane called Gunnar. He was 65 years old and had just ridden his Honda down the west side of Africa at a time when no one was supposed to be able to make it through. I was impressed that a man his age would even attempt such a thing, but he was quite matter-of-fact about it.

He said, "I may not ride as fast as the young people and perhaps I don't bounce as well, but with a lifetime of experience and a more gentle pace, I think I see things with more depth and quality."

I could see his point and was certain he was right. I pledged at that moment to slow down again and to get back into our more gentle style of travelling. In the recent days of haste we'd ridden past a few things that we really should have taken the time to visit. We'd nearly had an expensive disaster too.

Chapter 4

'When the World holds its breath'

'Life is what happens when we're making other plans.'

John Lennon

Namibia is a photographer's dream with wonderful roads, and this combination has you mentally battling with whether to ride, or to stop and take photos. Thankfully both of us were mad keen on taking pictures so we took our time and got the most out of both opportunities. If either of us hadn't been into photography, the constant 'stop, look around, take a picture, start again' way of riding our days might soon have rankled.

After one of these stops Birgit somehow didn't get her camera bag fastened onto the bike properly. The bag worked loose and she didn't notice she'd lost it until a long ride down a dirt road. She was instantly gutted. Not only was her camera an old friend, but the roll of film inside it was almost all used up.

We knew that we were highly unlikely to see the camera again. There'd been a fair bit of traffic on the road and that meant, to our too cynical minds, that the camera was long ago into someone's car and that the driver was scooting along congratulating himself on his unexpected windfall.

In fact on a road as bumpy as this, at the speed we'd been driving, the camera was just as likely to bounce off into the scrubby, dust-covered brush that lined the roadsides. In any event, the impact would almost certainly have wrecked it.

We'd just decided that we'd got nothing to lose by heading back down the road to check, just in case, when a beat up rusty panelled pick up truck pulled up and a hand dangled Birgit's camera out of the window.

"We saw you go past earlier – think this is probably yours," the man driving the truck said. We'd doubted the general honesty of human beings and were happily proved wrong. With hindsight, I suspect that most people passing along that road would have done the same. The only 'luck' about this situation was that the camera was only slightly damaged; the rest was down to the better side of human nature.

I was nervous, very nervous. We were heading north towards the Caprivi Strip. This finger of Namibia runs between Botswana and Angola until it reaches the border with Zambia. It contained the strip of desert road where, the first time through Africa, I'd hit a metre-deep pothole in a dust cloud and woken up four days later in hospital with 17 bone fractures. I knew that most of the track had now been tarmacked, but I was still nervous. It was a demon from the past that I had to face. Besides that, I'd missed half of it, being unconscious at the time, and there was something rather nice about completing the job, even doing it from the 'wrong' direction. It was also the road from which Birgs and I wanted to get down into Botswana, skirting along the western side of the Okavango Delta.

The improved road was easy and in a perverse way I was glad I'd ridden it when it was still a hard thing to do. With the demon laid to rest, Birgit and I cut southwards just past Bagani, took a quick squint at the Popa falls, and then headed for Botswana. The tarmac ran out at the border, and was replaced by glaringly white sand and gravel. I'd forgotten just how bright this stuff was and how easily it covered everything.

The border crossing was a doddle. The officials were polite, friendly and knew exactly what they were doing. No one asked for 'dash' (bribe money) and within an hour we were through. In front of us lay 195 kilometres of what our map said was tarmac, but our eyes told us was not. We were heading for a fishing village just south of a small town called Guzman and as we were through the border by ten am, we had plenty of time to deal with whatever the road was going to throw at us. Or so we thought...

In spite of our dual purpose tyres, the gravel had the bikes wheels skipping and sliding. The key when riding this stuff is to keep your speed up and to loosen off on the handlebars – let the bike go

where it wants to go – within reason of course. Riding with this gently meandering technique is a far sight less tiring than

fighting every directional demand the road gives the bike. It still needs total concentration though and particularly so when riding the white road – the glare could hide some real 'nasties' such as an un-noticed section of softer sand.

Depending on how deep or soft the sand was, it could throw your front wheel towards the bush and if it was really thick it could slow you so rapidly that you'd come off over the handlebars, or fall off sideways as your bike suddenly lost momentum. The key was to keep that throttle open. Scary sometimes, especially for a beginner, but it always worked.

We suddenly found ourselves riding into a game park that wasn't marked on our map. Weird. Bikes weren't normally allowed in game parks but that was where the road was taking us. With no one around to stop us we rode on thinking, "This is good, what a bonus! I wonder what wildlife we'll see?" Not a thing, was the answer and that was a real shame, so we decided to go off and do a little exploring on a side road. The pale beige track was harder to ride – it was rutted and sandy, with sharp twists that made it hard to keep our speed up. I felt a little like a naughty schoolboy doing something I knew I shouldn't be, but the tingle of adrenaline and the anticipation of what we might see, spurred us on. I told Birgit that whatever happened, she should always keep her engine running. She might need to make a quick getaway, and an engine that wouldn't start in a panic situation would have been pretty stupid. But I'd also been told that we were far more likely to see game without scaring them off if we kept the engines running. The sound, after initial suspicion, would become the norm, and whatever animal it was would happily carry on going about its business. The plan worked with a small cluster of antelope, but would it work with the large group of elephant that stepped out of the bush into the road in front of us?

The lead elephant was highly suspicious and stood between us and her family. The old cow's big ears were flapping furiously and she kept curling her trunk upwards, before letting out what sounded to me like shrieks of pure rage. I started to look for an escape route. There wasn't one and a three-point turn on this loose stuff wasn't going to be easy. All we could do was to sit there, not moving a muscle, keeping the engines ticking over – we just had to be patient. Around us the bush seemed to have gone deathly still, as if everything was holding its breath, waiting to see what would happen next. If I hadn't been so afraid of stalling the bike I'd have had my fingers firmly crossed.

Then, after a magnificent ten minutes of swaying back and forth, stamping the ground, snorting and ear-flapping, she simply turned around, trumpeted again and she and her family crashed off into the bush. She left Birgit and me sitting in the silence on our bikes, sweating furiously. I was conscious then that it was no wonder the elephant had been so agitated. The smell of our fear, combined with the scents of hot oil, metal and rubber from the bikes, must have made a really offensive and worrying odour. I knew that the old cow probably associated these scents with poachers. The elephant population had been wiped almost to extinction in this region, within her lifetime.

We knew that we'd been very lucky and that we'd just seen something really special. Back at the main track, we looked at each other and grinned. The day was turning into a goodie. Then the track turned it into a baddie…

The gravel disappeared and soft sand took its place. This stuff is a nightmare to ride on with a loaded bike. If the road twists you simply can't get enough speed up to hammer through and that means you have to resign yourself to paddling through. As I watched Birgit, I thought about how much she had learned over the past months. Now there wasn't anywhere I felt I couldn't ride with her. She was more than competent, and no longer got so frustrated with 'I can't do it' thoughts. Not that she'd ever let those thoughts beat her. I felt guilty though.

Libby, as I called my BMW R80GS, was a doddle to ride in comparison to Sir Henry. The brakes were better, the larger front wheel made off-roading easier and the fact that she was a longer bike, with much better and more sophisticated suspension, helped her to soak up bumps rather than crash into them. The GS in 'R80GS' actually stands for 'Gelände/Strasse' or 'on and off road' so it was designed with off-road use in mind; Sir Henry, as an R60/5, certainly was not.

Birgit had also learnt that if she was about to drop her bike then it was better to get off the thing rather than risk getting trapped under it. She'd gone well past the stage of not wanting to scratch the bike, and that's hard when it's your pride and joy. Now, her sensible attitude was that damage to the bike could be fixed, but damage to her might be a different matter...

We paddled on. I could now smell my clutch burning and wondered how much damage this section of track alone was going to do to it. The clutch now had over 120,000 miles on it and most of those miles had been hard. I'd no idea how much longer the bike would keep going, and I just couldn't get out of my mind the comments a mechanic had made just before we'd set off.

He'd listened to Libby's life story and had said, "Take this thing to Africa again? I wouldn't, the thing's a wreck, bloody trashed it you have." And then to add insult to injury, the mechanic kicked one of the tyres and said, "Yeah, heap of shit. You'd be better off dumping the thing." Every mile we did gave me a sense of satisfaction. But I just couldn't get his words out of the back of my mind when I was abusing her like this.

By the time we finally pulled into the camping spot right on the shore of the delta, I'd decided, again, that I don't like winding sandy tracks. The deep sand of the track to the main road would have to be ridden to get back out again, but thankfully, just before the turn off, the conditions of the main road had changed to rideable. For now though, the lodge was a great place to be. Below us the delta waters flowed smoothly and deeply. On the far bank a stork had nested amongst the tall, thick, dark green reeds and over the first hour that we sat watching, we saw some twenty different types of birds. We'd read that on a good day, it was possible to see over sixty different species.

The Okavango Delta is a phenomenon, and a superb chance to see wildlife. It's a geographical quirk of nature in that it's one of the few river systems in the world that doesn't flow to the sea. This river system flows inland and actually disappears into the desert. This is what makes it such a great place to see wildlife. In the rainy season the delta floods and the waters rush out into the desert. When this happens, vegetation that's dormant during the dry season comes fully and vibrantly to life, and the animals spread themselves across the land as they feed on new shoots. Drinking water is never a problem. But, as the season changes, the waters are swallowed up by the dry conditions and the delta begins to shrink. As it does so, the animals begin to corral themselves into a smaller and smaller area of land.

The delta is in fact at risk from global warming. The rainy seasons are getting shorter and the dry seasons longer and drier. This means that the delta is shrinking. As I sat watching the waters I had the feeling that I was watching something beautiful that was dying. It was a sad, but privileged moment – we had been some of the lucky ones. We'd seen this part of the delta as future generations perhaps would not. With this in mind we decided to ride on round to the town of Maun and from there to hire dug-out canoes and guides. We would use them to head as deep as possible into the delta. We wanted to see as much of it as we could.

Maun is a town on the edge of the desert and the Okavango. When we rode in I suddenly became aware of just how remote the roads we'd been on actually were. I begrudged being around people again. I didn't enjoy the smells of diesel split in the sand, the stench of burning plastic from the bonfire in the scrubby wasteland behind the sprawl of the town, the malodorous scents of toilet areas and the heavy stink of greasy fried food. I didn't like suddenly being around lots of people.

I didn't like the stupidity of the goats and dogs that seemed to think that they owned the road – they obviously had no conscious recognition of the 'I'm bigger than you are so I go first' rule. I didn't like the sight of so much litter, floating around on the breeze or hanging snagged on strands of rusting barbed wire. I didn't like the sound of a mechanic bashing a truck wheel rim with a sledgehammer – it was an offensive jarring noise. I didn't like the staring eyes that followed us wherever we went and I didn't like the prices that were being charged now that we were back in 'tourist land'.

I could only laugh at myself. These were the noises and smells of life on the edge – the sounds of survival in a harsh land. They were the smells of reality, and if we wanted to find some canoe guides we couldn't avoid people. Our aim was to escape out onto the delta where the ebb and flow of life is not directly dictated by man on a minute-by-minute basis. Out on the delta we planned to just float and see what there was to see. We'd no intention of rushing around looking for the things we were supposed to see out there. It was an opportunity to slow life down and let the things that really matter become important again. I wanted to soak up the atmosphere, the sounds and scents of the place, in case I could never return, or the delta itself should cease to exist.

Our guides were called Peter and William. (Good Botswanan names!) Peter was about five foot eleven, slim-waisted and broad-shouldered, with biceps that any teenager would be proud of. He was very black-skinned, wore his hair short and his grin wide. I guessed that he was about seventeen, though he didn't know for sure himself. He had the makings of a 'wheeler-dealer' about him, but his eyes had the gleam of sincerity. I liked him. He introduced himself to us in a very formal manner: "I am Peter. I am a businessman. We are going to do business, yes?"

William was the perfect sidekick. He must have been about thirteen, with a round face, wide lips and eyes that sparkled with enthusiasm. And he was skinny – probably from doing all the running around that Peter demanded. Or perhaps it was just that he hadn't reached manhood – he certainly didn't have the athletic and coordinated way of moving that Peter had, but they made a good team.

We settled on a price to include the canoe, their time, food and a charcoal brazier. We parked the bikes safely in a backpackers' hostel and set off down to the water's edge. Making deep paddle-strokes into the dark, tannin-filled water, the young lads propelled the heavy wooden dugout towards the delta proper with apparent ease.

The inside of the canoe was lined with reeds and we'd each been given a small plank of wood to wedge on either side of it. We could sit on that when it was firmly slotted into place. It was good to have them as the canoe leaked and it didn't take long before the water began to creep up through the reeds. William was a busy boy, alternately bailing and paddling. Peter stood at the rear of the canoe with a long pole and a paddle.

They took us gliding through channels in the reeds. The banks of reeds were often higher than Peter's head. The stems were thick and green towards the water and grew ever more tan in colour toward the fluffy tops. The gently moving water felt strangely thick to touch. Perhaps it was full of sediment, yet it looked really clear. It was like looking down through a giant piece of very high quality amber.

The only breaks to the mirror-like smoothness of the water were the ripples that the bow of the canoe made, and the brief stabbing motion of the paddles. As the canoe passed by, its wake gently rolled out in waves that disappeared into the base of the reeds and then the water would return to its glassy stillness behind us.

A kingfisher came zapping down and arrowed into the water with a minimal splash that an Olympic high diver would have been proud of. Moments later the bright green, turquoise and electric-blue bird flashed up from the depths, fluttered its wings madly as it hit the surface, and then took off towards the reeds with a small fish in its beak. It was all over within a few seconds.

In the distance we could hear the complaining 'onk, onk, onk' of hippos. The boys told us that we would be moving quite near to them and that we should keep our hands out of the water. They feared the hippos, but apparently nothing else. (Hippos kill more people in Africa than any other animal.)

That night we camped on a small island and it was almost as if the world was standing still and holding its breath as the sun went down behind the reeds. As soon as it had disappeared, the night came alive with the sounds of cicadas and the crackle and popping of our fire. I sat in its glow wondering what it is about the night that seems to amplify such sounds.

The next few days were perfect. We gently cruised the channels and Birgit had the chance to show off the skills she had learnt on Lake Malawi. Much to the delight of the boys, she poled or paddled the canoe along, meaning that for once the boys could become tourists in their own backyard. In spite of the fact that the day held nothing new for them, they too seemed to appreciate and almost revere the calm, mirrored beauty of the delta.

Too soon it was time to be on the move. Birgs and I confronted more elephants on the road across to Victoria Falls, but again without mishap. We camped alongside the great Zambezi river and rock-hopped out towards the middle of the flow. When I'd been here the last time it had been so dry a summer that I'd actually been able to walk right out to the middle of the falls.

I'd once said that if I could come back to just one place in Africa then it would be Victoria Falls, and here I was, back again and it felt exactly right to be there. I was quite amused by the proprietary feeling I had as I showed Birgit around. It was almost as if they were 'my' falls. Daft really.

We cruised south and up into the Chimanimani mountains where I'd almost killed myself with a tyre blow-out the last time I'd been there. The mountains were also where I'd stupidly thought that the malaria I had was just a heavy dose of the 'flu. We called at the ancient city of Zimbabwe and it looked just as magnificent the second time around. The monkeys were a mix of the original thieving bundles of grey fur, and a younger generation of thieves. Whatever wasn't locked away or tied down would go missing.

We slipped back into South Africa at the Beit Bridge crossing and rode through steep rugged hills to places with names such as Bandelierkop, Duiwelskloof, Blyderivierspoort, Witrivier, Nelspruit, and up Piggs Peak into Swaziland. From there we rode back into South Africa passing through rolling grass-covered hills and towns, many of which were steeped in bloody Boer War history. Piet-Retief, Ladysmith and Greytown to name just a few. Then suddenly we were back in Durban and this time nothing seemed to have changed at all.

It was serious business time for us now and I had a bad feeling about it. I had the nasty sensation that we were about to try to do the impossible. I'd been keeping my ear to the ground whilst around other travellers and had picked brains mercilessly whenever I could. The grand consensus of opinion was that we were going to find it pretty much impossible to get both ourselves and the bikes on a ship to South America.

Times had changed and it was not going to be easy to find a boat. The days of budget, round-the-world cargo ship travel were coming to an end and seemed to be long gone between Southern Africa and South America. The days of working your passage were long gone too. A little voice in the back of my mind said that if we found a ship that would take us it was going to be pure fluke – a case of being in the right place at the right time, doing the right thing. Another voice said, "Don't even bother with this. Just freight the bikes across!"

Neither of us was happy about that idea though. And we knew that if we could make it happen, not only would we share the magic adventure of being on a trans-ocean cargo ship, but we'd also have achieved something special by making it happen in the first place.

In the old days when it was relatively easy for travellers to hop a working passage on a cargo ship, there were only owners and captains involved in the decision-making process. Both were powerful people whose rights and responsibilities were clearly laid out. Now it seemed that many ships were owned by one group of people and leased by another plus there was still the captain to contend with (whose role was still much the same). Once upon a time, you rolled up to a port, spoke to a ship's captain, and you were either lucky or you weren't. It doesn't work that way now.

The changes meant that the owners, the lessee and the captain all had to agree to take passengers; an unlikely combination, especially since there was little or no profit in the idea. And insurance was the key issue.

Apparently some idiot travellers had sued shipping companies when they had had an accident aboard ship. I felt mildly infuriated when I was told that this was the main reason cargo ships wouldn't take us. That is to say, infuriated and then in a position of no choice and therefore having to be mild about it. The leap in premiums was too high, unless it was a service that the shipping companies advertised. There was one other issue that seemed to put captains and owners off: maritime law says that if you have an accident aboard ship then it's the captain's responsibility to get you to hospital as quickly as possible – even if that involves changing course and calling in at an unplanned port. The expense of doing that and the time lost could be enormous. Understandably, not many were interested in taking the risk.

Birgit and I set to work – we still wanted to try. We were sure that with effort, enthusiasm and a large dollop of luck we might just be able to make it happen. We called or wrote to every shipping agent's office in Durban. We made friends and chatted and cajoled. And to our surprise, just about everyone we talked to was inspired by the idea of what we were doing on the bikes, and wanted to help us. Quite a few said outright that none of the ships they dealt with went to South America, but those agents always made a point of giving us contact details for someone else who might be able to help. The weeks passed.

In fact so many weeks went by that we began to get worried about our budget. We were spending the same amount of money on general survival but accommodation costs were hurting the budget. Camping out in the countryside is cheap, hanging out in cities is expensive.

We didn't actually have to be in the city. We could do our telephoning and letter writing from outside the urban sprawl, so we elected to head up the coast to see if we could find a campsite that was more affordable.

To our surprise, any site that was within a day's ride of the city was ridiculously expensive – not much cheaper than staying in a hostel. This was a real worry. Despite being really frugal, our budget was really suffering. But we'd had enough of the city so when we found a site that had shade, wonderfully clean showers and plenty of space for tents, we decided to stay for a few days.

It took me a long time to get to sleep that night. I lay chewing over budget possibilities and tried to work out what to do if something didn't come right for us soon, but I was also kept awake by the silence. I had a little chuckle over that thought as I remembered how alien it had felt to be around mankind when we'd rolled into Maun. Here, it felt alien to be apart from the mass of mankind.

As always, the bikes attracted a lot of attention. They were dusty and scarred. They looked purposeful and well used for that purpose. They wouldn't have looked at all pretty to a concours d'elegance fetishist, but to us they were like two-wheeled diaries. Every scrape or dent told a story. This first morning was no different and as we were having our pan of maize meal porridge, one of the owners of the campsite strolled over. Welcoming people personally was something Peter liked to do anyway, but he stopped and chatted to us for a long time. He was fascinated by the bikes, and our trip.

Later on that day he hunted us out and offered us work. Would we be interested in renovating the three shower blocks and the recreation room? Would we like to do that in return for a free camping spot and, "While I'm thinking about it, we have a bungalow tent that you're very welcome to use."

Once again we'd had it shown to us just how amazing people are. The whole family took us under their wings and within days we felt as if we belonged there. We'd said that yes, of course we'd be delighted to do the work, but that we had a conscience problem. Surely this was something that his Zulu staff could do? Weren't we going to be taking work away from them? We weren't sure if we could do this, in spite of how much the deal was a good thing for us. Peter told us that quite simply the staff weren't trained to do a good enough job and that was why we were the perfect answer to one of his problems.

Birgit came up with a great idea. "How about if we do the work but you give us one of your lads as a sort of apprentice?" she asked. "While we're working we can teach him how to do it and then he will have a skill and you won't have a problem in the future." Problem solved, and the next day we set to work.

Johnson was all fingers and thumbs to begin with and didn't seem to have a very good attention span, but he was there and we'd made the deal, so we set to it with him. After a couple of days he seemed to click with the work and Birgit and I began to feel good about life. He was learning and the work was coming on well.

Then the next day he was late. "Oh oh", I thought, "Africa time". He said not a word but just came in and got on with his work, but very slowly. I wondered what on earth had happened. He wouldn't say. The next day the same thing happened and the day after that he was even later still. We began to get quite niggled with him as he started to mess up jobs he'd learnt how to do and had proved he could do well. As each day passed he became more and more frustrating to work with and we felt we could trust him less and less. We were at a loss. Had we done something to upset him?

We showed him how to do the work again and he did it, but so slowly that he might as well not have been there. Then we found out what the problem was from one of the guests on the site. He'd heard Johnson arguing with some of the other Zulu workers. They hadn't realised that every word they said was being understood.

Johnson was being threatened by the other workers and apparently he hadn't liked it one bit. They told him that if he didn't stop working so hard then they would ostracise him. They told him that he was becoming too friendly with us, the white people. They told him that there was no point in him learning to do this work because even if he did learn it, no one would pay him to do decorating jobs as he was 'just' a black boy!

We tried to put the situation to rights but failed miserably. We certainly couldn't push too hard. We were only going to be there for a few weeks and Johnson had to live there with the consequences of his and our actions.

On the Friday of that week Birgs and I took off into the city on Libby. To save on petrol costs we left Henry parked up on the site. We needed to get away from the site for a few days and we wanted to check out how our contacts were doing with the cargo ship hunt. We'd stopped at one of the sets of traffic lights when a man on a BMW motorcycle pulled up next to us. We nodded at each other, as you do. We then rode on to the next set of lights together and while we waited for the red light to change we struck up a conversation.

To our amazement the man said he was a shipping agent. "Is fate dealing us the cards we need?" we wondered; a BMW biker and a shipping agent! Before he zoomed off he gave us his card and said, "Call me. I may well be able to help you. I have ships going to South America all the time. I know the ships' captains very well. Yes, I think I will be able to help you. Call me tomorrow."

We did, were invited to tea in his house on a hill, and his wife made us very welcome. "This is going really well", I thought. Birgit was a little quiet though and I couldn't work out why. I wondered if she felt uncomfortable being around a man who dressed as Carlos did. He was about five foot seven, slim, swarthy with greased back hair and expensively dressed. His jewellery was almost ostentatious and there was a slightly fanatical air about him that I couldn't quite pin down. He had a way of walking that reminded me of the strut of a bantam cockerel. He also seemed to be keen on ex-army vehicles and drove around in what looked like an ex- German army Second World war 4x4, which was still painted olive green. "Each to their own," I'd thought, and I quite enjoyed meeting someone who was so different.

We explained more about our situation to Carlos, who turned out to be from Argentina, though living in South Africa with his South African wife. As far as I was concerned it was a really pleasant visit and such a relief to have such a positive flow of thoughts from Carlos. We rode away with me feeling confident that he would live up to his promises. He was absolutely convinced that there wasn't a problem. He was going to check the cargo and shipping records to find a suitable ship and would get back to us.

Days passed – no news from Carlos. We managed to link up with the local BMW motorcycle club for a Sunday breakfast run. They took us through the awe-inspiring Valley of the Thousand Hills. Real Zulu land this. Tiny villages cling to the hillsides, their round, thatched roofs a cool shelter from the mid-day heat. Small boys proudly herding lean, long-horned cattle, returned beaming white smiles to our waves. I was surprised at how friendly they were. Our new friends even took us to a party in the traditional Zulu village of Kwa Beki Tungi. The dancers were awesome, their feet stamping and beaded kilts flashing in the firelight. But the maize beer – well, you either love or hate it – I just had the one cup!

Time was passing and if the truth be known, some weeks it was hard to keep our spirits up. Day after day of disappointment pulls even an optimist down. The only things that kept us positive were simply that we were in a beautiful and incredibly diverse part of the world, with bikes. We ended up exploring pretty thoroughly, with a hard ride here and there, just to keep the adrenaline flowing.

Two hundred and fifty kilometres down the road from our camping site, the Drakensberg (Dragon Mountains) meet the sky with majestic angular arrogance. Down below the crags and peaks you find not only an important part of South Africa's history but also some magical biking roads. In just one day we found roads to suit just about every rider's taste. Smooth, immaculate tarmac on long, twisting roads that must have been designed by a biker! There are also plenty of fast, hard-surfaced gravel roads and we found the infamous Sani Pass which climbs 9,400 feet to the small Kingdom of Lesotho. It starts out as a fairly decent dirt road but as the climb begins, the road narrows and you find the first of the sharp, blind corners. We dreaded another vehicle coming towards us. The local drivers know every hump and bump in the road and obviously believe in fate. When the trees fade away, so does any chance to ride and look at the view. The road becomes so bad that you can't take your eyes of it for even a second. Not even for the scene that's unfolding magnificently in every direction. It's a view that demands that you stop, and be amazed.

In parts, small streams tumble over the smooth stone surface, adding a slippery tease to your efforts to stay upright. The road rose

steeply in brilliant sunshine but the altitude meant it was cold. We didn't mind though, we'd been told that the previous day there'd been thick fog at this height. V-shaped hairpin bends on sharp-edged gravel made us sweat in the crisp air as chunks of rock shot away from under our tyres with a rubbery thunk. The GS coped nicely 'two up' on the way up. But, after a rest stop, freezing in the stiff breeze on the top of the plateau, going down was a different story. The bike seemed to have a magnetic attraction for the edge. With twenty-metre drops down to the next sections of road, it was white knuckle-stuff with the adrenaline really popping. Gravity seemed, all of a sudden, to be doubly strong. With tyres skidding and slipping on the loose stones, Birgit wisely got off to walk the worst two hairpins. I managed to scare myself more than a couple of times...

Back down to level earth, we collapsed into our hostel's saggy armchairs. The wooden-walled former trading station of colonial days offered its guests these battered pieces of history as a sort of 'wrap-around comforter' for aching limbs. A cold beer and a big feed were all that was needed to top off an incredible day. With 'Lion' lagers in our hands we felt alive again and were ready to face the 'Ship Hunt' once more.

We tried to phone Carlos but didn't manage to catch him and had no answers to the messages we left. We had no luck with the other shipping agents either. The work on the wash blocks was just about completed and we began to get really worried. It seemed that Carlos was just a 'blow hard'. When we finally did manage to catch up with him, he was just as confident as ever, but there was something in his voice that didn't sound quite right. More days went by.

We'd been on the hunt for a ship now for nearly three months. The time had whizzed by, and so had the money out of our budget, in spite of all our efforts to be frugal. We were finally faced with a simple fact: no amount of door knocking, fax sending, letter writing or phone calling was going to get us working passages on a ship.

We sadly began to research the cost of flying ourselves and flying or shipping the bikes separately. This was 'Plan B' and we had steered clear of it for as long as possible. Flying seemed too abrupt a way to leave Africa but also, the Royal Automobile Club in England had warned us that if we arrived in Argentina separately from our bikes we would face a lot of hassle to clear them from customs and it wouldn't be a cheap process. We were wary of the inevitable maze of red tape and 'gentlemen' demanding 'fees' for oiling the system.

The sad truth was that we weren't sure that we had enough money left to pay for flights to South America, for the bikes to be shipped across, and then to get up to the United States where we hoped to find some work. It was also a sad truth that the long winter was coming to an end in Patagonia and unless something happened very quickly, we'd lose our summer 'weather slot' too. The chances of making that slot now seemed very remote.

We'd given it our best shot and it seemed that we'd failed. We mooched around feeling pretty miserable, yet we still had a tiny optimistic inkling that somehow, something would work out.

But we were facing the facts: our offers of special insurance, liability wavers and simple pleading just hadn't worked. We offered to pay for our passage too but no one would do it. Too much hassle. Sometimes you can go to an agency that specializes in booking space on the few cargo boats that will still take passengers. We'd checked one in London but they were well out of our price range and booked up a long way in advance.

The shipping quotes started to come in. Wow! The more we received, the more we realised that the hunt for a ship had eaten too large a hole in our budget. If we took any of these options we would be hard pushed to make it up to the States. What to do? Risk it and hope that nothing went wrong or just accept that the trip had been fantastic, but now was the time to go home? Go back to work and in a year or two set out again… maybe.

The thought of having to give up on South America was the pits. We could ride back up through Africa and that would be great, if that was what fate decreed. But it still wasn't South America, and it would also mean returning to 'real' life an awful lot faster. I didn't fancy that at all. Life on the road was simply too good, too much fun and too interesting to stop now. I'd been on the road for over five years and it had become a way of life that was far better than any I'd ever had before.

We stood at our usual place by the campsite pay phone, our open-air office! Friends we'd made waved crossed fingers at us as they walked past. We hadn't told them the real state of affairs.

We wanted to phone each of the agents who'd helped, or had tried to help us. Around us, South African holidaymakers were stirring. Breakfast brais (barbecues) were beginning to waft the delicious smells of bacon, steaks and boerewors (thick very tasty sausages) through the air towards us. Carefree laughter pealed out, underlining how miserable we were feeling at that moment. I was acutely aware of the taunting sound of waves breaking on the beach. Overhead, seagulls cruised a hell of a lot freer than I was feeling.

We started our way through the list. Each call added another level of disappointment. Each person we spoke to seemed genuinely disappointed for us, and didn't seem to know what to say. These people seemed to take the weight of failure on their own shoulders. I was amazed by their kindness and once again my faith in human nature was reinforced.

I nearly dropped the phone when I made one of the last calls. The agent said, "Wow, I'm really sorry it's come to this. But hey, have you thought about going across on a cruise liner?" I stood stunned for a moment. Had we explained what we wanted to do so badly? Had this man no concept of our tight budget? Had he not just heard me say that we were so skint we were going to have to go home? I thanked him and put the phone back on its rest.

"Birgit, you'll never guess what the agent just said! He's got to be crackers. I'm not going to phone any more. Let's save our money. We are going to need it on the way north." She listened to the full story and then said, "Sam, we have nothing to lose but some time and the cost of a few phone calls. Go on, try it."

All of a sudden it felt like a wonderfully bizarre thing to be doing – two budget travellers phoning in search of a passage on a cruise liner!

No luck at all with the first travel agent, but American Express sounded a little more positive. "Hello, can you tell us if there is any way that we can get on a cruise liner from either Durban or Cape Town across to South America. We don't really mind where to exactly but Argentina would be great?"

Martin the agent replied, "Hmmm, I'm not sure, hold on a minute and I'll have a look. When did you want to go?" "As soon as possible." I replied, and I could hear the noise of papers being shuffled at the other end.

"You guys are in luck. The Marco Polo is leaving Cape Town in a couple of weeks. The cheapest cabin is well below deck but it's only US$1,000. They have space – not many people want to spend ten days crossing the south Atlantic at this time of year."

I was stunned. This was just about affordable, but would the ship take the bikes and if so, how much extra it would cost? "Um, that's brilliant news," I replied. "There is one slight complication. We have two rather large motorcycles. What do you think the chances of getting them on board would be?" There was a moment's silence from the agent. Then he replied, "Well, now this is a challenge. Sounds like it could be fun. You leave it with me. Call me back tomorrow."

The only agent we hadn't phoned was Carlos. We elected to wait to call him until the next day. It would give him another day to come up with something, and it would give us the chance to have a definite answer from the American Express agent.

The next morning we paced up and down by the phone for about half an hour. We didn't want to call until the office had been open for at least thirty minutes. "Hello Martin, it's Sam here, as in Sam and Birgit. Have you any news for us?"

"Yes, I've great news for you. The captain of the Marco Polo is happy to take your bikes on board. They can stow them below decks for you. And, they'll go for free. They'll be listed on the manifest as 'hand luggage'!"

This was going to cost us less than two thirds of the cheapest 'fly us and ship the bikes' option. It would take the same amount of time and we'd arrive together. Nightmares of weeks for customs-clearing the bikes and suitcase-loads of 'baksheesh' disappeared. This by now rather scruffy pair of oily-fingered, leather-jacketed overland bikers was going to cross the south Atlantic on a luxury cruise liner. What a great way to leave Africa!

There's no doubt in my mind that if you are positive, when the chips are down, something almost always pops up to solve the problem.

It's not easy to be positive in these situations. But that 'something', when it does pop up, is usually far better than the solution you'd hoped for in the first place. The best adventures often seem to start when you're at rock bottom.

There's an addictive adrenaline rush that comes with an amazing solution. It grabs you by the scruff of the neck and throws you back into life, and it's this feeling that is one of the reasons that I love to travel so much. The only things left to do were to phone Carlos and then make a plan for getting down to Cape Town. I felt a real sadness for Birgit. Being on a cargo ship across an ocean was such an amazing thing to do and now she would miss out on that. She was quite philosophical about it and said, "Yeah, but what a consolation prize!" The bonus of course was that our budget was almost back on track. At least now we would have our, 'what if something goes wrong' financial buffer.

"Carlos, we have great news and are calling to let you know and to thank you for trying to help us. We have a ship to Argentina." I explained the story to him and as I did so he was quite quiet. I had a tiny feeling that somehow we had managed to offend him. But that feeling went away when he said, "Then you must come to us for a goodbye and good luck dinner."

At dinner we talked about how sad I was that Birgit wasn't going to get on a cargo ship, but how delighted we were that the trip was back on and how the whole concept of being budget travellers on a cruise liner was such a laugh.

Carlos looked over at me and said, "Then this is something that I know I can help you with. One of my ships is going from Durban to Cape Town in three days from now. I know it isn't a voyage across the ocean but it's the next best thing, no? I am one hundred percent sure that I can get you on the ship. I have known the captain and his officers for years. There are cabins on the ship and normally they are empty. They are only ever used when the owners or family members of the officers are on board. Leave this with me, I'll arrange it, I'll call you tomorrow."

I couldn't help but grin at Birgit. Another brilliant consolation prize, but I had the feeling that she was only trying to look enthusiastic. I should have asked what the problem was but at that moment Carlos took us on a guided tour of his house so my question was forgotten.

Down in the cellar was another world. The walls were lined with Nazi flags and mannequins stood to attention in all sorts of Second World War German army uniforms. Iron crosses were in glass cabinets and stacks of Nazi propaganda were piled on top of olive green desks. To one side of the cellar was a large gun rack in which were stored guns from that period and more modern weapons. Next to them, was Carlos's bullet-making equipment. Carlos proudly explained, "These kaffirs taking over are never going to get the better of me. They won't know what's hit them if they try anything!"

Birgit and I stood in stunned silence, and with hindsight that was exactly the right moment to walk away. But we didn't. He'd been kind – it would have been rude to walk away. He'd also offered Birgit the chance to be on a cargo ship – who knows if that opportunity would ever arise again. I was also aware of the fact that I was fascinated by Carlos and I wanted to be around him more – I always found myself wondering what surprise he would have in store for us next. It was the unpredictability of the situation that I liked. But I hadn't expected just how unpredictable things were about to get.

We said goodbye to everyone on the campsite and headed into Durban, aiming for the docks. Because I'd previously shipped out from the docks to go across to Australia, I knew my way around a little bit and finding the right jetty wasn't a problem. Carlos had told us to ask for the first officer when we got to the ship and had told us that he would take care of us. He then said, "Just give the cook some money towards your food." That felt odd as we had pointedly asked about the costs involved and Carlos had said that there would be nothing to pay. We were going to be guests as he was owed favours.

We arrived at the jetty to find that the ship was a giant car transporter. Its stern doors were wide open and inside it looked like a rusty-sided empty aircraft hangar. We asked for and found the first officer. "Carlos sent us," we explained. "He said that when we arrived

96

you would show us what to do and where to go. Thanks very much for taking us by the way – its a great opportunity."

This was the second sign that something was wrong. The first officer looked bemused, but as he was busy he passed us on to a crewman, who showed us where to park and strap down the bikes. The crewman then showed us up to a cabin, helping us carry our gear. I had to smile. The crewman obviously hadn't been ashore. The ship was still and calm in the harbour but the sailor's gait rolled easily from side to side. It was as if he were still compensating for the effects of the open sea.

It was great to be back on a ship again and the cabin was magnificent. It was far better than the cabin on the ship to Australia had been, and that had been pretty posh – a bit like a good quality motel room. The crewman said, "You wait here, someone will come soon."

We unpacked and waited for someone to come. The hours went by and around us the noises of a ship in everyday life swirled. The giant engines rumbled, doors banged, someone was hitting metal against metal, someone was shouting orders and way down on the docks a stream of cars were being driven into the hold. Still we waited. But somehow it didn't feel right.

At that moment a man who was so covered in gold braid and had such an air of authority that he could only be the captain, walked past the open door of the cabin.

I thought, "I'll get rid of this uncertainty", so hopped over the bottom of the bulkhead doorframe and scooted down the corridor after him. I caught sight of him disappearing through a door and after knocking respectfully, followed him in. "Excuse me captain. I just wanted to introduce myself and to say thank you very much for allowing us to come on your ship down to Cape Town. This is fantastic and you are making a dream come true for my girlfriend."

The captain stopped what he was doing, looked up with a very stern and somewhat annoyed expression, and said, "I've never heard of you. I have no idea who you are. What are you doing on my ship?"

He really had no idea. Carlos had simply lied to us. Nothing had been arranged. I apologised, said we would leave right away and chased back down the corridor to where Birgit was sitting looking decidedly unhappy. I hurriedly explained what had happened and for a moment I thought that she was going to burst into tears. I felt a bit like doing so myself. This was one of the most embarrassing situations I'd ever found myself in. Birgit's expression was actually a combination of pure rage at Carlos, and total embarrassment.

We grabbed our things and headed back down to the hold. Although it had filled up there was still just enough room for us to get the bikes out. We battled with the straps as the sound of the engine got louder and the deck vibrations increased. It sounded as if the ship was going to set sail shortly.

I couldn't get the bloody rope undone. I cursed and yanked at the cords and around us crewmen were stopping what they were doing to watch us. The sound of the last few vehicles coming aboard echoed around the hold.

Just as I got the cords untied, Carlos arrived. "Hey Sam, what are you doing?" He yelled at me over the noise. I shouted back what had happened and told him that we were getting off. I yelled that he had no right to do this to us and surely he must understand how embarrassed we felt. I shouted, "Yes, we are budget travellers but we don't cheat and we don't lie. The captain knew nothing about us and the first mate didn't look as if he did either. We're leaving!"

Carlos then made the big mistake of shouting, "Don't be so stupid!" I'm not at all proud of this, but I lost it. I was absolutely furious and at that moment I was probably quite dangerous. I grabbed Carlos and amazingly, (because I'm not exactly a weight lifter), I picked him right up in the air and began to shake him furiously. Although I was furious and embarrassed, I also knew that I was on the verge of being out of control. I seemed to know instinctively that if I put him down and hit him, I'd do him some real damage.

Crewmen came rushing across to separate us, with the loading officer shouting orders at everyone. Most people looked absolutely stunned and bemused by what they had just seen. Birgit looked somewhat stunned too – she'd never seen me do something like this before. Carlos thankfully had the good sense to keep his mouth shut for a moment, but as we rode out, I heard him shouting, "You ungrateful fool!"

I rode away with my heart pumping furiously, and both my hands and knees shaking madly. I was incredibly angry with myself. It was my fault – my wanting to see what would happen next that had really dropped us in it. And, I was angry that I'd lost control. "This is what happens when people kill people" I thought, as we rode out of the port.

We now had the ride to Cape Town in front of us and by waiting around to get on the cargo ship we'd lost vital riding days. We had to get a move on. Thankfully we'd explored to our hearts' content on the way down the first time, and we knew where there were some great places to stay – the journey would be quick but fine.

It felt a bit odd to start a day's ride so late in the day but there wasn't any point in battling through Durban's traffic to try to find somewhere to stay. We'd said our goodbyes and it was time to be on the move. One of the hardest goodbyes was to my cousin Ros, who once again had made me feel really welcome in her home and had stuffed us both with great food. She and Birgit had hit it off and we'd had the chance to meet John, her new fiancé. Ros's parting gift to Birgit was a long black evening dress, just in case it was needed on the cruise ship. John kindly gave me a pair of sports trousers that no longer fitted him. These were not the sorts of things we'd been carrying previously…

If I believed in omens I'd have turned round there and then, and gone home. The debacle at the port had been grim. What happened next nearly killed me.

Chapter 5

Marco Polo

'That is the charm of a map. It represents the other side of the horizon where everything is possible.'

Rosita Forbes

One of the things that niggled me when I was riding with Birgit was the number of loo stops she needed. When I was drinking enough, my bladder seemed to be happy to be emptied a couple of times a day. Not so with Birgit and for some reason, it did niggle. I suppose it's easy for a bloke to have a pee. When on the road, there's always a wall or a scrawny bush to face and at worst, one just turns away from everyone and no one seems to give a hoot. But girls need full-grown bushes since dropping their trousers to squat in front of everyone is obviously best avoided. It gives new meaning to the title 'public convenience'! It was irritating for Birgit and sometimes she'd have to ride with crossed legs for a very long, uncomfortable time. I was happy to be a bloke.

We'd just crossed the Kei River, from which Transkei gets its name, and Birgit suddenly pulled to a halt by some bushes. "Ahh, loo break" I thought, "but another one, already?" She jumped off her bike, but instead of diving into the bushes she stood behind her bike gesticulating towards me, with increasing agitation.

I'd no idea what she wanted, so just sat there, thinking perhaps I'd better go down to her to see what the matter was. Suddenly she started to run up the road towards me. She was shouting something I couldn't hear through my helmet and was pointing at me with ever-increasing frustration and agitation. I looked over my shoulder to see if something was behind me; nothing there. By this time she was close enough for me to realise that she was pointing at my knees. I looked down.

One of my front panniers had caught fire and was merrily blazing away right next to my 43-litre nylon petrol tank, which I'd only just filled to capacity! I leapt off the bike. I'd not seen or felt a thing. My protective trousers had shielded me from the heat and the chin-piece of my full-face helmet and been exactly in the line between my eyes and the blazing pannier. The breeze had been blowing the smoke straight behind me.

At that moment I learnt a vital rule of the road. Always keep the blade of your penknife as sharp as a razor. I felt a tinge of panic as I realised that my Swiss army knife blade was as blunt as a spoon; I might as well have been hacking at the blazing straps with a rock. But I had no choice. If I couldn't get the pannier away from the bike then I'd soon have no bike left at all. I wasn't thinking about it at the time but we were at the end of the dry season and an exploding bike could also have started a serious bush fire.

Well, thank goodness for decent bike gloves. I trashed the things over the next few moments but they were enough to stop my hands from burning and when I finally did managed to rip the panniers off, and put the fire out, I stood panting as if I'd just gone ten rounds with a heavyweight boxer!

I'd saved the bike and was instantly grateful to Birgit. "I saw a flash of light from you in my mirror; at first I thought it was just something shining reflecting the sun. I couldn't believe it when you just carried on sitting there. I thought you'd be blown up!"

I was alive and the bike was still in one piece, but there was some damage. The stitching on the panniers had probably rotted – they had been on the bike in all weathers for a long time. The bag had fallen onto one of the BMW's horizontally opposed cylinders and the heat from that had melted a candle that I bunged in the bag at the last minute. I'd forgotten to pack it in one of the aluminium panniers where it usually lived.

The candle had melted through the canvas of the pannier and turned it into a giant wick! As the heat from the engine increased, the bag had caught fire. Inside it were my waterproof trousers and my SLR camera. The good news was that I'd only just put a new film in it. The upside was that this blackened and melted piece of modern art was insured.

Standing in the brilliant sunshine next to my girl and our bikes, surrounded by rolling hills, amber-coloured grasses and scatterings of wild flowers, I knew I was lucky to be alive. And anyway, the camera had been playing up for months – it'd had a hard life. Now I'd be able to get something that worked properly.

By this time I think Birgit was just beginning to question her own sanity. Was she going to lose it by travelling on with me? 'Things' did seem to happen around me at a frequency that didn't allow for a peaceful life.

Lee was great again and happily put us up when we got back to Cape Town. We had a few last-minute things to organise. We'd got the visas we needed for the next few months, but needed to stock up on travellers' cheques and US dollars. We also had on-the-road food to get, as we didn't know what Argentina was going to be like food-wise. It had always paid off to have a few days' food with us when stepping out into the new. I wondered how welcome I would be, as a Brit, in Argentina. The Falklands War was probably still fresh in a lot of Argentinean minds.

We scrubbed and serviced the bikes. We bought more oil and air filters, replaced the spark plugs and gave both the frames a thorough check for cracks. We searched for clothes too; we'd been told that there was a dress code on board the Marco Polo.

Day one would be casual. That meant sports trousers and sports jackets and that one was not expected to wear a tie! Ladies should wear summer dresses. Day two would be smart. For women this meant getting togged up in cocktail dresses, while gentlemen had to wear lounge suits. Day three was due to be eveningwear – black tie for the chaps and long evening dresses for the ladies!

I'd expected to have to smarten up for the voyage, but having no knowledge or experience of cruise liners I'd no idea that clothes like this were going to be required. 'Black tie' was out of the question and so were suits and cocktail dresses; we would just have to do the best we could. After all, we were paying guests weren't we? They could hardly throw us out of the dining room for breach of dress code, could they? In a 'phone call my mother said, "Why don't you just get room service on black tie nights?"

The day before we were supposed to embark, Birgit's bike stopped working. It was annoying, but we quickly realised that the timing was perfect. In Cape Town we knew where to get spare parts whereas in Argentina we'd be starting from scratch. The snag was to work out exactly which part from which model of BMW had gone wrong when Sir Henry was such a hybrid 'bitsa'. Birgit couldn't get on the phone and say, "I need a starter relay for a 1971 BMW R60/5 please."

BMW Cape Town did their best and the next day our friend Wolf from Charlie's Garage came down to the docks with a replacement relay – it looked like the right part. There was no chance to fit it before sailing but we assumed there'd be time on board. I liked Wolf, his brother Gerald and their head mechanic Mohammed, a lot. These guys deserve full credit for their heroic efforts to keep travellers on the road.

Even during the days of sanctions against South Africa they managed to keep overlanders going. Their knowledge was superb and their desire to help travellers was something really special. They put themselves out for us and other people like us. We'd become friends and it seemed quite fitting that Wolf should be the one at the docks, doing all he could to see us safely on our way. He was a tall, balding man who had a great mane of white hair at the back and a bushy white beard. I never saw him dressed in anything other than faded blue mechanic's overalls, which were inevitably too short.

The jetty was full of excitement. The ship was immaculately painted in blue and white and stood firmly up against the dock protected by enormous woven rope buffers. A long stepped gangplank came down to the concrete from a hatch about half way up the side of the ship. The banners on each side of the gangplank railings proudly read Marco Polo.

We felt dwarfed beside her, and slightly the poor relations as we watched people arrive and start boarding. The guardrails above were lined with passengers already and we could hear speculative comments about us. In the distance, Table Mountain unfurled a summer-weight tablecloth of cloud across its flat top and I took a moment to stand and do a 180 degrees turn. This was going to be the last chance I'd be able to see anything of the city. Before long I'd be down below decks dealing with the bikes.

Our luggage was loaded first. Uniformed Filipino crewmen did this and I felt sorry for them as they manhandled our battered kit aboard. Four aluminium panniers, four tank panniers, four spare tyres, a jerry can for Birgit (Henry only had a 26 litre fuel tank) plus two kit bags, looks like a hell of a lot of luggage when they aren't strapped to the bikes.

The bikes were then hoisted aboard. Birgit stayed down on the dock to control what was happening there and I went up on deck to be on hand if needed. We had a problem though. The loading officer wanted to put the bikes on the deck. This was not part of the deal and having previously had my steed strapped to the deck of the MSC Sabrina all the way from Durban to Sydney, I knew how much damage salt could do to the bikes. Having been told that they were going below deck we hadn't even oiled them.

An alternative plan was made; the ship's carpenter very kindly agreed that Libby could be tied down in his workshop and at his suggestion, Henry was lowered down a long service hatch and also safely tied up below deck. While all this was going on, bands on the jetty had been playing, streamers had been thrown down from the guardrails and tickertape had floated away on the breeze. By the time I'd got the bikes tied down, we were at sea. I hunted Birgit out and we spent the last hours of daylight watching Table Mountain disappear into the rays of our last African sunset.

Though we were both sad to be leaving Africa, it felt like an absolutely fantastic way to be doing so – none of the instant abruptness of a flight for us, we were gently easing from one set of adventures and cruising into another.

Our BMWs had been excellent and every riding day had challenged, amazed, and changed us. Even Birgit's 27-year-old R60/5 had coped admirably with Africa's conditions. Our friends had been quite pointed with their remarks about Africa and vintage bikes. To Birgit their comments had been an added spur! And anyway, Ted Simon's bike for his *'Jupiter's Travels'* adventure was an early 70s Triumph that was essentially a 1950s design. Our twelve months had often turned into a fight with thick glutinous mud, soft, power-sucking sand, treacherous thorns and we had become experts at dodging the hundreds of potholes. African truck and bus drivers had been a challenge to 'share' the roads with. Those guys believe that, regardless of the road conditions, the only possible speed is flat out! We were always ready to take evasive action and a cheery wave and a toot of their horn usually accompanied the cloud of dust that we were inevitably left in. We'd enjoyed the people we'd met and had some very funny and warm times.

Every wild animal we'd seen was a delight – from the tall, elegantly swaying giraffes often seen grazing at the tree-tops as we sped on by, to the herd of zebra that pounded across the road in front of us leaving us stunned with our good fortune. Each elephant we spotted was a day's highlight. The domestic animals were not so delightful – no road sense at all!

Africa had been a collection of clear rich blues of sea and sky, providing a complementary contrast to the land's collections of greens, ambers and browns. The western sunsets had brought vivid reds and oranges to the panorama of colour. Even the pre-thunder storm clouds were a strong image of Africa. Their deep purple and charcoal colours had stirred our senses. A coming storm would be preceded by a cool determined breeze and then the clouds would release their heavy loads with such speed and strength that visibility would be immediately cut to a few metres. But we knew that after every storm, the sun would return to ride with us again.

Chapter 6

Land of silver

'I know in my own case that a trip has really been successful if I come back sounding strange even to myself'

Pico Iyer

For the next ten days we ate our way across the south Atlantic! We soon discovered that we could start eating croissants at 6am, have breakfast at 8am, a mid-morning snack at 10am, elevenses at 11am (of course), lunch at 12.30, afternoon snack at 3pm, afternoon tea at 4.30, dinner at 7pm, supper at 10pm and a late-night snack at midnight. The food was superb and once our shrunken stomachs had expanded, we were able to take full advantage of at least three meals a day. Lost weight piled back on and our fat supplies were restored. When we were back on 'budget street' I was sure we'd be glad of that new layer of blubber. I was also sure that we'd be burning it at a rate of knots when we made it way down south to the chill of Tierra Del Fuego.

Our cabin was great, though mildly claustrophobic. In cat-swinging terms, the cat could actually have had quite a long tail. The bed was a great size too, and the bathroom had a shower of the 'batter you into submission' type. Excellent. It made a real change to be using giant fluffy terry towels instead of our camping towels, which in reality didn't do much to wick away the water. Our bed was made for us every day and when we got back to the room at night, after having promenaded, disco'd, cabaret'd and eaten, our pillows would always be decorated with a couple of delicious Belgian chocolates.

There were a couple of downsides though. Booze wasn't included in the cost of the passage and it was extortionately expensive. As in you'd be better off buying the brewery or distillery type of prices. Fortunately we'd read the small print and had smuggled several bottles of gin aboard which, along with plenty of tonic, kept us well-lubricated and in happy mood. (Thankfully the bottles hadn't clinked when the stewards carried our kit aboard, although we could always have tried arguing that it was for medicinal purposes…)

Evening meals were amazing affairs, regardless of the dress code of the day, and we rather enjoyed the concept of dressing up. It showed me a completely new side to Birgit. I'd never seen her in anything other than Doc Martens, hiking boots or flip-flops, and not a dab of makeup had touched her face in all the time I'd known her. She looked gorgeous in her vividly coloured long dress and the makeup looked great on her tanned, healthy skin but high heels didn't do anything for her, in spite of being just 5'1". In fact they made getting to dinner decidedly dangerous. She'd not had much chance to practise wearing her heels before we'd set sail and the 'novice wobble' combined with the rolling motion of the ship had her bouncing from one wall of the corridors to the other. She managed to remain surprisingly elegant in spite of this, and the fact that she was scattering other guests as she wended her wobbly way to dinner. Good job no one knew about our sneaky before dinner gin sessions!

We'd been given a set table along with a group of other people who would remain our dinner companions for the duration of the voyage. Whoever arranged the seating plan, had done well. We were put with a group of very level-headed and interesting people who didn't mind in the slightest that I turned up for the first black-tie dinner looking like a candidate for a limbo dance competition.

There was something about my bright yellow long-sleeved cotton shirt that had people wincing. Not those at our table though, especially when they found out the reason for my lack of suitable attire. Birgit looked the part though and there were more than a few lecherous glances in her direction. One or two of the older, single ladies shot her a few stabbing looks, but she was impervious to those and giggled at the lechery.

The only time I had a problem was on a black tie day from a loud-mouthed, stetson-wearing, gum-chewing, self-opinionated giant, fat Texan. This man, doing an impersonation of a penguin at a cowboy fancy dress party, scornfully looked me up and down, and boomed at the top of his voice, "What the hayll is thayat?" Within a millisecond, everyone was staring in my direction – after all, I was the only blue-coloured blot on the black and white landscape!

I wondered whether my blue silk shirt made me look a bit of a gigolo, but the genuine gigolo at our table never complained about me threatening his trade. Brian had actually been recruited as a teacher of bridge and other card games for the single ladies. He told us that his role was also to accompany a lady each night to the cabaret or to go dancing. I suspected from the way he told the stories that he did a lot more than that, but he was too gentlemanly to go further than hinting.

The cabaret dancers filled me with admiration. I would have admired their shapely legs, tight bums and pretty faces anyway, but what really got me was the way these girls managed to dance on their 4" heels even through the roughest weather. Skill and talent abounded and I think that more often than not the applause they got was more for their ability to stay upright than it was for their version of the can-can.

The weather badly affected others too. Patrick Moore was a guest speaker on board and it was his job, as a famous astronomer, to keep us entertained with tales of outer space, distant stars and so on. The trouble was, every time he led a party to the deck to look at the night sky, cloud cover obscured even the brightest stars.

Patrick was reduced to saying things like, "Well, if there was no cloud, exactly there, you would see such and such a star, and if the grey matter above us would move away, then we would be more than likely to see a shooting star at this latitude." Poor chap, the only enthusiasm he managed to drum up was from his overly bushy eyebrows which leapt around looking like a couple of ferrets itching to mate.

Back at the dinner table, the food was fantastic. It was beautifully cooked and presented with real style. The waiters were all highly trained and seemed to notice everything. Once, within seconds of dropping my napkin, a waiter brought over a new one and whisked away the old one. I'd never had such service before and there were moments when I thought I could quite easily get used to this kind of life.

Birgit, meantime, had discovered that yes, she could have second helpings of desserts and that in fact she could have a dessert as starter, main course and er, dessert, if she really wanted to, and some days that was exactly what she wanted. "Life is short", she said, "so start with dessert!"

The cruise was a life of decadence and the only things that kept our feet on the ground were our daily trips through the working parts of the ship to check on the bikes, and the thought of what was to come when we landed.

Our journeys through the bowels of the ship taught us a lot about what went on behind the scenes, and gave us a chance to talk with members of the crew who were not normally allowed to speak to us. We learnt that most of them were only permitted to go up on deck in the very early hours of the morning when the vast majority of passengers had gone to bed. Apart from those brief visits they had to survive on artificial light and air.

Most of the service crew were Filipinos, the entertainers Brits, Australians and Kiwis, and the officers a mix from just about every maritime nation in the world. The Marco Polo was actually a former Russian troop ship! However, its 1930s-style décor would never have given that away to any but the most trained eyes. We also learnt that the ship had its own fresh water production plant and were staggered to hear that each passenger used the equivalent of 150 litres of fresh water a day.

Broken glass was crushed and poured overboard, and food waste was also mainly dumped into the sea – this explained the mob of sea birds that followed the ship from time to time. The ship was like a mobile service station for seabirds.

The quantity of food being wasted on a daily basis was staggering. We weren't surprised though. We'd seen the almost full plates of food being returned, with the food merely nibbled. We'd watched people move the richly exotic food around their plates, either as if they were totally bored, or as if they were discussing some sort of strategy. I used to think of the toyed-with and discarded food as desecrated, but good manners stopped me from saying so.

Sometimes long distance travel involves seeing two sides of the coin of life. I was conscious of how we had sailed away from the hungry and poor of Africa in this vessel of total, almost obscene, luxury. I couldn't slate it too badly though. After all, the Marco Polo was getting us to South America and we'd had a fascinating once-in-a- lifetime experience. I'd also thoroughly enjoyed eating steak and lobster. And the sea life along the ship's route must have been very well fed! We'd been incredibly lucky to get on the Marco Polo. We suspected that the captain had stuck his neck out for us and I hoped that we hadn't done anything to make him regret his good deed.

There was still no sign of land when the water turned muddy. At the same time, the air became pungent with earthy forest smells. The mud was the sediment that was constantly being washed down the Rio de la Plata or River Plate as we tend to call it, though the name actually means Silver River. It was given this name when the earliest explorers were presented with silver by the Indians. This of course caused great excitement amongst the conquistadors, but exploration later revealed that the source of the silver was actually far away in Peru, which had already been settled by the Spanish.

The drainage area covered by the Silver River is huge: almost a fifth of the whole of the continent of South America. And at 220 kilometres across, it is the widest estuary in the world. The River Plate also forms the border between Argentina and Paraguay, and within the next day we would be sailing right up it and into the port of Buenos Aires, the capital of Argentina. The scents of land were strangely exotic and sent my imagination running wild. As we stood looking out towards where land must be I felt increasingly excited, and nervous. We were about to step into the unknown again, (unknown to us anyway).

The last breakfast on board felt as if it was being eaten on the edge of a precipice. Most of the other passengers were staying on board the Marco Polo and were due to head down to Ushuaia, the southernmost city in the world. From there they would cruise down into Antarctica, cocooned in warmth and luxury. We would be heading south too, but for us the journey would be completely different and it felt strange to be leaving the security of the ship.

Birgit spent some of the last hours on board down in the access shaft with Henry. She had to fit the new starter relay. She wasn't going to be able to test it, partly because of where the bike was but also because the bikes had been drained of fuel. This latter point was a bit of a worry since we had no idea where the nearest fuel station would be when we landed.

We'd been told that everything would happen in a hurry once we docked so Birgit got herself ready to be down on the dock to take care of all the bike kit when it was off-loaded, and to help guide the bikes down when they were swung over the side. I stayed on board so I could ensure that all the ropes and slings were tied on in places that wouldn't do any damage. The crew was keen and friendly but only the purser, Chris, was a biker. In Cape Town I'd caught a crewman innocently and helpfully trying to attach a rope to one of the carburettors!

We'd spent quite a bit of time chatting with Chris about bikes and travelling and he'd offered to help with the off-loading process.

It was quite strange to be five decks down below when the ship was sailing into the port, but I consoled myself with the thought that I'd had the privilege of watching the ship's arrival whilst on the cargo ship into Sydney, so it was only right that Birgit should do so this time.

The motion of the ship changed dramatically when we sailed into the calm waters of the estuary. Then the engines died away and the gentle rolling of the ship changed to just a slight bobbing, then there was a thump. Down below, I assumed that this was the result of the ship being tied up to the bollards on the dock.

Then everything started to happen. The access hatch was pulled open and light flooded down into the shaft, highlighting Henry. Moments later the sling was eased down the shaft by the derrick operator. I'd already released Henry from all the straps that had been holding him steady and worked quickly to fix the sling and straps to him. Above me, three pairs of eyes from silhouetted heads and shoulders looked down, waiting to see when I would give the thumbs up. Henry was ready, and as he was pulled up I managed to keep him from spinning and bouncing off the walls with a trail rope. Then it was Libby's turn. She was covered in sawdust. The carpenter had been hard at work during the passage. (We knew from our visits to the hold that a whole deck of the ship was being renovated during the voyage from Cape Town).

Libby rose up to the deck without a hitch. I chased up six flights of stairs through a floating city and onto the deck. The bikes were there waiting and one of the crew had a large jerrycan in his hand. The First Officer was kindly letting us have a few litres of the fuel kept on board for the lifeboats. It's really strange to see your bike hanging out in the middle of nowhere, held only by a few straps and ropes. This time, Birgit had a hold of the trail rope and she and a crewmember guided the bikes safely to the dock. All the time Chris was on hand – I suspect, neglecting his other duties so he could help us!

Our kit arrived and we strapped it on the bikes. Luckily the dock was well organised and the area around the ship was cordoned off, so we could work in relative peace. Birgit tried Henry's starter: nothing. We connected jump leads from my bike to hers in case the battery was flat: still nothing.

Passengers lining the rails above us realised there was some drama going on so now the section above us was packed with spectators. In their holiday clothes they looked like rows of exotic birds lined up on telephone wires. A few of the passengers now understood why we had not had 'Black Tie' for dinner! We tried everything we could think of, fully aware that at any moment we were going to be told to move the bikes. (I trusted that Birgit would understand this command when it came; she spoke basic Spanish whereas mine was minimal.)

When the bulk of the passengers had disembarked to go on tours of the city, we noticed an Argentinean customs officer heading down the gangplank. He had two carrier bags stuffed full of booze and cigarettes. One could only assume that there was something wrong with them and that he had confiscated them, according to the law.

These carrier bags combined with a fact of bike shipping to ensure that our entry into Argentina was a breeze. The rules the RAC had told us about, whereby arriving on the same vessel as your bike allows a much simpler and cheaper procedure for getting it into the country, was correct. We didn't even have a crate to dispose of.

We were summoned to the customs office. This was a tired-looking two storey, flat-roofed concrete building. The large double wooden doors were battle-scarred, and the large dusty glass windows had both louver shutters and metal bars fixed to them. Inside, giant fans moved sluggishly in the heat that was collecting up near the ceiling, and down below stood rows of battered grey-painted metal desks that were almost overflowing with papers. There, amidst what looked like semi-organised chaos, sat the officer who had just come down the gangplank. Around him men were shouting and waving handfuls of official-looking paperwork. The official's minions were shouting back, sweating into their uniforms and rubber-stamping forms with pure venom and no style at all. In the background, typewriters were clacking furiously and out in the port, every now and then, a ship would blast one of its horns.

The officer knew all about us – the captain had explained who we were. The 'gift' he had paid the customs officer on behalf of the Marco Polo also covered us and to our amazement the whole process took just fifteen minutes. Then we were free, provided we could get Henry started.

By this time the crowd of spectators had expanded from the ship's railings on three levels, to the dockside. Van drivers, truckies, shipping agents, the sandwich seller and even an escaped ship's cat had collected to watch what the gringos were going to do next. With a couple of spotlights, we would have been providing enough atmosphere and entertainment to charge a fee! But Henry just would not start.

We took a step back from the situation, and with a deep breath, ran through all the other things that might be the problem. Points and condenser? Nope, new in Cape Town and both worked well. Some sort of corrosion on the electrical connections? Nope, Birgit had been through all of those before we'd left Cape Town and had checked them just before we sailed up the river. Battery knackered? It shouldn't be – it was only a year old and as the bike had been used almost every day until we had shipped that shouldn't be the problem either. And anyway, jump leads hadn't helped. Nope, the only thing left was to try to bump-start Henry. The relay from Cape Town must be for the wrong bike.

Push-starting was something that Birgit had never done before, and I'd never done it with her bike so didn't know whether it required any particular knack. She climbed aboard and Chris and I looked at each other. It was going to be down to us and at that moment my respect for Chris rose even higher. Though he was dressed in his immaculate, brilliant white, gold-braided port uniform, he was still prepared to push a beaten up old lump of a fully-loaded bike up and down a dirty dockside in the mid-day heat. This is a good example of the connection that most bikers have with each other, but it also says a lot about the type of guy Chris was.

Well, our audience got a top-value performance and some of the customs officers even came out to watch the show. Finally, just as Chris and I were beginning to feel we'd had enough, Henry started with a puff of black smoke and a throaty roar. I couldn't see under Birgit's helmet but knew that she had an ear-to-ear grin on her face.

Now we had to try to get right across the city, to the southern outskirts and BA's only campsite, without stalling the bike. We'd heard terrible stories of how bad the traffic could be, and to make things worse we hadn't managed to get hold of a decent city street map. The campsite was only US$3 a night and was even supposed to have a swimming pool, but it didn't exactly have rave reviews. The only other option was to find a 'hostal' (hostel) in the city and if they didn't have any form of parking, use a guarded car park, but we weren't sure how safe the bikes would be there – we'd heard a few disaster stories from other travellers.

The journey started well with a handy petrol station, and we managed to fill both bikes, whilst keeping Henry's throttle open. No one batted an eyelid at that. Obviously it was the norm for people to fill up with their engines running.

It happened to be a Sunday. On this single day of the week the traffic is a whole lot quieter. It gave us the chance to fumble our way around the potholes and giant cracks in the roads in relative peace, and fortunately there were enough signposts find our way. But as with riding in any new country there are local quirks and rules of the road that one really should learn. Normally we had the time and the opportunity to sit and watch drivers and their antics for long enough to understand what the quirks were. This time, no chance, we just had to get on with it.

The roads were wide but cluttered and nothing seemed to have been finished. Many of the buildings were either going up and unfinished or were falling down and gravity hadn't quite finished the job yet. Even the dual carriageways and flyovers hadn't been finished, but that wasn't stopping the traffic from using them. I lost count of the number of potholes we rode round when we weren't being forced through them. The thing that really got me was the kerb-like step that always seemed to join a concrete flyover to the road at ground level.

A step? Yes, and it would often be a good 15cm (6 inches) high. The traffic would slow right down to bump up and down it. With an ailing bike each of these steps was a major obstacle. If Birgit didn't get it exactly right each time then she would have either stalled the bike, or would have damaged her wheel rims. Her off-roading experience in Africa now paid real dividends. We weaved our way through the elegant historical buildings of the city centre, with time to look. Many are beautiful. All have a story to tell. We even bumped our way past the balcony that Eva Peron had made her famous speeches from.

The heat was becoming a problem for Birgit. We didn't worry too much about sweating on the bikes – it had become normal. But for Henry, the stop-start of the Sunday traffic was becoming tricky – especially as Birgit had to keep the throttle open all the time. She didn't dare let the bike tick over. Sooner or later the bike would overheat and then we'd have other problems to deal with. To top it all, the road signs ran out and suddenly we were lost. We found ourselves in a residential back street, and it didn't look right at all. There was nothing for it but to stop the bikes and ask directions. It was only when we'd made that decision that we noticed a big sign saying Bombaderos: Fire brigade. Surely they would know where the Lomas de Zamora campsite was?

We pulled up in front of the giant doors and peeked inside to see an enormous bright red American-style fire truck. I'd only ever seen these on television or as models in a toy shop. As we stopped, Henry decided that enough was enough, and stalled. The firemen were great and took a real shine to Birgit, and soon she was chatting away to them. Luckily one of the firemen spoke English and it turned out we weren't far from the campsite and, "Hey, no problem, one of the crew will take you." No sooner had Birgit been presented with a Bombaderos embroidered shoulder patch, than one of the guys was on his bike and indicating that we should follow him. But Henry didn't want to start.

Well, we entertained the neighbours and the firemen as we chased Birgit up and down the street with Henry still refusing to start. I think the Bombaderos were just beginning to regret their kind offer of help when Henry fired up. The bombadero on the bike shot off with a flamboyant riding style that had his pegs a centimetre away from shooting sparks as he belted around the corner, obviously expecting us to keep up with him! Two fully-loaded overland bikes aren't quite up to back-street ballet and it wasn't long before he left us well behind. He came back though and carried on showing us the way.

The campsite was big, and ramshackle. Everything had a layer of neglect and nothing seemed to have been cleaned or painted in recent months. But the site fees were reasonable, there was space, we were there, the showers worked (sporadically), and there was a nice shady eucalyptus tree to camp under. It would do. The plots on either side of us looked as if they were being lived in permanently and each was surrounded by junk. We couldn't have travelled much further from the luxury of the ship in a single afternoon. Even the streets surrounding the campsite had a moody, perhaps sullen and dangerous air to them.

We'd just got the tent up, had sorted our things out and were feeling pleased that we had a stash of food, when it started to rain. It was one of those moments when you know that though grim, things had worked out just fine. It would have been an awful journey from the port to the campsite in the rain.

Next day, having worked out how Argentinean payphones worked, Birgit called the BMW garage belonging to Ruben Monni and his son in Buenos Aires. Carlo in Namibia had recommended him to us. With some awkward stumbling she managed to make them understand what the problem was – the Spanish names for motorcycle parts weren't things that she'd learnt in school, or on her trip to Bolivia as a teenager. If she'd had a new bike they would have been able to get hold of the part she needed without a problem. The mechanic asked her to phone back in a couple of days, which would give him time to hunt through their boxes of odds and ends. It would give us the chance to catch the bus into the city and do some sight-seeing. I couldn't be asked to ride the bike in the city and the chance to use public transport was part of the reason for travelling. Experiencing as many local things as possible was the only way to learn, to discover and to explore. On the bike in the city I suspected that all I'd be learning was how to survive! Buenos Aires is massive. If you include the suburbs, the whole sprawl covers roughly 4,400 square kilometres (1,700 square miles).

Bus numbers 540 and 141 took us right to the Plaza Italia in the city centre. With hindsight, we could have just  followed those buses out and they would have taken us straight to the campsite. We became proper tourists over the next few days and did exactly what tourists are supposed to do – we went to see the places of interest that make a place like B.A. a 'must visit'. That included hunting out tango dancing haunts. This is the national dance of Argentina and it's danced with fire, verve and full flamboyant passion. They dance it in clubs and bars, in cafes and on the streets wide pavements. I liked the city and those days of being a tourist acted as a sort of halfway house between the luxury of the ship and the squalor of the campsite. It was always a bit hard to go back to the campsite but we hoped that we wouldn't be there for long.

Argentina is the world's eighth largest country, and the second largest in South America (after Brazil), with an area of 2.8 million square kilometres (over a million square miles). Argentina declared itself independent from Spain in 1816, which was about the time that Bolivia, Paraguay and Uruguay were doing the same thing. I often wonder where the names of countries come from, and there always seems to be a story attached. In Argentina's case, it was simple and delightful. Having just come up the 'Silver River' I was tickled to find that the name Argentina is based on the Latin word for silver – argentum.

As a country it's been heavily influenced by immigrants from Europe, with the greater percentage of those being from Italy and Spain – we could see their influence all over Buenos Aires. On some of the streets you could imagine you were strolling through Rome or old Madrid. It's estimated that between 80 and 90% of the population come from Europe and when you look at a map of the country you can often see where small settlements of different nationalities have been established.

Politically, it's been a turbulent country since the Second World War. In part, the Falklands war was an effort by the military dictatorship of the time to distract the population from internal woes. They weren't the first; what is it about governments that makes them think that a bloody conflict will solve a general crisis? Blinkers, desperation, or perhaps an ignorance of world history and economics?

By the time we arrived, President Carlos Menem was in power, and he was in trouble! In the early 1990s hyperinflation had been a massive problem and to try to put a stop to that, Menem introduced a system where the peso was linked directly to the US dollar. He also changed the way the country did business with the outside world and this combination was doing some real good. The problem was that there was a flaw in the plan. The peso was linked at a really high rate and this could only be maintained by flooding the country with dollars, and so the plan began to crumble around the edges. Foreign debt increased enormously and when the home market was opened up to foreign imports, local industry collapsed. This meant that while some

118

of the population were living like kings, most people were struggling with poverty and high unemployment. The signs of this were all around us at the campsite.

We'd now given up on the idea of being in Ushuaia for Christmas. It wasn't going to happen. Even when Birgit's bike was fixed we'd still have to ride like nutters to get there in time and in the end, what would be the point of that? There was still the chance we could be down there in time for the New Year though.

The guys from the garage had found a selection of potential relays in their boxes of bits, and to our amazement insisted on travelling from the other side of the city to bring them to us. We were stunned by this kindness. It was generosity at its best. When they arrived they insisted on doing the work too. Birgit hated other people working on her bike, but it seemed churlish to argue. The second relay worked. The fee? "Nothing, nada," Señor Monni said, "You just have a good Christmas and a fantastic trip."

It was also over these days that I discovered South American mosquitoes are just as ferocious as their African cousins. I hate the sound of the things and I intensely dislike the fact that they frequently outwit me with their zillion and one ways to sneak up and zap you without getting swatted. We discovered that the mossies on this campsite seemed to have developed a resistance, if not a taste for Deet. Every time we lathered on 'the only repellent in the world that really works' we would suddenly have a swarm of F16 fighter jets performing dog-fights around us, and attempting to refuel in mid-flight. I sometimes wondered, as the curtains on our neighbours' caravan twitched, whether they assumed that the nightly dance we performed as we tried to swat away the bloodsucking mini-monsters was some strange, northern hemisphere form of foreplay.

If they'd walked past our tent at night they would certainly have thought that some sort of bizarre ritual was going on inside. Birgit, being the smaller and therefore more manoeuvrable of us in a confined space, and with far more talent, was the designated destroyer of interior invaders. It didn't matter how careful and how quick we were

119

getting into the tent, some mosquitoes would always sneak in. There were times when I had the feeling they were mocking us. They were stealth stingers and would lie in wait until we were settled and had put our torches out. Then they would start their campaign, and they'd commence with mental torture. Somehow they seemed to have the ability to whine at an inordinately annoying pitch, loud enough to work its way through even the best earplugs. But then, once you had raised yourself out of your sleeping bag, had followed the sound and were just about to swat, they would instantly fall silent. This would leave your opened hand swatting empty air up against the side of the tent, again. It was the ultimate tease and some nights, from the outside, our tent must have looked as if it contained a pack of quarrelling dogs, but the sounds emanating from within were definitely human: "Gotcha!" "That'll teach you!!" "Damn, missed it!" "Cor, that one had been feeding – my blood or yours?" and of course, the inside of our tent began to look as if a mad axeman had been at work.

Our neighbours on the other side were no curtain-twitchers. Esther and Esteban seemed to accept us for who we were and invited us to join them for a Christmas asado. Asado is Argentinean for barbecue, though I think that any self- respecting Argentine would be insulted at having one of their favoured ways of cooking meat compared with anything Australians, Brits or North Americans do on their 'BBQs'. They certainly didn't incinerate everything until it bore no resemblance to meat – nor did they feel the need to keep vegetarians happy by adding a few strips of capsicum to a mass-incineration exercise. An asado in the hands of an expert is almost an art form, and it's one of the great social traditions in South America. (If you're vegetarian you probably won't appreciate the concept).

By this time we'd discovered that the reason vegetables were so expensive in Argentina, especially after African prices, was that there was an alternative food source that was much cheaper: beef. We'd spent the first few days in a state of mild panic over the price of veg. We could hardly ever find any fresh bread either and had to put up with prefabricated squares of yellow carbohydrate that Birgit advised me was special toasting bread. Not having a toaster, and with our petrol stove being useless for anything more than adding a tang of gasoline, we never managed to taste this stuff at its best. We had steered clear of meat because in Africa most of it was lean, stringy, tough and had almost always stood in a seething jacket of flies for some time. But now we knew how cheap top quality beef was in Argentina, we weren't too embarrassed at the quantity that was stacked up on the asado. The only thing we hadn't realised was that we were the only guests and were expected to help our hosts to devour the lot. Our neighbours lived on the site on a semi-permanent basis and had added a pergola with a canvas roof to cover their asado, which consisted of a metal grill on breezeblocks that was a good metre and a half long.

Esteban set to work. First, in one half of the grill, he made a good blaze using kindling and chunks of wood that he'd prepared earlier. Once the blaze had almost died away he used a little shovel to tease out a couple of scoops of coals that were glowing a brilliant red orange, but didn't have any flames. He placed these under the grill adjacent to the section where he had the fire going. Then he added more wood to the original fire, and some meat to the grill over the embers. He followed this routine as the four of us proceeded to eat what felt like most of, and every part of, a whole cow. He never cooked over flames, only over the embers. This meant that the food was never burnt, just beautifully cooked. Even the chitterlings and sweetbreads tasted good.

As we ate, the sky was filled with fireworks. The display went on for four and a half hours and the air above us was literally filled with them. The noise was phenomenal and even now I associate the taste of grilled meat with the tang of gunpowder. I wondered about the expense of the fireworks. It sounded as if the country's munitions budget had been burnt in one night, and the areas around us were incredibly poor. We'd seen thin-faced children walking barefoot and unwashed. The dogs we'd seen looked as if they all ought to be put down and the women seemed to be joyless, and worn out. The men seemed to be either unemployed or earning a pittance. But underlying all this there was an air of pride and I admired the people for that. I

121

suspected that the fireworks, though expensive, were a way for everyone to join together and have a big happy party. Christmas was a reason to celebrate and they were going to do their best to enjoy it.

I supposed that if each family in the whole area bought just a couple of fireworks then such a display was possible and enjoyable. Esther and Esteban set off no fireworks themselves but seemed to enjoy the way that every few moments the world was lit up by flashes of intensely brilliant multi-coloured lights. Enormous bangs filled the air and I hoped that the local hounds were deaf as well as skinny. The bangs were so frequent that it sounded as if we were at some sort of weird drummers' convention, and from time to time the bangs even sounded as if they were keeping up a beat.

The next morning, the mosquitoes only lazily tried to eat us. Perhaps they were still stunned from the noise, or were intoxicated by the gunpowder smoke but more likely they had eaten their fill of party-goers during the night.

It was time to move on. I had really itchy feet by now and with both bikes working well, we hit the road. The plan was to ride a fairly short day, as we knew that it could take us quite a while just to get out of Buenos Aires.

As we rode, a huge rainstorm hit us. It was almost as if a giant, waterlogged cloud was following us, and as the rain heaved down, open manholes became mini whirlpools. The edges of the flyovers became mini waterfalls and the ancient car in front of us, which was held together by kilometres of brown parcel tape and had smoke pouring from several holes, began to fall apart as the rain dissolved the glue on the tape. Navigating was something that Birgit, up in front, seemed to be managing surprisingly well in spite of the fact that our visors were misted up inside and rain streaked on the outside. Fortunately the town of Azul was quite well signposted and when we finally made it to the edge of the city, the rain stopped.

Not only was Azul just 264 kilometres south of B.A. but it was supposed to have a really good campsite. We both liked the town as soon as we hit its streets. It made me think of old Spanish hill towns.

Terracotta roofs topped many of the buildings and the main streets were lined with carefully shaped orange trees, which at this time of year were covered in vividly coloured oranges. I wondered why nobody had picked and eaten them, but when I tried a windfall I understood immediately. They were incredibly bitter. "Never judge a fruit by its skin," I thought with a grin.

The camping site was easy to find and superb. It was green, grassy and well taken care of. We put up the tent and then flopped. We were shattered. We'd not ridden the bikes for more than a couple of hours at a time for nearly three weeks and our muscles had lost tone. I didn't think about that much at the time, but I soon wished that I had...

Chapter 7

An angry wind

'Men stumble over pebbles, never over mountains.'

Emil Caddy

We treated ourselves to a glass of red wine in celebration. We'd discovered by this time that Argentinean wine is incredibly cheap, and very good. Even the cheapest plonk sold in litre cartons was well worth drinking. Although Argentina is the world's fifth largest wine producer, almost 90% of it is consumed locally. We could see why!

Both of us looked up when we heard a motorcycle arrive and circle round at a distance. This bike was soon followed by another. After a moment's conversation the bikers rode across the grass towards us. They were members of the local bike club and it was their turn on the rota to ride to the campsite to see if any bikers had turned up. They would invite visitors to their new clubhouse and to meet the other members; perhaps even to go out and party. Would we like to join them?

We left Henry locked and parked up, and followed Neldo and his mate back into Azul. They had only just purchased the building and renovation had not progressed much beyond a new sign saying 'Clubhouse'. We were taken around and introduced, and Birgit chatted happily with everyone. With my lack of Spanish I suddenly felt quite left out, but after a while I got talking to one of the guys who knew some English.

We chatted about bikes and travel, about Azul and about the guy's dreams for the club and the clubhouse. They wanted the club to become the biggest and friendliest motorcycle club in Argentina. It didn't matter what bikes people rode, it was the fact that they were on bikes that was important. The clubhouse was being sorted out so they had a big meeting room and were going to organise sleeping rooms so they could invite visitors to stay over. "If you come back next year you can sleep here instead of the campsite," one of the guys said. It turned out that the guy I was talking to was the club President. Jorge had no fancy airs about him, but he had a magnetic personality.

I'd dreaded the subject of the Falklands. I didn't want to get into an argument and I didn't want to be labelled. I wanted to be treated just as me. Fortunately Neldo, who also spoke some English, had been confused by my GBJ number plate (Jersey Channel Islands). Birgit's German number plate had muddied the waters nicely too. So I was safe, but really sad when he rattled on passionately about how Las Malvinas (The Falklands) belonged to Argentina and how the British had been murderers in the war and so on. I was non-committal and didn't respond to his comments and managed to steer the conversation away from the war to the club and travelling. We chatted on.

Then Neldo said, "So where is this GBJ?" I said, "It's one of the islands in the English Channel between England and France and is part of Great Britain." I stood feeling very uncomfortable about deceiving him by omission. Neldo shot a look at me that made me even more uncomfortable, and moved away without saying a word. I looked around for Birgit. If things were going to turn nasty we would probably have to make a rapid exit. I moved across the courtyard towards her. Before I got to her, Neldo caught up with me and took me by the arm. I tensed as he swung me around, expecting to be thumped.

But he looked me straight in the eye and said, "You have made me think. Before we talk I don't like English. The Malvinas war was terrible. But now after we talk, I think that maybe you English not so bad." With that he turned from me and strode determinedly through the crowd of club members, and I didn't see him again.

He left me feeling a little stunned. I was absolutely impressed with how he moved his thoughts about so rapidly and how sensitive he was underneath his burly biker image to the fact that things often need to change, and how the actions of some should not label all. It was also my first experience of just how passionate conversation can be in Latin countries.

It reinforced my feeling that travel is not only about having adventures and learning about the wider world. It seems to me that a lot of the problems between nations stem from ignorance and a lack of one-to-one communication rather than greedy tussles for power or wealth. It's easy, when we are dealing with a faceless, depersonalised group, not to see them as human flesh and blood. We fear what we don't know or understand. Every traveller can act as a peacemaker by keeping an open mind and by questioning their own prejudices. On the other hand, those who travel with an 'I'm better than you' attitude, just make things worse.

I stood in the middle of the courtyard, thinking these thoughts and suddenly realised I'd been oblivious to everything else around me. Birgit was being asked if we wanted to go into the town centre to eat and drink. No one had yet had dinner even though it was now 11pm.

We declined because we wanted to be in Ushuaia in time for New Year and needed to be on the road early in the morning. There was a stiff breeze blowing as we rode home. Sheets of old newspaper, empty crisp packets and clouds of dust billowed around us as we rode. With two of us on the bike it was like riding a mini sail. I hoped the wind would have gone by the time we were ready to ride in the morning, but it increased during the night. In spite of the flap of the tent fabric, we knew after the Wild Coast storm that it would deal with far worse than this, so we still slept soundly.

In the morning we awoke to find that we'd been lucky. A branch of a tree had missed the tent by barely a metre. As we un-pegged the tent

 it made a break for freedom but we managed to get it packed away as the wind continued to fight with us. Around us the treetops were whipping back and forth a good two or three metres as the wind gusted. While still in among the buildings we were able to ride reasonably sensibly, but as soon as we passed the last house, all hell let loose. It was almost as if we had offended the wind somehow. It was absolutely vicious and seemed determined to knock us off the road. In front of us lay over 3,000 kilometres across the Pampas and Patagonia. It occurred to me that the famous 'Roaring Forties' had to roar from somewhere and this was where we now were...

As we passed level with the city of Bahia Blanca, the price of fuel halved. We'd heard about this but it had seemed too good to be true. It would make an amazing difference to our budget, bearing in mind the number of kilometres we planned to ride over the next few weeks. The idea behind the government doing this is quite sensible and I suspect that the majority of people living across Patagonia would not be able to afford to do so without fuel being so cheap. We'd heard that fuel was the only thing we'd find that was cheap when we got into the far south.

As we headed on down, the wind added a chill factor to temperatures that were already too cool for my liking. The countryside opened up and we began to ride a road of a thousand gently rolling valleys. This really is 'the open road'. To the sides, foot-high tussock grass waved its resilient yellow stems like silk in the wind, like a vast field full of blond heads whose hair is streaming out according to the whims of the fickle gusts.

There were no trees and nothing, except the very occasional town, seemed to be able to slow down the wind. The strong gusts turned into vicious, unpredictable attacks as we headed further south. When I wasn't battling to keep the bike upright, I wondered what on earth I was doing there. I rode heaving at the handlebars and felt as if I were arm-wrestling with a giant and that he was toying maliciously with me; teasing, pushing and shoving. Every so often he would abruptly change his mind. All the strength I was putting into stopping the bike falling one way would suddenly tip the bike the other way as the wind dropped momentarily.

Each day of riding felt like a marathon and my slipped discs began to complain. They were the pivotal point between my shoulders, which were flexing in the wind, and my legs that were gripping the bike with the effort of staying on. I should have guessed that this would happen. The reading I'd done on the ship had made it very clear that we were going to be riding through one of nature's unique regions. I'd heard Patagonia described as being like one giant wind tunnel, and I'd read that wind speeds frequently got up to 190 kilometres an hour. I'd also read that some windstorms were strong enough to hurl stones through objects, like bullets, or small cannonballs. A friend had said to me, "You do realise that Patagonia starts when the rest of the world finishes. Why on earth are you planning to ride a bike down there? It has the worst weather in the world!"

Human nature is a funny thing isn't it? When someone says "Don't touch, the paint is wet." we often go right ahead and touch it just to make sure. We'd had all the warnings but we still had the urge to go and touch Patagonia's paint.

What makes the wind so strong is that it's westerly and promoted by extremely low temperatures in Antarctica. The intense contrast between the temperatures there and at the Equator build low-pressure systems called cyclonic centres and it's these that hammer across the arid plains of Patagonia. The Andes play their part too in that they channel the winds, and the ice cap that covers much of the mountain range rapidly cools temperatures. The more I read the more I felt that the Andes were having the same effect that a stick stirring a snake pit would have.

Pitching camp in Patagonia was a two-person job. We'd carefully unpack the tent with one of us making sure that nothing blew away, while the other clipped the tent poles together. Then with one person, usually me because I'm the heaviest, holding the inner and fly sheet down, the other, usually Birgit, would scurry round feeding the poles into slots on them both. We would both then hang on for dear life as we erected the tent. This was the critical time. If one of us lost our footing or a handhold then the tent would be gone and we would be facing a very cold night plus the loss of a couple of months' food budget. When Birgit had got as many of our six inch nails into the stony ground as she could, she would leave me sprawled out over the top of the flysheet like some sort of human splat against the fabric, while she collected rocks and used them to weigh down the pegs and the snow-skirts that fringed the flysheet.

Tent secure, we would park the bikes as a sort of windbreak, but in such a way that they would not be blown onto the tent. This happened to a friend's fully-laden BMW! Then we would collapse into the windless, dustless tent, shattered but nice and warm from our efforts.

Sometimes we were lucky and managed to find a small, well-drained gully to set up in, though we were wary of flash floods. At other times we were able to camp next to petrol stations. This was actively encouraged by many of them and was a godsend for us. The owners often planted hedged bays in between which we could put the tent up. The battered hedges were enough to keep the worst of the wind off the tent erection process, and that made the sighting of a fuel station towards the end of a long day's ride seem like a mirage made real.

Fuel stations like these were a bonus in other ways too. They usually had good washrooms and sometimes, hot showers. But the best bonus was the never-ending supply of hot drinking water. The drinking of maté (as this tea is called) is an Argentinean custom that everyone agreed was a good thing. Maté is traditionally referred to as the 'drink of friendship', and it is in fact the national drink of both Argentina and Uruguay.

Fuel stations have vast urns that are always full of hot water so that people can fill their maté gourds or their thermos flasks. It's quite normal to see people going about their daily business with a gourd in one hand and a thermos in the other. Birgit grew to like this tea made with the leaves of the yerba plant, but I remained unconvinced. The taste is rather like a combination of green tea, tobacco and oak. I simply couldn't understand why everyone raved about the stuff. To me it tasted disgusting, and it brought on nicotine cravings! I used the hot water to make neat, pure coffee and got my buzz from the caffeine instead.

In the morning though, it saved a lot of time to be able to pop into the fuel station with our billy, fill it with water to boil for tea or coffee and then use the rest for making our porridge. We'd found maize meal flour in the supermarkets so were able to continue our African habit of maize meal porridge for breakfast each day. It's a cheap stomach-filler that gave us a lot of energy. I think that Birgit secretly liked the stuff because we'd often stir in a lump of chocolate as a treat!

But I'm not giving maté due credit. I liked the fact that something as simple as a herb drink could bring so many people together. There's a whole routine that has to be followed to make a decent gourd of maté, and this would often lead to people sharing that gourd together. Getting this drink just right was something that people treated with respect, concentration and pride. I make cups of tea or coffee on autopilot. I don't need to think about what I'm doing, but Argentineans never seemed to make a maté without total absorption.

Maté is usually served in either a decorated calabash gourd or a ceramic, gourd-shaped container. The size of the gourd is such that it can

be held easily in the hand. Each stage of the routine is followed religiously – even the length of time, and the way in which a calabash is seasoned so it becomes ideal for drinking maté, is known and traditional.

The exact amount of yerba has to be added and the water must never be boiling or the leaves get scorched and that affects the flavour. When the process has been followed, a sort of straw with a filter on the end is inserted into the mix in the gourd, and you drink the maté through that. This straw, or bombillia (bombija), is often made out of intricately decorated pure silver and many are handed down from one generation to the next. You can find nickel silver, stainless steel and even bamboo straws but I never saw one made of something as mundane as plastic.

A gourd of maté will often be passed around a group of friends or in the family. Some will take a suck or two on the straw before passing it on, and others will drink the whole gourd before filling it with hot water again and then passing it on. You can re-use the same 'mash' quite a few times and in fact it's frequently the first brew that tastes the worst. In a sharing session the host will usually drink that one themselves. I'm afraid I saw the whole thing as rather unhygienic. For starters the water wasn't boiled, so in out-of-the-way places you never knew what bugs were lurking within the brew. If anything I suspected that the hot water was just what some of the bugs needed to be able to multiply at maximum potency. As for using the same straw, that was always going to be a leap of faith, but I supposed that this was part of how the whole friendship concept worked. It was a trust thing!

The days went by with hours of long, open and very remote roads. Oncoming drivers were so happy to see something else alive that everyone flashed and waved enthusiastically. Derelict fuel stops with their wind-blasted, dried-out old wooden buildings and metal signs that swung and squeaked from their posts, were home to rusting wrecks from a bygone age. Oil-pumping 'nodding donkeys' stood squat in the landscape looking like leftover props from a Star Wars movie. At first glance, wild sage and yellowed feathery clumps of grass seemed to be the only vegetation. But on closer inspection we would often find small clumps of fleshy-leaved 'cushion' plants nestling out of the worst of the wind. On some, small vibrant flowers bloomed, defying the near-hurricane-force winds. I discovered later that the yellow-flowered plant we'd seen was a member of the pea family and that started me wondering just how big the pea family might be, and how widespread throughout the world. There are 13,000 different species! They survive from gardens to rocky mountain slopes and desert fringes. The more I read about them the more I liked their determination, and their ability to add a vibrant splash of colour where little else could flourish.

Towns seemed to be of the bleak Eastern Bloc architectural type and their windswept streets were hardly more welcoming than the open lonely roads. Some of the town squares even had giant statues as monuments to oilmen or miners. They were very much in the stark angular Eastern Bloc style too, and though they seemed to be more of a political statement than a memorial to the men and women who had worked the land, they were very impressive.

We didn't see any birds until we were travelling along sections of the coast. Here, the inevitable seagulls wheeled and cawed as they buffeted their way along the shore. We also saw a few cattle, a few scattered, dirty-looking sheep and a very occasional guanaco. I'd been looking forward to seeing these creatures, which are from the same family as the llama. In many parts of Argentina they had been hunted almost out of existence and when we saw some we felt privileged, but I'd read that they were herd animals and was sad that the ones we saw seemed to be loners.

Another loner we came across rolled onto the campsite at Comodoro Rivadavia. He was a North American Indian called Dr Greg Frazier. The bike, I could just see under the mountain of luggage he had strapped to it, was a BMW R100GS, a 980cc version of my own 800cc R80GS. From it's beaten-up appearance you knew that every ding told a story, and that the collection of dust that clung into the exposed nooks and crannies came from the roads of many countries. Greg and his bike made a perfect match – weather-beaten and road-worn. Lean and loose-limbed, Greg exuded an air of quiet confidence.

Greg offered us a mix of olives and fatty pink luncheon meat that had been roughly diced into two centimetre cubes, and a swig of his vodka. He was soon explaining to Birgit that he was on the hunt for a rich woman to look after his home, and him when he was there, and did she like the sound of it?

I was a bit gob-smacked as he made it sound like a marriage proposal. He had approached Birgit with total seriousness, no hint of humour in his voice and total disregard of my presence. Later that night as we huddled out of the wind in our tent, we pondered the question. Had he been serious or was he joking? If he was serious then that made him a very strange and lonely character. If he had been joking then he had a wild sense of humour, had mastered the poker face, and we'd missed the punch line altogether. Perhaps there were no connections between European and Native American Indian senses of humour! He said nothing more in the morning, so we presumed he'd been joking. Good taste though, I teased Birgit!

Greg had given us a good tip – as we headed further south we should try to ride in the mornings only. The wind would be much calmer in the early hours and due to some quirky mix of climate and geographical influences this was something that could be depended on.

The ride south was becoming an endurance test, and I wasn't sure how much more I could endure. In spite of very early starts, my back hurt from the blasting wind and I couldn't find a comfortable position on the bike anymore. I wasn't sleeping well because of the constant niggling pain, and the cold riding was now beginning to knock chunks off my usual optimism. But I decided that the pain wasn't bad enough to start taking painkillers – I'd pumped so many chemicals into my body since I'd originally slipped the discs in Australia, I felt it would be good if I could hold off taking any more for as long as possible. Beside that, I was an adventurer; I could beat the pain with 'mind over matter'. I also knew from my old days of physio exercises that a daily five kilometre, striding-out walk would sort out most back problems. When we were camping in the middle of nowhere I loved the looks that I'd get when someone drove past this man striding out along the roadside without so much as a small knapsack on his back. A lift? "No gracias, I'm out for a stroll actually."

Some way to the east of our route stood the small town and port of Deseado. I didn't feel like battling the extra kilometres to get down

there, in spite of the fact that Deseado is where, in 1586, a Welshman is supposed to have come up with the name 'penguin' for the strange bird he found in vast colonies there. The Welsh version of penguin is pengwyn, which means 'white head'. This was one of the things I liked about travelling. Had I not been on the road reading up about each place as we went, I probably never would have known that. Learning this sort of thing made me question many things I'd taken for granted.

By the time we made it to the port of San Julian, I'd had enough. My back now really hurt and I was only keeping myself going with thoughts of how well I'd done to be able to ride my motorcycle at all for the past two years. They counted as a bonus after being told that I'd never ride a bike again when I'd badly slipped the two discs on my last day in Australia. I'd thought my travelling days by any means at all might be over.

I'd put my back through a lot over the years. I don't remember thinking about it when I was younger, but if I had, then I'm sure I would have felt that I was pretty invincible. In my youth I'd played a lot of rugby and I'd mostly bounced easily. Then over the years of travel I'd done all sorts of labouring jobs on building sites and fruit farms and the like. I'd walked away from those jobs with money in my pocket to keep travelling, and feeling stronger and fitter as a result of the work. But with each game or job I was probably inflicting a little more damage, and I was sure that the 17-bone fracture accident I'd had coming across the Namibian desert the first time through had contributed to the accumulating damage. Some work with a film crew in Darwin had been the last straw.

But I was sure that a good long rest would do my bones some good, and that a few days of walking and not riding would do the trick. In fact the truth was that my body was now screaming "Enough!" and I should have listened to it four days ago. Fortunately the beach campsite was well sheltered by great swathes of bushes and that meant Birgit could get the tent up on her own. The rest was easy and while she put our home together, I took my first painkillers. Two hours later they didn't seem to have done a thing.

It may have been the pain, or the permanently grey skies, or the ever-blasting wind, but I soon decided that I didn't like the town of San Julian. I was very happy I didn't have to call it home; the five days that we stayed there trying to get me fit again was too long. The roads in the town were straight and wide. The buildings that lined the streets were either old and tired render, or new and tired concrete, or dull grey breezeblock. They looked as if they had either given up on life or were bland defences against the elements and nothing more. There didn't seem to have been any attempt to make the town look attractive. Or perhaps attempts at beauty had been so constantly wrecked by the environment that people had just stopped trying. There was very little traffic and those vehicles that were around were either 4x4s, an occasional articulated truck, or rusty saloon cars suffering from the effects of the sea air. The few shrubs that survived would probably have withstood anything short of a nuclear blast and though it wasn't really cold, it certainly wasn't sunbathing weather either. The wind made me feel cold though, and I was despondent.

Was my round the world dream going to die here? What an ignominious end that would be. But I consoled myself that if it was going to end at least it would be out on the road and not stuck at home in 'real life'. Yet I had to smile at the thought that, after all the mad things that had happened over the years, and all the dramatic disasters I'd walked away from, I was finally going out with a whimper not a bang!

Birgit was bravely trying to hide her disappointment as it became clear that I wasn't going to be riding anywhere in a hurry. It had been her dream to get to Ushuaia and now that dream was potentially in tatters. I suggested that she should ride on alone but she wouldn't hear of it. She didn't want to leave me in such a state, on my own. I was selfishly glad when she told me, but also felt guilty and somewhat impotent.

Even if I'd been able to manage short hops on tarmac, we'd been told that two long stretches in front of us were rough gravel and I knew I couldn't manage them. In a strong wind on loose gravel your bike feels as if it's doing a madman's waltz. The bike floats sideways as a result of the wind, and even faster sideways as a result of the gravel. Gravity suddenly becomes magnetic and the more tired you get the stronger that magnetism is. When you are fit, riding in these conditions can be a buttock-clenching, teeth-grinding challenge but if you aren't fit, it's downright foolish.

Our options were either to put the bikes on a truck and go north, hoping that the absence of wind and warmer weather would help get me fit again. Or else we could stay where we were and carry on the mind-numbing, uncertain and painful day-to-day slog of trying to get fit again in a cold, bleak place. Neither option had much appeal.

Then, one night when we were huddled in the tent drinking cheap red wine out of a carton – the kind of painkiller I do like – Birgit had an idea. "Why don't we hitch-hike down to Ushuaia?" I wondered what the chances of hitching were and where we could leave the bikes.

I didn't really mind not being there on the bikes. It was sad in a way but I'd always been on this journey with the idea that I wanted to use as many different forms of transport as possible. This looked as if it was going to be just such an occasion. And at least we'd be getting there.

Someone once said to me, 'There's no point in travelling, it's all been done before." I had a wry grin to myself. Others might have made it to Ushuaia before, but I doubted that anyone would have done it with the collection of events we were having. It was just proving the point that everyone has their own trip made up of a unique mix of jigsaw puzzle pieces. To illustrate that point, I remember a friend telling me that he'd been chatting with someone and discovered that they'd both been to the same city. Yet the things that each had seen and done were so different that their visits might as well have been to completely different places. They'd made a plan to travel back to this city with each showing the other what they had discovered and experienced. I loved the concept.

We were still looking for the pieces of our jigsaw puzzle, or perhaps it was more that they were all there in front of us, but that we hadn't yet worked out how they'd fit together. We'd no idea if we could actually make it down by hitching but felt that it was well worth a try. After all, we'd have our tent and we could carry enough food and water for several days. We could just camp near the roadside if we had to wait for a long time.

I rather liked the sound of the new adventure that was beginning to unfold. It beat the hell out of plodding around the town, hoping. And it certainly beat the idea of giving up and heading north with the bikes on a truck. It also meant that we would be rubbing shoulders with Argentineans, and that should be interesting. For the last few days we'd spoken to no-one other than shopkeepers, fuel station attendants, and the owners of the campsite in San Julian. We'd become quite friendly with Señora Jacinta and she'd realised that something was wrong. It was highly unusual for anyone to stay on the campsite for more than a couple of days. It was a bit of a giveaway that I almost had to be winched out of the tent and then could be seen walking round in circles looking like an old man with a broomstick up my backside.

Birgit explained our problem and what we were thinking about doing and this very kind woman arranged for the bikes to be stored at the garage of her brother, Pinocchio, if we could get them there. I was sure that I could manage a ride of less than a kilometre. Much later, someone asked me if I wasn't worried about leaving the bikes with strangers. I replied that there was never the remotest doubt in my mind that the bikes would be safe in the care of our campsite host. I don't even remember thinking about it. Señora Jacinta and Pinocchio were good people; it was as simple as that.

The clinching factor in the decision was when we realised that the Argentinean customs in Buenos Aires hadn't stamped the bikes into our passports. We'd be breaking the law by leaving without them to go through the strip of Chile, but if no one knew about it...

As a final touch of kindness Señora Jacinta arranged for a friend to drop us off at the main road near the fuel station. Potentially we were in for a long wait, but we felt as if perhaps, if we got our hitching technique right, then the gods would smile on us and we'd be on our way without having to spend the night on the roadside. Strangely, we felt rather vulnerable without the bikes.

A truck went past us, with the driver paying us no attention at all. That was strange – we'd not seen a single hitchhiker on the way down so we must have stood out as an oddity. Perhaps our 'thumbs up' technique was actually some sort of insult. I vaguely recalled reading that it wasn't the way they hitched here. That same thought process filtered up the idea that the way to let people know you wanted to hitch a ride was to use a slow flapping motion with palm down and arm straight, moving your hand up to your shoulder and back again.

The next vehicle to approach was a beaten-up 4x4 pick-up that looked like a relation to the 'parcel tape car' we'd seen in Buenos Aires. At least this time the driver stared straight at us. He looked just like a large blubbery bulldog that someone had plonked behind the wheel. He had a round, bald head, with bristle- covered jowls and a nose that looked as if he'd spent too much time with it pressed up against windows as a child. On either side of this flattened nose ran deep gullies that headed down to curve up out of sight under his chin. His round shoulders were so big that he seemed to overflow from the driver's side of the car into the passenger's side. As he went past he slowed and indicated that he was turning off. While he did so he gave us a friendly grin that transformed him from wrinkled hound to interesting character. What a pity he'd been turning off.

Happily the traffic was heavy this day. Within the hour another vehicle had passed us, with the cowboy-hatted driver giving us a friendly wave, and also indicating that he was turning off. At least it seemed that we were getting our technique right.

Moments later a small burgundy-coloured Datsun saloon car pulled up. The young driver was so skinny that my mother would have wanted to give him a good hot meal. He had shoulder-length, straight black hair and sported a day's stubble on his chin. In spite of being so lean, he looked moody and handsome – I could imagine girls going weak at the knees over him. He leant out of the window and with a white-toothed smile asked where we were going. His companion was a looker too. Her skin was the colour of a very dark tan and she too had black hair that fell to her shoulders, but hers was wavy. She had a heart-shaped face and also sported a friendly smile full of even and brilliantly white teeth.

The car was packed with camping kit and clothes and my first thought was, "Thanks for stopping, but I can't see how we're going to fit in!". Miguel and Toni told us that they were heading the 400 kilometres down to Rio Gallegos and that we could have a ride. Before Miguel had even finished speaking, Toni was out of the car and bundling their things together. Before we could say "Yes please", she'd stuffed most of the things in the boot. We could fit in, just, but we'd be travelling with our rucksacks on our knees. There wasn't another car in sight, so we gratefully accepted the ride. It was a good first hop, as Rio Gallegos was the last major town in Argentina before the border with Chile. The car sagged on its suspension under our combined weight.

Miguel and Toni were both drama students and were on their summer break. They'd saved like mad to be able to afford a holiday down in Patagonia, and were now seeing where the road took them. Miguel seemed a little put out that my Spanish was so poor, but the two of them soon struck up a conversation with us in English, with Birgit helping when they stumbled over words. The tarmac hummed under our wheels as we headed south.

Inside the car I felt decidedly insulated from the world, and that was quite a disconcerting feeling. But I was delighted. The car was being pushed and shoved, sometimes from one side of the road to the other, but wedged in as we were I felt totally unaffected by even the worst that the wind could do.

Miguel had been training to be a lawyer but with great regret had decided not to continue with his studies. He told us that the legal system in Argentina was so corrupt that he wanted to have nothing to do with it. He also said that actors on the stage in Argentina were some of the few people that could get away with criticising the generals and now President Menem – albeit 'tongue in cheek'. He seemed aggressively proud of his rebellion against authority, but there seemed an air of uncertainty about him with regard to the future. He gave me the impression that he had decided to live for the day, and that studying to become an actor was largely because Toni had already been doing the course.

Miguel muttered that Menem had been a complete disappointment. The people had expected wonders from him when he became president. After all, he was from the Peronist party and Eva Peron had built up a party set on a specific, people-friendly code. I suspect the reality was that Menem had to deal with such a dire situation that it was impossible to make anything happen quickly, and therefore impossible to make most people happy.

As they got used to us, their conversation became more passionate, revealing their deep frustration that a country such as theirs should be in such dire straits. The economy had been suffering badly for generations and from time to time inflation had soared. They reinforced what we'd read: poverty was rife in Argentina, but there was also a stratum of super-rich people.

This distrust of the government had been earned over generations and it seemed to me that people swung from being resigned to their fate, to showing flamboyant displays of outrage, many of which ended in tears.

Miguel said, "The linking of the peso to the dollar has stopped much of the black market money dealings and you must be careful with this as the black market is infiltrated with informers – it isn't worth the risk." It felt odd to be able to draw US dollars directly from hole-in-the-wall machines. We could pay for things in the shops with them too, though we always got local currency as change.

The two of them talked about the war with Britain, and often those conversations were sparked by the many 'Las Malvinas son Argentinas' posters, billboards and paintings on roadside rocks that we passed. They were angry that Argentina had been got into the war and were furious at the number of people that had been killed. Toni called the whole thing a 'political trick'. But in spite of this, the two of them believed that the Malvinas did actually belong to Argentina and that Britain was squatting there illegally.

By the time we'd made it to Rio Gallegos the two of them let us know that they were in fact heading down to Ushuaia and that if we'd like to travel all the way with them, then we would be very welcome. Just as they told us that, the grey sky disappeared for a few moments, and brilliant sunshine transformed the countryside around us from rather daunting drab shades of mustards and sages to crisp yellows and greens. Even the wind in the bright blue sky seemed to be friendly for that instant.

It seemed strange to be crossing our first border in South America without the bikes, but at least it gave us a chance to see how things were likely to work. It all looked incredibly easy. For Miguel and Toni it certainly was and even with us tagging along it only took an hour to clear through both sides. The officials knew exactly what they were doing and were friendly and courteous; their uniforms had not turned any of them into mini-dictators.

Almost immediately after the border, the road turned to gravel. This would have been easy to ride the bikes on. It was well compacted by the passing of thousands of vehicles. The gullies and occasional potholes were hard work for the little Datsun though, and I had the feeling that Miguel and Toni were wondering if it had been so wise to give us a lift all the way.

The occasional runs of 'washboard' surface had the car meandering from side to side as the wheels skipped across the tops of the ridges. The stones that the tyres flicked up under the car sounded as if they were doing real damage and it bottomed out several times on ridges of gravel.

Conversation died away inside the car and Birgit and I looked at each other. It was 56 kilometres to the ferry across the Magellan Straits, and if the road continued to be like this it would only be fair to say goodbye to the two of them. We had no wish to spoil their dream. If we were going to part company with Miguel and Toni, then the ferry port would be the place to do it. We could walk round and tap on windows of the stationary vehicles to ask for a ride. But Miguel and Toni felt that we should stay with them, even though the next 80 kilometres after the ferry were still gravel. They'd talked to a truck driver while we'd been looking around and he'd said that the ride was going to be better. I was glad. My nest in the back of their car had become very comfortable and I was loath to have to find another way to travel. And while large chunks of the conversation went over my head, all the talking was helping me to learn more Spanish.

The ferry takes just half an hour to cross the straits and bearing in mind how little traffic we'd seen, I was surprised at how many vehicles there were waiting to get on. As we stood in the queue the sun came out again and it stayed out. The water and land around us sat under a sky so piercingly blue and clear that they looked sharp- edged and vibrant. It was almost as if everything around us had instantly blossomed. I could feel the warming rays on my face and hands and around us, hardier souls were even stripping down to T-shirts!

I felt a surprising sensation of happiness and pride to be on the ferry. After all, these were the Magellan Straits, steeped in history. Though the strait is only about 4km wide at its narrowest point, before the Panama Canal was built it was considered to be the safest way from the Atlantic to the Pacific Ocean. It was first navigated by the Portuguese sailor, Ferdinand Magellan in 1520, one of whose ships went on to become the first to circumnavigate the globe. (Magellan himself was killed in the Philippines only two thirds of the way round).

Others who explored it in those early days were Sir Thomas Cavendish and Sir Francis Drake, the first Englishman to sail around the world. The Spanish made several attempts at colonising the region but all failed – it's a harsh land. By the time Sir Thomas got there in 1587 there were only ruins left to show that any attempt had been made. He renamed the original settlement Port Famine! Chile took possession of the channel in 1843 and it has remained theirs ever since.

My happy mood was made even better by the sight of a black and white dolphin, which had decided to follow playfully alongside. At first I'd thought it was a baby orca but I'd never heard of an orca doing such a thing and Birgit was pretty sure that this was not killer whale territory. I felt completely privileged that the dolphin had come to play and it felt like the start of good things to come. When I walked back down the steps into the vehicle bay to get out of the stiff breeze, I was lucky enough to find a sunny corner to stand and ponder what we were doing.

Below my feet I could feel the rumbling and grinding of the engine and the screw turning. The smells that surrounded me were those of hot car engine, the sea, ancient spilt diesel from 4x4s and trucks, old paint and the occasional wafts of exhaust fumes from the ferry's blackened sooty exhaust funnel. It was a strangely exotic mix that smelt of travel and adventure.

As we eased on down into Tierra del Fuego – 'Land of Fire' – it got significantly warmer, and all of a sudden I realised that there wasn't any wind. The land had become hilly and this seemed to be deflecting the winds. It was Magellan who gave the area the name Tierra del Fuego. When he first sailed past in 1520 he could see fires that had been lit by the Yamana Indians. The Yamana wore little clothing so these fires were vital to their survival – they even carried a lighted fire aboard their canoes!

It felt strange to be seeing hills after all the rolling plains and there were trees too. Most were gnarly, thick-barked loners. These were dotted along the higher slopes and leant in the direction of the prevailing wind. Many of their branches sported trails of beard-like tree moss. They made me think of hardy but arthritic old men staggering along the hillside paths, leaning forward under the weight of their loads.

Before long we were treated to clusters of evergreens nestling in the valleys. I was surprised at my reaction to seeing all the trees. It was almost as if I'd been suffering from tree withdrawal symptoms!

Apart from the road that looped round through the gold rush town of Porvenir and the last 80 kms into Ushuaia, the road was mostly tarmac once we made it past Rio Grande. This city is home to one of the biggest meat-processing plants in South America, but I'd read that overall, the city was struggling to survive. It had boomed on the back of Chilean government financial incentives to business, but when those incentives were withdrawn, the city began to run down. The city also boasted the most southerly oil refinery in the world. The area we'd been driving through had been dotted with more of the slowly nodding 'donkey pumps' and it seemed pretty obvious to me that the reason Chile hung onto this area so tenaciously was a combination of national pride, control of the Magellan Straits, and oil.

When Birgit had first said that she'd come to South America with me I hadn't realised how much she loves cold climates. Her insistence that we should make it to Ushuaia was a combination of that love, and her geographer's desire to make it to the southernmost point of the continent. She's also a sailor and she said, "If I can't sail around Cape Horn, then at least I can get to this part of the world by land."

Ushuaia isn't the southernmost point but it's not far off and can boast being the southernmost city in the world. For two thirds of the year it can be minus 21 degrees Centigrade here. It's also the city with the most suicides in Argentina.

I didn't feel suicidal when we first arrived but I did think it was a bleak place to have to live. In the early days it was also a place that a government had to pay people to come and live in – they would have had to pay me a hell of a lot. Now though, tourism is booming and gleaming navy-blue and white cruise ships moor in the green  waters of the Beagle Channel below the town. It was strange to think that at some time over the past two weeks the Marco Polo had called in here. At that moment she was probably sailing near to the ice mass of Antarctica. I was surprised to see how many cruise liners there were in the harbour area and I was also surprised to see scores of fishing boats. I'd read that fishing was a mainstay industry but I hadn't realised just how important it was.

Ushuaia struck me as being an oasis in a cold bleak land, and prices reflected the short season. Everything was expensive unless you wanted to buy electrical goods, which for some reason were amazingly cheap. Food was astronomically expensive.

Actually, the town reminded me of photos I'd seen of alpine towns. The streets were steep and lined with many houses that either looked like Swiss chalets or like gingerbread cottages. Restaurants and cafés threw multi-coloured lights out in to the chill night air. Menus and brightly-painted boards advertised mouth-watering dishes that reminded me of the menus on the Marco Polo. The scents of asado wafted through the streets and the sound of laughter inevitably accompanied an opening door.

Miguel and Toni kindly dropped us off at the Rugby Club campsite, which was a good three kilometres outside the town. This was close enough to walk in and out, and we were anxious not to impose on the guys. But, before we split up for a few days we did arrange to travel out to the National Park and the end of the road with them.

It was cold, dark and raining as we set up our tent and as we did so I wondered what it would really be like to live in a place with no sun for eight months of the year. This was the middle of the summer and the ground was still sodden, snow was still around in places and we could see our breath. We learnt a lesson that night too: if you put your tent near fast-flowing water in conditions like this you'll have a cold night. It seemed as if the constant rush of the river pulled any warmth away from us as soon as we created it. Where further north our candles would warm the inside of the tent quite quickly, here they seemed to have no effect at all. Thankfully we had excellent sleeping bags, but even so we slept fully clothed and in the morning moved the tent as far away from the river as we could get it.

When we arrived, there were only two other bikers on the camping site, which was a rough field with sporadically placed damp bushes, and dripping evergreen trees along two sides. There were a couple of Swiss style wooden buildings, which the manager and his family lived in. They also had a sparsely furnished hall which acted as a restaurant, and was the only warm place in the vicinity. A log-burning stove threw out waves of cheering, luxurious heat. If you could get a table near the stove you were onto a winner and it was more than worthwhile blowing the budget on a beer, just for the pleasure of being in out of the damp and cold.

Sometimes we were treated to the owner's son singing to us in the evening. Sergio had a dream. He was training to be an opera baritone and to my untrained ears he sounded good enough to make the grade. Birgit was brought up in a house that was frequently been filled with opera and as Sergio sang, I watched for her reaction and she clearly approved. I settled back to revel in the rich and powerful sound of his voice passionately rolling out songs that Domingo, Carreras and Pavarotti had sung at their 'Three Tenors' concert. We were lucky Sergio was at home on holiday.

The other bikers were Guy and Marlene from Belgium and they told us that just a couple of days ago there had been a score of bikes there. Everyone had started to turn up just before Christmas. They'd partied and explored the area until the New Year had been welcomed in, and then everyone had split for the north. Guy and Marlene weren't in a hurry and were enjoying the peace. We didn't know it then, but they were going to become two of those special sorts of friends one occasionally makes out on the road.

Guy was a tall block of a man, over 6 foot tall, with broad shoulders that must have been a real problem to get a bike jacket big enough to fit. He had a round face and closely cropped hairstyle. At first glance, he looked a bit of a lout, but as I looked closer I realised that before me was a kind man and a real gentleman. He had enormous hands that, though firm in the handshake, had a controlled gentleness about them. When I learnt how he made his living I was amazed.

Marlene was roughly half Guy's size. A slim girl of 5'5", she had a daintiness about her that seemed quite incongruous when she was standing next to Guy. But in spite of this, the two of them complemented each other perfectly. The old saying is that one should never judge a book by its cover and I always thought Guy and Marlene were the perfect examples of why one should not judge people by the way they look.

Guy had struggled through school as an undiagnosed dyslexic and left school at sixteen with virtually no qualifications at all. This didn't stop him choosing an unusual career and making a major success of it. He became a hairdresser and was so talented, and so good with people, that he became the world champion hairdresser. It was really hard to visualise Guy working in this environment, but in spite of his size he never seemed to be clumsy at all and in fact moved with gentle, graceful, purposefulness.

In time he built his own hairdressing business and Marlene had worked with him in this building exercise. Eventually they sold the business for a small fortune and were travelling on their earnings. They were the most well-off people we met travelling the budget route around the world, but they seemed to deal with this in such a way that no-one they met was left feeling envious. The levelling factor of being on the road certainly helped, but their values had a lot to do with it too.

When Birgit and I stood by the Fin del Mundo sign in Ushuaia I felt really pleased that we'd made it. We'd missed the Christmas overlanders' party and we'd just missed being there for New Year, but that didn't matter at all. We had made it. This was a real turn up for the books – now to get to the end of the southernmost road in South America.

Then it was time to head north. There was disappointment for both of us at this stage because it was now that we realised that we weren't going to be able to ride the fabled Routa 40 along the base of the Andes – from what we'd heard it was just too rough and with my back being the way it was there was no way that I'd manage it.

In fact there were quite a few places that it would have been stupid for us to attempt to get to. We both felt a major sense of loss over the fact that I simply wasn't fit enough to get to the Torres del Paine National Park. We'd both read amazing things about the park and it'd been our plan to go hiking there for a week or so. We'd planned to get there by riding to the small town of Porvenir and then catch the ferry across to Punta Arenas. There was a dirt road that headed almost due north from there and linked up with the '40', which then skirted the National Park. It just wasn't to be, and I had to kick myself for thinking such negative thoughts. After all, we'd made it to Ushuaia when we'd thought it wasn't going to be possible. We just had to concentrate on what we *could* do.

Chapter 8

Olga the shot-putter

'Life is a hypocrite if I can't live the way it moves me.'

Stephen Fry

Birgit and I pored over our maps. We'd been through Porvenir on the way down so we didn't need to go back that way. We could try to hitch back up the Routa 3. If we were lucky over the first 665 kilometres we could head inland along the southern section of the Routa 5. We could then try to hitch the 430 kms out to El Calafate, from where we might find a way to get out to one of the largest glaciers in South America.

The Perito Moreno drops down into the Lago Argentino and this sight was supposed to be stunning. If all was still going well then we could try to hitch on up to El Chalten at the base of Mount Fitzroy. We could then hitch the 600 odd kilometres back to San Julian to pick up the bikes.

That became the plan. We would use the time I needed to heal, wisely. We weren't going to sit around waiting for it to happen; we were going to get on with the trip as best we could and thank our lucky stars that we were able to get to see anything. But it all depended on how well the hitching went. The buses seemed amazingly expensive, though in reality, bearing in mind the distances and the remoteness of this part of the world, they were not. They were in pretty good condition too – unlike many African buses, these had tread on their tyres!

It snowed the day we left Ushuaia and suddenly I was really happy to be back on the move. Now we'd made up our minds what was going to happen next, life took on a positive air again and I started to feel less guilty about stopping Birgit from doing things. She dealt with the knocks courageously and tactfully by cheerfully saying things like, "Well, we've got to have some things to come back for another time haven't we?"

Hitching worked well. For some reason there was much more traffic and the cars heading away from Ushuaia had less luggage – that was quite logical I supposed. At the border crossing back into Chile we picked up a ride in a truck, and as we did so Guy and Marlene passed us with a cheery wave as they too headed north. We wondered if we'd bump into them again.

The truck was a bright yellow round-nosed Mercedes with rusty patches. Birgit leapt up when it pulled over, and started to chat with  the driver. While she did so I took a closer look at it. The yellow bodywork was battered and bashed, cut and grazed and in some places looked as if it was being held together with wire stitching. The windscreen was spangled with cracks that had been formed by stones thrown up by other vehicles on the gravel roads. Amazingly, all the cracks had managed to avoid the sticker of the scantily-clad woman that the driver had placed on the glass.

The truck didn't look promising, but the big engine was still ticking over and it sounded reassuringly smooth. It was a meat transporter and a rumbling and very rusty refrigeration unit was attached to the front of the freezer compartment. I could smell the sour scents of old meat and wondered how hygienic the freezer compartment was. The underside of the truck was filthy and great gobs of heavy oil had collected passing dust in little mountains that wept shiny runs of viscous fluid, but the tyres looked almost brand new. They weren't even the retreads that so many vehicles in poorer countries seem to use.

Birgit looked across at me and I gave her the thumbs up. Moments later we were travelling in a rolling 'room with a view'. The world looked quite different from the height of the truck cab and to a background of some very enthusiastic salsa music on his cassette player, Felix started to chat with Birgit. When we hit the first pothole my initial happy thoughts about this ride disappeared. From the way the truck had leapt into the air, the freezer compartment must be empty and that meant that we were going to be in for a rough ride. It was now a toss-up: stay with Felix and his view, which continued to be superb and we knew could only get better, or cut the risk to my back and get off, potentially offending him and hope that a better vehicle would come along.

In the end it was the time of the day that made our minds up. We were now well away from any town and if there'd been a sun to see, it would have been about half way through its fall to the horizon. It didn't seem sensible to stop, but if we stayed aboard it would be for quite a while. So we stayed and it was fine – when Felix wasn't leaning across to try to include me in the conversation, he was a great driver. He was also a good-looking bloke and told us that he was twenty six and had a wife and two year old daughter whom he really missed when on the road. The ferry was a pleasure ride again and Felix, being a truck driver, knew exactly what was happening with the crossing times. But by the time we'd made it to Rio Gallegos it was the middle of the night. Felix had stopped to repair the truck.

The radiator had developed a major leak and with the background of a superb sunset to keep us entertained in a truck stop called Sombrero, he battled to bodge the leak. As he was doing so, five Argentinean bikers blasted into the truck stop. They were all riding Brazilian-made Honda Transalps and were carrying mountains of kit. None of them had panniers. All of their kit was strapped onto their pillion seats with stretchy rubber cargo nets and the piles of bags were stacked up higher than their heads. It must have been like riding a two-wheeled sail. And the fact that the kit was so loosely strapped on must have meant that it shifted around all the time as well.

The lads seemed oblivious to any such difficulties. They had left one of their mates further down the road where he'd stopped with a puncture. They had ridden to the truck stop with his wheel, hoping to get it fixed. They were full of total enthusiasm and were bouncing around like a bunch of puppies. They were living their adventure and were having a ball. It didn't matter that they were learning some lessons the hard way. They were having fun! Their enthusiasm was completely infectious and we watched the way that other people seemed to instantly warm to them.

With my unease about walking around strange cities at night in mind, we asked Felix to drop us off at the fuel station on the outskirts of the city. With luck they would have room for us to put up our tent.

The truck rumbled out of the pitch-black night, into the brilliantly glaring lights of the petrol station. Birgit and I climbed down from the cab and stood blinking for a few moments. The combination of the stiff breeze and the bright lights had brought tears to our eyes. Felix yelled "Adios" and we yelled "Muchas gracias", and he rolled out into a night that had no stars and no moon. We suddenly felt lonely as we stood in the chilly quiet light of the deserted forecourt.

The petrol station wasn't really set up for campers but the man behind the counter told us that if we could find a spot where we wouldn't get run over by the trucks then we were welcome.

In the morning, after a surprisingly noisy night, the sun was shining and we could take stock of our surroundings. In the early hours, there wasn't any wind which meant that though the bare ground along the roadside was rubbish-strewn, the carrier bags and bits of discarded paper didn't look as if they were taking part in some sort of manic kite-flying battle. It was a world strangely at peace and we took it to be a good omen. We planned a big hitch this day and sunny, wind-free weather would be a major bonus. But first we had to get to the Routa 5 turnoff.

Our luck was in: within a few minutes an old pickup truck stopped for us and we were on our way. The driver, who said nothing but grunted a lot, indicated that he wasn't going along the 5 but that he'd drop us off at the junction. That would do very nicely thank you. The 30km hop was a useful start.

The junction is a windswept three-way connection of roads in a featureless spot that even the most eloquent estate agent would struggle to describe in desirable terms. It was a pretty God-forsaken place. On the positive side, at least the road was tarmacked and it looked in pretty good condition too.

Four hours and seven vehicles later we were beginning to wonder if the 'good omen' had in fact been a warning. We tried every trick in the hitchhiker's manual but with no luck at all. Some of the cars were so loaded that their wheels were splayed outwards and the people inside looked as if they were pasted to the windows. Most of the other drivers indicated that they were shortly going to be heading off the road, but those few seconds of contact with other human beings were moments to be savoured.

By two o'clock in the afternoon we had a problem. The wind had got up and had been blasting us non-stop for several hours. Though it was quite sunny, the wind-chill meant that we'd put on almost every item of clothing we had, and were still cold. Birgit had six layers on! For me, the wind made it only marginally better than sitting on the bike, and by this time my back was beginning to feel sore. But the wind and sun were having an even worse effect on Birgit.

Little by little the skin on her lips was being peeled away, and lip salve wasn't making any difference at all. By three o'clock she'd had enough, and so had I. At just the right moment a car going the wrong way arrived and pulled over. "Do you need any help?" the driver said. "Yes please, can you take us to the petrol station?" we asked. "Of course." No sooner said than done, we were back at the petrol station again. At least this time we could pitch tent in daylight!

Birgit's lips continued to peel. We'd left the roadside far too late. By 6pm she looked as if she'd been six rounds with Muhammad Ali. All the skin was gone and she was left with a bloody mess akin to third degree burns. It didn't take long to decide that we weren't going to hitch hike again. It just wasn't worth it. Blow the budget, we'd catch a bus!

The next morning we booked ourselves on the bus for the 320 kilometre journey to El Calafate. It cost us $35 each on El Pinguino. To put this in perspective, $35 was more than we would have spent on food for a whole week. In fact, travelling without the bikes had meant that we were spending less on food than we had been. To save weight in our rucksacks we'd not taken our cooker, fuel bottle and pans with us. That had cut our options. Our diet had been cheap but rubbish. We'd been surviving on white bread that tasted great so long as it was eaten straight away. By lunchtime the stuff was stiff enough to build walls with. Tinned tuna saved the day, though other than carrots and onions, vegetables were horribly expensive. From time to time we would find a supermarket that stocked the pre-diced mixture of spam and olives that Dr Greg had introduced us to, and they were a bonus! We had one pot with us so when it was dry enough and we could find a wind-free spot, we could make a little fire to boil water to make tea and coffee, or maté for Birgit. Our one daily treat was to have a sachet of grapefruit juice powder to mix in our drinking water. We were amazed by how authentic it tasted and there were days when it was like champagne for us.

The ride on the bus was pure luxury. The seats were comfortable, the driver only mildly lunatic and the scenery was stunning. And we were blessed with yet another day of brilliant sunshine. The ride was really smooth too, partly because the road was tarmac initially, but also because we were driving straight into the wind. Then, when the road hooked us north, we were so close to the bottom of the Andes that the wind seemed to pass high above us.

The land spread out beside us in an almost continuous prairie of golden splendour beneath a cloudless deep blue sky. In front of us, the Andes reached up powerfully through that sky, and the snow-capped peaks glistened in the sunshine. For once I didn't miss my bike a bit. It felt like an absolute privilege to be inside in the warm and to be surrounded by views that I had all the time in the world to enjoy. It made a real difference not to be spending most of my time scanning back and forth in the never-ending search for the next pothole or ridge of stones. The sun of this morning had been a good omen!

The bus stopped for a driver's break at a ramshackle fuel station with weather-beaten concrete buildings. As we drove over a snaking black pressure hose, it pinged a battered red bell that hung from the wall by the peeling, once-white main door. Faded and warped painted metal signs skirted the length of the building at roof height. Once, they had brightly advertised famous names; now they were merely ancient reminders of brands that no longer existed. The sun-bleached wooden outhouses and sheds looked as if they could fall over at any moment. Their corrugated roofs were rusty and the edges were disintegrating in patches of flaky, lace-like strips. In some places the wind had bent the iron sheets back over as if some sort of giant tin-opener had been at work. Weeds grew in amongst the broken bottoms of the pale grey and splitting timber planks, and spiky trailing plants had crawled over rusting machinery as if they were attempting to pull the iron back into the ground.

A few eucalyptus trees provided some shade, and a rather straggly windbreak. The petrol station sign squeaked as it swung back and forth in the wind, as was traditional, and a solitary bony cow chewed cud as it watched us all pile off the bus. A yellow dog, whose fur looked as if it had been designed by a punk hairdresser, watched us from a sunny and sheltered spot on the dusty forecourt. He had one eye open and one ear raised. The tip of his tail seemed to twitch whenever he thought someone was looking at him – it was obviously the best he could do by way of enthusiastic greeting. The wind whipped up little dust-devil cones that twisted fallen eucalyptus leaves upwards as it swirled around anything that was either brave or stupid enough to get in its way. Our footprints were soon blown smooth, hiding all trace of our passing.

When the bus pulled back onto the road everything except the wind seemed to be slumbering again. The wind was already erasing the bus's tracks. The only evidence that it had been there was a blotch of leaked oil where it had been parked, but even that was quickly being covered over. In spite of the faint tinge of sadness that surrounded the place, there was also an air of quiet and 'wise old survivor' about it. And in a way, the collection of faded colours and irregular shapes were rather beautiful in the sunshine against the yellow and blue Patagonian background.

Sunshine transformed Patagonia. Yet another confirmation of this was the brilliantly turquoise and pale shimmering grey glacial water of Lago Argentino (the silver lake). To get to El Calafate we had to skirt the edge of the lake and were treated to a collection of colours that ought to have no right to be next to each other, but in this setting simply looked stunning and quite natural.

El Calafate was surprising too. It was set up for tourists and as such it was almost manicured. That was strange after the sporadic, rough-and-ready countryside towns and villages we'd seen to date. Even Ushuaia was rough-and-ready by comparison. A campsite for $4 a night, with hot showers, a kitchen and a wind-free spot to put the tent, in such an interesting part of Patagonia, was a real bonus. There were even a few sporadically-timed buses that could get us to and from the head of the lake where the Perito Morano glacier pushed down into the water. On the downside, it was here we discovered that a lot of Argentinean campers had no regard for thin tent walls and no desire for sleep before 2am.

I'd seen glaciers in New Zealand but nothing had prepared me for the stunning beauty of the Perito Morano. It was a vast, craggy, brilliantly white, 55 metre high wall of ice that seemed to be constructed of one cathedral after another. The 'cathedrals' looked as if they were separated and sculpted with pale turquoise fissures, and every so often a vast chunk of ice would crack off the wall with a distinctive 'boom' and fall into the lake with a huge splash. The chunks would sink deep – often disappearing from sight for a moment but then they would bob back up, creating more waves. With a small part of the chunk showing above water they would float off as another of the icebergs that dotted the opaque, turquoise and silver waters.

At the head of the lake stood the magnificent snow-topped Andes and as we stood turning slow 360-degree revolutions on the spot, we decided that we had rarely been anywhere so beautiful. The air was so clean and clear that it felt as if we could reach out and touch anything we could see. The sun-filled scene was sharp-edged and vibrant. White glacier matched puffy single white clouds, which matched equally white and glistening snow on the peaks. The dark greens of the forest complemented the bright clear blue shades of the sky, and the lake's turquoises acted as a firm line to anchor the world to. It was one of those moments no camera could ever do justice to.

Having been so inspired, we were keen to get on to the town of El Chaltén, or to be more precise, we wanted to see Mt. Fitzroy. The mountain has a quirky history which makes it quite unique. It's right on the frontier between Argentina and Chile and the precise route of the border has never been agreed. Though it's just 3,375 metres high, it has a reputation for being a fiercer and more technically difficult climb than many of the world's great mountains, including Everest. Fitzroy is named after Robert Fitzroy who was the Captain of Darwin's ship the Beagle, which he used to explore a large part of the region in 1834. The original name for this angular and magnificent rock of giant proportions came from the aboriginal Indians, the Tehueche, who called it Chaltén. This means 'Smoking Mountain' and came from the cloud that usually forms around the top of the highest peak. This cloud was considered to be sacred by the Indians. Now, the mountain is considered sacred by more experienced climbers, and by those who want to hike the many trails, including us.

The road to Chaltén from Calafate would have been a pig on a bike. Loose dirt combined with wind and tyre-formed corrugations to make for a bumpy, slippery ride. This combination would have had bikers tempted to grip their handlebars so tightly that it could easily turn into a muscle wrenching, white-knuckle ride. Instinct just does not want to let you ride with the better looser grip. Instinct says go slow, and it also has you tempted to watch what is happening immediately in front of your front wheel. In the bus it was warm, calm and very easy, with no challenges to deal with. I feared I was getting lazy and that I was beginning to forget why I loved riding my bike so much, even in such challenging places.

The town of El Chaltén was more like a small village or a large hamlet. The buildings were mostly widely spaced apart on a fairly level plain that looked as if it had been marked out with a lot more people, and buildings in mind than actually materialised. It was the epitome of 'windswept'. The few people we saw looked like walking bundles of clothes. The wind coming off the mountains ripped down at a rate of knots and brought with it a freezing air that Felix would have loved to be able to have in his freezer truck. It didn't help that the wind was also bringing showers of rain with it. Needing to get the tent up and straight inside it pronto, we headed straight for an area on the outskirts of the town that had been designated a free campsite. Birgit got the tent up in double quick time, battled with the tent inner zips and within minutes we were inside, protected and feeling somewhat stunned.

She had had to battle with the zips because after almost a year of constant use in windy dusty environments they had become increasingly difficult to operate. They either jammed or the teeth popped open shortly after the runner had clicked them together. She had to deal with this battle on her own too. The tent wasn't big enough for me to be crawling around in with a stiff back, and to make it worse she was inevitably the one who had to get up in the middle of freezing nights to go for a pee. One night I heard her come back in muttering, "Now I know why they call this a bloomin' expedition tent! Hrrmph, it's an expedition getting in and out of the thing!"

It wasn't fun but we couldn't fix the zips out on the road. We tried soap and silicone spray to no avail. We just had to accept that the

 tent was getting worn. In fact the flysheet was now beginning to sag and if we didn't get the pegs banged in exactly right then we'd have drips of water coming inside. We also had a problem with the seams. The sealing tape on some of them had completely disappeared and that meant that where the stitch holes had opened up over time, water was now easing in. Weather conditions like these pushed the tent to its limits.

It rained all day for the next three days. The only thing that was good about this was that it rained hard enough to wash away the piles of faeces that other free campers had charmingly left behind them. Sad that people would treat such a place with this lazy, despoiling attitude. When I saw mini mountains, with the inevitable toilet paper streamers flying from them, I used to feel like hunting down the culprits and giving them a good thwack, or rubbing their noses in it. The trouble was, it was a cultural thing and the further north we went the more often we would find piles of poo – often in such obvious places that the original owners must have had no sense of discomfort at entertaining passers-by with their ablutions. Fortunately we'd put our tent on top of a raised up area so the polluted run-off waters missed us.

Suddenly the rain stopped, and then the wind stopped too. There was an ear- tingling, almost eerie silence that was only broken by the rushing, tumbling sound of the stream running close to the site, and by water pitter-pattering from the trees onto our tent.

If the weather hadn't broken when it did we would not have had three fantastic days hiking through the dwarf beech trees on the slopes of the mountains, nor would we have followed trails that led us past more turquoise lakes. Nor would we have had the pleasure of drinking from crystal-clear streams. We were getting pretty smelly by that time so it was great to be able to wash in the icy waters, and then dry off in the surprisingly warm sunshine. The wind was still blowing up on the top of Mt Fitzroy and we could see sheets of snow being whisked up from the slopes and flung into the air, to float down catching the sun as it went. The sun also quickly dried off fallen twigs and branches and we were able to collect enough to make a fire and have our first hot meal in four days.

The better weather also gave us a chance to see if there was a pharmacy in the village. Birgit's lips had got even worse. The last couple of days had been agony for her – a thick scab had formed on both of her lips and every time a scab cracked she had to deal with some real pain. Sometimes it had been bad enough to bring tears to her eyes and to have blood streaming down her chin. I had been banned from making any jokes – the last thing she needed to do was smile, or laugh at anything. In a way it was a good thing that the weather had been so gloomy or there might have been more things that would have tempted her to smile!

There was a small pharmacy tucked away in the corner of the village, and the pharmacist gave Birgit some zinc-based cream to smear on her lips. As she did so she stared hard at me. The look she gave me needed no translation. It was clear she thought I'd been hitting Birgit. Although the unwarranted visual chastisement made me uncomfortable, we were just pleased to have found a lotion that seemed to help straight away. But it was nearly a month before the last section of scab finally healed.

Time to go! Back to Calafate, and then on to Rio Gallegos to catch another bus up to San Julian. No more hitching for us. We wanted to enjoy the last chance to stay out of the wind and we were itching to head north. We got back to the campsite in Calafate on the 19th of January. I'd been on the road for six years to the day. I'd been through Africa twice, across Asia and now down to the southernmost point in the Americas. It was time for a celebration.

That night, making good use of the fully equipped campsite kitchen, we tucked into a mega meal of steak, potatoes, salad, carrots, biscuits, and plums, all washed down with the excellent red wine that was always available. The next day, Birgit's stomach complained bitterly at all the unfamiliar food and she was wracked with diarrhoea for hours! How unfair was that?!

Back in San Julian the bikes were fine. Pinocchio had looked after them really well for us. I nervously rode the kilometre back to the campsite and was delighted to find that though my back was a little sore, riding the bike was fine. The month of hitching and hiking had paid off.

But the back trouble had scared me. I decided I should look for some medical advice. I was already doing an hour of physio exercises every day, but perhaps I should be doing something else as well. I was very conscious that Birgit had missed out on some opportunities because of me and I was determined to do all I could to ensure that nothing went wrong again.

We decided to head for the hiking and ski resort of Bariloche. There I hoped I would find some sort of sports physio or specialist doctor who could take a look at me and give me some advice. I was tired of being an invalid. It wasn't the way I liked to be at all and even though I'd been dealing with the slipped discs for a couple of years by this time, I still hadn't got used to the fact that I couldn't throw myself into things as I had once been able to.

We were sensibly cautious over the next days and stopped every half hour so I could have a walk around and ease the kinks out. These stops were a pleasure and each one added a new facet to the trip. I told Birgit that I'd never whinge again at her pee breaks! I'd see them as opportunities now, and anyway, I no longer had any right whatsoever to be impatient with her – though she had with me!

With the spaces being so wild and open, and the distances so vast, it was always tempting to crack on, to cover the kilometres. But stopping as frequently as we now were meant we were seeing things

 that we would otherwise have blasted past: the different shapes and colours of the grasses, the tiny flowers that nestled out of the wind, the tea-coloured water that flowed in some streams and the crystal clear water in others. The two gauchos (cowboys) we saw silhouetted on a hilltop against the blue of the sky was a sight that we'd never have noticed, and if we hadn't stopped, they would never have bothered to give us a wave. I wondered if it was they, or the truck drivers. that had been using the road signs as targets. Nearly every sign we passed was riddled with bullet holes! Was it boredom, or rebellion at being told what to do in such out of the way places?

The road changed between tarmac and gravel and it began to curve in great swoops along valleys whose slopes were covered in evergreen forests. The Andes stood tall, proud and beautiful to the west of us. Sometimes the tops were clear and at others the snowline seemed to be cloaked in cloud. The bikes were behaving perfectly, as if they were glad to have us back and even happier to be on the road again. Riding behind Birgit, I could hear the comfortable growl of Sir Henry the Hybrid. Beneath me Libby ticked and purred. Her load seemed to be in perfect balance and when we were on the gravel sections her dual-purpose tyres seemed to be happily working overtime to keep the bike rolling steadily forward.

We'd planned to ride short days of just 150 kilometres but with this stunning riding we just wanted to keep going. It was as if all the pieces of the jigsaw puzzle had finally fallen into place. Life couldn't possibly get much better. This was why we were out on the road. We were free and at the same time we were part of something amazing. We were in control again, but that didn't matter – we were quite happy for the land and the road to tell us where to go. If a town looked interesting we stopped for a wander round. If a view from a nearby hillside looked as if it might have potential, we climbed it. People waved at us when we passed them, or they passed us in their always overloaded cars, and from time to time truck drivers cheerfully hooted their horns at us.

There seemed to be plenty of places we could camp and they always popped up at the right time, though one turned out to be so dire that we only stayed for half an hour. We found an old and derelict ACA (Argentine Motoring Organisation) petrol station. It was all closed down but it looked as if someone was living there and there was plenty of space to stick our tent up without getting in anyone's way. Birgit went and knocked on the door. Moments later a man who looked just like a shrivelled old mountain goat stuck his head out. He had a long, thin face which was topped by long straggly white hair, and his chin sported a perfect goatee beard. His voice didn't match his face though – it was deep and humorous. "Si, of course you can camp here – choose your spot and make yourself welcome." The cost? "Nada, you are very welcome." When Birgit asked if it was safe to drink the water from the water tank on wheels outside his cabin, he replied with twinkling eyes, "Of course it's safe to drink. After all, the worst that will happen is that you'll die!"

A peaceful spot, free, and a landlord with a sense of humour – perfect. But what we hadn't realised was how many flies were going to descend upon us as soon as we took our helmets off. They swarmed around us and weren't happy with just sucking on our sweat, they wanted blood too. Within moments Birgs and I were doing arm-waving war dances on the cracked and split old tarmac as we tried to bat away the swarming flies. We'd never come across blood-sucking flies like these before and couldn't get away fast enough. As we rode away I had a vision of a black crowd of the things following us tasty humans down the road. No wonder the station was derelict and no wonder that its owner looked the same. I did wonder why he put up with the flies; perhaps they'd got bored with the way he tasted and now left him alone.

At the town of El Bolson we filled our tanks to the brim, along with every container we had. This was the last place we were going to be able to get cheap fuel. The sun stayed with us all the way to Bariloche. Life continued to feel great and we were totally enthralled by the scenery surrounding the town. After the extremes of Patagonia we were riding through another world. Lake Nahuel Huapi, the forests, and the flower-filled meadows around it were the things of Alpine picture postcards. There was nothing around to say that we were riding through South America except for the signs in Spanish and the Argentine number plates on the vehicles. Bariloche itself was organised with what seemed like Swiss efficiency and I had thoughts of Swiss chocolate, schnapps and après ski parties floating through my mind as we explored.

There were some really good camping equipment shops, the best we'd seen since Cape Town so we were sure we'd be able to find somewhere to replace the zips on the tent. By this time Birgit had just about gone on strike as far as they were concerned and was muttering about 'binning' the tent.

Though it was out of season in Bariloche, the entire infrastructure was functioning and most of the businesses were open.

We felt as if we could get anything done there and when we found a really good hostel to stay in, we realised we were at great risk of getting stuck – again! The hostel was called the Bolsar del Deporte and the owner Carlos spoke Schweizer-Deutsch – Swiss-German – which meant that for once Birgit could have a language holiday. For the last year and a half she had been bouncing between speaking English or Spanish, and until I heard her rattle away in German to Carlos, I hadn't realised how much she missed being able to speak her native tongue.

It was also a real treat to be staying indoors out of the wind and the rain. To have a warm dormitory to wake up to and to be able to potter along to the wonderfully hot shower in just our sarongs was total luxury. It made a change to have four gas rings to cook from instead of just the one and little things like the steamer pot and the wok that were part of the kitchen equipment made staying there a pleasure.

For some reason the hostel seemed to attract good people. There never seemed to be any inconsiderate behaviour and there was always a great, multicultural atmosphere. One thing I did notice though was that I seemed to have aged on the road. Most of the backpackers in the hostel were a good ten years plus younger than me! That was an odd thought. But it was also a satisfying one. I still felt 26 at heart and was, I thought, living the life of a 26 year old. Perhaps I should stay out on the road forever and that way I'd never grow up. But nah, I didn't really fancy being the Peter Pan of the travellers' world!

We found a sports physio who specialised in hiking and climbing injuries. Back problems were his forte, he said. Unfortunately I couldn't help thinking, "Latin wide boy" as soon as I saw him – he was so darned smooth. But to begin with he seemed to know what he was talking about so we went with it. We explained the history and in particular what the past few months had been like. He was very sympathetic, again, to begin with.

But then he seemed to make up his mind about something. Just as he had finished telling me to stop doing one of my physio exercises as it was damaging things further, he said that he thought most of the problem was more than likely psychosomatic. I was obviously imagining things!

Then he said, "No, continuing with your journey will not do any further damage to your back. It will be absolutely fine. You must just think positive."

Well, no, I wasn't imagining things, but I was delighted that I wasn't likely to do any more damage and thinking positively? I was good at that! With my mind at rest I happily accepted the prescription for painkillers and for a course of anti-inflammatory injections, which is how I met Olga the shot-putter.

One of the quirks of how medical things worked in Argentina was that 'Mr Wide Boy' was licensed to issue prescriptions but not to give injections. In many places the pharmacy actually has a nurse and it was her job to deal with them. We chose the biggest pharmacy in town and handed over the prescriptions. Moments later I was given the box of pills and was told to go into a side room.

To my horror, inside was a squat, muscular, pug-faced woman who had crammed her Russian shot-putter's build into a nurse's uniform. She grinned a sardonic, no-nonsense, broken-toothed grimace at me, rolled up her sleeves, flexed her muscles (which were far bigger than mine) and stabbing her finger in my direction, ordered, "You, trousers down! You bend over!"

If I hadn't been told to bend over I would have instinctively leapt to attention. As it was, for fear of immediate punishment, I couldn't get my trousers down quickly enough. "Back pain? No problem, I'll bend over. How far would you like?"

Seconds later a squirt of liquid hit my backside, and then I felt a needle being thrust into my poor buttock with an impatience that that would have impressed a time and motion inspector. The complete lack of tenderness would have shocked any human rights activist!

Back pain? Nah, for a moment, bum pain was a far greater issue. The next I knew was a now happy Olga ordering me to "Trousers UP! You go! I see you tomorrow!" I usually like to meet people who enjoy their work...

Within an hour my back felt so good I would gladly have kissed Olga and any insulting thoughts I'd had about her hairy facial mole had completely disappeared. For the first time in months I had no back pain at all. 26? I felt like a 17 year old! Whatever it was, this stuff was good. I wanted more and decided that I actually did like Olga after all.

With the course of injections finished and me now wonderfully pain free, Birgit and I headed for the border with Chile. We were keen to crack on. We had some adventuring to do. Everything was going well and even the repairs to the tent had worked out. The first time we put the tent up Birgit couldn't resist sitting in front of it, opening and closing the zip. She told me she was conducting a quality control check but I knew she was simply enjoying the sensation. The bikes had been serviced in the back yard of the hostel, supplies restocked and all our equipment was now clean. We were ready.

We rode out though the 'Swiss' countryside and up into the mountain pass towards the border. The road was tarmac and the ride was a cruise in the sunshine. The only drama was when we stopped to look at a strangely pale rock and discovered that it was volcanic tufa and wasn't firm enough to support the weight of Birgit's bike on its stand. Of course she went over, but no damage was done as the stuff was so soft.

The officials on the Argentinean side of the border were efficient and friendly. They thanked us for visiting their country and wished us very happy travels. Nice.

The 50-kilometre road through the pass to the Chilean border was an adventure. It was rough gravel and no one had got round to repairing the road where it had been broken up by ice heaves in the winter. But Birgit rode the stuff, with her bike leaping all over the place, as if she had been riding beaten-up, pot-holed gravel for years. The difference in her riding style from just a year earlier was phenomenal. I felt that now she'd be able to tackle anything. Not only was she keeping her bike upright, but she seemed to really enjoy the challenge.

I like the fact that border crossings often mark a dramatic change in conditions from one country to the next. Riding from the Argentinean side of the Andes to the Chilean side we noticed that the weather was instantly milder and that the trees changed from mainly evergreen, to a wide variety of deciduous.

The scenery felt less dramatic, until we rounded a corner and saw the snowy top of the extinct volcano Mt Osorno. We wanted to get closer so we hopped off the asphalt and headed along graded gravel roads through the meadows and wood-fenced farmed fields until we reached a village called La Molina. The volcano had sat on our left for most of the day and at times it had been hard to work out whether we should be riding or just standing in awe of its beauty. I was also struggling with the fact that it was pure joy to be on a dirt road with no pain – not even a hint of it. We couldn't have wished for a better welcome into Chile.

Birgit said some of the villages could have been plucked straight out of Germany. Over the past century and a half, Chile has been a major emigration destination for Germans and at times it felt  to Birgit as if she was actually riding through a German history book. To my delight the local beer was based on German recipes and to Birgit's delight the cakes in the bakeries tasted as good as they looked. We relished the hours of riding and exploring fun in the area. Little did we know what was hiding over the horizon...

We'd read good things about the island of Chiloe, which sits off the coast of Southern Chile and is the largest of an archipelago of hundreds of islands that stretch right the way down to the tip of South America. This thought had been reinforced by one of the locals on the campsite that night who had walked straight over to our tent, given us two huge tomatoes, said "Bienvenido a Chile", spun on his toe, and headed back to his own tent. When we'd got over our surprise we got into conversation with him and he had raved about the island. So, we had to go.

To get to the ferry dock at Pargua, we had to ride down a good length of very boring dual carriageway. We'd not been on a road like this for ages and it simply reinforced our view that motorways and the  like are to be avoided whenever possible. This one had traffic delays too, and I nearly ended up adding to them. At one stage the four lanes narrowed down into just one lane, to accommodate road repairs. It was at this precise point that my clutch cable decided to snap. There was no warning at all and I suddenly found myself in heaving traffic struggling to change down and trying not to stall. The other road users must have wondered what the gringo on the bike was playing at, and as soon as the road opened out again I cut the engine and pulled to a halt with a jerk – I'd not been able to snick the gear lever into neutral.

I think my guardian angel had been awake for that one and because I'd got a spare cable strapped into place, disconnecting the old one and linking in the new didn't take long at all. That was why I kept them there and also because it meant that they weren't taking up valuable space in the panniers.

Over the next few days we meandered south over the island, exploring the picturesque wooden towns and fishing villages as we went. Then we made a fateful decision that led to nearly four months of disaster.

One of the things I'd been gagging to do in South America was to ride Chile's Carretera Austral or 'Southern Highway'. In reality, it's more of a track than a 'highway'. The whole region is extraordinary. It's a temperate rain forest. There are only two other remotely similar places on earth, one in New Zealand's South Island and the other in the Pacific state of Washington, USA. The flora and fauna were supposed to be intriguing and the track had the reputation of being one of overlanding's greats.

The road is 1,240 km of dirt and gravel. It twists and turns through dense virgin rainforest and past towering cliffs from which ribbons of waterfalls cascade downwards. There are several ferry crossings along the way and because of the weather they can usually only run for two months of the year. President Pinochet initiated the Carretera Austral in 1976 with the intention of connecting the whole country and twenty years later it was still under construction. The expense must have been phenomenal and we felt it would be rude not to ride at least part of it and since my back was doing so well we decided to risk it.

 It's a five-hour crossing from the port of Quellon to the tiny port of Chaiten, and though the crossing was calm, the rolling motion of the flat-bottomed, landing craft type of ferry for this length of time, started to do undo Olga's work on my back.

We didn't want to splash out on a hostel in Chaiten, though it was tempting because the ferry left much later than scheduled so we arrived at night. The gravel road out of the town in the dark didn't help me – there was no time to brace myself for potholes. We were both very tired by the time we made it to the campsite, which was a magical little place right on the water's edge. Wood was provided for barbecues and the showers were heated by stoking a log fire under the water tank.

I didn't say anything to Birgit about my back, though I couldn't hide that I was feeling sore. We wanted to do the ride, I felt we had committed to it and therefore we should just get on with it. Perhaps everything would be OK. It felt fantastic just to be standing there.

The next day was a delight to ride. Birgit took Henry swooping along the gravel road which led us up and down through stunning scenery as we headed north again. I kept expecting to see a dinosaur come crashing out of the forest, as the whole scene seemed so 'prehistoric'. Giant ferns grew next to plants that looked like 2-metre tall clumps of rhubarb. Neck-achingly high trees were hung with beard moss and lianas, and everywhere we rode we could sense the desire of the vegetation to reclaim the thin strip of track. Libby skipped and hopped over the gravel as if she were thoroughly enjoying doing what she had been designed to do, and to begin with the pain stayed away. The only battle we were fighting was with the bloody horse flies. They were vicious little blood-suckers who would quite happily bite through cotton clothing. The only parts of us that were safe were the tops of our heads, when we kept our helmets on, and wherever our leather jackets covered. The flies made stopping really difficult, so we didn't as often as we would have liked to. Then we discovered that the horse flies didn't like flying over water. It was really weird. If we stopped on bridges, they didn't bother us at all. Brilliant, but I didn't get much walking done, as few of the bridges were more than a couple of metres long.

The gravel continued to challenge us, and the bikes. The scenery continued to be stunning and to our great good fortune the sun stayed out, letting us see the Carretera Austral at its very best. But little by little I started to feel a pain building in the top of my left leg, which then spread to my back. I couldn't find a comfortable sitting position on the bike and by the end of each day's riding I was aware that there was just a hint of numbness in the back of my left thigh. That was new, but I carried on with my positive thinking. The physio would have been proud of me. I was living my dream.

We were going to have to use two of the three ferries which connect the different sections of the track. The first was a one and a half hour crossing from the village of Caleta Gonzalo across to the town of Hornopiren. We camped just before the little port and were there in good time. I wasn't sure how I was going to cope with the passage. If the first ferry across from Chiloe had done damage, what was this one going to do? I couldn't go back and I shouldn't really go forwards. What we did know was that in a week's time this ferry would stop running for ten months.

When we parked the bikes on ferries we always put them on their centre stands and left them in gear. We used our spare luggage straps to fix them to whatever looked solid enough to stop the bikes falling over if things got rough. With that done we watched all the vehicles grind aboard into the open vehicle bay.

Beaten up old cars, that looked as if they'd barely survived the track, hobbled aboard. Trucks with engines roaring and exhausts blowing clouds of black smoke almost bullied their way aboard, and a couple of beaten-up old buses joined them, all making the ferry rock as they heaved themselves onto the deck.

Amongst the arrivals was a serious-looking 4x4. Its owners were a young couple and their two daughters. It didn't take long before Sarah was over talking with us – once again the bikes were an ice-breaker. It turned out that Sarah and Joe owned the top quality tent we'd been admiring in the campsite earlier, and meeting them was one of the best things that happened on the Carretera Austral. Not only did this meeting turn into a lifelong friendship but they had a fascinating tale to tell, and that kept my mind mostly off the damage that was slowly being done to my back by the rocking motion of the ferry.

Joe was a mineral prospector and that caught my attention straight away. As I'd been travelling, I'd been keeping my eyes and ears open for people with my surname, Manicom, and there was a prospecting connection to it. As a child I assumed that my father and I were the only people called Manicom but as I travelled the world I discovered that there were other Manicoms about. And to my amazement, many of them had either personality or physical characteristics that I recognised. I also heard about some who were real characters. There'd been a highway robber in Australia for example, and one of the things I wanted to do in Chile was to see if there was any trace of the Manicom who'd come across to prospect for gold in the Chilean Andes.

Sarah, Joe, Emily and Hannah all lived in Santiago, the capital of Chile. They seemed to have very much the same priorities in life as we did, and though our lives were quite different they seemed to value many things in exactly the same way – it was quite a strange feeling.

Sarah and Joe really appreciated the amazing opportunities that travel gives. They had travelled extensively as a couple and were now in the process of teaching their children how valuable an experience travel can be. By the time the crossing finished we'd got on so well they'd invited us to stay with them when we passed through Santiago.

But first I had to ride the bike again – I was in trouble and I knew it – we were down a bloody long dirt road where there weren't any hospitals, and doctors were going to be as rare as hen's teeth.

The weather clouded over and the air now had a real chill to it. The gravel dropped down a really steep and dangerous slope, and the stones that made up the surface ranged in size from knobbly walnut to angular fist. The bike's tyres did not enjoy this at all, and each obstruction had the handlebars whipping from side to side. Somehow I managed to stay upright, but Birgit took a tumble. If there'd been any boulders or big rocks lurking she'd have been in horrible trouble, but fortunately she just had earth and the loose, knobbly gravel to deal with – both she and Henry survived with just dings and hurt pride.

Birgit had to undress me that night – I could no longer bend down to reach my feet. The tablets from Bariloche made not a jot of difference and my paracetamol was as much use as feeding the pain with chocolate buttons. I ate so many of the things, just to take the edge off the pain, that I was probably close to overdosing on them.

One more ferry crossing to do and then we would be within reach of proper medical facilities. Or we could stay where we were and hope that with rest and walking I'd be OK – the thought of going through the whole Patagonia exercise again filled me with gloom, verging on despair. For the first time I felt totally knocked. I felt as if all optimism had been battered out of me by the road. I felt painfully helpless.

I also felt frustrated and it was that which probably helped me through the next thirty-six hours. We decided to take the earliest ferry we could get on, and try to make it to the nearest city, Puerto Montt. We knew there was a hospital there – we'd seen it from the main road as we'd ridden down to catch the ferry across to Chiloe. Perhaps there'd be an 'Olga' there.

The ferry companies conspire with their schedules to keep you stranded in between the two crossings and that was fine by us. A rest day was a good plan, but all through it, the pain level edged up and I began to wish that we could just get across the final stretch of water so I could get to some help. The hours couldn't go by fast enough.

Next morning the day dawned dull, damp and cold. The chilly waters now looked dark and dangerous. When a fishing boat puttered past the dock it sent its wake in a V-shaped, rolling swell that seemed to ease its way through water that was as dark as oil and just as thick. When the wake hit the rocks it seemed to do so with no more than an exhausted whimper. The pungent scents of rotting vegetation and old seaweed filled the air, and every so often I caught the unwelcome hint of stale urine from the concrete wall we were queuing next to. The sky hung dark and heavy with the colour of washed slate, and the rock faces dripped runs of water as if the very rock itself was shedding tears. Not a single bird was in the air and even the horseflies seemed to have given up and gone home. In spite of my bike gear I shivered. No one around us was speaking and even the ferry crew went about their business with their heads down, and none of the usual banter. As a heavy mist began to roll down from the mountaintops, rain started to fall in slow heavy motion – each drop hitting the water as an individual, causing an ever-changing pattern of rings to form across the still waters around us.

The thirty-minute crossing went smoothly and while the ferry's engines throbbed away below us with an almost melancholy tone, my back throbbed with growing pain. I could barely get my leg over the bike and I needed help from Birgit to even stand it upright. I wondered how much longer I was going to be able to hang on. We let the other traffic go on past us. There was no point in jostling for position on the narrow gravel track; it was going to be hard enough just staying on and keeping the bike pointing in the right direction.

We passed a couple of potential free-camping sites, but I didn't like the idea of being stuck in the middle of nowhere. We knew that there was an organised site coming up soon and we aimed for that. Just as we reached the point on the road outside the campsite at Puerta Lenca, I knew that I couldn't ride any further. Pain was shooting through my back and when I tried to change gear to slow down, I realised I no longer had any feeling in my left leg. It was completely numb from my toes right up to my buttock. There, the numbness changed within millimetres into a pain that was so excruciating that I started whimpering inside my helmet.

Somehow I got the bike into the campsite, but I couldn't get off it on my own. I could see my left foot on the ground but had no idea if it would take my weight. I stayed sitting on the bike until Birgit had parked Henry and had put the tent up. She unpacked my sleeping bag and inflated my sleeping mat, and then reached down beside the bike to put the side stand out. I let the bike fall onto it. The resulting jerk shot fireworks of pain through my body, but at least Birgit could then ease me off.

My back now felt as if it was falling to pieces. There seemed to be no strength or support in the lower back area at all. It took ten minutes of slow-motion movement before I was finally, and for a moment, blissfully lying down flat. Then the pain returned. This time in rolling floods that had no rhythm at all – I could feel myself going white and I could feel a cold sweat rolling down the side of my face. I was well and truly stuffed.

Chapter 9

Two formidable women

"Once a journey is designed, equipped, and put in process, a new factor enters and takes over. A trip, a safari, an exploration, is an entity, different from all other journeys…A journey is a person in itself; no two are alike. And all plans, safeguards, policing and coercion are fruitless. We find after years of struggle that we do not take a trip; a trip takes us."

John Steinbeck

When I'd been travelling on my own before, and things had gone badly wrong, I'd had to rely on fate and my 'guardian angel'. Most overlanders will think about mishaps from time to time, but will try hard not to contemplate them too often. You know that, as a stranger in a foreign land, you will be vulnerable to all sorts of disasters. Some can come from not understanding the local lingo, some from not knowing the local customs and others simply from catching an unpleasant local lurgy. Some will happen because you are pushing yourself in an unfamiliar environment. Or you can just run out of luck. Riding a motorcycle increases the risk of a drama too of course. That's a lot of chances for something to go wrong. In the end though, aren't some of the best adventures things that start with a disaster? If we weren't prepared to take risks then we'd simply stay at home.

As I'd travelled on my own for so long it was still a novelty to have a disaster as a member of a team. I trusted Birgit implicitly and as a result I never doubted that everything would turn out OK. I knew that she would get things sorted out, and so she did. She told me later that one of the hardest things was handling Libby. My bike stands almost as tall as she does and in comparison to Henry, is really heavy. Not easy to woman-handle at all, especially at five foot one.

The owners of the camping site were amazing. Victor and Gladys allowed Birgit to use their phone to talk to the hospital in Puerto Montt, and translated for her when she stumbled over Spanish descriptions of what was wrong. The key question was whether an ambulance could and would come down the Carretera Austral to get me. I certainly wasn't going anywhere on the bike. Eventually they got back to her and said that an ambulance was on the way – they'd found a crew who were prepared to drive down to us. Birgit then set to repacking our stuff as best she could – after all, we were going to be away from all our kit for goodness knows how long. The bikes and all would be standing out in the open on the campsite, and nice as they were, Victor and Gladys couldn't keep an eye on everything all the time.

When the ambulance arrived the crew climbed into our tent with their stretcher. They pumped me up with painkillers and managed to get me onto it. Then I was loaded into the back of the ambulance on the stretcher and Birgit was invited to join me alongside one of the crew.

The driver drove off slowly and I could feel with each sway of the ambulance that he was doing his best to miss the potholes and chunks of rock that were sticking out of the track. Thankfully I was flying on whatever the drugs were, and for the first time in five days I was virtually pain free. Birgit told me later that I'd even tried to crack a joke in Spanish! That must have been excruciatingly bad as my Spanish at this time was still pretty grim.

Hours later, when we arrived at the hospital, the drama kicked off again. Though Birgit could show the hospital administrators that I  was fully insured, they weren't happy until they had written confirmation. So, I was placed on the stretcher in a corridor for four hours – during which time the painkillers slowly wore off and the pain returned. If I was prepared to sign a Visa voucher with a limit of one million pesos, then the hospital staff would get to work. As perspective, this was over two thousand two hundred US dollars at the time and that was almost exactly my budget to get up into and through Central America.

We were both very nervous about signing the voucher. We'd heard tales from other travellers about hospital bills that had soared out of control, especially where the equivalent of a blank cheque had been handed over, but after four hours in the corridor I'd have signed just about anything! There are times when you have to trust; you have

175

to forget that you are vulnerable, and you have to place yourself in other people's hands quite completely. You have to remind yourself that most people in this world are honourable and decent. But it's a daunting leap of faith when you are in pain and struggling. As soon as I signed the voucher, I was put in a room of my own and despite the pain I still took in the fact that the hospital looked spotlessly clean and properly equipped. The sense of relief was phenomenal.

Things got even better when the hospital's spine specialist introduced himself in perfect English. Dr Denton's family had emigrated from the UK when he was a small boy and he'd kept up his English ever since. He sounded as if he knew exactly what he was doing. I was sent to be scanned and X-rayed, and set up to go flying on morphine.

While I was lying happily floating in the clouds, Birgit was told she couldn't stay in the hospital room until confirmation from the insurance company was received. One of the things we'd liked about our policy was that in a disaster situation this option would make life a lot more comfortable and a lot safer.

She set off wearily into Puerto Montt in the very late evening to find that most of the hostels were full. Eventually she found a dive of a place with a strange atmosphere. Yes, they had a room, but looked at her bit oddly. The receptionist looked round, and past her, as if she was expecting to see something else there. When Birgit asked for a key and for a business card for the hostel the staff looked at her as if she was very odd.

As she unpacked, she began to suspect the reason for all the odd looks. From the rooms to either side came rather distinctive sounds. When she stepped outside the room later on and met a man in the corridor, the way he looked her up and down confirmed her thought – she'd booked into a brothel.

It took the insurance company 24 hours to respond to the telephone calls and faxes from Birgit and Dr Denton. But they came up trumps. Yes, whatever the bill was, it was going to be covered and yes, Birgit could have a bed in my room.

Meantime Dr Denton had advised us that I should have an operation to take out the damaged discs. The extreme pain had come from the fact that somehow I'd managed to slip another disc, or to be more medically correct, another disc had prolapsed. I now had a set of three damaged discs and the combination of the ferry and the dirt road had been just too much for the two already damaged discs to deal with. I tried to think when the third disc had 'popped' but couldn't pin the moment down. It was almost as if the disc had taken a slow motion dive and had prolapsed out of the spine as a gradual thing over the five days on the Carretera.

Dr Denton said that he did this sort of operation all the time and that I'd be back on the bike and riding in just a few weeks. Now that sounded good to me and if he could take the pain away forever then that was what I was going to do. If the authorising paperwork had been in front of me at that moment, and I'd been on my own, then I'd have signed up for the operation.

I didn't doubt him – he sounded absolutely positive and quite matter-of-fact, but what worried us, when Birgit managed to get the thoughts to sink into my morphine-sodden mind, was the fact that he was the only person we could communicate with clearly. He was the only one that we had understood 100%. What would happen with aftercare and what about the physio that would be needed? Getting it right with a language barrier was likely to be a big problem and potentially fraught with risk.

There were times when even morphine couldn't control the pain and it would have my back arching and rigid. The pain seemed to shriek its way viciously through my body, sending white-hot knife-stabs to every extremity. My forehead throbbed constantly and I could feel the wriggling worm of my veins pulsing on my brow. The only pain-free part of my body was my left foot, which I couldn't feel at all. Thinking positively made no difference at all and in between bouts of pain, I wondered if I'd ever feel my foot again.

Up until this time I'd had sprains, bone breaks and the two original slipped discs, but I'd never had pain like this. I kept trying to tell myself not to be a wimp and that others were far worse off than I was, but it didn't make the pain go away. In moments of calm I understood something of the pain that those who lose a limb on the battlefield have to go through. I understood a little of the pain that a villager in the mountains would have to deal with, but they would have to travel to get help with no painkillers and no ambulance – if they could afford medical attention at all.

I thanked my lucky stars that I was wealthy enough to afford the travel insurance, and that I was in a country that had such good medical facilities, and that Birgit was there. Without her, in spite of the tender care Dr Denton and the nurses gave me, I'd have felt incredibly alone. Without her sorting things out in her calm and efficient manner, all sorts of things could have gone wrong.

Over the next seven days the insurance company decided that I shouldn't be operated on in Chile but that I should be flown home to be operated on in the UK. It took ten days to get everything sorted out because of the problems with finding an international flight with enough seats available for me to get on board. There would need to be three rows flattened down to get a stretcher in.

Dr Denton's son Alan had been an amazing support for Birgit while all this was going on. He'd been out to the campsite with her and they had managed to get Libby on the back of a pickup. Dr Denton had very kindly agreed that he would store the bikes in his back yard in the nearby town of Puerto Varas when we were flown back to the UK. Birgit said that Alan was a skilful driver and that he had managed the journey back along the Carretera without mishap.

Once Birgit had both bikes safely in storage she went to see the Chilean customs officials to find out what the paperwork deal was going to be with us flying out without the bikes. What we really didn't want was them saying to her that we had to ship the bikes out of the country. Dr Denton's offer went half way to solving the problem of what to do with them but in the end it would come down to the customs officials.

Bribery wouldn't have made any difference. Chilean officials have the reputation for being the least corrupt in the Americas. Strangely enough it was Birgit's bike that was causing a problem. Somehow, when we entered Chile, my entry card had never been marked that I was coming in with a bike. I could have left it there and no one would have been any the wiser.

As things started to move towards getting me sorted out, I started to feel more positive and even to have 'what next' thoughts. I didn't for a moment entertain the idea that we wouldn't be back to continue with the trip. Another bonus of our insurance was that Birgit would be flown back to the UK with me, and then, when I was fit again, the insurance would cover for us both to be flown back out to the bikes again. The policy, for a situation like this, was quite amazing.

Customs told Birgit there wasn't a problem under the circumstances and that was that – easy. We were set. Now it was a case of dealing with the pain and waiting for the insurance company to tell us how they were going to get me back to the UK.

On day nine the news came that a doctor and nurse were going to be flown in a private jet ambulance from Buenos Aires to the airport at Puerto Montt. They'd pick me up and fly me over the Andes to B.A. There, after a night in another hospital, I'd link up with another doctor and a nurse, who'd flown out from the UK and would fly us back in a British Airways 747.

On the day, things didn't start too well. The plane bringing the doctor and nurse, Guz and Gabriella, was held up by heavy winds over the Andes. Then, when we'd said our goodbyes to Dr Denton and the nurses, and I'd been taken to the airport, customs wouldn't let us leave. We didn't have the right paperwork for Birgit's bike to stay in Chile without her!

What happened next, with me lying on the stretcher, linked up to a morphine drip watching life go by on the airfield through the open door of the plane, was a touch of farce that had a nice slant. The hold-up was due to the officials being so honest that they weren't prepared to break the rules, but they were still keen to find a way to solve the problem. Gabriella and Birgit eventually managed, with essential assistance from Dr Denton and Alan, and loads of chasing around, to have Henry signed over to Alan for the time we were going to be away. It must have been a really strange feeling for Birgit to be giving her bike away to a person she'd only met a few days before.

The farce continued in an adventurous way. The plane eventually took off and then, after hopping the Andes, had to land at the international airport in Buenos Aires. Only when we'd cleared Argentine immigration was the plane allowed to take off again and fly to the other side of B.A. where the hospital was. Birgit said the bonus was that she was able to see the city from the air, at night.

The farce continued when we got to the hospital, and found that all the paperwork relating to us had been left on the plane. But the English doctor and nurse were there waiting for us and that was a really positive feeling, though it was rather sad to say goodbye to Guz and Gabriella. We'd only known them for about six hours, but they had played a key part in the saga.

Oliver and Karen, the team from the UK, had a problem. They hadn't been given the right paperwork to be able to get morphine on the plane – the thought of being on the flight for 13 hours without any was scary, and that was when I was still sedated! They had also expected to be able to pick up syringes and needles of the right size to be able to administer the painkiller, when and if they eventually got it. The only needles they could come up with looked like four inch nails to me and even Oliver said, "This will probably hurt." Dammit, wasn't he supposed to be reassuring me?

In the middle of the night an air bubble somehow got into the drip, but something woke me up just in time to get it dealt with before it eased on into my bloodstream and gave me a heart attack. The wake-up call must have been from my guardian angel. Birgit was fast asleep, totally exhausted and well aware that we had a really long day ahead of us

We were supposed to be at the plane at 6pm for a 7pm departure. At 5pm the ambulance still hadn't arrived, but the permit for the morphine had so I couldn't give a toot. I was totally in the hands of others and selfishly all I cared about was that the pain stayed away. At the rate we were going we weren't going to make the take-off time of 7pm – the whole point of us being there at 6pm was so that I could be loaded on with some privacy.

The ambulance driver, when he eventually arrived, drove with the flare and flamboyance of the racing driver Emerson Fittipaldi. He shot through the rush hour traffic in B.A. with siren going and blue lights flashing. I felt every pothole he hit, and every drop at the end of each flyover made the ambulance shudder violently. Birgit said I was being bounced all over the place and that Oliver, Karen and she had needed to work hard to keep me steady. We made it, just. I was loaded up into the rear of the 747 on one of the 'concertina' lifts that you usually see feeding your in-flight meals into the plane.

Inside, every head turned – the plane was now delayed and I was the reason. I was probably quite good entertainment really – not a bad effort for someone lying flat on his back. Six seats out of nine in the three rows had been laid flat and my stretcher was lifted up onto a special framework. I had roughly 40cm of space between my nose and the bottom of the hand luggage compartment – a very weird and slightly claustrophobic feeling. That feeling though was of no real concern – the pain was back with a vengeance. The journey had set all the relevant nerve endings a-jangling again and I just wanted to be unconscious. I was totally unaware of the tears that Birgit later told me were running down my face.

Lying on the stretcher was like lying on a bed that sagged in the middle. But at least it didn't sag from end to end. If it had I would have felt like a banana - very uncomfortable. The trough-like shape and the closeness of the hand luggage compartment closed my world into a small place and when a curtain was drawn around the stretcher that completed the effect. Had it not been for the roar of the engines, the hiss of the air-conditioning system and the distinctive smell of airline food, I could have been in a confined space anywhere. It didn't matter that I've always been a tad claustrophobic – the drugs kicked in and I was soon asleep.

The cabin crew were brilliant and as I hadn't been able to take advantage of the in-flight goodies, they even gave us a bottle of champagne. I'd not eaten anything because I had no appetite but I'd not drunk anything either. The thought of having to have a pee on the stretcher… Nope, I was taking my liquid in injection form and that was enough!

After we landed at London Heathrow we were driven the 200 kilometres to Nottingham University Hospital in an ambulance, and then lay in a corridor for quite a while… Then it was time to say goodbye to Oliver. He'd been great, as had Karen – we'd said goodbye to her in London. The hospital was expecting us so I didn't have to join the three-hour queue in Accident and Emergency. But after a few checks the doctor announced to Birgit, and to my mother, who'd arrived by this time, that they could take me home. Well, they may not have immediately had a bed for me but the doctor simply hadn't realised that he had two formidable, straight-talking women on his hands. My mother and Birgit refused point blank to take me! Even in my drugged-up state the expression on the doctor's face amused me – he looked absolutely stunned at their reaction.

What we didn't know at this time was that if I'd not been admitted that night, I would have had to wait 18 weeks for the scans that were needed to find out what the problem was. Admit me they did, and thank goodness, they put me in a room all to myself. I'd been overseas and that meant I needed to be 'barrier-nursed' – a sort of mild quarantine – and that was fine by me! In the morning the scans were done and the doctor, slightly red-faced said, "Hmmm, I can see now why you were flown home. I'm glad we kept you in." He then said he was worried about doing an operation on my back. "It's so bad that there is more than a 50% chance that you'll come away from the operation permanently in a wheelchair."

The other option was physiotherapy, months of specific muscle-building work, and a lot of luck. When I asked how long it would be before we could go back and carry on the journey, the doctor looked over his glasses at me with an expression of total surprise. He hadn't realised that I intended to get fit and carry on with the trip.

Having decided to give the risky operation a miss, I was off the painkillers and walking again after three months of hard work. I'd actually developed the start of a six-pack stomach from all the

182

exercising, and Birgit and I decided that it was time to risk flying back to Chile. The only way to find out if it was going to be possible to carry on was to try. I still had to walk six kilometres and do an hour of physio exercises every day. Looking on the bright side, after all that exercising I was certainly a lot fitter than I'd been before, and who knew what amazing things we were going to discover on my daily six kilometre walks.

On the 15th of May 1998 Birgit and I were at Birmingham airport, waiting to fly back to Puerto Montt. In front of us was a 31-hour journey, via Amsterdam, Buenos Aires and Santiago.

Chapter 10
The longest 'motorable' road in a small world

'You gain strength, courage, and confidence by every experience in which you really stop to look fear in the face. You must do the thing which you think you cannot do.'

Eleanor Roosevelt

The bikes were absolutely fine when we got back to Puerto Varas. They were covered in dust though, and the tarpaulin that Birgit had wrapped around them had flapped itself to bits in some recent storms. We spent the next couple of weeks checking the bikes over and going for walks and short rides. The first day's ride was a very scary thing to do – a hell of a lot rested on how my body would react to the tensions and stresses I was about to put it through. I dithered, putting off the moment that I knew had to come.

It was tempting to find an excuse not to do it for another few days. The thought of provoking another bout of excruciating pain was frightening but I had to confront the demon and pray that I was going to be able to ride. I simply hoped that since I'd successfully ignored the doctor's prognosis in Australia, I'd be able to do so again. But now, faced with putting this confidence and perhaps arrogance, to the test, I hesitated. Perhaps I wasn't fit enough yet – rushing it could make things worse. Perhaps I just needed to be patient for another week or so…

I felt like a young bird must feel, facing its first flight from a cliff-edge nest. I'd worked hard to get to this point, it would have been daft to chicken out, I knew I had to try. Behind me, Birgit waited anxiously – her dream was riding on the next few moments too.

I was totally focused. The outside world ceased to exist. It was just me and the bike. She sat in front of me – totally inanimate, but threatening. I felt a little bead of sweat trickle down my spine, which made me think, "For goodness sake you are being spineless, just get on with it!"

In slow motion, I gently eased my leg over Libby, carefully pulled her upright and pressed the starter button. She burbled into life at once. A sense of relief hit me and at that moment, even

ZANZIBAR PARADISE

HAVING FUN ON THE GRAVEL

REED CANOES IN THE OKAVANGO

STUNNING NAMIBIA

FETCHING WATER - UGANDA

MOUNT FITZROY - ARGENTINA

FIST SIZED GRAVEL + GRAVITY = OOPS!

THERE'S A ROAD HERE - HONESTLY!

A DIP IN THE VOLCANIC BATH

THE ANIMAL MARKET - OTAVALLO

SAM IN THE AIR AMBULANCE

BIRGIT & SIR HENRY - ANDES

GIANT 'RHUBARB' - CHILE

FANTASTIC COLOMBIA

DAWN PEACE

BATHTIME IN ECUADOR

THE WOOD COLLECTOR

OTAVALLO MARKET

GUATEMALAN COLOUR RIOT

PANAMA BUS & LIBBY

GUATEMALAN LADIES

before her wheels rolled over the dusty tarmac, I knew that everything was going to be ok.

I rode for just ten minutes and that was enough. I seemed to have lost all the bike rider's muscle tone I'd had. But I'd ridden. I'd not had to stop because of pain, but simply because even those few kilometres had been quite exhausting. I felt a flush of triumph as I got back to Birgit and parked Libby on her sidestand – pulling her up onto the centre stand would have to wait a few more days.

In a way, being stuck in Puerto Varas was a bonus. Though it was an enforced stay, it meant that we had plenty of time to explore and to soak up life in a small Chilean town. We liked  it and took long walks around the particularly pretty lake Llanquihue, which is pronounced 'yownkeeway'. In the summer the town is very popular with Chilean holidaymakers. It's right in the middle of their Lake District and it's back-dropped by three stunning volcanoes – Osorno, Tronador and Calbuco. These three rise majestically over the town as if to act as guardians and protectors. On a sunny day the view is simply magnificent. On a grey and wet day you are reminded of the brooding power that every volcano has.

As we became regulars in the bakery and the superbly stocked supermarkets, locals started to nod to us when they saw us out and about. By the time we decided we should bite the bullet and get on the road we were sad to be moving on, but we had a long way to go and would now be riding in the wrong season.

We'd pored over all our maps to work out a new route. Our original route was going to take us through some of the most inaccessible areas in South America, along some of the most difficult motorcycle riding conditions the continent could offer. When we'd been planning the route, there had been an element of 'crossed fingers' but Patagonia and the Austral Highway had proved a point, so now we had to adapt.

Yet again the road and the adventure were making the journey happen. It underlined that it's all well and good to have a master plan laid out in advance, but the road rarely lets you stick to it. Birgit and I liked to have a plan though. In part because it meant that we could budget, but also because it meant we could do a lot of pre-trip drooling over the exciting places we hoped to visit. A plan was also important to make sure that we weren't going to be in places when the weather was at its worst. We also liked to know what there was to see in a region and a key factor was how long a visa would last. While some countries' visas weren't activated until you actually entered the country, those of others would start running out from the moment they were issued so you might only have six weeks left of a three month visa by the time you got there.

We'd originally planned to steer clear of the Pan-American Highway as much as possible; now we decided to treat it as our main road, but to scoot off it into the plains, deserts or mountains where we could find roads that looked acceptable. We also decided that we wouldn't let my back prevent us from getting to places we really wanted to see. If necessary we would use some form of public transport. The trip was back on.

The Pan-American Highway is a key route for all the Americas. It's 48,000 kilometres long and apart from the 87-kilometre Darién Gap between Columbia and Panama, you can drive from the southernmost reaches of South America right up to the northernmost stretches of Alaska, at Fairbanks. The Guinness Book of Records has the road listed as the longest 'motorable' road in the world.

This route was first mooted in 1889 but the original idea was to make it a railway. In 1925 the idea was finalised, but as a road. Mexico was the first Latin American country to complete its section, in 1950, and over the years there have been many discussions about the pros and cons of forcing the highway through the rainforests of the Darién Gap – more on that later.

First we had a country to explore that is never wider than 242 kilometres but is over 4,346 kilometres long. Chile also has just about every climatic condition to be found anywhere on the earth. In the south it was obvious that we were out of the summer and well into winter. The three months in England meant that we were now facing some very chilly rides in Chile.

The shortest road to Santiago was just over 600 kilometres, but we weren't bothered about that. We were ready to do some exploring and with the idea that we'd ride no more than a maximum of a hundred kilometres a day, we set off slowly. It was insidiously damp and cold, so we piled on every layer of clobber we could, topped off with our rain gear. The combination helped but I was glad it didn't snow because my hands were forever cold as it was. If we'd known they existed, heated grips combined with 'elephant muffs' would have been a good idea. I'd started off the trip as a novice and Birgit was a novice. The only things we knew about biking were the things we'd learnt along the way. Heated grips had never come up in conversation – quite logically as for most of the trip we'd been in warm countries.

The days eased on by in a jumble of typical traveller's days. Good hostels and bad. Warm and dry rooms and those so cold that you could have stored beef carcases in them. In one of these the only way we could get warm was to go to bed and curl up around our drinking water bottles. We'd fill them with hot water and they worked perfectly as an on-the-road alternative to the more traditional hot water bottle.

Bland scenery alternated with stunning views as we rode. Some of the towns were pretty and some singularly ugly. Some had interesting

buildings, and others suffered from a surfeit of function over form. When we saw ugly buildings with a back-drop of volcanoes or the Andes, it underlined to me that man has a great ability to despoil. But perhaps such buildings were the result of a lack of funds rather than a lack of appreciation for the surroundings.

Good roads with smooth tarmac alternated with those beaten up by the weather and traffic – the roads were really heavily used by big trucks. Friendly drivers waved and smiled, compensating for those who were in a 'me-first' hurry. I was surprised that we never saw a motorcyclist.

Every so often we'd see a police car tucked by the roadside with the occupants watching the traffic. One policeman waved at us, the others just stared. For some reason I always felt guilty when they did and I wondered how long it would be before we came across a corrupt policeman who would demand a dollop of palm grease.

To our delight my back stayed fine. It was still sensitive and adjusting to all the things one usually does in a day on the road, and then adding the physio and the walking was quite strange, but slowly we got used to it. As each day passed we felt as if we'd been given a bonus, and Santiago seemed like a really important milestone.

Henry was suffering though. He'd developed an oil leak from the final drive by the rear wheel and his battery wasn't charging. We'd run cables from it so we could start him with jump leads from Libby, without having to remove any luggage from either bike. These things seemed minor though, as did the small crack that had appeared in one of Libby's pannier racks. They were all things that could be fixed when we got to Santiago, and from another traveller, we had the name of a chap who was supposed to be extremely knowledgeable about older BMWs.

Santiago had a population of around five million people, which was well over a third of the population for the whole country. It was about one and a half times bigger than Berlin, or five times bigger than Birmingham, England. We could have just eased our way round the side of it but we'd heard that it was an amazing place to visit. Plus, Sarah, Joe and the kids were there, and we needed to get Henry sorted out, so we had to stop there.

It turned out to be a great city, with such a good atmosphere at Sarah and Joe's that we stayed for almost two weeks. This is one of the things that I really liked about our style of travel. Mostly we weren't in a hurry and that meant that when a situation or opportunity arose, we had time to explore – to grow an 'oak tree adventure' out of 'an acorn opportunity', if you like. After all, learning and having fun were the reasons we were out there.

Sarah gave us great directions to get to the suburb of La Cumbre where they lived. The only wrong turn we took was completely our fault. As we approached Santiago and the density of the traffic dramatically increased, the dense bubble of smog sitting over the city was visible and defined. We could see that some of the suburbs stretched up the sides of the mountain bowl that Santiago lives in, and that they were just peeking out above the curve of the smog, but the rest of the city was right in it. The smoggy brown, yellow and orange tints reminded me of the colour of the water that my parents had washed off the walls in the kitchen of a house they bought from a family of heavy smokers.

Amazingly, the nicotine yellow air didn't smell bad, or perhaps it was just that driving into it was such a gradual process we didn't notice a change. In a perverse sort of way as we approached, the nicotine skies seemed to suit the city. The tall skyscrapers all seemed to have a brown tint to them which meant that they blended together and there were none of the usual grey tones of modern skyscrapers in other cities. What made the colour a great contrast was the broad band of blue, snow-topped Andean mountains that towered behind the city in a cloudless, crystal-clear sky. I'd never seen this collection of colours together before, and though I knew that what I was seeing was quite an abnormal collection and should be despised for its filth, it still looked strangely attractive.

The Andes around Santiago are high – the volcano Tupungato is 6,570 metres (about 20,000 feet), and you can see three other volcanoes – Tupungatito, Maipo and San José. The highest mountain as such is Cerro El Plomo which stands at 5,424 metres. It was used by the Incas for ceremonies, and in 1954 the mummified body of a nine year old child was found burried on its upper slopes.

One of the best ways to explore a city and to get to know it is to use the local transport. It makes for great people-watching opportunities too and I always enjoyed them. Riding on public transport was such a contrast to battling with the traffic on bikes where every second of attention had to be on what everyone around us was doing, and trying to keep up with Birgit who does a very good eel impersonation. We still rode with Birgit in front and me tagging on behind. In dense traffic this made particular sense as my bike handled so much better.

The downside was that she always had to do the navigating, but we'd found that if we obeyed two golden rules then our riding was hassle-free, and we got where we needed to be. The first rule was to decide in advance where we were heading, and if there was a change in that plan then to stop and talk about it. The second was that I had to submit myself completely to Birgit. She was the boss and the decision maker and my job was to keep up, regardless of what the rest of the traffic thought I should be doing.

Sometimes it felt really odd for Birgit be so completely in control, even after a couple of years of riding together. If I hadn't trusted her judgement completely then the plan would never have worked and we'd have been arguing all the time. As it was, the trade-off worked and we cruised.

To get to the recommended mechanic, Guillermo de Freijas, on the other side of the city, we could catch a collectivo down into the city and then hop on the metro. A collectivo is a mini-bus which runs to a set route but without designated stops, you just flag it down. If it has space then you climb aboard and pay your fare. If not, then another one will be along soon. They reminded me of the matatus in Kenya and other parts of Africa, except that they lacked the jolly banter that bounced around the squashed interiors of the matatus.

Guillermo was an old-fashioned mechanic working in an old-fashioned garage that was really just a giant shed behind his house. It was racked out from floor to ceiling and each shelf was filled with an amazing jumble of BMW bits. Around the edges of the oil-soaked, metal-strewn earth yard were at least six BMWs in various stages of dismantlement. I suspected that Guillermo always had a number of projects on the go at any one time. The walls of the shed and the yard were hung with old wheel rims and had parts of old oilcans, BMW logos and black and white photos nailed up in a montage that could keep you occupied for hours. There was no need for magazines to read while waiting – there was a world of fascination displayed everywhere.

I felt a little as if I had stepped back in time, but also that I'd walked into the operating theatre of a master.

When he finished his conversation with another customer, Guillermo came across to us, wiping his oily hands as he came. This action didn't have much effect. As we got to know him a little over the following days I wondered if he had any blood in his body at all. I suspected that he ran on engine oil and from the colour of his skin, it was probably old engine oil!

Birgit asked the questions and Guillermo endeared himself to her immediately by addressing his reply to her rather than me. (Often, when Birgit would start a conversation with a mechanic or sales person, these guys would listen intently to her, looking at her as they did so, and then they would give their reply to me!) Guillermo told her, "Si, I can fix your bike – just a seal is needed and if you get one from the BMW stores I can do it. Also yes, I can fix the other bike, I weld many things."

Santiago was fun to explore. In the city centre the buildings are, in the main, great to look at. The city was founded by a Spanish conquistador, Pedro de Valdivia, in 1541; I bet he never imagined it would develop into one of the most modern and dynamic cities in South America. In spite of its early start it didn't really grow until the 1930s when a lot of money came into the area from the burgeoning nitrate mines. But in 1985 a massive earthquake knocked down a large percentage of the old Spanish colonial-style buildings. The Andes are the most seismically active mountains in the world and with Santiago nestling right amongst them it was inevitable that the city would suffer from earthquakes. Those older buildings that remain, stand next to the modern ones, many of which have mirrored glass walls. I rather liked this effect as it meant that the modern buildings almost camouflaged themselves into their surroundings by cladding themselves in reflections of mountains and the older buildings. The feeling of unity is also increased by the fact that all buildings are restricted to a particular height, due to the earthquake risk.

After travelling through open plains and rain forests, the opportunity to see some of the cultural history of South America was right there before us. Birgit loves museums and though I am happy to take a stroll through them I don't often do it. This was one of the things that I was enjoying about travelling with Birgit. Thanks to her, I got involved in things that I perhaps would not have done had I stayed travelling on my own. We visited the Bellas Artes Museum, the Contemporary Art Museum of Santiago and the Museum of Pre-Colombian Art. The latter was my favourite. The exhibits weren't strictly Chilean but that was fine by me. What the exhibits did was start to visually connect the ancient cultures of the lands we were about to travel through. They ranged right the way down from Mexico, through Central America and on to Chile.

If nothing else, the displays taught me to have considerable respect for the ancient cultures. Nothing did that more than a quipu that was on display. In simple terms, a quipu is a data recorder that was used by the Incas. They usually consisted of threads or strings that had been spun from llama or alpaca hair. Sometimes cotton was used too. It was a system of accounting and the Incas worked the quipu with a code that was based on a decimal system. Some of them were quite simple with only one or two strands but others were quite magnificent and highly complex – they could have up to 2,000 strands of knots. It's thought that not only would merchants use them to keep records but that perhaps they were also used for taking population censuses and the like too. One major advantage of the system was that they were easy to transport, and some of them even look like intricate necklaces.

We visited the magnificent Metropolitan Cathedral, and sat to eat sandwiches under the shade of the trees in the Plaza de Armas. These plazas are found in just about every city and town of significance. As the name suggests, they were built on a military basis. The idea was that these town squares could be easily secured and fortified in case of attack, and around the edges you'll usually find the majority of the government offices, churches and buildings of importance. They were supposed to be a place of refuge, and for our aching feet they certainly were.

Sarah had recommended that we should go to eat in the central market. "There's a great atmosphere and the food is really good." She was right. The market building has been described as an architectural wonder and we instantly loved it. The inside is set up in 'onion ring' layers across the ground floor with the outer ring being the place where you'll find dozens of butchers' shops. Then you have seafood, shops which instantly have the mouth watering. I love the smell of seafood and fresh fish in particular for me is really enticing – the colour of all the different types of fish is the clincher. Quite logically with these outer rings in place, the centre is a collection of restaurants and the smells that came floating out from them made me want to move in!

But the biggest surprise was Santiago's superb wall art. Some would call it graffiti but as far as I was concerned they were extremely skilful murals that made building site hoardings an attractive addition to the city. The paintings were a long way away from the illiterate daubing of so much graffiti we usually see in cities. The thing was, seeing the 'graffiti' just brought it home to me that beneath the city's shiny surface was another world where life was not so bright.

When we were travelling in and out of the centre on the collectivos and the buses, the harsher side of life was evident. Sarah had told us that most people in the city worked long hours for wages that were hardly above survival level. Street vendors would try to leap onto the buses or would crowd around the windows of the collectivos to try to sell everything from ice cream to pens to matches, newspapers and safety pins. There was always an air of desperation about them and they always looked underfed and totally exhausted. Reality checks are never a bad thing, but they do tend to bring me back to earth with a thump that is sometimes harder than I would like.

I frequently muttered about being on a careful budget but for me the decision might be whether to have the more expensive cheese with the better taste, or the budget version. For many of the locals the choice would be 'cheap cheese' or 'no cheese' that week.

Back at Guillermo's the bikes were ready. By the time we left it was dark and we were really glad that we now knew our way around the city. The only bits we didn't know so well were the outskirts where the metro ran underground, or where the buses had special lanes, but we knew enough to have confidence that we'd make it back to La Cumbre.

But as I followed Birgit I worried about her. Her night vision was still pretty grim and at its worst when she was in a situation where the light changed rapidly from bright to dark. That's city driving. She was driving along the multi-lane freeway much slower than she would normally. I felt like an old mother hen clucking and fussing behind her. Once or twice vehicles had come rushing up behind me, expecting me to be moving at the same pace as the rest of the traffic. I could imagine the expressions of surprise on the drivers' faces when they suddenly realised that they were about to bounce their bumpers off me. I started flashing my brake lights on and off – must have looked like a mobile disco from behind – but it worked, and we eased our way through the heavy traffic. All went well, for a while.

Things went pear-shaped when I realised that Birgs wasn't indicating to turn off where we should. I pulled over to one side of our lane and indicated, hoping that she would see my blinker going, realise her mistake and take the turning. As I was doing this I allowed a gap to open up between us so she had space to brake when she saw me indicating. That was my mistake. Another vehicle popped in the gap and taking the turning off, did so in such a way that I had to go too, or hit him. Birgit carried on riding down the main road, and then realised that I wasn't there any more.

We were both instantly irritated with each other, and then worried. I was annoyed because in spite of Birgit's night vision hassles she hadn't seen me indicating, and she was annoyed with me because I'd apparently broken the usual rule. I hadn't done as I was told! Thankfully there wasn't any real harm done, but both of us rode our separate ways up to Sarah and Joe's, worried that the other might be lost in the dark in this massive city.

By the time we met on the street outside Sarah and Joe's house, we were pretty ticked off at each other. She was furious with me and I was outraged at her level of anger, but the reality was that for both of us, the state we were in came mostly from a combination of fear for each other's safety, and relief that we were both safe.

If any of the neighbours in this terribly posh area had been nosy, they'd have been entertained to a shadowy but full-on shouting match, complete with much arm-waving, in the yellow light of the neon street lamps. Terribly Latin behaviour! Pressure relieved, we both laughed and were still chuckling at ourselves when we got inside – Sarah wondered what on earth was going on.

Staying with Sarah, Joe, Emily and Hannah was the easiest thing in the world and when it was finally time to move on, doing so was hard. We all knew that there was a very good chance that none of us would ever see each other again, and that felt like an awful waste. Libby had also caught the mood – she didn't want to start on the day of departure and that turned a hard leaving session into a long, drawn-out, one. But, once we'd reached the city limits, had filled the tanks with fuel and had hit the open road, it felt exactly as if that was where we were supposed to be.

A glow had been put on this first day back out on the road, at the petrol station. We'd just finished re-fuelling, and paid, when a man came striding over, thrust a bar of chocolate at each of us, smiled, turned and strode off again. I sat on the bike, with her engine turned off, and marvelled at his thoughtfulness. I vowed that one day, when I saw some foreign bikers in a petrol station in my country, I'd do exactly the same thing.

South of Santiago we'd been passing farms and lush green fields. Now, as we rode on north of the city, the landscape changed rapidly to dry range, where candlestick cactus was quite at home. The temperature changed too and for the first time we were able to take our rain trousers off. Doing so gave me a tingling anticipation of freedom. I hoped that over the next few weeks I'd be able to peel all the layers off until I was back down to just bike jeans, T-shirt and leather jacket.

Routa 5, the southern Pan-American Highway, pulled right down to the coast and we began to ride with the spectacle of the ocean on one side and the Andes on the other. As we got warmer, the Andes started to feel like old friends – a good thing, as they'd be keeping us company for much of our ride. The Andes stretch almost from the Caribbean to Cape Horn, some 8,000 kilometres.

But the road had a 'mind tease' in store for us. My brain was accustomed to 'low level' and 'seaside' equalling 'nice and warm'. Not here it wasn't, thanks to the bitterly cold Humboldt Current, which flows down the length of the west coast. It plays climatic games all the way and its effects were going to hold quite a few more brain teasers for us as we continued north.

Some of the towns were right down on the shore and the number of fishing boats either pulled up on the beach or moored at jetties, and the stench of old fish made it obvious that fishing was the main form of employment. The boats were mostly made out of chunky wooden beams and looked as if they had generations of paint layered upon them: bright yellows, blues and reds — such a contrast to the weather-beaten shoreline warehouses, shops and houses.

Back streets were usually dirt-surfaced and potholed, though I was surprised at how clean they were kept. Even piles of disintegrating metal seemed to have been purposefully placed. Along the beaches we'd find pale silver sand that was beautifully rippled by the wind and the tide. Drying racks for giant fishing nets stood where they could catch the breeze, and overhead wheeled some of the largest seagulls I'd ever seen.

One little cove right next to some fish-sorting sheds had a gaggle of pelicans, who I suspected were probably quite happily resident there. I liked these funny-looking creatures and we sat watching their antics for hours. To my mind, like penguins, they look totally different when they are in their element, the difference being that pelicans seemed just as happy in the air as they did in the water. However, it was only when they took to the air that we could appreciate their true gracefulness. They seemed to have built-in radar which helped them judge the exact number of centimetres they were flying above the surface of the water. One metre appeared to be the optimum height and they would swoop over the rolling waves and down the other sides as if they were glued to the surface by a metre-long leash. It was a most elegant and precise display of formation flying.

Many of the towns that were slightly inland had more of a Spanish colonial architecture and layout. These towns, with their  cobbled side streets and ornate buildings, were more interesting to visit than I'd anticipated. Terracotta tiled roofs sat upon ornate cream-coloured walls and the inevitable Plaza de Armas provided a focal point around which the towns would function. For us the squares were attractive location-fixers. The plazas were well signposted which meant we could get hopelessly lost in the labyrinthine back streets with total confidence that we'd have no trouble getting back on track again. There were many occasions when the road we were riding along narrowed down into single lane, and then narrowed further until we would be riding through cream-walled walkways where motorised traffic seemed completely out of place. Then quite abruptly these walkways would open back out into a two lane road again. These pretty bottlenecks weren't the places to be riding in rush hour!

It was in a town like this, La Serena, that we met Winnie and Manuela from Dachau in Germany. Manuela was riding a red and white Paris Dakar R100GS BMW which was pretty much the same size and stature as Libby. But Manuela was the same height as Birgit – we couldn't understand how she was possibly coping with a bike this big.

She'd had some pretty major alterations done to the bike so that she could get her feet down, but she quietly admitted that the bike was too big for her in towns like this, with its cobbled squares and twisting sloping streets. But Winnie was having an even harder time.

Winnie had broken his back. Not on this trip, but it had been enough to make him think that he'd never travel again. All the whimpering I'd been doing over my piddling slipped discs seemed quite pathetic when I found out what Winnie had been through. It just reinforced to me the thought that when things have gone pear-shaped for you, there's always someone who is worse off!

Because he didn't think that he'd be able to cope with riding South America on two wheels, he'd had a bike and sidecar set up for him with an emphasis on off-roading in its design. It looked superb and it was the first such beast I'd ever seen. One of the bonuses of the outfit was it meant that they could carry a lot more stuff. The sidecar was stacked up with spare parts, spare tyres for both bikes and spare fuel canisters. Winnie said that the plan wasn't working though. "I think for me that this outfit is harder to ride than just two wheels."

There were two problems. The first was that whereas on two wheels one could slalom through potholes and other obstacles, with three wheels one of them is always hitting something. That meant a constant jarring for his back. The other problem was that the sidecar demanded a different sort of riding style. It wanted to pull to the right all the time, so Winnie was battling with the strain of that for every kilometre they rode and it got far worse when they were riding off road or on tracks.

The outfit also gave them another problem. Already in South America we'd found that the cheaper hospedajes or hostels didn't always have off road parking, but they were usually quite happy for us to squeeze the bikes through into their courtyards. We'd quickly learned that it paid to carry a piece of string that was exactly as long as the widest point of the bike. That way we could easily check if we could get the bikes through the gaps involved. Henry wasn't usually a problem, but Libby had really wide handlebars and they could be a hassle. To date though, none of the alleyways or entrances had defeated us and normally we'd even been able to get the bikes through with our aluminium panniers still on.

Not the case for Winnie and Manuela. They were stuck with either having to pay out considerably more to stay in a class of hotel that had car parking, or risk leaving the outfit out on the street. With it being so unusual it always attracted a lot of attention and that meant doing so was a risky business. They were between a rock and a hard place, but we liked them a lot because they weren't letting the hassles get in the way of them enjoying their trip.

Accommodation in the old Spanish colonial towns was usually far more attractive than the options in the newer places. Concrete seemed to be the building material of preference in the newer towns, and the rooms always made me think of soulless boxes. But the Spanish buildings had real charm. Walls weren't straight, nooks and crannies abounded; floors weren't level, and there was a lot more wood in evidence. Instead of plain concrete, the floors in the old places would usually be a mosaic of traditional floor tiles. The outside walls were thick to help keep invaders and the heat out, but the interior walls were often so thin that getting to know your neighbours intimately without ever meeting them was quite possible. In a way though, it was quite a generous thing. If someone was having a party, you were invited. Many of these old buildings also had cobbled or tiled courtyards. From the roadside they could look a little plain but once through the gates the buildings took on real character. The courtyards would frequently be filled with large terracotta pots of lush green plants and the almost inevitable balconies would be homes to tubs of flowering shrubs that tumbled over the edges. When you'd come in from riding through a pretty barren land that had little shade, these places looked like small oases. And with the outside walls being so thick, the traffic noise was blissfully deadened too.

I taught Winnie some of my back-strengthening exercises and during conversation we discovered that they knew a friend we'd made years before in Kathmandu. Volly had talked about his trip across Asia to Winnie and Manuela and had described us to them during the tale. That we were on two bikes had confused them for a moment because when we'd met Volly, Birgit and I had been two-up on Libby. Small world though – particularly the world of overlanders. We also found out that they knew Connie and Thomas, whom we'd last seen on the road from Uganda into Kenya.

Now, over 600 kilometres north of Santiago, a niggle started with Libby. Oil was spewing out from the final drive on the bike and flicking itself in rather pretty streaks over the rim and across the walls of the rear tyre. The centrifugal forces produced a fine piece of oily modern art. But this is not such a pretty sight to an overlander. It wasn't an issue that I'd ever heard being chatted about by other people on bikes so I had no idea of the potential seriousness of the problem. We stripped all the luggage off the bike and removed the back wheel. A big gloop of thick black oil treacled its way out of the housing and dribbled down to form a shiny black puddle in the beige roadside gravel. Fortunately the brake pads looked completely dry, so if the leak continued like this then at least it wasn't likely to be a safety issue, in the short term. The only thing I could think of was that the seal in the final drive had gone. It had been in there for over 140,000 miles by this time so I couldn't complain, but of course Sod's law said that this was one of the seals that I wasn't carrying as a spare.

We had a choice to make. We could go back to Santiago and get it fixed there – Guillermo would be the man for the job, and if he didn't have time then we could at least take it to the BMW Dealership. Fingers crossed that they would have such a seal.

Or we could see if we could find Winnie and Manuela – perhaps they would have one amongst their mountain of spare parts, and the special tools required to do the job.

Or we could ride on to Antofagasta to see if the BMW mechanics there could fix it. The other option was to ride on with fingers crossed that it didn't get any worse.

We actually did bump into Winnie and Manuela but they didn't have that seal as a spare either. Winnie did say, "I have a friend who rode 10,000 kilometres with oil coming out like this – it was no problem." I didn't feel comfortable with doing that. In an emergency yes, but now when there were so many options, no, not the best idea. But I really didn't want to have to ride all the way back to Santiago. I had the feeling that perhaps each day we were on the move was a day riding on borrowed time. If I had a riding quota that I'd been allowed, now we were back on the bikes, then I didn't want to waste part of it by going all the way back and then having to deal with the ride north all over again.

We made two phone calls that afternoon. The first was to BMW in Antofagasta. The lady we spoke to there wasn't sure if they'd be able to fix the problem. She sounded so uncertain, this alone made up my mind about that option.

The other call was to Bob Porecha in London. Bob told us that we shouldn't worry. If we needed him to, then he would be pleased to send out a replacement seal to wherever we asked. In his typical way he didn't seem at all bothered. He was one of the calmest, most pragmatic people I knew. No disasters, just issues to be solved, and there was always a solution.

In the morning we decided that we would ride 100 kilometres back towards Santiago and if the leak got worse then we would keep riding down. If it stayed about the same then we'd risk riding north and we'd ask Bob to send us a seal out.

At the 50-kilometre point we stopped to inspect the wheel. To my surprise there was hardly a hint of oil on the rim. When we whipped the back wheel off it was as dry as a bone inside the casing. Birgit helpfully spouted, "Oh-oh, now you've got trouble. No oil leak means no oil left in the drive unit!" She was just pulling my leg – we both knew that I'd filled the compartment the previous night. But what an odd turn-up for the books. This was not what I'd expected at all, but it made our minds up. We'd ride north. We'd ask Bob to send a seal out just in case, and so he did, but the seal never leaked again – not even a tiny drip.

The location of fuel stations was now an issue. As we headed up towards the Atacama Desert the gaps between towns became far greater and we fell back into our African practice of filling up every time we saw a fuel station, even if the tank was only half-empty. I mostly didn't have a problem at all but Henry had a far smaller tank and if we were going to be able to meander on and off the Pan-Am as much as we wanted to, then we needed to keep a close eye on fuel.

Riding the Pan-Am was a bit like riding giant corrugations. The valleys all seemed to come down to the coast, across the highway at an angle of roughly ninety degrees. I supposed that this was a result of the climate. Rain didn't happen often, but when it did, it really poured, and the waters would make channels in the most direct possible way in their attempt to escape down to the sea.

The long open roads were good for thinking and that's one of the things I enjoy most about travelling on a bike. I never tired of the sound of my tyres on the road. I loved the sound of Libby's engine tapping away beneath me. The feel of the breeze on exposed skin was a comfort and a reinforcement of the sense of freedom travelling gave me. I loved to smell the changes of the land as we rode and sometimes the difference in temperature between a sunny section of road and a section in the shade was a real attention-grabber. But the opportunity to be so in tune with my bike that I didn't have to think about what I was doing was a fine thing. This left me the chance to think about all sorts of wild and unrelated things.

I thought about my family, I thought about school friends that I hadn't seen for years – I wondered where they were and what they were doing. I thought about the people who had helped me along the way, and there had been many of those. I'd never forget Captain Joseph in Tanzania who put up his farm as bail to get me out of jail. My friend Kulap the prostitute in Thailand was another who had saved my life. Then there was Peter and Edith, who had picked me out of the Namibian Desert with seventeen bone fractures and both eyes full of broken glass; there was the little old lady on the desert track in northern Kenya who gave me her boiled eggs – because I needed my strength for a journey such as mine… and so the list went on.

I also thought about the characters of the road that had made travelling through the world such an eye-opening place. The child who had hooked an open umbrella on the back of my bike in Egypt; the aborigine I'd sat chatting with in the Australian Outback, the shipping agent in Madras who, eventually, had freed my bike from the clutches of the port, and of course the other travellers I'd met on the road.

There was a special sort of camaraderie between travellers and I hoped that this feeling was something that would never disappear between one traveller and the next. For many travellers there's also a sort of code that they try to stick to. It is based on the old countryside saying, 'Leave only footprints behind you'. It also includes the aim to make nothing more difficult for the next person to come travelling the way you have just been. Sadly there are a few selfish, ignorant pillocks who believe that they have the right to ignore any sense of responsibility and will do exactly what they want, when they want, and don't care about the damage done – they won't be there again so it doesn't matter.

I'd seen travellers hit local people because they had problems with the language barrier. I'd seen a traveller throwing all his rubbish out of the window of a train. I'd seen travellers happily handing over backsheesh at the first request – thus encouraging corruption in countries that were being bled dry by it. I'd even seen travellers leave their budget accommodation in third world countries, without paying for their stay. I'd seen travellers behave with arrogance and superiority towards local people, and I'd seen the humiliation and in some cases, hate, that this had caused.

On the balancing side, I've seen some beautiful things happen between locals and travellers and they always restored my faith in human nature. They reaffirmed that one of the points of travel is to break down the barriers of ignorance – and to show that we are all fundamentally alike, with the same basic priorities in life, and that real happiness comes from helping each other. The reality was that the rogue travellers were few in comparison to the many that travelled with open minds, a hunger to learn, humour and consideration.

Sometimes I'd be so far away from myself with my thoughts, on roads like these, that I could ride most of a day without remembering much about where I'd been. Those were special, but dangerous days. I didn't want to ride past anything without being able to remember it. That was why I usually wrote a journal and to my constant surprise, even when I thought I'd noticed little, my journal-writing sessions at the end of the day would bring thoughts and visions flooding out of my sub-conscious and onto the page.

The road here was too fascinating to be away with my thoughts for very long. Just before the Atacama proper starts, you loop up through a series of bends in the road that are so magnificently proportioned they must have been laid out with biking in mind. And what's even better is that as the road rises through the hills it swoops and curves through some stunningly colourful rock changes. The colours went from cream, to pale yellow, to orange, to russet, to amber and finally to a sharp, rich, red that had a thin layer of flame-coloured desert dust on it. Once through this section that's it. You are in the fabled Atacama Desert, the driest place on earth.

Chapter 11

Valley of the moon

'The journey of a thousand miles begins with a single step.'

Lao-tzu

I have a passion for deserts that started in Africa. It was reinforced in Australia and again in the Sind in India. I was really pleased to be back in this sort of landscape, and the Atacama has a fine reputation for adventuring. It also has a reputation for being a killer and a wrecker of dreams. It's a place that demands respect. To live there you have to be incredibly hardy – both physically and mentally.

The most depressing thing was the amount of rubbish discarded on the roadside. If you could look past the bottles and bags, the bits of old car and burnt-out tyres, then the desert was well worth staring at, but this low-lying barrier was a mess. There were even road signs telling people not to burn their tyres on the hard shoulder!

In contrast, we didn't mind the shrines that sporadically dotted the roadside; most were fascinating, even looked like miniature whitewashed chapels, but all were sad since they marked the spot where someone had died. We read that the most common cause was people falling asleep, or letting their mind wander too far away from what they were doing. Every time we saw one it acted as a sharp reminder to pay attention. We'd also read that the intense heat was a contributory factor in the accident statistics, as was speed. When roads are as open and as lightly used as this one, it's tempting to open the throttle and get a move on.

But there were plenty of nasty surprises to catch the unwary. Fiendish bends would follow a blind brow so you had no advance warning. Even at our steady 90 to 100kph we were caught out a few times. Spending a second too long admiring the view at the wrong moment could literally be fatal. There were occasional speed warning signs, but really it was up to you to keep your eyes open and be sensible. It was sobering to think that some of the people who were being commemorated could have been just like us, but had let their attention wander just once, at the wrong moment.

To our surprise there were police out on the open road with speed cameras, and yes, we got zapped. Luckily they didn't signal for us to stop, but when we slowed right down, the two policemen wagged their fingers at us in admonishment and then waved us on our way. It was a timely warning, though we had only been a little over the 100kph speed limit.

This road is a pure history lesson and it was in such good condition that we were easily able to maintain a good average speed, so there was plenty of time to stop and look at points of interest.

It's a road of broken dreams and fortunes made. Every so often you come across the sad sight of a ruined mining town. Mud brick walls which are slowly returning to the ground are all that remains of the family homes, shops and businesses. These ghost towns made me think of old candles that had dwindled down to mere stubs. It wasn't hard to imagine them as bustling busy places with all the sounds of human life and endeavour that you'd expect from a small mining town. Now, the wind whistles and the only other sound comes from the geckos that scuttle across the sun-baked walls and rounded mounds of disintegrated mud brick.

The cemeteries were particularly bleak and sad; stark reminders of lost dreams, they always seemed to be set a hundred metres away from the villages. The perimeter fencing was mostly made of picket-length strips of iron and barbed wire, which in some sections looked as if it had been twisted by time into a mad woman's hair do. In other places it sagged and drooped as if it had simply given up any idea of protecting anything. The headpieces, either fallen, or leaning at crazy angles over the mounds of earth, were mostly made of iron too. Anything that was iron was pitted and had turned the distinctive flaky burgundy or orange colours of rust. A few graves were marked with bleached and splitting lengths of wood that in any other climate would have long since rotted away. All these shapes amalgamated to form an intricate and sad silhouette. I wondered if my mining ancestor had ended up in one of these graves – there was no way to tell.

The area around San Pedro de Atacama was on our list of top one hundred things to see. The town itself was a quaint place with an attractive white painted church with the remains of a pre-Colombian village and fort. Nearby were El Taito, a geyser field with more than eighty active geysers, and the Salar de Atacama, a giant saltpan that's plonked right in the middle of the desert. Also not far away, was the Laguna Miscanti, an unusual lagoon to find at this altitude in a desert and there was the dramatic sounding Death Valley too. But the Valley of the Moon was what we were really keen to see.

San Pedro was more of an Indian-looking town than anything to do with modern Chile or old Spain. Under the snow-topped gaze of

the Licancabur volcano, rough meandering lanes worked their way between the thick-walled houses, and flowers seemed to be popping out from just about everywhere. Like the indigenous human inhabitants, they had developed a strange tolerance to a chemical element that would kill the rest of us if taken in quantity. The underground water was naturally blended with arsenic. Even the local donkeys and llamas seemed to have developed a tolerance for this particular brew. Nowadays a filtration plant has been built – after all, bikers and backpackers were visiting the place, and sending too many poisoned and pallid visitors on their way would do little to enhance the town's tourist trade.

Exploring under a clear blue sky was fun. The sun was bright and seemed to put a happy glow over everything, so long as you smeared on plenty of sun tan lotion. It was almost as if the thin air did little to filter the effects of its rays.

The road through the Valley of the Moon is a rough track of sand and gravel with occasional sections of rock, or boulders. In spite of a few stretches of slippery corrugations it was absolutely fine to ride and I was delighted that we'd decided to chance it. The landscape was well named. Most of the surrounding rock is actually salt and over thousands of years the elements have worn and weathered it into magical twisted shapes. But most of the shapes were'nt sharp-edged, they were rounded and smooth, and their colours magnificent. The valley was a world of pastel shades of blues, pinks, creams, mauves and purples. I'd never seen anything like it. Birgit and I spent hours just sitting looking at the views. There was an air of total peace to the place and for a brief moment I envied the miners whose ruined houses could still be seen. But I envied for only a moment or two – in the end, the colours might have been stunning and the peace magnificent, but the realities of living and working there must have been harsh.

Our zig-zagging route now took us near the town of Chuquicamata, and past the world's largest open cast copper mine, then on toward the coastal town of Tocopilla. The road past the mine was a pig to ride. A never-ending stream of heavily- laden trucks had ripped the road surface to shreds and every vehicle threw up a cloud of dust, which, with no wind to dissipate it, hung as a permanent yellow fog that could gum up my nostrils in minutes. It made for grim and rather scary riding as you'd no idea if anything was about to blast out of the dust, on your side of the road – if you could even tell where your side of the road was. This happened several times but Birgit, up in front as usual, managed to avoid the oncoming vehicles and by the time they got to me, they were back on their side of the road.

Tocopilla was the starting point for a road that ran 244 kilometres along the beaches and cliffs up to the duty-free town of Iquique. We'd heard that if we needed bike tyres then this was the place to get them – we were curious to see how cheap they'd actually be. Barring disasters though, as we'd been sponsored by Avon with their excellent dual-purpose Gripsters we hoped that we'd have no need to buy tyres anywhere.

As we rode into Iquique, all hell was breaking loose with a wonderfully excited atmosphere. Chile had just beaten Cameroon in a World Cup football match and it was as if everyone had decided to have a holiday as a result. Cars overloaded with youths leaning out of the windows waving flags and scarves in the red, white and blue of the Chilean flag, belted through the streets with horns blaring and headlights flashing. Groups of men and youths responded by jumping up and down, waving their flags and scarves and chanting "Chi-Le! Chi-Le! Chi-Le!" Above the streets, windows had been opened and flags had been unfurled over windowsills, and everywhere we went people beamed with happiness. It made riding the bikes very unpredictable but we thoroughly enjoyed being completely wrapped up in the atmosphere. I couldn't resist adding the sound of my horn to those of the locals, prompting thumbs up signs and grins in my direction.

The duty-free zone was a bit of a disappointment and all we bought was a packet of biscuits. The tyres on sale were made by Pirelli in Brazil, and were reasonably priced rather than cheap.

The other place we wanted to see was a street lined with the houses of the former nitrate 'barons' and these homes, with their ornate columns and balconies, are an opulent sign of those times. Most of them, built out of imported wood from Oregon, are still in really good condition.

We were now nearly out of Chile and we had a choice to make. Also on our 'top one hundred' list, was a visit to Bolivia. The country had been Birgit's first taste of Latin America, where she'd learnt some of her Spanish and first been fascinated by the continent. The family that she'd stayed with still lived in the capital city La Paz and she was keen to see them. But it was the middle of the winter and getting there was a problem.

We could cut inland from Iquique, past the Salar de Uyuni, another famous saltpan, and from there head across to La Paz. But long stretches of this road were supposed to be heavygoing dirt roads that had been mangled by winter conditions and big trucks. I was very nervous at the sound of this.

The other option was to head up the coast of Chile, to the town of Arica, and then turn inland. We'd heard that the road up to Cochabamba also had sections of dirt but that most of them were well graded in preparation for the asphalt that was being laid on this road. That sounded like the best option and the insurance policy to this plan was that we'd heard about a train that ran towards Cochabamba. We thought that with a bit of luck we'd be able to get the bikes on that if the road was too grim.

The day's riding couldn't have been better or more adrenaline-buzzing. We dropped down into amazingly deep canyons along roads that twisted and turned so tightly that full lock was needed from time to time. The scary bit came from the complete absence of roadside barriers. One slip and you'd be over and falling hundreds of feet into the abyss below. The bottoms of the valleys were lush wind tunnels and the climbs back out again were just as precarious, but what fun. I love it when the adrenaline pops and buzzes from something that requires such total concentration and I love to sing at the top of my voice when I'm riding roads like this.

Music is the lifeblood of South America and for the traveller it acts as one of the connecting themes between adventures. It's always there in the background. It may be nature's music: the collective sounds of the birds and the singing of the breeze as it floats through the treetops. But it's more noticeable as the mellow sounds of the panpipes, the flamboyant tango, or the vivacious sounds of the brass bands. The music has identifiable roots too; the influences of Spanish and African cultures being the most easily recognisable.

High up in the Andes the music sounds free and magnificent. Cafés and bars of the towns and city centres almost spring to foot-tapping life as hot and passionate music bursts from within. Worried faces turn to smiles and people's footsteps take on a new and jaunty life as they allow themselves to be unconsciously affected by the beat as they pass by.

People seemed to use music as both the chance to break free from the hardships of their lives, and to celebrate that they were alive. Their music is uninhibited and addictive, and sometimes I found myself happily locked into the inside of my helmet with a tune I'd subconsciously taken on board. And as we headed north and I started to understand the words, it was as if a whole new world had been opened up to me. Now, as I rode singing my way through the villages, I got appreciative grins rather than startled bemused looks. They may not have liked the standard of my singing but I got points for enthusiasm. In canyons such as these, Libby and I bounced happy echoes off the steep rock walls.

When we found a hostel in Arica, we couldn't get the bikes off the road and into the garage. The man with the key had gone. However, as far as Christina, the girl on duty at the desk was concerned, there was no way we were going to leave our bikes on the street. With a big rock and a length of metal she battered the hasp, loop and padlock off the wooden garage doors, and swung them open for us with a flourish. As soon as we'd parked up, she took the same rock and hammered everything back together again. Apart from some shiny bits of metal and a few dings in the paint on the door, no one would know that she had been 'breaking and entering'. Now that's what I call service, and I was delighted that we didn't have to leave our bikes on the street. At that moment Paraguay won a football match and the streets suddenly filled with rushing, cheering, excited people who were coming out in support for a fellow South American country, or were just using the win as an excuse to go wild. It was certainly better for the bikes to be out of the way of any untoward over-exuberance.

At the Bolivian Embassy in Arica we had bad news. There'd been heavy snow for a week and the pass up from Arica was totally blocked. The weather forecast was for more snow and they advised that it could be weeks before the road was clear. We both felt a little stunned by the news. Heavy snow hadn't been something we had taken into account – even now I'm not sure why we didn't think about it. But at least that meant the other road would have been impassable too, and we might have spent loads of time on a hard road riding up to find that the way was blocked. And anyway, there was still the train option. Wasn't there?

No there wasn't. Though the train was still running – the last few had made it through the snow – the train service had stopped carrying passengers just a few weeks earlier. No amount of enthusiasm from us made any difference. They could carry the bikes, but not us. As we stood under the palm trees on the street outside the railway station, it dawned on us that perhaps fate was giving us a clear message that Bolivia wasn't for us. At our backs lay the Pacific Ocean, before us lay the Andes in a hundred and one shades of snow-topped blue, and to the north was Peru.

211

Chapter 12

A living epic

'Adventure can be an end in itself. Self-discovery is the secret ingredient…'
Grace Lichtenstein

Peru. The very name conjured up images of Incas, the Andes and beautiful roads, of squat, flamboyantly-dressed indigenous Indians, of Spanish conquistadors and their hunt for gold, of Cuzco, the 'Shining Path' bandits and desert mummies.

Fine, if Bolivia wasn't for us this time then Peru sounded like a prize alternative. In fact, with its amazingly diverse landscape and well documented historical past it didn't feel like 'second choice' at all. Peru is a pearl among the jewels in the South American crown, and if we were being guided that way then so be it.

We hit the road as soon as we could – the only delay being a wait until 9am for the man with the key to the garage! The bikes were fit, we had food supplies on board for a couple of days, just in case, and the tanks were full. We'd not managed to change any dollars into the Peruvian currency but we had managed to get a 'Relaciones de Pasajeros'. We'd been told that this was a vital piece of paperwork and without it we'd not get across the border. We wanted everything to be right because for the first time outside Europe we were going to try to cross a border without using our carnets for the bikes. We could have been travelling all the time in South America without them, but as we still had time left on them we'd been using them. From what we'd heard they made border crossings simpler but they weren't a requirement. Our carnets were due to run out in about three weeks and we planned to be in Peru for a lot longer than that. So, with the aim of not complicating things we decided to bite the bullet and try the crossing without. It felt quite strange to be suddenly cutting out a very familiar part of crossing a border.

Just outside Arica, a long line of trucks spread like a sleeping snake up the road towards Bolivia. It didn't look as if anyone was going anywhere quickly. Engines were off and the drivers were milling about in the pale morning sun, sending wisps of cigarette smoke to join the cool mist that gently floated over the foothills.

It was a Sunday and that meant the border crossing was quite quiet. While I stayed with the bikes and our gear, Birgit set off to work her way from one building and one counter to the next. From the way the officials reacted to a petite lass dressed in leather, it made a lot of sense for her to deal with them and the paperwork. They'd all try to politely chat her up. The expressions and body language were all flirtatious and fun. Some of the blokes were quite funny as they postured and posed in front of her. Images of bantam cockerels came to mind. Some of them were good looking, but they all seemed to share an unshakable belief that they were God's gift to women!

By this time I'd learned enough to hold basic conversations and to understand the jokes that were being made about my surname. Said in bad Spanish, Manicom sounds very much like maricon which means homosexual. In a culture that's as macho as South America's, that always caused great hilarity among the prats, and resulted in embarrassed, 'I don't know where to look', expressions from those with manners. Either way, I itched to find enough Spanish to bounce back at the joke makers with a suitable retort. My Spanish however, was producing some laughs as well.

The previous day I'd yelled "Bosta!" at a street trader when he'd been just far too hassling. He'd stopped abruptly in mid rapid-fire sentence, so it had worked. It was only later I'd realised that where I'd meant to say "Basta", which means, "Enough!" what I'd actually yelled at the guy was "HORSESHIT!" No wonder he'd looked so startled, but it had worked.

Birgit returned surprisingly quickly. She was waving a fist full of papers at me and had an expression of triumph on her face. "Done it, let's go," she said. We were about to ride from the Second World countries of Argentina and Chile, into a third World country. Peru was very poor and very unstable in comparison.

As always, riding across no-man's-land gave a moment for reflection. Chile had literally put our backs against the wall but in the main, it had been a kind country with generous, open-hearted people, systems that had mostly worked well, and scenery that was both unique and stunning. We'd mostly had the feeling that we'd been safe too. The fact that corruption was such a small issue in Chile had helped us to have this feeling. All in all, our months in Chile had been good to us and the quality of the roads running north from Puerto Varas had been good enough to allow my bones to settle and for me to rebuild my biking muscle tone. Life was good. What did it have in store for us next?

Reams more paperwork and endless rubber stamps on the paperwork, all of which was beginning to wear Birgs down a bit, but eventually she was back from the Peruvian customs. "OK," she said tiredly. "I think it's all done, lets ease out of here."

It wasn't to be. At the last checkpoint the border control guard checked the collection of papers and clicking his tongue, said that we didn't have the papers we should have had. We needed a Relaciones de Pasajeros, for each bike. We suspected that Birgit had got as far as she had because the officials had thought we were two up on one bike.

Birgit's face dropped. We'd have to go back to Chile and start all over again. But no, I was to stay where I was, the guard told Birgit. He would come back with her to help her speed through the process. I could see him puffing himself up with macho pride – he was going to be the one who would help this damsel in distress get through. Fantastic as far as I was concerned, but I hoped for Birgit's sake that it wouldn't get to bum-pinching stage or something equally OTT. The two of them set off on foot, her leathers squeaking as she walked.

Birgit told me later that he'd been very helpful but his flirting became quite annoying and ultimately rather insulting. He'd alternated between trying to chat her up and watching the football that was showing on screens throughout the offices. I told her that he'd actually honoured her – wasn't football more important than anything else in Latin America?

In spite of the time taken to cross the border, there was still a good chunk of the day left. We decided to ride on. We'd skirt the city of Tacna and head for Moquegua. It was only a couple of hundred kilometres and since it was Sunday there was hardly any traffic on the road. We sat back on the bikes and cruised along gently, remaining comfortably within the speed limit. A customs checkpoint roughly half way to Tacna let us on through without any real hassle. This was promising and gave a good feeling to the country and a sense of relief. We'd been hearing some very dodgy stories about the shenanigans the Peruvian police and officials got up to. One person we'd met coming out of the country had warned, "Look out for the police. They have guns and aren't afraid to use them." Other travellers had told us tales of bikers who'd been involved in accidents and had their bikes confiscated. But the feeling that life was good got even better as we neared Moquegua. The landscape quickly changed from arid, beige and unkempt desert, to lush, green, and cultivated valleys. The tarmac was in good condition and everything felt well with the world

Hayricks and wooden huts dotted the fields, none of which seemed to have much in the way of fencing. The soil was a dark, rich colour and the grass, where the land had been given over to meadow, was green and moist. Cows had been tethered to graze and without fences they were kept in place by stakes and ropes so that they could graze their own crop circles. The Moquegua River rushed along beside fields where we could see maize and long runs of grapes – I was surprised at how warm the air now was.

The town itself was a mix of cobblestone streets and alleyways. Many of the buildings looked quite rough and ready, but some of them were grand in comparison and had imposing wooden doors with metal studs and spikes pounded into them. We bumped on the cobbles past the market area, which was packed with people who were much shorter than most Chileans we'd seen, dressed in simple clothing. Another big difference was that they were far more curious about us than most Chileans had been. We managed to stop quite a few conversations as we rode past looking for signs of a hotel, hostel or campsite.

Up in the steep and narrow backstreets we found the Hotel Limones. It looked a little grand for our usual budget but there was nowhere cheaper and when we peeked through the gates, we knew it was the place for us. So what if it was a little on the expensive side, entering a new country deserved a splurge!

215

Beyond the wrought iron and chunky wooden gates was a garden filled with citrus trees, hence the name of the hotel. The branches were laden with large, bright yellow and very knobbly lemons. Around the garden was a raised stone walkway bordered with a low stone wall, upon which stood columns that supported a tiled roof. Dotted in between were white urns planted with flowers. Along the walls of the walkway were solid-looking wooden doors and windows with ornate wrought iron bars. Yes, we could bring the bikes in, and yes they had a room for us.

The room was quite large with whitewashed rough-rendered walls and an almost Spartan feel to it. It made us think that perhaps the building had once been some sort of monastery. However, the room was clean and the sheets on the large wooden bed were sparkling white. We didn't normally stay in places that ran to sheets, let alone clean white ones, so this was a real novelty. The walkway in front of the rooms was wide enough to park the bikes on the worn and uneven stone without getting in anyone's way, but they did look road-worn and rather dusty. The surroundings emphasised that the bikes had done some rugged kilometres – I just hoped that neither of them would leak any oil!

A visit to the market was a must. A food shopping expedition also gave our daily six-kilometre exploration exercise an objective. We arrived back at the room armed with a rosca, a very sweet, very dry bread almost powdery in texture. Dunked in coffee or tea it tasted good, but on its own it seemed to explode as soon as it was bitten into, and then would soak up all the moisture in your mouth. It made you sound like the village idiot when you tried to say anything.

We also came back with some great little avocados. These had cost buttons, and we'd found a round slab of superb but rather pungent goat's cheese. We settled down on the walkway to eat. It looked as if we were the only guests, so we sat back enjoying the wafted scents of the lemons and the feeling of the gentle warm breeze as it floated though the gardens. Welcome to Peru.

Peru is the third largest country in South America, and it's divided roughly into three regions that run more or less north to south.

Along the coast are dry and frequently barren lands that are bordered by the cold waters of the Pacific. The majority of the moisture that these lands get comes not from rain, but from dense chilly fogs which roll in off the ocean from May to November. The coast is the most highly developed and this is where what industry there is tends to be based. Fishing is one of the main industries as the chilly Humboldt Current literally teems with fish – so much so that it's rather like a fish motorway running from north to south. There is quite a bit of farming going on in this section but only where it's possible to irrigate. The soils are actually quite fertile but sufficient water is a major problem, and the reason for the barren nature of the area.

The middle region is the high sierra. This is stacked with dramatic mountains and split by gorges, but its gentler slopes and  valleys are suitable for cultivation. Most of the inhabitants here are indigenous Indians and the area is far less affluent than the coast. In part this is due to custom and education but it's also due to too much of the population surviving on too small an area of cultivatable land. Potatoes and cereals tend to be the main crops and some cattle are farmed, but in the main the land is too poor to support much cultivation. There are vast sections where cattle can't survive but the more hardy Llamas can. So farmers eek out a living breeding them for meat, milk and wool – it must be a harsh and vulnerable life.

As soon as you are over the mountains, the slopes fall away to become heavily forested, and eventually drop down into the Amazon Basin. Though this region is the largest, it's the least populated. The terrain and climate don't encourage many to try to live here. The main form of transport is by boat down the rivers. Roads are few and dangerous – mostly because they are dirt roads and are subject to constant landslides. Most of the people live right on the riverside, but these difficulties make for a completely different, rather cut-off way of living.

For me, it wasn't just the extreme diversity of the land that fascinated. It was the history. This land had had civilised nations living in it for four thousand years. Some human remains have even been carbon-dated back to 7500BC. I'd read that, in spite of the conquistadors' eager search for gold, and in spite of the modern rape of historical sites for artefacts, we were in for a treat. There were more than enough buildings and artefacts left to enthral us. I was particularly keen to find out more about the Incas. These people had controlled the largest empire that South America had ever known. Inca lands included Peru, Bolivia, Ecuador, and much of Argentina and Chile. The empire began in roughly 1197.

Keen to get exploring, Birgit and I left the Hotel Limones in good time. We didn't want to leave too early though because the dawn was decidedly chilly. The sun needed to be well and truly up before we ventured out onto the roads. We were heading for the city of Arequipa. We'd read that Arequipa not only had some magnificent Spanish architecture, but stood in the valley below the El Misti volcano. It was also a major station on the railway that ran from the coast up into the mountains. I'd read that this train journey was an erratically running epic, so we were keen to find out more about it.

We were back on the main road and heading north by ten o'clock. The road was good and the bikes were running smoothly. It was a fine sunny day and we were full of anticipation. Suddenly, we were confronted by a police car and two policemen who were making it perfectly clear that we had to pull over. Oh-oh, their body language did not look good. My instant reaction was to check our speed. Nope, not a problem, we were well within the limit. Perhaps it was just another customs checkpoint, or perhaps there was some skulduggery about to begin.

Birgit pulled over and waited for me to do the same. We pulled our helmets off and looked across towards the policemen, removing our gloves as we did so. We'd long ago learnt that when confronted by officials it paid dividends to let them see your face, and to have your hand ready to give a firm handshake. If they were accompanied with a smile and a hello in whatever the local language was, potentially tense situations were defused quite quickly. It was a simple matter of showing respect.

None of this worked this time. "Papers!" the policemen demanded. Birgit asked what the problem was. "You were going too fast. We have laws in this country you know. There will be a fine to pay!" he said abruptly, with a tone that bordered on vicious.

I knew exactly what was going on. The stories about the corrupt policemen were at the forefront of our minds. I felt a tingle of anticipation for what would happen next. There were three issues. One, we'd not been speeding. Two, they wanted money and were sure that the power of their uniforms was going to get it for them. Three, we were not going to pay a bribe.

The fact that Birgit was a female motorcyclist on a big bike threw them for a moment. It also threw them that she knew more than enough Spanish to make a very clear and indignant refusal. It was enough to put them momentarily on the defensive, and that meant they said too much.

They thought we'd ridden all the way from the border and to do that by this time of day we must have been riding fast, much too fast! But we had a joker to play. As always, we'd hung onto our hotel receipt and the one from the Limones stated the date of our stay very clearly indeed. Once Birgit had pointed this out to them, they didn't have a leg to stand on and very begrudgingly let us go. Brilliant – one up to Birgit and Sam! But they still made us deal with an intense, face-saving, finger-wagging lecture on the evils of speeding before they let us go.

The next Peruvian oddity was a tollbooth. The only thing we knew about these was that bikers blissfully don't have to pay a penny to go through. What we didn't know was how the system worked. In the UK you just ride up to the booth and when the operator sees you are on a bike they lift the barrier and you are through. Simple, but it doesn't work that way in Peru. They have an even simpler system. To the right of the tollbooths is a marked out lane wide enough for a bike but not for any car. To make sure that cars don't even consider attempting to slip through, reflective red and white boards are mounted at knee height on galvanised angle-iron posts. The arrangement was perfect for bikes – you just line yourself up with the passageway and filter through. The little walls that border it are usually low enough for your panniers to clear with ease.

Sometimes I would feel a bit guilty about wearing out the roads in a third world country with my big bike, and without any contribution to the road fund. But at other times it was highly satisfying not to have to pay. Sooner or later we were going to be overcharged for something, or 'charged' for something that we shouldn't have been, and these 'free passage for bikes' toll booths helped to balance things out.

At the next tollbooth Birgit misjudged her approach and hammered into one of the red and white boards. She hit it hard enough to make her bike wobble horribly, but she managed to stay on and at the last instant successfully heaved her bike in the direction of the entrance to the bypass lane. Behind her she left me, and a sign that was now bent over at 90 degrees.

My first reaction was to try to work out how to say in Spanish, "She's nothing to do with me – look, she's German, I'm English." While these thoughts were filtering sluggishly through my brain and the translation was forming, sort of, Birgit had ridden zippily up the road with a good attempt at complete innocence. She didn't stop until she was just about out of sight and even then kept herself distanced from the 'incident' by only watching what was going on through her mirrors.

Thankfully, none of the officials or police at the tollbooth seemed to have noticed. I rode up to the sign and parked Libby so it was blocked from their view. When I thought no one was looking I leant over and tried to straighten the sign. To my complete amazement, it pulled back vertical with almost no effort at all. I then noticed that the upper and lower sections were only held together by a sliver of metal – it had obviously been hit several times before. Now, a breeze would probably be enough to snap the top right off.

It was time to scoot, and I did so with as much innocent, 'Who me?' body language as I could muster. We rode the next few kilometers expecting to hear police sirens at any moment, but thankfully none came. We dreaded the thought that the police would have phoned ahead to stop us the next tollbooth, and we felt like a couple of fugitives. It was partly guilt at the damage done and partly the fear of the unknown. In Europe we would have gone to find the relevant person and apologised for the damage, but here? We battled with our consciences, but fear of Peru's corruption got in the way.

It was easy to feel paranoid here. Values change dramatically when you go from First, to Second to Third World countries. 'Life is cheap' is a hackneyed saying but it's often not so far from reality. Bolivia is also very much a Third World country and a friend riding there had the extreme misfortune to hit a child with his bike. Our friend made the 'mistake' of getting the child to a doctor's. He probably saved its life, but the next thing he knew, his bike had been confiscated and he'd been thrown in jail. The police and guards treated him as if he was complete scum and it wasn't long before the 'fine' was demanded. He knew that this was going to happen and was quite prepared to pay whatever was needed to get out of jail, but he had wanted to use some of his money to help the child. As far as the police were concerned, he didn't have enough money – strangely, the 'fine' increased with each payment. It did so until he had almost no money left. He used the last he had and told a very tall tale about how he'd need to be out of the prison to get more money. As soon as he was out, he lost the man tailing him and headed straight for the airport where he bought a ticket on the first plane out, accepting that he'd never see his bike again. This confirmed that he'd been dealing with pure corruption. If it had been official then he'd have been stopped at the airport. He paid with his credit card which the guards had given him so he could get them more money. Of course, he'd had his passport too, so that he could 'prove that his card was his when he went to the bank'. Our friend had felt that if he hadn't left then he would probably still be in jail now. There are hundreds of westerners in jails across Peru and Bolivia. They are lost souls. Many have tried to smuggle drugs, but there are also those whom I called 'The Unfortunates"; people who had simply been in the wrong place at the wrong time. As we rode away from the toll booth I wondered whether, if something dire happened to us, we'd be quick-witted enough to talk our way out of trouble.

In the end we could only be happy that in this instance Birgit's angel must have been on hand. Her bike was dented, but hardly damaged, and she had stayed upright. Had the sign not been dinged already, the story could have been a very different one. We might have had no chance to get away unnoticed.

The police weren't the only danger. The first couple of days in Peru taught us an important, potentially life-saving lesson. As we'd rolled through the mountains towards Arequipa we'd learnt that Peruvian drivers think that they own the road – both sides of it. Corners were potential nightmares.

It was quite normal to be riding gently around a blind corner to be confronted by some ancient heap of ex US junk on wheels, being driven with flare, panache and a total disregard for any other road user! I decided the Peruvian drivers must come from the same gene pool as Indian and Pakistani drivers. Either that or the god they all worshiped, regardless of name, must be the same controller of fate and destiny. As in "If it's God's will that I die today then keeping to my side of the road won't make any difference anyway". The roadside shrines continued, but in greater density!

We liked Arequipa as soon as we got there. It's set in a valley full of crops, and even from a distance we could see the sun reflecting off the city's famous churches. They are made of a white volcanic rock that seems to glow when the sun hits it. To the romantic in me it looked a little as if each one was surrounded by a halo.

The traffic was busy and the layout of the streets didn't help the flow much. The streets running into the city were your typical workshop-lined industrial areas but then, passing an invisible line, the character changed dramatically. Apart from the cars and the television aerials it was a bit like stepping back in time. Big bikes really aren't easy to manoeuvre in busy traffic on cobblestones, so we were determined to find somewhere to stay and park up as quickly as possible. Expensive hotels and restaurants dotted the edges of the ancient main square so we took to the backstreets in search of somewhere cheaper with off- road parking. Most of the buildings were either one or two storeys high and I guessed that once again we were in the earthquake zone.

Fortunately we found the El Gobernador quite quickly. The young and very friendly owners had safe parking, spotlessly clean rooms and hot running water: perfect. It was located in what looked like an OK part of town, only a few minutes' walk from the town centre.

Birgit and I spent the next few days ambling through the sights of the city – the convent, the churches, the cathedral, the Plaza de Armas and the markets.

The Plaza was bordered on three sides by impressive Spanish colonial buildings that were fronted by shady arcades. On the fourth side stood the cathedral, and in the middle, trees and flowering shrubs provided splashes of colour against the backdrop of creams and whites of the buildings.

The markets were fantastic. Even the streets to get to the markets were fascinating. Mostly they were narrow and winding, bordered by small shops selling everything from wrought iron work, to enormous wedding cakes, to clothing shops and old-fashioned hardware shops.

The wedding cakes were both works of art and architectural masterpieces. Some were like miniature wedding cities, with bridges between the 'buildings'. Some were layered and columned so high that I suspected the lower levels must have been made of concrete, or they wouldn't have been able to support all the upper layers. They were small girls' fantasy cakes – white and fluffy pink with amazingly ornate and intricate piped icing. When Birgit had wanted to take photos of these edible works of art she had a fat finger from a fat señora waved firmly in her direction. There was no mistaking the message. 'No photos'.

The hardware shops were full of dusty displays of everything. Buckets of nails stood next to rusting reels of chain, which stood next to reels of galvanised chain – for those who could afford it. Meat cleavers hung next to hammers and pickaxes. A steel-shod, wooden-wheeled wheelbarrow stood leaning against a wall right next to a collection of gleaming scythes and machetes.

The fashion shops made us laugh. There were none of the serious-faced, skinny but elegant mannequins that we were used to. Our mannequins sell us images of how retailers think we would like to look. The mannequins in these shops sold clothes with their smiles. They all had beaming grins and looked as if they were on the verge of breaking into full-blown fits of laughter. The psychology was interesting! Would you be happy if you bought this set of clothes? Absolutely!

The markets themselves were rough and ready buildings whose cream-washed rather dingy walls could probably tell real tales. They had stood watching over and protecting generations of market traders, who probably had sold pretty much the same produce for all that time – tomatoes, oranges, lemons, grapefruit, cucumber, maize cobs, ten different types of beans, lettuce, carrots, sweet potatoes and avocados.

The fruits and vegetables were stacked up in great piles of colour every pace or so. Mingled in between the fruit and veg stalls were the butchers and the sellers of imported plastic things – none of which looked as if they would survive a journey back to a village. They were colourful, but in a fake sort of way. After all, they were competing with the natural colours that the other stalls proudly displayed.

Both of us wanted to get up into the mountains to Cuzco, and if we could make it to Machu Picchu then that would be a bonus. But we'd heard all sorts of stories about the roads up into the mountains. None of them was tarmacked and all were supposed to be very dodgy to ride.

My back was playing up a little and the thought of getting stuck out on another remote dirt road was quite unsettling. I'd slipped on a wet cobblestone outside the market, and had then, almost immediately afterwards, put my foot down expecting to find that the pavement was there, only to find that it wasn't. The jolt to my back had sent a shiver right through me – it wasn't painful, but was a warning that if I was unlucky many more times, then I'd be in trouble. I wasn't happy with myself, but knew that I should stop being so bloody ungrateful. I could still do stuff.

We knew that scare stories are notches on travellers' metaphorical 'gun handles', and that such stories were always the ones told with the most glee and embellishment. Of course storytellers weren't trying to put others off, just making sure that their own experiences were told with suitable depth of warning. Drama helped! Normally we'd listen, but take such stories with a certain amount of salt. We'd go and find out for ourselves. But my back cast a different light on things. We'd just have to find another way up to Cuzco, and that was where the possibility of the train suddenly changed from being a traveller's story into an epic that we experienced for ourselves.

We were surrounded by the warm yellow neon glow of Arequipa at night. Dark shadows and amber reflections stained the intricately carved white volcanic rock buildings of Peru's second city. And after a brief bargaining session with the driver of the mustard-coloured Toyota taxi, we were on our way to the station.

Our driver soon eased his taxi into the gloom of the railway station yard and I was surprised at how quiet it was. There were hardly any people around, just a few stalls selling bread, sweets and the inevitable soft drinks. The yellow, bubble-gum flavoured Inca Cola was displayed proudly at the front of the stands in two-litre, clear plastic bottles.

The scene was harshly picturesque with stalls lit up by single, bare, electric light bulbs. In the fringes of the light, the dark-skinned stall keepers huddled like fairytale goblins. One could almost see eager hands being rubbed together at the thought of profits that this night would surely bring. We'd discovered that the train ran on a somewhat erratic basis and that there were days in between each departure. This meant that the straight-faced stallholders had to make a killing this night, or they'd be in trouble. We could sense the tension.

I pondered the precariousness of their livelihoods. If the train broke down, or there was a strike, a landslide, or any one of many other potential problems, these people and their families would be going hungry. For those who had invested in hot or fresh foods, there was perhaps real difficulty to be faced. They were all gamblers living on the edge and behind their blank expressions I was sure there were sharp minds waiting to take advantage of any opportunity that came their way.

We hoisted our backpacks and wandered into the glaring fluorescent light of the waiting room. We'd allowed ourselves plenty of time, and having picked up our boletos de viaje – tickets to ride –- the previous day, we settled down to wait. We knew that trains in South America ran on 'South American time', so it could be a long wait. As our eyes got used to the brightness, we saw that there were other tourists already waiting, but no locals. The hands of the large, heavy, wood and brass wall clock ticked slowly by. I began to wonder if the locals knew something we didn't, but there wasn't anyone to ask so we carried on waiting patiently.

At 8.30 p.m. new sounds began to filter through into the expectant atmosphere of the waiting room. For some reason I felt the need to look the calm, experienced traveller. I casually studied, for the fourth time, the curly edged landscape wall poster that graphically described how high we would be travelling, hopefully this night. The ride would take us along the highest railway in the world.

Some of the people waiting had gone to investigate the sounds and when they didn't come back, the rest of us hoisted backpacks once more and followed them through the worn double doors. There in front of us stood six rickety old carriages. The dim platform lights showed that the carriages had once been painted a neat two-tone orange. Now they were battered and seemingly unloved. Birgit and I exchanged glances that needed no words.

The cars nearest to us were economy class – very basic, with firm, straight-backed seats, no light and no heating. I was suddenly very glad that we'd decided not to rough it. The next two in line were smartly called 'Pullman Class'. This is the tourist section. Inside were saggy and stained reclining seats of dubious vintage, and single sex toilets that were equally ancient. These were located at opposite ends of the carriage and were surprisingly clean. The forward two cars were for cargo.

I walked the platform for the last half hour; stretching muscles that I knew would be cramped and sore within a few hours. I watched the last minute rush of locals and tourists alike get settled for the twelve-hour journey through the desert and up into the Andes. The locals staggered across the platform loaded high with brightly-wrapped bundles and plastic-clad parcels of goodness-knows-what. The blue and white enamelled wall sign said 'No live animals' (in

Spanish and in English) but said nothing about the proverbial kitchen sink! With a last frantic rush, the economy coaches were finally stuffed, 3D jigsaw style. Bundles, both human and merchandise, were wedged in tightly in the cold and dark.

The tourist section filled now with the eager and the anxious. Most were backpackers, but a good percentage were locals who were decidedly better dressed than the Indians who had been piling into the economy class compartments. One was a toothless old lady, whose face was so wrinkled it looked like a baked potato that had been left in the oven for far too long. She was bundled up in a heavy quilted blue satin jacket and over her head she had a peach-coloured chiffon scarf. Her companion was a small boy, who was obviously at her beck and call. I guessed that this was the first time he'd been on a train, as he fearfully looked around the compartment and started at the unfamiliar noises. He also jumped at the brusque orders that were being rattled out by his imperious mistress.

People found their seat numbers and slotted their packs securely into overhead racks that for once had plenty of space for you to stash large bags on. I thought that our train designers at home could learn a thing or two! The more cautious and the more experienced travellers locked theirs with padlocks to the metal bars. Chunky matt black 'local' padlocks from China and Taiwan were clicked into place alongside sleek brass padlocks from Germany and Scandinavia. Those packs that didn't fit above, were placed in the gangways as traps for the unwary.

The cargo section had its passengers too. Large waxy brown cardboard boxes were being stacked aboard. These were packed with bewildered cheeping young chicks, bound for the dinner tables of the Incas' descendants and tourists alike. With a whiplash jolt, a thundering diesel engine of matching orange livery was fastened to the coaches. The heads of the unsuspecting moved with shocked unison inside the tourist section, and with experienced acceptance in economy. The chicks' heads could no longer be seen. Still on the platform, I was anxious. I just hoped the last minute welding job I'd watched being done on the engine coupling would hold. Little did I know how worried I should have been.

With another jolt, the train began to heave itself away from the reassuring security of the station. I jumped on board. Engine thundering and horn blaring, the mish-mash of life on wheels was persuaded arthritically through the peace of the darkened suburbs. I was sure there'd be no-one setting their watch by us – inevitably, the train was late.

A tall floodlit cross on a hillside marked our departure from the confines of the city, and a cold, strangely musty smelling air welcomed us to the desert. Up ahead, the engine blared its horn as if in a soulful mourning at our passing from man's hustle and bustle to the secret calm of the night. The panorama of stars threw a pale light over the bleak nothingness outside. We could see no further than the carriage lights and the stars conspired to let us. Even the platform lights had been bright in comparison to the tunnel of flickering shapes and shadows that we now found ourselves passing through. But a hard bright cone of light shone out from the front of the engine. Sand dunes and cartoon style cacti flared quickly with the rushing darting probe of its ray – the night's secrets exposed and naked for one fleeting moment.

Inside, as the train picked up speed, we looked at each other with a mixture of resignation and horror. How, we wondered, was the carriage managing to stay on the track? One minute we were leaning crazily to one side, teetering almost at the point of no return. The next, with the smoothness of a hiccupping pendulum, we were rushing towards the rock face or sand dune on the other side. This manic and uncomfortable motion was accompanied by a cacophony of sounds. Creaks, groans, grinding, banging, and rattling filled the air assuring us that we were still alive and still in forward motion. We had eleven and a half hours still to go.

Amazingly, we both managed to sleep. I don't remember dropping off. In the absence of a gentle rocking motion, nervous exhaustion obviously did the trick. Tea made from the famous coca leaf helped us too I'm sure. It was poured by a blue- uniformed steward, from a battered pale blue metal-sleeved thermos flask whose perished cork seal was helped by a wedge of pink plastic carrier bag. We reasoned that at this lower altitude, there was a chance that the water it had been made with had been boiled long enough to have annihilated the microscopic dangers. If not, well, at least one of us was sitting close enough to their appropriate toilet! Tea or maté de coca is an old Andean Indian remedy for the equally dreaded altitude sickness. Not wanting to turn our Sacred Valley dream into a nightmare, we drank the overly sweet maté with enthusiasm.

Only twisting and turning with clockwork regularity helped ease the aches that soon pained us as our bones refused to form to the shape of the reclining seats. These seats could not have been made for bodies of European size. I consoled myself with thoughts of those to the rear in cold, dark and rigid seats. I wondered how they were faring. Worse? Or maybe better off from being so tightly wedged together.

The dawn came with a gentle lilac mist that changed rapidly to a romantic orange glow. This clean, hard light, which can only be found at high altitude, followed as the sun raised itself above the craggy mountains. We rattled on through the waking world, our passage at first seeming to abuse the beauty that surrounded us. But then again, the orange colours of the train were matching the sunrise and our movement was in keeping with the stirring of life in the new day. In mud and sod huts, bleakly placed in a sort of no-man's-land, I imagined arms being stretched, eyes being rubbed and kettles being put to boil on fires of dried Llama dung.

At six thirty a.m. we climbed stiffly from the warmth of our carriage onto the bitter, freezing cold air of the platform. We had reached the halfway point – the mud- walled Juliaca railway station. We searched

quickly for a spot in the gentle warmth of the sun's early rays. My eyes wandered around our strange new surroundings, my chest tight and short of breath in the thin air. I couldn't quite believe that I actually wanted to be back sprawled in the discomfort of seat number 14.

We had three hours to wait for our connection, which surely couldn't be as rough a ride as that of the night had been. We sat on our backpacks, tiredness making us feel a little vulnerable but also philosophical. Battered bananas and day-old rolls, fellow survivors of the night, went down well as breakfast. Russian-doll-shaped Indian ladies scuttled past us. Their peculiar scuttling movement was a way of walking that seemed to be a cultural characteristic. Their babies were casually slung across their backs in brightly-woven shawls that seemed to just about hold them safely. Outsized bowler hats or fedoras with rounded crowns topped twin jet-black plaits that hung to their waists. The ends of these were woven together in some sort of simple crochet. Respectful greetings passed between these mothers of the mountains and the crisply uniformed railway officials. We were ignored. For them it was just another day and as foreigners merely passing through, we were of little interest.

The surprising habit of most Indian women to wear a bowler hat strikes you as soon as you arrive in this part of the world. Some wear hats that look like fedoras, with their softer felt domes rounded out, but most sport hard-topped hats that look just like the bowlers that were so popular in Europe and the USA between the two world wars. You see both types of hat in black, brown and even white. One thing they all have in common is that they look much too small for their owners. They perch precariously on top of the women's heads, looking as if they are defying gravity.

There are plenty of legends as to why exactly this particular type of hat is so popular here. Some say that a clever salesman solved a problem when his firm had imported bowler hats of the wrong size for Irish railway workers to wear. Apparently the hats were something that they liked, perhaps from a safety point of view. The hats are hard-topped and would give an element of protection if some sort of building material were to fall or if struck over the head with intent – these were tough, hard times and the railway builders in this part of the world in the 1920s would have been a rough bunch. The tale has it that when the supply of hats arrived and were too small for the navies, the salesman persuaded the local women that they were the height of female fashion in Europe, and a custom was created. Some say the salesman added to the bowlers' appeal by telling the Indian women that they guaranteed fertility!

There are other theories. One is that the Spanish conquistadors started the fashion as a result of being seen wearing their own round-topped, firm-brimmed hats of the times.

Whatever the truth, these hats are now a part of the culture and both southern Peru and Bolivia would look completely different without them. Now they are a sign of position in society. They cost at least month's salary for the average Quecha or Aymara family, but apparently the position and angle at which they are worn is significant. It can indicate whether a woman is from a powerful or wealthy family, or whether she is married or single.

When the wearing of bowler or derby hats died out in Europe in the period between the 1950s and 1980s, the main manufacturer in Italy, Borsaline, closed its factories there and decamped to Bolivia. Apparently, the best South American bowlers are stamped with the Borsaline logo.

Their continued popularity may be down to the simple fact that they keep the sun off the top of the head and the felt that they are made of in Bolivia is easy to keep clean.

The women look so much at home with their headgear and wear it with such panache that it's easy to forget that these hats used to be de rigueur for English butlers, city bankers, lawyers and civil servants. But, as you see their heads bobbing along above the scuttling walk of their owners, it's easier to recall Charlie Chaplin or Laurel and Hardy. In Europe and the USA the hats have all but died out, but up in the Andes they've taken on a new lease of life and remain of great cultural importance.

When our train arrived, it was just as battered and noisy as its relation. We climbed aboard feeling confident that we knew what we would find inside. Instead we found seats that didn't recline, and their cushions were damp with a wetness of unknown but worrying origin. The ever-useful carrier bag came into play and we settled down to a crinkly journey. Our closest travelling companion in a carriage filled mostly with local people, was a very drunk Dutch guy who was knocking back vodka and coke for breakfast. He was drunkenly and very loudly trying to chat up two Brazilian girls, who sat rooted to their seats with the stunned expression of rabbits caught in headlights.

With a by now familiar roar and a hard jolt, the train pulled out of the dusty platform with horn blaring. Fully awake at this hour, the townsfolk paused their dealings as the train rumbled right through the middle of the market place – the track was the market place. Dark brown fedoras and black bowlers bobbed, and eyes squinted at our disturbance to the business of selling wares that looked both familiar and simply bizarre. Plastic toys and combs from Taiwan, with their cheap and cheerful colours, were next to buckets of chicken legs and rolls of Alpaca wool. Aluminium kettles gleamed in the sun, neighbours to bales of wire and tubs of sheep's stomachs. A baby sat squalling on the ground next to a bucket of what looked suspiciously like eyeballs. As the train passed out of the market, the people swept back across to cover the tracks with their wares and within seconds it was as if we'd never been there.

The train rolled like a drunken sailor from the outskirts of the town onto a great plain covered in shaggy tussocks of grass and bounded on two sides by low ranges of craggy mountains. These were almost purple against the vivid blue of the sky. To me, the straw-coloured plain contained a surprising number of rugged, mud-walled farms. Some had corrugated iron weighted down with large rocks, but most of the farms had sod or straw roofs – all had wisps of smoke coming out of holes in the centres of their roofs. I wondered at the farmers' survival in this starkly beautiful but seemingly waterless world. The clumps of grass were steaming little clouds as dew evaporated in the now warm sun, but there wasn't even a hint of a stream or a river, and I could see no wells.

Dogs with thought-provoking features always shot out from the trackside farms. A gleeful race would be on – dogs versus train – hind legs scrabbling for grip on the loose trackside gravel. The giant steel wheels of the train emitting loud screeches as they spun on shiny steel ribbons that seemed to be the only things even resembling straight lines in this world. Tongues flopping, ears sleeked back and coats often clumped with dried mud, the dogs would always chase faster and move more nimbly over the tussocks and ditches than we thought possible. Then we would remember that this rattling old set of creaks and groans on wheels was going to take twelve more hours to cover the final 350 kilometres. But we couldn't fail to be impressed with the enthusiasm and endurance of our fleet little four legged escorts as they stayed with us for several kilometres at a time.

A new tarmac road was being built through the mountains. For much of the time it followed alongside the railway tracks. We pondered the continued existence of the little orange train. My body cheered at the thought of a smooth, relaxing bus ride through this fabulous beauty. But my mind romantically viewed the passing of such an old friend to the mountain people with a touch of sadness. The length and discomfort of the journey had made me feel a little more in touch with the harsh life of the mountains, and with these tough little people living in their world of constant challenge.

We climbed slowly through valleys that were neatly terraced in the style of ages past – many having been built by the ancients themselves. We climbed past buildings that had hardly changed in design for hundreds of years. Browns, yellows, sage and bright clear blue  constantly surrounded us. This collection of colours was only broken by the white of a snowy mountaintop, or the human colours of an occasional village. There, posters advertised beer or washing powder, and the vivid distinctive colours of Andean knitwear flapped on washing lines. Above us condors soared, floating effortlessly on their giant wings. From a distance condors are quite magnificent with their three-meter wingspans, but close up, these fifteen kilo bruisers are one of the oddest-looking birds I'd ever seen. Their wrinkled bald heads make them look like devious and wizened old men. On the ground, they look comically clumsy and totally out of their element, but in the air...

The river rushed cold and glacier-blue beside us as we moved through the Urumbamba valley. Its waters were opaque with swirling ice-ground sediments. It was a bringer of life to so many along its banks. At brief stops in the dusty villages, vendors of hot spicy pies, chocolates, 'alpaca' sweaters and singly sold cigarettes would tout their wares to the red-eyed passengers. Like us, our temporary companions were glad to take the opportunity to stretch and stroll, however briefly, on a surface that did not rock and roll. We were missing our bikes. The glimpses we had of the road showed us that this section at least held no fears and no dangers that we couldn't handle.

In the day's last yellowing light we arrived exhausted and sated with beauty. The fabled Inca town of Cuzco lay before us. We worked to unscramble our brains, to encourage them to take in our new surroundings. Our senses told us that this was a city with an air of proud difference – Cuzco was the historical capital of the sun worshiping Inca Empire.

Cuzco is a city surrounded by beauty and it has a history of war and peace, of love and cruelty. We were welcomed to the cobbled streets with the blare of car horns, and a taxi driver wanting to overcharge us, but we didn't care. We had made it. We had survived a magnificent 27-hour body-wreaking journey through time and had landed in living history. Cuzco, city of the Incas, Spanish conquistadors and now invading travellers eager to marvel at the skills and stories of days gone by. The Sacred Valley awaited us – a dream and the unknown.

Chapter 13

A dream and the unknown

'Action may not always bring happiness, but there is no happiness without action.'

Benjamin Disraeli

Birgit and I spent the next two weeks immersed in Spanish and Inca history. It was an exciting, action-packed time, but we had a problem: Birgit was suffering from altitude sickness. She'd never suffered from it before, but this time the height was causing her problems. We were monitoring her carefully – altitude sickness can kill. She felt queasy all the time and had a slight headache that took some of the joy out of the days for her. We thought hard about dropping down to a lower altitude than Cuzco, as we knew that this would clear up the problem but since she wasn't experiencing the signs of severe altitude sickness she decided to carry on exploring.

We hoped the feelings would go away as she became acclimatised, but were both aware that it could get worse. If it did then we'd go straight back down the mountain to Arequipa, though not on the train if we could avoid it. We'd already worked out that we'd probably have been better off riding the bikes up!

In spite of Birgit's sickness we loved Cuzco. We'd had so many warnings of how dangerous the city was that we were expecting it to be like a gangland war zone. Even Peruvians had warned us about the pickpockets, muggers and beggars. They had told us that Cuzcoans had no pride or morals and that this ancient city was now a whore to tourism.

We could see where some of these comments had stemmed from but we also realised that these warnings had come from people who had heard things second-hand, and the tales had changed with a Peruvian version of 'Chinese whispers' with each telling. And some of the stories had come from people who couldn't see beneath the surface.

For us, Cuzco was a delightful place to explore. With a little imagination we could easily get a feel for how life must have been in the days of Spanish colonialism. We could see from the still-visible layout of the ancient Inca city how the streets and buildings would have been. Some of the present-day buildings grow upwards from the original Inca foundations and lower walls. The markets too were fascinating and the mountain light added a unique tone to the place. Of course, large sections of the city were devoted to supporting tourism but we only had to take a few steps to find ourselves in more down-to-earth parts where the priority was mere survival – a roof overhead, food in the stomach, education for the kids and something stashed away for old age or a medical emergency. Survival looked the same, and frequently smelt the same, from one Third World country to the next.

We spent the next few days flitting from the tourist world to the real world and back again. We particularly liked the Santa Ana market, though this was one place we'd been severely warned off going to. In the very early mornings, when the sun was still low in the sky and so pale that it had almost no colour at all the market looked as if it was bathed in silver. The rooftops in front of the sun's rays took on dark and mysterious shapes that blended and connected the forms of the different buildings into one sharp-edged, jagged line. Where there were streets in line with the rising sun, the cobbles took on the look of a river full of ripples and eddies. The silver below the buildings hid the years of old grease and the grime on the stalls. Men's breaths billowed out, clouding the air and women breathed into their shawls, leaving dewdrops of condensation that glittered in the sun. Dogs shivered beneath stalls made of chunky blocks of wood, plastic drinks crates, old bicycle wheels and sheets of tin.

It was rather like a mediaeval farmers' market, and if you wanted something to work your farm with, make a home with or to

feed a family, then this was the place to come. It was easy to spot the people who rarely came to the big city. Like us, they were uncertain and rubber-necking with open eyes at the unusual sights. The touts and thieves were following them down the street with almost as much care as they were following us. When I spotted a dodgy character

watching us I soon found that a brazen, and confident "I've seen you!" smile in their direction removed the risk.

Our hotel was basic and had no glass in some of the windows – a cold wind blew through until we blocked them off with our sarongs. The shower water was ice cold but it still cleaned you and a shower always left us raring to go. From the way the locals in the markets smelt I suspected they were far too smart to subject themselves to a daily dousing in freezing water!

We stayed well clear of the tourist restaurants and found ourselves little local places tucked away in backstreets. Though very poor, all had been set up with pride. Paint often wasn't much in evidence but the restaurants were scrupulously clean. Walls were often a sort of rough render, and floors would either be bare, uneven concrete, or tiled with old ceramic or terracotta squares that might have been salvaged from ancient buildings. Chairs were basic wood, and in keeping with the size of most of the patrons they were short enough in the leg for me to feel like a giant. The Formica-topped tables in our favourite restaurant actually matched each other and had bright blue wooden legs. On the wall was a small blackboard on which the day's offerings were displayed. For a set price you could have a three-course meal. The main course was always a challenge; a voyage of culinary discovery.

There were plenty of things on offer that we simply don't eat any more. Dessert would often be a slab of some sort of cake or other. These cakes didn't taste of much, were incredibly sweet and their colours were grotesquely artificial: strawberries are never that red! The last course would be a cup of maté de coca and it seemed to have a way of settling the stomach very nicely.

You need a stomach-settler when your main course has been a thin vegetable gruel, enhanced with a chicken's greasy yellow claws. (You discover this when your soup's level has dropped far enough to reveal the black tips of the upside-down claws). On other days our soup was enriched with grey chunks of tripe that still had strips of half-digested grass stuck to the follicles.

Most of these restaurants didn't have menus posted at all – you had what was on offer that day – though the choice didn't change very much. When she asked what was on that day, Birgit frequently struggled to understand the reply.

The combination of Cuzco-accented Spanish and unfamiliar words sometimes foxed her. I was always impressed with how much effort the restaurateurs took to try to explain – they never seemed to get impatient with us and though other patrons always gave us long, curious stares, the looks soon stopped and people would get back to their meals again. Strangely, there was never very much chatter going on – I hoped that wasn't due to our presence, but it seemed to be quite normal that people just got on with stoking their boilers. Conversation simply wasn't a compatible activity.

It was always interesting to see what was served up as a result of these strange-sounding words. But it was easier for me. I wasn't feeling permanently queasy. But even Birgit admitted that chicken claw soup was better than the dodgy-looking burgers and chips that were being sold to the hungry tourists in many of the budget establishments on the main square. On tripe days though, I always ate well!

One of the advantages of not being in a hurry was that we could wander Cuzco to our hearts' content. Another was that we had the time to get to know people a little and that came in very handy when we were bargaining in the markets.

One of the things we wanted to do in Peru was to buy more materials for making jewellery. We'd bought a pile of things made out of soapstone and ebony when we were in Africa, and we'd posted them to the USA. We knew that funds would be low by the time we got to the States and I knew that I had to find a way to fill the coffers enough for us to be able to enjoy this massive, and comparatively expensive country. The backstreet markets were the perfect source of potential jewellery ingredients.

Most of the items were being sold by little Indian ladies who sat on steps or under Spanish arches with their vividly-coloured shawls or blankets spread out on the stone beside them. These would be covered in carefully laid-out hand-made goods. Most were quite beautiful, but some were brightly-coloured, mass-produced junk. We bargained for leather straps, bangles and necklaces. We looked for pendants made out of stone or silver, and for semi-precious stones that we could set into silver.

The ladies sat like dusky dolls with their brightly-coloured skirts and jackets. Their multiple layers of vividly-coloured petticoats puffing up their skirts so as to require constant squashing down in mid-bargaining session. I supposed that these petticoats must have become customary over the centuries of Spanish occupation.

I can imagine the fascination of the Indian women for these strange, tall foreign women who appeared to have no legs but still had feet that popped out from beneath their hourglass clothes. The strange thing was that the Indian women's skirts and petticoats didn't reach to the ground – they stopped just below the knee. Was this a practical issue or a way for the Indian women to stamp their own identity on the fashion?

We got to know one of the ladies quite well one quiet trading day. She seemed to be happy to talk to Birgit and the two of them sat side by side on the steps of a long walkway that led from the bustling main road up to a square lined with palm trees. The pale stone steps had been smoothed by centuries of passing feet and in recent times those stones had been polished to a shine by the skirts and blankets of the Indian ladies.

The two of them went about their business as if they were in an invisible box, protected from the distractions of the rest of the world. They were oblivious to me as they focused on the woman's woven woollen straps with an Inca design, her plaited leather bracelets and necklaces, and more bizarrely, her bunches of vividly-coloured neck cords for keeping reading glasses to hand. As they bargained, the Indian woman taught Birgit how to weave the woollen straps, which was a real bonus.

The deals were being done but Birgit had her eye on one more thing. The woman had her wares spread out on an old hand-woven cloth whose colours were those of the high Andes. The stripes and geometric designs were picked out in rich sky blues, in the mustards of the high pastures, the glacier blues of the rivers, the deep greens of the valleys' wooded slopes, the browns of the mountain rock faces and a shade of pink that we'd only seen on some of the flowers that had decorated the last stretches of the train ride into Cuzco.

I could tell from Birgit's expression that she'd fallen in love with it – it would make the perfect souvenir of Cuzco – it had real meaning. But, the astute, sharp-eyed Indian lady had also seen the expression change on Birgit's face as she decided that she really would like to have it. The bargaining game continued, with a mixture of smiles, firm headshakes and sign language. Birgit knew that she was paying too much, but had worked into the deal that we could take a close-up photograph of the Indian lady. The clincher was the promise to send her a copy of the photo. The address she gave Birgit didn't look like much, but we supposed she knew what she was doing. The bargain was struck!

We made a daft decision the next day, or rather I did. I signed us up for a tour round some of the local sights. With Cuzco having been the centre and capital city of the Incas, it's surrounded by forts and towns that for me were 'must sees'. But I didn't want to have the hassle of finding and then chasing around the local bus transport system to get to them. I booked us on a tour.

The tour served its purpose, but we were forced to cram a hell of a lot into the day! We arrived at a site, listened to the guide make well-worn and sometimes crude jokes that raised a few elderly eyebrows, disembarked, hurried around whichever site it was, leapt back on the bus, and then travelled on through magnificent scenery to the next place. Then we did the same all over again, and listened to yet more crude jokes that diminished rather than enhanced the experience of looking at the magnificent sites. I had the feeling that I was 'doing' them, not exploring.

It was rather like being given a choc-ice at regular intervals throughout a day, but then after one bite having the thing snatched away and thrown out of the window of the bus. It was a mistake, it was too fast for the likes of us, but it was very easy and what would have taken a week of effort in the exhausting thin air, was done in mind-numbing comfort in a single day.

One of the stops had been to the market in the famous town of Pisaq. The brief visit was enough to convince us that we had to go again, and we did, but this time on the local bus.

The bus station in Cuzco was a dirty, busy place where things happened with an air of intensity that we'd not really seen in Peru before. If someone was on the move, they did so with head-down determination that would have pleased even Olga the shot-putter's time and motion expert. If they were waiting, people sat wherever they could and seemed to go into semi-hibernation. A ripple of life flushed through the clusters of people every time a new bus heaved itself into the rutted yard. The rush would be on and people would chase the bus across the yard until eventually it stopped. There didn't seem to be a pre-ordained spot for the incoming buses to stop at so the chase was necessary, if you wanted a seat.

Inside the battered and rusty cream-coloured bus to Pisaq, the seats were wooden and were so small that even Birgit felt they'd been made for another race. Baskets and bundles were thrown up onto the giant roof rack, and even a tightly-trussed pig was passed up squirming and screaming to be tied on next to the bulging patchwork of belongings. I just hoped that it hadn't been allowed to drink anything before the journey – from the sound of it the distressed creature was strapped right above our heads and there were some suspiciously thin spots on the roof. Neither of us had our waterproofs with us! The bus filled rapidly and before long even the standing room was taken up. The bus literally wallowed out of the station. As it swayed back and forth I wondered when the thing had last been serviced and if its brakes had any chance of stopping us on the mountain roads. The tour bus had been complete luxury in comparison and even it had filled the air with the smell of very hot brakes as we'd worked our way through the mountains. I reasoned that if we were going to have an accident on this bus, it was far better that we were crammed in as tightly as we were. There would be little chance of anyone rattling around like an egg in a biscuit tin. The only thing that bothered me was that one of the Indian men had a viciously sharp machete stuck in his belt, and every so often the cold steel would rub against my ear. It was a worry.

When we could see past the people, we were treated to majestic views and when we couldn't see past, we could still tell what was happening. The heavy lurches of the bus told us when we went through potholes; nerve-wracking, one-sided wobbles told us that we were going round corners and blasts on the horn told us when another vehicle was stupid enough to get in the way. The smell of burning brakes told us when the driver was trying to slow his rumbling monster down. The whitening knuckles on 'machete man' told me when it looked as if the bus driver was losing the battle.

If you have ever played or watched rugby then you'll have an idea what it was like trying to get off the bus when it made it to Pisaq. Passengers are so tightly packed that no amount of saying a polite "Permiso" – "Excuse me" – is going to make any difference at all. If you want an up-close experience in Peru then you can do no better than to go on a bus like this.

Pisaq is a combination of Inca town, old decaying village, former Spanish business centre and thriving market for both tourists

and locals alike. Most of its streets are either beaten earth, cobbled, or raggedy, dust-covered tarmac. Gullies run down the centre of the cobbled streets which act as a drainage ditch. In the wet season I could imagine that they were a well-designed godsend, but in the dry season they were quite capable of twisting the ankles of the unwary. They also formed collecting points for any rubbish that the dogs, goats or wind hadn't disposed of.

The town centre is where the market is held and a giant tree plays host to the stalls, all of which are protected from the elements by bright blue plastic tarpaulins. These shimmer in the heat and wobble and crackle in any breeze that makes its way into the square. The hillsides around the town are heavily terraced, as if a giant has groomed the countryside with an enormous broken-toothed comb.

We were lucky. The day we'd arrived was traditionally the main local market day and as a result there weren't many tourists around. The stalls were set up, in the main, to sell giant mounds of healthy-looking produce. It was the first time I'd seen just how many types of maize it's possible to grow; there were pale cream, gold, brown, red and black. Stacks of gnarly potatoes sat next to heaps of perfectly formed carrots. Onions and garlic competed for space with cabbages, and the meat stalls, for once, sold meat that didn't have the usual black cloak of writhing flies.

The cholitas (women farmers) distinguished themselves and their origins by wearing very different hats. Some wore their fedoras with the tops rounded up. Some wore them with a crisp pleat in the top and some wore bowlers, but all were decorated with a particular emblem that belonged to an individual village. Some villagers sported miniature lace fans tucked into their hatbands, some had a particular coloured feather and some had clusters of coloured ribbon. The one thing that each had in common was a stumpy, heavy-footed gait – no spring in the step at all.

Down by the river it was obvious that market day was also washday. Scores of women seemed to be having a party down on the riverbank and around them on the grass, on bushes and over the small straggly trees were spread a lumpy quilt of drying clothes. In between the clothes sat groups of women chatting in the hazy sunshine, baskets of food by their sides. With no road in sight and the terraced hills forming the backdrop, it was easy to imagine Inca women doing exactly the same thing for centuries.

But Machu Picchu was the prize. This Inca city had lain hidden in the jungle for hundreds of years and had only relatively recently been discovered and cleared. I'd seen photos which had impressed me, but nothing like as much as the glowing smiles of those who had been up into the mountain jungle to get to the site. Their faces said more to me than any guidebook could.

We had intended to hike the 33-kilometre Inca trail up to the old city but with Birgit still struggling with the altitude, and getting very frustrated with herself, we decided that the hike wasn't a realistic plan. We'd go up on the train instead. To ensure that there was still a strong element of adventure, we decided to go up on the train that was usually reserved for the local people. It also helped that the tickets were cheaper too. That also meant that we didn't have to go up and down in a day as you were expected to do when you bought a tourist train ticket. The 'Indian' train moved slowly, stopping at all the stations along the way; it sounded much more like our cup of tea.

Cuzco nestles in a deep valley and the thought of building a railway out of the valley and up into the mountains must have been a

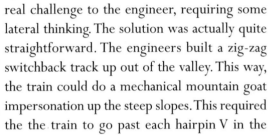

real challenge to the engineer, requiring some lateral thinking. The solution was actually quite straightforward. The engineers built a zig-zag switchback track up out of the valley. This way, the train could do a mechanical mountain goat impersonation up the steep slopes. This required the the train to go past each hairpin V in the track, then stop and reverse after the points had been manually changed by the brakeman or the engine driver. They then hopped back on until the next V had to be negotiated. The simplicity of the idea was awe-inspiring and it reminded me that the simplest ideas are often the best.

It also made me think about the hundreds of thousands of problems that had been solved over the years that had passed from man's first footsteps on the continent, until this time. Some, such as the mortar-less buildings of the Incas had been quite inspired. They had no mechanical tools and never invented the wheel, yet these giant blocks of stone had to be transported kilometres up mountainsides, and then chipped away at with great precision resulting in the almost gapless joins; an awe-inspiring thought. Some of the blocks were as big as small houses, but no-one actually knows how they did it. The Incas couldn't write and there is no known record of how such feats were achieved.

The train pulled away from the busy platform with a series of warning bells, each more urgent than the last. Inside the train, we were cosy amongst the mass of travelling humanity. There are no roads into this area of the mountains so everything goes by train. This meant that each passenger was loaded high with purchases from the big city. Bolts of cloth, aluminium pans, a paraffin lamp and a smelly container of paraffin were stacked close to me. I was glad that Birgit didn't seem to smell it and I suspected that the rich oily odour would have had her heaving.

As we climbed upwards we had a wonderful view out over the valley. The surrounding mountains were wreathed in clouds but the sun was already reaching the fields where farmers were out ploughing impressively neat furrows with ox-drawn wooden ploughs. We passed wooden, tin-roofed houses that had been sited prudently beside the railway track. On many were crosses decorated with two oxen or with two small bottles.

With no heating in the train, our feet were freezing, but up over the crest, the track settled down to run across the high plains and then at Ollyantaytambo it dropped down to the river. We followed along the banks for quite a while and this river was very different from so many of the others we'd seen at this altitude. Instead of being glacier blue-grey, the water was a more normal muddy brown and rich tea colour. Rapids and small waterfalls churned the surface.

The village on the river at the base of Machu Picchu is called Agua Caliente, which means hot water, or hot springs. We were going to try to find somewhere to stay in the village but didn't intend to hang around there until the evening. We pushed and shoved our way through the milling mass of people who seemed to be velcroed together by their belongings. We manoeuvred on past the touts, who swarmed around the Puente Ruinas railway station selling tickets for everything from guided walks to the hot springs, which we knew were a hop skip and a jump away, to Indian crafts, and tickets back down the hill on the train.

The town was ramshackle and had an air of impermanence about its concrete walls and corrugated iron roofs. But many of the small gardens had flowers growing in them and others were meticulously tended vegetable gardens. General stores, cheap restaurants, tourist gewgaw shops, and a mix of hotels lined the streets. None of the hotels looked particularly classy but that didn't surprise us as it seemed that most tourists that visited Machu Picchu came up in the morning and went back again at night. This was the very reason we wanted to stay over. Once the day visitors had caught the train back down, we hoped that we'd have the site virtually to ourselves.

A small fleet of buses was on hand to take those who didn't fancy the three hour trek up the hill to the ruined city. That included us. We'd read that the walk back down was an hour at very best, so we knew the hike up would be a real effort. Birgit wasn't up to it and being lazy, I was quite happy to use her as a face-saving excuse for not having to stride up. Though I wasn't suffering from altitude sickness, pretty much everything was still an effort.

We dumped our bags at the reception centre at the top and then set out to explore Hiram Bingham's discovery. He had literally stumbled across Machu Picchu in 1911 and as the Spanish had never found it, the city remained very much intact.

We walked the final stretch to the city along with other visitors, most of whom seemed to be part of various organised tours. When I saw their brightly-coloured, clean and patch-free clothing I looked down at my gear and it occurred to me that though clean, in the UK I'd probably have been mistaken for a tramp. With my hair now pretty long, I could have fitted into the hippy drop-out scene quite well. I had no desire to cut my hair though. My monthly beers still relied on the fact that I wasn't paying to have my hair cut!

Machu Picchu is thought to have been built in about 1450 but it wasn't a very long-lived city. It's thought that it was abandoned about 100 years later at roughly the time the Spanish conquistadors arrived. There have been many speculations as to who lived in the city but it seems likely that it was the private estate of the Inca Emperor Pachacuti. It wasn't hard to see regal aspects to the buildings as we wandered around, but we'd also read that there was a religious significance to the city. It was said to have been laid out along lines through the mountains based on astrological considerations.

From our layperson's point of view, the city was simply inspiring. There was something about it that gave a sensation that we had very rarely encountered elsewhere. We even felt a tingle of spirituality when we were down in the ruins with all the other visitors,

but the feeling was greatly enhanced when we climbed out of the city to sit and look down over it from one of the steep-edged surrounding hills.

The people down below were too far away for us to be able to recognise them as First World visitors. From our vantage point it was quite easy to imagine that the bright colours of fleeces and cardigans were robes made of exotic bird feathers, or hand-woven garments dyed with vibrant natural tones. The grazing llamas help to conjure up this image of days gone by.

Strangely, almost six years before at the start of the trip, I'd found myself doing the same thing at the ruins of Delphi in Greece. The main differences then were that I'd imagined the visitors into togas, and I'd been on my own – I'd had a feeling that something was lacking and I'd written, 'For a moment up there on the terrace I felt lonely. The day was beautiful and it seemed wrong not to be sharing it with someone special. I tried hard not to let the feeling spoil the day. If there had been someone else with me, perhaps I wouldn't have had the time to recognise the beauty, or feel the freedom to fantasise about the city, and these special moments might not have been there at all. It seemed very healthy to be thinking these thoughts as I was on my own, and the situation was unlikely to change.'

Now, up there on the grass overlooking the ruined city, a tingle of pure happiness flooded through me. How things had changed. Not only did I have a friend, travel-partner and lover, but she had exactly the same mind-set in situations such as these. My fear at Delphi had been disproved. I lay back into the grass and stared up at the cloudless sky. With a happy glow I realised that Birgit thoroughly enhanced my adventuring. It was almost as if we'd been made for the purpose of travelling together. I hoped that, as she lay quietly on the grass just inches away, she was thinking the same sort of thoughts about me.

Another impressive moment came when most the visitors departed, leaving just half a dozen of us floating around. Until that moment the surrounding mountains had merely been impressive. Now they were stunning, imposing and quite beautiful. Now I could see where all those 'we visited Machu Picchu' smiles came from. We too would be telling our story with similar smiles of enthusiasm.

Back in Agua Caliente we found a small hotel quite quickly and settled into a room that was basic but clean and had everything we needed. Outside in the flower gardens, papaya trees hung heavy with orange and green fruit, birds sang in the jungle trees across the river and a bright blue and yellow parrot sitting under the eaves welcomed us with a raucous screech. I hoped he was a heavy sleeper – this was one noise that would definitely penetrate my earplugs.

He was an inquisitive bird and a great conversationalist. While screeching at us, he looked as if he expected us to understand every word  he was saying. At the end of each screech he would drop his head towards his left shoulder and look at us as if to say, "Well, what do you think then?" I like parrots. Not only because it seems totally illogical that they should live in a mostly green and brown world, yet be so brightly-coloured, but because most live far longer than I expect to – up to ninety years.

I wondered how old this feller was and how much he had seen in his lifetime. He somehow seemed to be a wise old bird and I wondered if he had held screeched conversations with Hiram Bingham way back when. It was a nice thought, but if he had, then he was probably going to fall off his perch at any moment!

The train back the next day was an education. When we'd come up I'd sat thinking that the line could have done with a few professional Japanese railway system 'pusher-oners', but the way back just made me laugh. Though we didn't heed it, the advice is to just get yourself on that train and then worry about your ticket later. The pressure comes from the people who travelled up on the morning train but are now heading back again, the usual mob of locals on their way to do whatever real life was demanded, the few of us who'd come up in previous days, and all the people who had hiked the Inca trail. And these guys all had seemingly giant rucksacks to try to squeeze on board.

When the train arrived, the atmosphere of patience combined with extreme tension, exploded with energy and action. Everyone leapt to their feet and made a mad dash for the train. People fought tooth and nail to get aboard. Good manners disappeared and those who had done this before were plain to see. Those of us who had not stood out like sore thumbs as we wavered between good manners and joining the mad scramble.

Further down the platform I saw a guy grab a chair from one of the restaurants, put it by the train, climb up on it, push his package through the open-topped window, and follow it through – head first! Moments later his face appeared at the window with a flush of exertion and cheerful cockiness that he'd got a seat.

When the train pulled out of the station it was stuffed to the gunwales inside and the outside was festooned with people and their belongings. If there had been an accident there would have been considerable loss of life, but no one cared about that. What mattered was that we were all on board. Next to me a French tourist's armpits oozed a noxious mixture of chilli, garlic and the strong need to have a shower. Fortunately we weren't standing. There were an awful lot of raised armpits at that altitude and I suspected that the air up there was becoming rather ripe! The train moved slowly enough for those hanging on the outside to be picking flowers from the trackside trees and bushes as we went, and we didn't arrive back in Cuzco until a very dark ten o'clock at night.

We were on a roll though. Birgit was feeling a little better so we decided that as we were so close, and we'd heard that the snow had cleared, we'd head across the altiplano (high plateau) to Bolivia. There was no way we were going to go on the train again. The ride was too mad, and besides, this was a chance to try another form of transport. We'd take the long distance bus.

The only bus we could find at short notice was the night bus to the town of Puno, which is just before the border with Bolivia. It left

Cuzco at seven pm and we drove out into a world of pink. The setting sun cast a score of shades of pink across the sky and the land. The mountains stood as black silhouettes against this rose-tinted world. And as night fell, we realised that there wasn't any heating on the bus. And to make matters far worse, the bus driver had his window open to keep himself awake. I missed my bike!

Travelling by public transport was fun and interesting but at times like this I felt out of control. I sat huddled in my jacket and was thankful that we'd decided to bring our sleeping bags into the bus. If we could keep them off the mess of dust, dirt and spit on the floor then we'd be OK. We'd manage. Strangely, Birgit seemed happier than she had for days. It was almost as if there was more oxygen in the chill night air.

The bus arrived in Juliaca at two in the morning and just sat there until five, waiting for the bus agent's office to open. We wondered why the bus hadn't left Cuzco three hours later – we could have been sitting in a nice warm bar instead of sitting in the bus in the pre dawn freezing hours. As the light came, we could see that everything was covered in a crisp layer of frost.

I grumbled to myself, "I thought South America was supposed to be warm! Should have brought another pair of long johns!"

I felt reassured by the behaviour of the officials at the border with Bolivia. One sat in front of a computer, keying in our details. His colleague sat next to him entering all the same details into a giant ledger, by hand. I didn't much trust computers either!

I could feel Birgit getting excited as we rolled through the town of Copacabana and on closer to Bolivia's capital, La Paz. The landscape was golden and hilly with the ever-present, snow-topped mountains as a back-drop. As we drove, Birgit gave me a running commentary describing what had changed since she'd been there as a teenager. The biggest change seemed to be how big La Paz had grown. It now overflowed up out of its famous valley and onto the altiplano itself.

The following days passed in a blur. It was a great time to be in the capital city, the highest in the world. It was the time of the four hundred and fiftieth anniversary of its founding. The steep streets were festooned with flags and bunting and people had been travelling in from the surrounding countryside to join in with the celebrations. The atmosphere crackled.

We also managed to link up with the Schillings family, whom Birgit had last seen when she was seventeen. They ran a company called INTI and one of their products was a pick-me-up tonic. It was supposed to help people who were suffering with the altitude, and in Birgit's case it worked. She seemed to sparkle under the influence, but that was in comparison to how she had been. She still wasn't herself though, lacking her usual, 'have-a-go-at-anything' attitude.

I liked La Paz, but was irritated that we weren't going to be able to spend much time in Bolivia. There was a lot we'd planned to do and there were some exciting things we'd wanted to look at. But, we just had to be philosophical and be glad that we'd even made it to here. Six weeks earlier, that had seemed highly unlikely. The time off the bike had done my back some good. We'd walked miles and it seemed that the combination of the two things had enabled my back to recover, and strengthened it. I felt that once we'd made it back to Arequipa and were on the bikes, I'd feel the fittest I'd been in South America. This feeling boded well for the rest of the trip and Birgit commented on my lighter mood. I was also happy that she'd agreed that we should avoid the hell ride back to Arequipa by train and take the bus instead. It had to be better than the train!

I liked the ride from La Paz back to Puno, and seeing the kilometres in reverse revealed some new things. The colour of Lake Titicaca was different – a much richer blue. The hills seemed to have shades of violet and sage mixed in with the golden colours I'd noticed on the way out. The border crossing felt like an old friend but an air of edginess grew when we hit the first of the roadblocks.

The farmers of Peru had been on a countrywide strike while we'd been in Bolivia and the roads were strewn with boulders and barricades. Inflation was a major problem in Peru and the life of the farmers was getting worse and worse. The price they were paid for their produce in the mountain market towns was buttons in

251

comparison with what was being charged for it by the time it was sold in the big city markets. Then, the seed and the equipment they needed to buy would cost a fortune by the time the goods had made it to the rural areas. The difference was crippling, it had been going on for years and the farmers had had enough. I felt sorry for them. For us, the raging inflation was fine, so long as we didn't change too much money at a time. It actually made our time in Peru quite cheap, but for most of the inhabitants it was a time of financial hell. Once again, the government wasn't getting it right. I found myself wondering if any government of a country like this would ever get it right.

Was corruption just too strong? Was the traditionally corrupt and inefficient way of doing things so strongly rooted that it would never change? The situation in Peru reminded me of Kenya and Zimbabwe. The one thing that most people seemed to have was hope. Even the farmers must have had some hope that their strike was going to make a difference somehow. But hope needs fuel – it needs to be proved worthwhile from time to time, or there is no point in hoping for anything. Were miracles more likely to happen in an environment such as this?

Sitting on the bus, observing life as a visitor seemed such a wealthy position to be in. My observations and thoughts felt as if they were a complete luxury in comparison to the real life going on around us. In Puno we sat in a square that should have been teeming with life, filled with the sounds of a market in full swing. But that day it was almost silent and the few people moving across it walked heads down and feet shuffling in the old newspapers, bits of string and the dust.

Unusually, the bus to Arequipa only had a driver. All the other buses we'd been on had had a driver's mate too. It didn't seem to be a problem though as the bus set off on time, and for a change we were on a vehicle that was merely full rather than completely overloaded. The driver was a cheerful chap who looked about fifty, although it was easy to overestimate people's ages; the mountain air seemed to do nothing for a person's skin, except ensure that it crinkled. And the life of the mountain people seemed so hard that I had the feeling that each facial gully held a story of some trial or tribulation and smile-lines stayed in place even when they wasn't amused. Yet their faces were transformed and sparkled when something funny did happen, and as I'd seen in other poor parts of the world, humour seemed to be present in great quantities.

The driver had these smile-lines on his dark, tanned face, and I could see where his came from. He laughed and joked with the passengers as he supervised the loading of the bus, and laughed with those sitting near him at the front of the bus. The mood he set made me feel as if we were all off on our summer holidays and annoyingly, Cliff Richard's 1962 hit song Summer Holiday came to mind. Annoying, because after humming it to myself for the twentieth time it felt as if I was trapped inside the bus with it! Thankfully we had a puncture and this brought the old Beatles song A Hard Day's Night to mind instead. I could live with that song. The driver flashed a gold-toothed grin at us when he'd finished changing the tyre and we were off along the dusty track again. I'd checked the bus's tyres just before we'd left and been surprised that all six of them had had a good quantity of tread. The spare he'd just put on was as bald as a billiard ball and as it was a front tyre, I hoped that it wouldn't give us any problems once we started to drive down off the high mountain plains.

We drove on past grazing llamas, and past a dry salt lake bordered with small grey-brown heaps of salt. We could only guess that someone was farming it. Then, just before we started the real descent, we stopped at a ramshackle set of mud brick buildings and the driver indicated that we were taking a break. By this time most of the passengers were bursting for the toilet, but unfortunately there wasn't one. You just found whatever bit of privacy you could, were careful not to put your feet down where other people had already left their waste, and then enjoyed the sense of relief. This was not a place for the squeamish, or for those who lacked a good sense of balance! The people who had travelled this route before must have known about the lack of facilities here as they had all legged it off into the bush earlier, when the bus had its puncture. A lesson learned.

A heavy dust, laden with dried human waste rolled over us every time a bus came or went. I felt as if we were standing in the middle of an enormous Petri dish. The bacterial cultures must have been having a party – I wondered how many new versions of stomach bug were inventing themselves on the ground and in the air around us. I just hoped that we'd already built up enough of a tolerance to whatever the bugs were scheming.

This was obviously a crossroads and I was surprised at how busy it was. Every so often, to add to the layer of dust that was constantly being topped up, a heavily overloaded truck would waddle over the ruts and park up with air brakes squealing. With a last puff of compressed air that lifted a mini cloud of dust, the trucks would almost sigh as they finally came to a halt.

We couldn't wait to get on the move. So far the ride had been surprisingly smooth and the road condition had been very good. Our bikes would have lapped it up. If it continued in the same way then our bikes would definitely have been the most comfortable way to get up into the Andes at this point.

The descent started and several hours of hairpin bends followed. The track remained dusty and the underside of the bus sucked up so much into the air that even when we were a couple of bends further down the hill, our original dust cloud would still be billowing over the road. Anything that stood within one hundred metres of the road was an almost unrecognisable beige, ghost-like shape. Amazingly, some of these shapes had to be plants, but how they managed to get enough sun to grow under their dust cloaks was beyond me.

Then, almost as abruptly as the hairpins started, the ground levelled out, we were back in Arequipa, and I could stop playing with my virtual worry beads – that front tyre hadn't popped. After checking that the bikes were OK, our first target was the shower. Our clothes were so impregnated with dust and sweaty grime we decided not to wash them ourselves but to splash out on getting everything professionally laundered.

The laundry was behind an ancient, very thick, dark brown wooden door that hung in a deeply arched stone doorway. A small Indian woman was behind a green, glass-topped counter that was the perfect height for us, but high enough for her to have to stand on a wooden block behind it. Birgit was wearing her sarong, her swimsuit, a thermal vest and her bike jacket. I was wearing my sarong too – which had raised some eyebrows on the way to the laundry – and my bike jacket. Neither of us quite had the nerve to go there dressed in black bin bags, though we'd been tempted! Our 37 items of clothing (counting each sock as an individual item) disappeared in the arms of the Indian lady who didn't blink an eye at how dirty they were. We actually felt embarrassed and we'd even been tempted to give them a pre-wash before handing them over, but that would have just been daft.

When we got them back the next day they were crisp and clean but everyting smelt of chemical cleaner – perhaps the clothes had been so grubby the laundry people had decided that they'd needed fumigating!

With our bike boots and leather jackets waxed, we were now ready to hit the road again. We handed over our 'thank you for looking after the bikes' bunch of flowers and box of chocolates to the owners of the Gobernador, and eased out through the hotel gates, bumped up the steeply cambered cobblestones and wobbled through the traffic in the Plaza de Armas. As we did so, a smartly dressed policeman called a halt to the traffic to let us on through. As we passed him he somehow managed to combine a salute and a wave. Next stop Nasca.

Chapter 14

The Hotel Casanova

'You must not judge people by their country. In South America, it is always
wise to judge people by their altitude.'

Paul Theroux

The road dropped us from the mountains, through a series of police
checkpoints, past small, weather-worn villages and firmly into the
coastal desert. By the time we'd made it to Camana we were riding in
a thick sea fog. The fog was so dense and cold that we had to stop to put
more clothes on, and then had to resort to sitting behind a truck.
Neither of us felt completely comfortable following close to a truck
but it was either that or sit beside the road and wait for the fog to
disappear. We reasoned that even if the truck driver couldn't see much
better than us, he probably knew the road and at least had his
windscreen wipers to keep clearing away the moisture. That was a real
problem for us. The fog was not quite thick enough to make the
moisture bead and slip away in the breeze we were making as we rode
– though that breeze was pretty pathetic at a speed of just 40kph.

Camana was an eerie, dangerous place to ride through in the
fog. The locals knew exactly where they were going and made small
concession to the denseness of the damp grey air. Cars, trucks and
mopeds buzzed in and out of the swirling fog as if it wasn't there at
all. For us this meant that we had to be on full mental alert. At any
moment a vehicle could come blatting out of the fog and then for all
of us there'd be a dash for a last minute escape – every time it
happened I prayed that we wouldn't both decide to evade each other
in the same direction!

A stiff wind cleared the fog on the other side of the city. By now
the Pan American Highway was following the beach and in sections
there was absolutely nothing to stop the wind from snatching at us and
throwing us around. Fortunately the road was almost deserted and that
meant we could let the wind play its game without fear of being on the
wrong side of the road at the wrong moment.

Sand dunes stretched away inland and though we passed through a few tiny, tired-looking villages, there was little to be seen from the road. The towns of Oncoña and Atico looked as if they were about to roll over and die. The streets were filled with paper that thrashed around in the wind, flapping against buildings and swirling in mini tornadoes where wind currents joined each other at the corners of buildings. Bits of rusting old wire lay haphazardly by the roadside and the people looked downtrodden – they walked like automatons whose batteries had almost run down. The few restaurants looked as if they couldn't give a damn whether anyone came and ate in them or not, and even the bars looked as if they couldn't be asked to even try to portray an air of rest and relaxation – partying was obviously totally out of the question. As we rode through, I had the feeling that the bars were where people went to drown their sorrows, and no more.

The wind was blowing miniature sand dunes across the road and if we stopped to look at something that might just be of interest, the grains of sand in the wind would spin away from our wheels twisting into little cones. My mouth felt dry and gritty and I could feel sand collecting in crusty scabs inside my nostrils. When I eased my neck I could feel a sort of sandpaper effect from the collar, and I wished I hadn't waxed it quite so enthusiastically in Arequipa.

By the time we made it to the town of Chala we'd had enough for the day. Chala was like a big bus stop and as we slowed, people glowered at us. No one made even the slightest attempt to smile a greeting – they just scowled blank or slightly angry stares. The main road was lined with restaurants, with fish being the main offering. The water tasted horribly brackish and my shower left me feeling stickier than when I'd first climbed in. We were both missing the mountains and the cheerful friendly people we'd met up there. This part of Peru was the most uninspiring we'd been to and I was extremely grateful we didn't have to live there. What freedom we had, that in the morning we could just get on our bikes and ride away from the gloom and the squalor.

The 173 kilometre ride the next day to Nasca was more of the same, but a little better. The wind had died a touch and we were treated to the sights of oasis farms. These farms in the middle of the sand dunes had wells, and the regular supply of water had allowed people to farm in what looked like some of the most unlikely places in the world for doing so. The outer reaches of the farms were obviously ongoing projects, as sand grasping vegetation was planted out in equal rows, but behind them stretched lines of lush vegetable cultivation.

As usual, we took regular 'bum breaks'. Some days the temptation was to just ride, ride, ride but every time we stopped, had a bum rest and had a little walk around, we were getting the chance to look closely at the land we were travelling through. Each bum rest was like a mental snapshot of the journey. But these breaks did attract some attention – I mean, who of sane mind, would stop for a break in the middle of nowhere? Sometimes I would get the feeling that we'd done the equivalent of stopping on the hard shoulder of an English motorway to set up our deckchairs and have a thermos of tea and a slice of cake!

This particular day we attracted the attention of a pair of cruising police officers. I wasn't sure what it was but there was something about Peruvian policemen that made me feel guilty, vulnerable and on edge. Birgit and I looked at each other – perhaps this stopping in the middle of nowhere wasn't such a good idea after all. Were the policemen about to find something wrong with the bikes, or tell us that we'd contravened some obscure Peruvian law? Were their hands going to come out with the demand for a bribe to 'help us solve the problem'?

The green and white car crunched to a stop beside us on the gravely hard shoulder. The policemen both wore mirrored aviator sunglasses – the ones that the bent cops wear in movies. They sat in their car and stared at us – intently. I could hear Birgit shifting her boots on the gravel beside me. The bikes were still ticking as they cooled from the heat of the ride, but the only other sounds were from the breeze and the pounding of my heart. One of the car doors swung slowly open and a policeman climbed out. He hitched his gun belt, and then stepped towards us. "Is everything OK?" he asked us with a nicotine-stained smile.

Phew! They had only stopped because we were stopped in such an odd place. If we'd had a problem they would have been only too pleased to help us. The second policeman got out of the car now and the two of them walked around the bikes making admiring comments to Birgit – they'd already sussed that she was the one with the language brains.

The second policeman, who was a lanky, knees-and-elbows sort of bloke with crooked teeth and a long almost horse-like face, smiled at me and then proceeded to tell me the names of every single member of the English 1966 World Cup-winning football team: "Banks, Cohen, Wilson, Styles, Charlton, Moore, Ball, Hunt, Charlton, Hurst y Peters" he spouted with a smile and a Spanish accent.

He said the names as if he too was frustrated at our lack of ability to communicate. These were his only words of English and he said them as if to make sure that I knew he was a friend. Once again my preconceived ideas had been blown away.

A visit to the famous Nazca lines was a priority. These giant etchings in the Nazca desert were made by removing the surface  layer of iron oxide gravel to expose the light-coloured base earth beneath. But they aren't just lines in the gravel; many are drawings of animals, insects and people, and some are 270 metres long. We had decided to splash out and treat ourselves to a flight over the lines.

Despite some of the best brains in the world putting their minds to trying to discover why these 'geoglyphs' are there, stretching out hundreds of miles across the desert, no one has come up with a definitive, provable answer. They have survived for well over a thousand years since the time of the Nazca people because the area is virtually windless and is extremely dry. There's a constant temperature of about 25 degrees Celsius year round and this combination has helped to keep the lines clear enough to be seen from the land, and stunning to see from the air. No human feet have trodden in the area of the lines for years – apparently jail is the punishment for doing so.

The theories about the lines range from the plausible to the outlandish. In his best selling book, Chariots of the Gods? Erich von Däniken speculated that the lines were drawn to indicate landing pads for visitors from outer space. Others say they were built to be admired from hot air balloons – there is no evidence that such things existed at the time, but the materials to make balloons large enough to fly were available. And some say they were racetracks for sporting events, but my favourite theory was that they were drawn as a sign of respect to the gods.

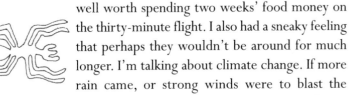

It's thought that at the time they were drawn, Peru had a series of major eclipses of the sun and anyone who has seen an eclipse will be able to confirm that the image is very much like that of a giant eye looking down to earth, blinking. If I'd seen such a thing in the time of the Nazca I think I would have felt that something major, magnificent and of vital importance had happened. I would have wanted to show respect and perhaps I would also have wanted to find some way of communicating.

For me, the reason for their existence is less important than the simple fact that they are there, and are magnificent. It was going to be well worth spending two weeks' food money on the thirty-minute flight. I also had a sneaky feeling that perhaps they wouldn't be around for much longer. I'm talking about climate change. If more rain came, or strong winds were to blast the plateau, then the lines could disappear very quickly – they are only ten to twenty centimetres into the sand.

The flight in the little Cessna aeroplane was a stomach-wrenching nightmare until we got high enough for the desert thermals not to bounce us around quite so much. And then the view was quite magnificent – until the pilot started to play games with us.

I wasn't sure what Birgit was enjoying the most – the flight or the sight of the lines. She certainly didn't seem fazed by the way the pilot was flinging the 'plane from one wing tip to the next so that we could both see the shapes in the sand below. I thought he was either a sadist or had an over-developed sense of duty. There was something rather disconcerting about hanging vertically in the ether hundreds of feet above the desert.

Back on the ground Birgit told me she'd always wanted to learn to fly and that this flight had just reaffirmed that dream. I wasn't surprised and I knew that one day she'd make it happen or at least would take some lessons just so she could see how the whole process worked. I just hoped that she'd concentrate on learning how to fly on the level!

The only slightly sour taste to our visit to Nazca was the ride out into the desert to the tombs. These tombs have been ripped open by grave robbers, and the mummified occupants have been left exposed to the elements to disintegrate. The dry, windless desert air stopped the mummies from disintegrating totally, but our gawping at them somehow felt wrong. Once they had been people just like us – they had loved, laughed and cried. They had had their dreams and their disappointments – but in a very different time. I looked briefly at them and wondered if they were looking down from a spirit world at us. Were they unhappy about having their resting place exposed or were they glad that the memory of their lives lived on thanks to people travelling out to stare at them?

Lima now loomed on our horizon, 500 kilometres to the north and I was not looking forward to it at all. In fact, I would have preferred to avoid it altogether. Peru's capital sounded grim. The potential draw of the various museums and other sites of interest was not enough to persuade us to stop there; the only attraction which might have done was the chance to drop in on the famous and supposedly very helpful South American Explorers' Club – but it didn't.

The best way to avoid the city at its worst seemed to be to stop just short of it for the night and then face the traffic mayhem that we expected in the morning, when we were both fresh. The road into Lima was dual carriageway. To begin with this was so quiet that I began to wonder whether we'd somehow missed the 'Road Closed' signs. But as we got closer to the city the density increased. The condition of the vehicles was even worse than that of the the heaps in Buenos Aires. Here it seemed that people couldn't even afford brown parcel tape to hold their cars together. The foggy air was thick and yellow with belching, unfiltered fumes, and as we slowed down in the traffic I had the chance to make a closer inspection.

The truck in front of us looked like a thundering potential death trap – I wondered how it wasn't shaking itself to bits. The rear number plate was held on with a knotted old shoelace. The bumper was only fixed on one corner, so every time the truck crashed through a pothole the bumper hit the ground and sparks flew. The rear flap of the load bed was missing and the wooden sides were so battered and splintered that the passengers riding in the back must have been afraid of being stabbed. A trail of oil dribbled down every time the truck slowed and so much was pouring out that I wondered how long it would continue to run before the engine seized solid. All four of the rear tyres were bald, and three of them were down to the canvas. The exhaust pipe was blackened, disintegrating and vibrated madly with the combination of engine-induced rumbles and those that came from the road surface. The suspension had collapsed on one side, so the truck leaned like on old drunk. The driver's horn presumably no longer worked as the lad with him sat on the roof of the truck banging madly on it whenever anyone even dared to come close. When a vehicle got too close, he screamed obscenities at the driver. He must have been burning calories at a massive rate as a result of his furiously enthusiastic, arm-waving, cab-bashing, traffic-parting system. He was so efficient that the mess of junk on wheels cleared a path rapidly through the mayhem – I just hoped that Birgit would keep following it, and that nothing would fall off it in front of us.

Then we got lost. Somehow we'd not seen a Pan American Highway sign or we'd missed one to the city of Barranca. We parked up, creating a small traffic island and everyone got on with their dashes to wherever they were going as if we were no more than a rock at the side of the stream.

Road signs seemed to have stopped altogether and street names were non-existent. The road was wide enough to be a dual carriageway but the drivers treated it as an 'any' way. Left and right lanes of traffic didn't exist. People just drove straight at each other as if playing a constant game of chicken. The edges of the street were lined with dust-covered, paint-peeling shops and small workshops, in front of which probably a decade of detritus had collected. Dust, orange peel, newspapers, ripped magazines, the remnants of political posters, old bent nails, blackened banana skins, twisted lengths of reinforcement bar, a rusting rear truck axle, a broken plastic washing-up bowl and wooden ice lolly sticks lay next to a yellow dog which surely must be dead, and a 125cc motorbike with four milk churns strapped to it.

But even in our dirty state we must have stood out like a couple of sore thumbs. A policeman came to our aid. Happily we hadn't got too far off the route we needed and with some very nimble work we managed to get back out into the stream and rode hard. There were two ways to ride this sort of traffic – give way to everything and take a month of Sundays to get through, or push and shove as hard as the next person. For the latter you had to convince yourself that no one meant you any harm, and then ride with Latin flare or even arrogance.

That all worked well until a car driver rammed me out of his way! He was very clever at it too. He found a way to nip in just alongside me by my panniers, and then gave an almighty shove that had me wheeling out in front of everyone else – who of course reacted as you'd expect. Horns blared and fists were waved! The car driver gave me a cocky grin and very cheerful wave as he moved into the gap he'd just created. But I was furious – he'd got the better of me! I was also more than a little shaken.

Nearly 200 kilometres north of Lima, the city of Barranca looked a real hole. As we rode into this dump of a town, I knew that we had to get back up into the mountains. We needed a fresh air and beauty fix. The only reason we stopped in Barranca at all was because it was a comfortable day's ride away and after Lima we didn't want to have to ride too much further. But our hotel that night was the worst we experienced in the whole of South America.

It started off quite well. We found the Hotel Casanova really easily, they had a room for us, it was affordable and at first glance didn't look too bad. And, "Si Señora, you can bring your motorcycles inside." The parking wasn't in a courtyard but in the reception area. My piece of string came into play and luckily we could get the bikes up the step and through the door without having to take any panniers off. This seemed like a major bonus as the scruffy reception area was full of greasy men who were uniformly dressed in sweat-stained, grubby shirts unbuttoned low enough to expose equally grubby undershirts stretched over bulging bellies. All were smoking as they watched the television, all were unshaven but some sported thick black Pancho Villa moustaches. With these villainous characters sitting in our new 'garage' we were quite happy not to show off just how easily our panniers could be removed from the bikes.

We made a show of unlocking all the locks on our boxes and carefully locking them up again when we'd retrieved the few bits of kit we needed. As we did so, the TV was forgotten. We were much better entertainment. My friendly nods to the men were ignored with dead eyes and expressionless faces. Not a soul spoke to us, except the greasy-skinned, stubble-chinned receptionist who was one of the surliest men I've ever met. Everything was too much effort for him! But at least the bikes were off the street, though I wondered how long they would survive in the reception area – would bits be unbolted or fiddled with to breaking point?

Our room was the first down the corridor from reception and that was fine, even though we could hear the reception TV in the room. The walls were streaked with rivulets of grime. They might once have been white – it was hard to tell. Years of cigarette smoking in the room had turned the walls into a blotchy sepia. The dark green lino floor held a sticky grip on our feet as we walked across the room. The sagging, iron-framed bed had a filthy sheet spread across it. On the wall round the edge of the bed at mattress level was a grubby line encrusted with pubic hair. Blood was splattered in between the sticky black curls.

Birgit and I looked at each other. Should we stay or should we go? The thought of getting loaded up and then having to ride some more was daunting. It was getting dark outside and we knew there wasn't another affordable option close by. So we stayed.

We put our tent ground sheet on the bed; that way we could keep our sleeping bags off the walls and if there were going to be bugs in the bed then they'd have a hard time getting at us. A selling factor for the room was that it was en-suite. But the bathroom held a cracked mirror that reflected five versions of my grubby face back at me, and the toilet was full of the last inhabitant's turds. The smell was grim, but fortunately the flush worked reasonably well – used repeatedly it finally cleared everything away. The toilet seat was missing but that didn't faze us – we'd have preferred not to sit on it anyway! The killer item was the shower – almost literally.

It looked like something out of Dr Frankenstein's laboratory. The shower rose had a collection of electrical wires coming from it that showed bare copper and the once-white porcelain shower basin looked as if it was rimmed with tar. That was OK, we'd just use our flip-flops, but the wires were a worry. We'd heard about showers like this from other travellers and it seemed that though freakish looking, they actually worked quite well, and no one we'd talked to had been electrocuted...

Tired, we set up camp and made a dinner of white bread rolls and wedges of soggy cheese which when combined with tomatoes weren't too bad. We washed carefully, then climbed onto the groundsheet. Mosquitoes were already beginning to buzz as we lay listening to the rapid speech and overly dramatic sounds of a Spanish soap opera from the television in reception. Beneath that layer of noise came the sounds of trucks rumbling past us in the street outside and the quiet murmur of voices coming from somewhere that was hard to pinpoint. It could have been worse – we dozed.

Suddenly we were woken with a jolt. We'd not realised that the room's only window, a small affair high on the wall, opened out right into the restaurant next door. Someone had turned a jukebox on. Then moments later, the disco on the floor above us in the hotel started up.

The barrage of noise was hitting us from two sides and above. Birgit and I looked at each other horrified. What sort of place was this?

We lay in the sagging bed and giggled hysterically. It couldn't get worse. The bare walls of the room bounced the sounds around until I began to feel that the room was spinning. With a booming salsa beat coming from above, I now knew what it was like to be inside a loudspeaker. Even the ceiling was drumming and vibrating – I think Birgit was still giggling but I could no longer hear her.

It was a long night. The people of Barranca liked to eat late, but eventually the diners left for their homes and the jukebox was turned off. Much later, in the early hours of the morning, the disco-goers clattered down the stairs and headed off drunkenly into the night. Out on the street, only the occasional night-running truck yammered, air brakes blowing, off into the night. The only sound we were left with, apart from the ringing in our ears, was yet another soap on the reception TV.

In the morning we were woken by the sound of tables and chairs scraping across the floor in the restaurant next door. We stared at each other, bleary-eyed. We didn't need to speak. We automatically fell into our routine, though the sensation of flip-flopping across the sticky floor was an odd one. Birgit took the first shower. Seconds later she yelled out at me. The electrical current was running right into the stream of shower water. If she'd not been wearing her rubber flip-flops she'd have had a nasty shock for sure. As it was, the tingle wasn't even at free perm voltage, thankfully, so a shower was quite manageable, unless you made the mistake of touching one of the pipes. That resulted in a nasty surprise that almost bounced your hand away from the pipe, and left it tingling madly. Time to leave.

Our map told us that if we headed a little further north along the Pan American Highway, we'd come to the turning for the town of Huaraz. It nestles between the towering Cordillera Negra and the snow-covered Cordillera Blanca (in Spanish, the black and white ranges, respectively). We'd read that the mountain scenery was stunning and that small picturesque villages were scattered across the Callejón de Huaylas valley. It was time to head for the hills. We were ready for some fresh air, some beauty and keen to get away from the coastal people. The bonus was that we had two choices for getting back down to the sea again later. One was a fairly short loop of just a few hundred kilometres and the other ran right through the Cordillera Blanca until it reached the mountain town of Cajamara. There, the road dropped back down to the coast again. Things were looking good.

Life felt as if it had taken a turn for the better as soon as we were outside Barranca. Almost instantly we found ourselves riding a series of valleys full of sugar cane plants swaying in the breeze. We rode on over small concrete bridges spanning gullies full of cold-looking water. The riverbeds themselves were wide and told of seasonal floods when the snow melted.

The turn off for Huaraz was well signposted; it started level but soon began to climb steeply. It snaked in ever-tighter bends, first following a river and then the contours of the hillsides. It felt really good to be free and climbing into the mountains again. The only worry was that Birgit's altitude sickness would come back. She'd been so knocked by it that even all these weeks later she was still feeling a little off-colour.

But right now, this road demanded our full attention. The drivers of the trucks, buses and cars heading downhill obviously felt they had the right of way and their egos demanded that their descent be made at the fastest possible speed. Every blind corner was a potential 'meet your maker' moment and we were extremely grateful that we had such relatively narrow vehicles. Burnt-out and smashed up wrecks told the tale of those who had not got out of the way quickly enough, or had misjudged the corners in their lemming-like rush to the sea. Some of the smashes must have entailed considerable loss of life, but the wrecks did nothing to deter the speeding macho men.

Each of the buses was like a small slice of Peruvian life collected together on one set of wheels. Coastal dwellers would be hunched into seats with their more western clothes getting scrunched in the squash. Indian people would be colourfully piled in higgledy-piggledy, and their bundles were always easy to spot. No suitcases for them, just brightly coloured cloths and large woven, stripy plastic zip-topped bags. They also seemed to be philosophical travellers, never wide-eyed as their bus rounded a corner on the wrong side of the road almost on two wheels. The other passengers tended to be backpackers and when I saw them scrunched in, and very wide-eyed, I was incredibly happy to be on the bike. Libby was doing me proud – she was giving me the liberty that I craved.

Not far past the village of Cajacay, the road levels out and heads straight on for the long road through the Cordillera Central and then on down into the jungle. Or it turns left across the high plains towards Huaraz. The colours at this altitude are fabulous. Everything looks as if you are seeing it through crystal-clear lenses. Objects are sharp-edged and the colours of the plains and the mountain ranges are vibrant and crisp.

The air in the shade was bitterly cold, but out riding in the sunshine was incredibly pleasant. One side of my body was warm while the other was being chilled. But long, sweeping curves allowed every angle to catch and soak up the sun – with the layers of clothes we had on neither of us was cold – just exhilarated. With hardly any other traffic and good visibility we could let the bikes do their own thing, and they cruised seemingly unaffected by the thin air.

The road meandered alongside a river for much of the way along the valley, and dotted along its banks as we neared Huaraz we found very pretty, traditionally-built clusters of houses. These were occupied by Quechua Indians whom I found to be friendly and always open for a laugh or a cheerful smile. The women wore pretty, traditional layered skirts called Llikllas but the men now dress less traditionally. We liked their sandals made out of recycled vehicle tyres. The families seemed to grow crops at subsistence level around their houses and always had a few pigs and chickens pottering around. We were told that the Indians also bred guinea pigs for the table, but we were never invited into a home so we didn't manage to check that out for ourselves.

To some, Huaraz would have been a disappointment. It certainly wasn't pretty. In the 1970s a major earthquake had almost flattened the city and more than 10,000 people had died. Prior to that, the city had been a maze of small, cobbled streets and a combination of beautiful old adobe houses with tiled roofs, and others made from basic mud bricks. Now the streets had been widened and most of the buildings were made of concrete. But the passing of time and nature were softening and reclaiming to a certain extent. Flowering shrubs were looping up and over buildings, easing the hard edges, and down in the streets the sheer diversity of inhabitants and visitors made the town into an intriguing place. Huaraz is the centre of life for many of the mountain people and from it they get all the things they can't grow. The market was busy and people moved with a bustling intent. Horses and donkeys inhabited the streets just as much as cars and buses. But where the vehicles left a tang of pollution in the air, the animals left the smell of fresh dung and the acrid scent of urine behind. To me that was preferable to the carbon monoxide.

For me the best thing about the place was the view. From the centre of Huaraz I could see Huscaran, Peru's largest mountain, and around it we could see twenty other snow-capped peaks, all of which are over 5,000 metres high.

The cheese that we found in the market was good news too. I'd been craving hard cheese. In fact a strong mature cheddar and fresh milk were pretty much the only items from home that I missed. Most of the cheese we'd been able to find since Chile had been soft and white which though quite pleasant, had no 'bite' at all. This stuff was superb in comparison.

The bad news was that the roads we wanted to take down out of the mountains were both closed. Landslides were to blame. No one knew how long it would take for them to be cleared and each person we asked was certain that we'd not manage to wiggle the bikes over or past them.

It was our chance to ride the reckless road back down to the coast and because we knew the bends we could have some fun. But we weren't going to push our luck quite as far as the trucks and buses had!

We'd have to stay in Barranca again – though nothing would have persuaded us to return to the Casanova for a second night. We'd spend the extra money and find a better alternative. We made sure we arrived back in the town with plenty of time to hunt for a decent hotel and found the perfect place just a kilometre from the Casanova. The Los Paroles was from a different planet; it had sparklingly clean rooms, a courtyard to park the bikes in, and there wasn't a restaurant or disco within either sight or earshot. Perfect – and it only cost about twenty cents more! The moral of the story is to avoid arriving in a town just before it gets dark, unless you really have no choice.

The words El Niño had been on people's lips ever since we'd come back to South America. While we'd been in the UK and I'd been working my way through the physio exercises, thinking that I was living in a disaster, a real disaster had been going on. The effects of El Niño had hit the coastal areas of Peru and Ecuador with awesome results. Thousands had died and more than half a million people had been left homeless. The fishing industry, Peru's second largest, had been devastated with a drop of ninety percent in production in some areas. The news had been on the television in the UK but it had been the usual downplay of anything foreign that wasn't to do with a war that we were involved in. We'd arrived back in South America with no concept of how bad things had been, or how much it was going to affect our journey. We were about to move into the region that had been worst affected.

The landslides on the roads between Huaraz and Casma, and Huaraz and Trujillo were the first time that we had been directly affected – that we were aware of. I did cast my mind back to the downtrodden and sullen inhabitants of the coastal towns and villages further south. From what I'd now learned it was quite reasonable for the people to have behaved this way because they'd recently been well and truly battered by the storms. Many had lost their jobs and their belongings. What reason did they have to smile? I suspected that in their shoes I too would have regarded those passing through my world with tired disinterest.

El Niño simply means 'the little boy' in Spanish, but it also means 'The Christ Child'. It comes from the fact that the phenomenon starts around Christmastime. El Niño occurs when there are changes in the normal patterns of trade wind circulation.

270

These winds usually move westward, carrying the warm surface water to Indonesia and Australia. This allows the cooler water to well up along the South American coast. No one really knows why, but sometimes these winds can be reduced, or even reversed. This moves the warmer waters toward the coast of South America. At the peak of this occurrence, a pool of hot water the size of Canada and up to four hundred metres deep was measured, stretching out from the coast of Peru and Ecuador. When the water is warmer like this, it causes heat and moisture to rise from the ocean, resulting in storms and torrential rainfall. Also, as the cooler coastal waters of the Humboldt Current are prevented from welling up, this seriously disrupts the oceanic food chains.

Every three to seven years, an El Niño event is a big one. During the past forty years, ten of these events have been recorded, and the worst one by a very long way had just happened. Storms had pounded the coast in apocalyptic proportions. Rivers burst their banks and the sea surged inland, in some places for fifteen kilometres. Cities that could often go a decade without any rainfall were suddenly flooded, and hundreds of kilometres of roads were completely trashed. In just one area – La Liberdad near the city of Trujillo – forty three out of fifty six bridges were wrecked. The collateral damage was grim. Apparently, the city's cemetery was washed away leaving hundreds of cadavers and coffins to float around the city streets.

Throughout Peru over three hundred bridges had been destroyed and entire villages had been washed away. The former Peruvian Prime Minister, Alberto Pandolfi, said, "There is virtually no aspect of life in this part of the world that was not affected by El Niño this time."

Reports from Ecuador, the next country on our route, were saying that the damage was so severe that it would take the country a decade to recover. Outbreaks of cholera were being reported. After Ecuador we planned to move on to Colombia. There, the bandits and drug smugglers were playing their dangerous games and the country was becoming politically unstable again. It looked as if we had some difficult months ahead. But some interesting facts were beginning to emerge.

I read a report on El Niño that proposed the idea that the French Revolution of 1789 came about partly as a result of a severe occurrence of El Niño. The phenomenon doesn't just affect South America. It can cause hurricanes and tornados, and cause drought and therefore poor harvests in many parts of the world. Just such a poor harvest was thought to be part of the cause of the uprising in France.

In northern Peru the recent storms had created a lake in the middle of the desert three hundred kilometres long, forty kilometres wide and ten metres deep. The myth surrounding the lake was that it was stocked with fish that had been lying dormant in the sands and had come to life with the rains. That idea had to be rubbish, didn't it?

We set off riding tentatively into the deserts of northern Peru. Birgit had picked the brains of the owner of the Los Paroles and she'd marked the back of our map with the following comments: road to Chimbote – open; road to Trujillo – open; road to Chiclayo – closed; alternative road through mountains could be possible. Road to Tumbes – passable; road to Piuria – closed but an alternative route possible.

The things I remember most from this section of our journey are the heat, the trashed roads, and the absence of warnings about the missing bridges. On some bridges there were a few rocks scattered around but hey, that was quite normal so why should we take any notice of them? The tell-tale warning was a track heading off into the scrub in the direction of the river just before the bridge. Night driving would have been distinctly dodgy.

Some of the rivers were now only centimetres deep and for us they were fun and rather exciting to ride across – even with soft sand beneath the surface they were just an adventure. At one crossing Birgit got talking to a local man who was mooring a small boat. He told us the nightmare story of the day the bridge came down. Above us stood the mangled concrete, tarmac and twisted steel remains of a thirty-metre high, two hundred metre long bridge.

He said, "It started with a strong breeze that shook the bushes and the trees. As it built in intensity it picked up the desert sands and began to hurl them against anything that got in the way. My boat once had more paint on it than this. The wind then blew incredibly strongly and the rains started to come. At first the rain was good to have, but within minutes it was raining so hard that the road flooded. As the water came off the desert the river filled fast – very fast. I'd never seen the waters rise so quickly. We had white water out there and the river was pulling trees and bushes out by the roots. These came rushing past us and if anything got in the way you could see it being pounded. At this time vehicles were still crossing the bridge, but they were doing so very slowly. It was impossible to see for more than a few metres. The river came up over the banks here, and it washed much of the bank right away. I was sheltering in my hut but the wind took my roof off and once it had done that, the walls started to give way – they were made of mud bricks you see. Then I saw something strange. The bridge was moving! All around the pillars, things were collecting and the river was flowing faster and faster. I'd never seen it like this. Then the bridge started to fall. It was lucky no-one was on it at the time – there was a big queue on each side but no-one dared to go up onto the bridge. They were afraid of being blown off, but they didn't think that the bridge would collapse. Yes, they were very lucky. Now we have no bridge. I wonder if they will find the money to build a new one."

When we heard this story Birgit and I knew that we too had been very lucky. If we'd not flown home to the UK when we did then we would have been on this road when El Niño had struck.

At the Casa Suiza hostal in the fishing village of Huanchaco we had a very nice surprise. We headed for this town because we both wanted to see the caballitos that the village was famous for. These are one-person reed boats that the fishermen use on a daily basis. Their fat-bottomed, high-pointed bow design can be traced right back to the Incas. If we were on the beach at 5am, then we'd be able to see the fishing 'fleet' heading out through the surf. It was supposed to be an impressive sight.

We headed for the Casa Suiza on the advice of other travellers. They told us that the owners, Elizabeth and Oscar, were great hosts and that they ran an immaculate hostal. We'd also been told that they had off road parking for the bikes and were extremely biker-friendly people too. It sounded like a bit of overlanders' paradise, so this was a town that just couldn't be missed.

Guy and Marlene, whom we'd last seen in Patagonia, had also decided that this was a 'must-see, must-stay' sort of place. Just a few hours after we'd arrived, they rolled up on their big red BMW R1100GS. We'd thought that, with the three months we'd had off the trail, they'd have been long gone, even though we knew they were slow travellers.

Peruvian wine is not as good as that of Argentina or Chile, but it was certainly good enough for a reunion party. With our friendship re-cemented and endless tales of our separate adventures told, we all decided that it would be rather fun to travel together for a while. This was unusual for Birgit and me, as we mostly felt that we were better off on our own but those thoughts didn't apply with Guy and Marlene. In any event the plan to travel together was going to be a loose one; we could go our separate ways any time we liked.

We set off across the Sechura Desert together. Before we'd come to Peru I'd had a picture of the country being a green and rather lush place. That image was in my mind, perhaps, because the bulk of my knowledge of the country came from television programmes about the Incas living in the mountains, and tales of the Amazon. Perhaps the desert just wasn't interesting enough to be filmed very often or perhaps it was an area of the country that Peruvians just weren't keen on publicising.

As always with a holiday or an adventure, even on a long trip such as this, there never seemed to be enough time to do everything. The choice on the road was either to spend loads of time swotting up about the next country and miss out on the things to discover where we were, or else arrive in each country knowing enough not to make cultural blunders and knowing enough to have a taste for the history and the sites that one 'should' see. Birgit and I preferred the latter option, and we really enjoyed the combination of word-of-mouth recommendation and stumbling across things.

The amount of Peru that was pure desert was a shock. We'd spent weeks riding through cold desert lands where my instinct had told me there would be none. The Sechura – all 188,735 square kilometres of it – was more of the same but with a difference. Numerous short rivers cross this desert and the banks of those rivers have supported human settlements for many generations. The people survive on fish, guinea pigs, squash and peanuts. When the moisture from the rivers combines with dense fog life can flourish. The fog rolls in off the cold sea currents. When it condenses it allows quite a few very hardy species of plants to survive well away from the rivers. This desert was also the place that La Niña lake was supposed to have been formed by El Niño. We wanted to see it for ourselves.

It was true. There, in the middle of the desert, stood a lake. By the time we got to it the waters had shrunk to a fraction of their original size. And yes, there were people out fishing on the lake. I was stunned. Was the story true? Was it possible for dormant fish to have come to life?

I knew that happened with plants but had never heard of it happening with fish. Perhaps there were some sorts of fish eggs that could survive and come to life in this way. It just sounded really far-fetched. But how else would the fish have got there? Another theory was that the waves from the sea had been so big that they had thrown fish up into the clouds and the clouds had carried them overland to deposit them in the newly-formed lake. Was that possible? It sounded far too daft. There were even sea-going fishing boats on the water, and the shore of the lake was covered in so many fish-drying racks that there must have been a considerable quantity of fish in the lake.

Another story was that the government had rapidly stocked the lake with fish, but I couldn't understand that either. Surely they'd been too busy dealing with the chaos of the aftermath of El Niño to be messing around with collecting, carrying and delivering fish in a large enough quantity for this level of industry to have been warranted?

There weren't even any rivers running close enough to have overflowed and stocked the lake. It was a total mystery. Deciding that I really liked the whole concept of the lake in the desert and its fishy mystery with no obvious answer, I chose to leave it that way. When we left the lake I asked no more questions and read nothing more on the phenomenon. The mystery would remain, for me at least.

Chapter 15

Chaos and loving it

'Fear is that little darkroom where negatives are developed.'

Michael Pritchard

The border between Peru and Ecuador is one of those rare lines on the colonialists' maps that makes perfect geographical sense, and doesn't stomp over historical tribal lines. In fact much of the border remains more or less the same as it was in Inca times.

On the southern, Peruvian side are the deserts and mountains that were ruled from Cusco by one regal Inca brother, and on the other side of the frontier the countryside is made up of more mountains, jungle and the wet sierra coastal lands which were ruled by the other regal brother from his base in Quito, which is now the capital of Ecuador. Soon we would be crossing the equator, from which Ecuador takes its name, but first we had the border crossing to contend with.

As we rode in convoy towards Aqua Verdes, the last town in Peru, I knew that the situation was politically tense between Peru and Ecuador. There had been a major argument between the two countries over land down in the jungle and this territorial dispute had recently resulted in fighting right along the border there. Peru was supposed to have won but Ecuador still disputed their claim to the land and relations between the two countries were fraught, to say the least. I wondered how this might affect our passage but there was no point in worrying about it: what would be would be.

The day had started sadly but still with a positive twist. We'd stayed in a small beach hostal called the Casa Blanca on the edge of the town of Mancora – close to the border. Before loading up the bikes, Birgit and I went for an early morning stroll on the beach. It might be a long day and a limber up on the sand seemed like a great idea. It was also a moment of peace before the hassle of the day began, and a chance to take stock of our time in Peru, before getting into the new adventures that were about to begin.

The light was the typical pale silver-blue which heralds the dawn so often along a coastline. The air tasted strongly of the salty tang of the sea, and the beach sands were a very pale grey which seemed to blend perfectly with the colours of the sky. Even the water seemed to be conspiring to tone itself in with the land and the air above. Gentle and opaque, grey waves rolled in and crested just short of the sand before hurrying up to the high water mark. After a moment's hesitation the water streamed back towards the ocean, pulling with it grains of sand and tumbling small seashells and bits of wood as it went.

Out of this, a large elderly dark grey seal staggered and stumbled to dry land. Every movement he made looked as if it was incredibly hard work. He manoeuvred his bulk in slow jerks, with each flipper digging deep into the sand. His head bobbed heavily each time he moved forward. He huffed and puffed and wheezed. He looked and sounded as if he were suffering, as if he was about to keel over and die. I stood watching this painfully sad sight, wondering why he had chosen this stretch of sand to come to die on. It felt odd that he would choose to die so near to people. Just a kilometre in either direction he would have had the privacy and peace of empty beaches.

When he came to a stop he flopped his head heavily to the sand, and lay there motionless. The only signs of life were a slight flaring from his nostrils and the occasional blink from large brown and tired eyes. Every so often we could see small puffs of drying sand lift up from where his nostrils were almost touching the ground. We were not alone though. Seagulls screeched and called to each other as they swooped and curled above us – it was almost as if they sensed death, and a feast, but they weren't the real danger.

A local man had been attracted by the seagulls and had decided to act. Where we had elected to let nature take its course and for the seal to die at its own pace, and in relative peace, this man had decided he was going to speed the process along. Before we knew it, or could stop him, he had found a large rock and to our stunned surprise, set about trying to pound the seal to death with it.

I was horrified, but then I remembered the road back in Africa when the dog had run out in front of Birgit and I was faced with trying to put the beast out of its misery. I'd chickened out; perhaps this man was just braver or more matter-of-fact about things than I was. The seal might have been dying but he still had some survival instincts. He heaved himself up, flinching as the rocks continued to beat him, and before we could stop the man, the seal shuffled back to the water.

Seeing the seal move off and us running towards him, the man dropped his rock, turned around and strode away across the beach. The seal made it back to the safety of the sea and disappeared into the waves. This set the mood for the day, but in a positive way. The seal's determination and gentle dignity seemed like a message to us, in some bizarre way.

Chaos started early at the border – but I found myself loving it. The atmosphere was electric. It seemed as if everyone was supercharged. Being early in the morning, everyone still had energy. There was laughter, hurried movement, wheeling and dealing, cursing, noise, eclectic colour, worry, stress, anxiousness and more laughter.

Every traveller's need was being catered for along the roadside to the border. All sorts of goods and services were on sale: bags, coffee, tamales, biscuits, shoes, a porter to help you with your bags, a tout to obtain your photocopies, a Peruvian flag, a hunk of meat, dried or fresh fish. And the moneychangers buzzed around us like persistent flies. They didn't have any luck at all. We'd spent the last of our soles on petrol just before we'd got to the border. This was a risky thing to do, but we knew that there'd be no official fees to pay to leave the country and if we didn't have any money then the unofficial fees would be very hard to pay.

This was the first time we'd done this. Usually we had some money within reach just in case we hadn't understood the rules and there really was a fee of some sort that had to be paid. But this time we knew there wasn't and were darned if we were going to be tempted to pay a bribe. That would have broken my record – I still hadn't paid anyone any baksheesh anywhere.

At one time this border crossing had had an appalling reputation for bribes and 'additional fee' demands, but now it was supposed to be OK. The government had cracked down, or so we'd been told. The new levels of enforcement didn't stop one of the customs officers from demanding fifteen soles each for the privilege of getting the bikes out of Peru. Birgit and Marlene dealt with this man admirably. They refused point blank and made it clear that they knew the rules.

I was glad for Birgit that she had a friend who spoke good Spanish to help her through the system. Guy and I did our manly duty of guarding the bikes and the kit.

Peru and Ecuador are separated by a river at this point, which is spanned by the 'International Bridge', as it is called. It was packed with people rushing in a disorderly manner from one country to the next. I had the feeling that all of them were muttering "Time is money, time is money". But the reality was probably only that they knew how long this border crossing could take, and we were far more relaxed because we didn't. By the time we were rolled onto the bridge it was 12.50, but at least we were half way there.

As we rode under the 'Welcome to Ecuador' banner that hung over the bridge, four hours and ten minutes of farce and fascination began. You can do nothing without your immigration papers, but the immigration office where you got those papers was three kilometres away and we were not allowed to take the bikes to get there. Birgit and Marlene took a taxi, only to find that it was closed and that they should come back at two-thirty. Rather than have Guy and I worrying about them, they hitched a ride on the back of a truck, back to the border. When they arrived it wasn't hard to find us. We were the ones that looked like a couple of honeycombs with moneychanger 'bees' crawling all over us. They had extraordinary persistence.

After much discussion about much they would give us for our dollars, a figure was agreed upon. We knew what the official exchange rate was and theirs was slightly better so it seemed like a good idea to go with it. We'd earn ourselves a few beers out of it, but it was a good thing to have a little loot to hand, and of course we could enjoy the experience to the full. And so we did, but not in the way we thought we were going to.

The moneychangers didn't want to give us the money before we gave them ours. They counted the money so quickly it was hard to keep up with them. There was some real sleight-of-hand going on too. Pre-counted notes would be eased out of the bundle until there was nothing like the number there should have been in the wedge of loot. Very clever stuff – but we were smarter. We'd seen every one of their games before and were watching out for them. Having four of us really helped too. While Guy and I bargained, the girls were able to take over bike-watching duty. It's at moments like this that you're most vulnerable to things going missing off the bikes.

We had the advantage over the moneychangers: we didn't actually need any of their money. We had fuel, food and our credit cards. If the worst came to the worst we could even change money in a bank! Finally, when we thought they'd got the message that they had to deal fairly with us, they tried it on once more, and lost out. The moneychangers were outraged that they'd put so much effort in, but had come away with nothing. Birgit admonished them: "We may be foreigners but that doesn't mean you can treat us unfairly!" Enough said and we certainly didn't feel as if we'd lost out. If anything, the guys had been good entertainment in spite of their hassling style, and the time until the immigration office opened had passed quickly.

Before long Birgit and Marlene returned, this time having hitched a ride in a police car! We suspected that a little flirting had been going on! Then, after the customs check, we could all weave our way through the stalls, shops, goats, children, a snuffling pig scoffing something disgusting right in front of a stand selling what looked and smelled like pig burgers, in and out of pot holes and around a few kamikaze cyclists. When we'd done this, we had to argue to be allowed to park the bikes anywhere near the immigration office where we had to get all the papers stamped and signed off. It seemed that the car park around the edge of the building was not actually intended for cars but for queues of people to snake their way towards one or other of the various offices.

Inside the concrete building, in a first floor office, sat a young man who for once had no film star pretensions – though the large wart on the end of his nose wouldn't have helped him to get a starring role. At the other desk sat an older man who didn't smile and had no distinguishing features at all. He had one of those faces that would fit a thousand passport photos; he would have been better suited to being a smuggler rather than an immigration officer. He didn't smile as he gazed at us; if anything, the look on his face was a sleepy and bored "I should be having an extended siesta" expression.

El Jefe, the colonel, wasn't back from lunch yet – he was off at the hairdresser's. This didn't stop the younger man diligently and painstakingly attaching the various stick-on and rubber stamps to the four sets of documents that were spread out before him.

As he finished doing this, the older man got up, picked up a large bowl of water and emptied it out of the open window. The sounds of numerous people spluttering came from below – he'd just water-bombed the queue. Birgit asked him, "Why did you do that Señor?" "Because it's fun!" he replied with a wicked grin.

Eventually the colonel returned. His hair was spiffy and he was the one with the film star looks. His crew were probably hand-picked so that he didn't have any competition. He was incongruous though – instead of an impressive military uniform he sported an old and baggy rose-coloured jogging suit. His tongue seemed to have been well oiled and with Guy and me outside, he had free reign to flirt with Birgit and Marlene. They told us later that it'd been hard not to laugh out loud.

By the time we finally escaped it felt as if we'd all achieved something. We were in. If the truth be told, it was Birgit and Marlene who'd done the real work while Guy and I were doing our 'heavy' act by the bikes. It was too late in the day to ride on, so we stopped for the night in Huaquillas, the Ecuadorian border town. Ecuador loves its checkpoints. Close to the border, the police, the army, immigration and customs all had a go. By the time the army were demanding to know where I was carrying my AK47 assault rifle, Guy had had enough and had blasted off down the road in disgust.

The solders on the gun hunt seemed to think that this was very rude of him, and were quite perplexed that I wasn't carrying a gun. I had the feeling that they were sure I was travelling with one and that they were very frustrated that my hiding-place for it was beating them. Eventually they let us go and we found Guy and Marlene down the road and round a corner. Guy was still fuming at the stupidity of the soldiers – normally he was incredibly laid-back but this episode really pulled his chain. I was glad he hadn't hung around!

Then we took a wrong turning. We'd had enough of the El Niño-lashed coastal roads and were delighted at the sight of jungle. We wanted  more and our map showed a useful-looking secondary road that headed roughly in the right direction. The road we ended up on, only headed very roughly in the right direction. It was a mixture of dirt and gravel. Had El Niño not trashed so many roads we might have become suspicious a little earlier. I was already having problems with what my internal compass was telling me but ignored it – the map had to be more or less right, didn't it?

If it had been raining, the road would have given us a grim, slippery ride. Luckily it was as dry as a bone and the graded, dark reddish-brown earth track took us swooping through the jungle with such a contrast to the rides of the previous days that it was a complete and utter joy. Even the bikes seemed to revel in having something interesting to do. Our loads were perfectly balanced and though the occasional ridges and potholes kept us awake, the ride was almost done in a jungle green dream – except when there were army checkpoints that is.

The number of checkpoints should have made us realise that we were riding along a little-used track that skirted the border. The fact that the soldiers were so surprised to see us should have been the next clue – though we were used to being stared at, because of our novelty value. It should also have struck us as being strange that there were villages where our map said there were none, and where there were supposed to be towns we didn't find any. At the time I wondered if they were off a side road that we'd missed. Not a logical thought really, though the map we had was probably the worst I'd ridden with to date. Eventually one of the soldiers at a big checkpoint helped the penny drop. Thankfully we didn't seem to have trodden on anyone's toes, the guards had been happy to see something new going on, and we were pretty much at the end of the track anyway.

By this time we were back up in the mountains and they seemed like old friends. I loved the constantly bending roads and the views were stunning. I like riding above the clouds. It felt quite unnatural and was a delightful thing to be able to do whenever the opportunity arose. It's bizarre to be on a bike looking down at clouds, as if you were doing so from an aeroplane. The downside was that it was much colder at this altitude. Birgit said that the temperature and landscape reminded her of Austria.

As we approached the market town of Vilcabamba, Henry's exhaust started to make strange noises. I was riding in my favourite position as 'Tail-end Charlie' and I could hear the tone change and wondered what was going on. It sounded nasty. By the time we stopped for a break, Birgit had noticed it too. It wasn't strange that she hadn't heard it earlier because the slipstream carries a lot of noises away with it – particularly those that are created behind you. It was nothing major but the problem would cause a bit of a tease over the following months. Henry's exhaust was rotting and as holes were appearing the bike was becoming noisier. As a temporary repair we cut open a soft drinks can and stuck it over the holes with heatproof tape. It worked for a while.

The road between Loja and Cuenca was supposed to be one of the most beautiful in Ecuador so we didn't want to miss it, particularly since there were Indian villages along the way that were described as  places where time had virtually stood still. In one of them, Saraguro, there was supposed to be a market on a Sunday that was pure Indian and nothing for the tourists. We were a little sceptical as we thought that if we'd heard about it then surely the locals would have found a way to make some money out of visitors. But since it was an out-of-the-way village and as we were going to be arriving on a Saturday night, it seemed too good a chance to miss.

The Indian inhabitants of Ecuador dressed very differently from those of Peru. The women seemed to favour dark, loose skirts and cloaks of a rich blue-black which they draped over brilliantly white blouses. The cloaks were held in place by large and intricately decorated silver broaches and they wore dark, wide, flat-brimmed hats which kept the sun out of their eyes

The men in this town were very different. They were all wearing shorts and sported a sort of apron of a type I'd never seen before. I thought they looked great, but that they must have been really hardy people to be wearing shorts on a day that was so cold I could see my breath! I felt at home with the men as we all sported long plaited ponytails.

The people were incredibly friendly and were quite taken by Birgit being so fascinated by their technique for spinning wool. Birgit seemed to be able to make friends anywhere we went and I think it was due to her genuine interest in people and their skills. The women here happily showed her how to spin wool in their style.

They had a long stick onto which they had twisted a large clump of knotted rough wool. With one end of the stick gripped firmly under an arm they would tease out a twist of wool and fix it to something that looked like a cross between a knitting needle and a spinning top. As the women sat talking, they were all happily twisting and spinning away at the clump of wool until it almost miraculously found itself wrapped in a regular-sized thread around the 'needle'.

The road north was hard going, not so much with its technical difficulty but for the fact that the surface was frequently wet. It also varied from loose gravel to mud and there were some impressive potholes. To be able to enjoy the view we had to stop and look. Life was very different up here and along the roadside were things that were endlessly fascinating.

We passed a brick factory, tucked into the side of a hill, where the labour was done by stocky, tanned men who controlled equally stocky horses, whose job it was to work straw into the mud with their hooves. The horses were tied to a pole fixed to a spike in the ground.

They walked around this pole, heads down, for hours while the men added more water, more straw, or took shovels of the mixture which they then smeared into moulds. The horses of course were adding their own special ingredients to the mix as the day went on. Metres of brown bricks were being laid out to dry in the thin mountain air.

A little further on we passed a man and woman, both traditionally dressed, who had both just finished cooking a pig, whole.

 It was a giant of a pig with all its extremities still attached. They had it skewered on a long pole wedged into a sort of trestle as if it was important for the pig to be able to watch passers-by with its dead eyes. Its skin was completely blackened and the people were using large machetes to shave off any remaining bristles. The scraping was also rasping off the layer of soot, and this was leaving a golden reddish-brown layer of crispy skin.

Small boys were out collecting firewood. They were doing so on wooden-wheeled, wooden-framed scooters. These things were very low to the ground and the kids piled them high with branches that they'd cut to roughly a metre in length. I was stunned by the speed at which they scooted down the hillsides. The things had no brakes that I could see, and with their wooden wheels they must have given a really bone-shaking ride. Having said that, perhaps riding one required the same technique as riding corrugations – go fast enough, and you smooth out the bumps.

It was now time to split up with Guy and Marlene for a while – our plans didn't match. If things worked out, we'd all meet up again in Quito and perhaps we'd travel together some more.

Riding on through the mountains, we were now following a meandering route towards Quito, but first we wanted to get down into the jungle on the Amazon side and then we wanted to get up close to one of the many volcanoes that dot Ecuador's countryside. Even though we'd seen quite a lot of volcanoes in Chile and in Peru, the sight of them never failed to fascinate Birgit and me. And as we were getting towards the end of the Andes we knew that we'd soon be running out of volcanoes to look at.

The road into the jungle was fun. It was beaten up, potholed, gravel upon which we battled with the buses for right of way. Well, we mentally battled with them, but gave them the right of way – size matters!

These buses were great. They were beaten-up old truck-beds upon which a roof had been built to give protection from the rain. The sides however were almost completely open; they were painted bright colours and were always packed full. Their drivers had decorated them with tinsel, swinging tassels and pompoms, and the buses reminded me a little of their Pakistani cousins.

To add an element of fun to the road as it dropped ever downward and got dramatically worse, the cliffs from which it had been gouged shot plumes of water over us. Below these waterfalls the surface was always an adventure. The gravel had been washed away leaving rounded boulders in its place. Of course with the water teeming down it wasn't possible to see exactly what we were riding over, but thankfully neither of us fell off.

Back up into the mountains again we skirted the majestic Chimboraso Volcano, which thrust up to tower above us. It was a beautiful day but the price for the clear blue sunny sky was the chill in the air. My hands in particular were freezing. They hadn't been as cold as this since southern Chile, but up here at least there wasn't any wind to deal with. The road continued to be good, varying from gravel to asphalt, and back again to gravel. It felt absolutely superb to be fit enough to be riding roads like these. Admittedly I was keeping any 'Paris-Dakar' bursts of enthusiasm under control, but at least I was riding them. It had only been a few months since the doctors had told me that I was probably going to end up in a wheelchair. That thought made me realise that I was incredibly happy.

I had a great girl by my side, I had a bike that was a joy to ride and I was travelling through a sun-filled land packed with one awesome view after another. Life couldn't get much better – warm hands would have been nice though!

We wanted to get up to the tiny Indian Village of Zumbahua and then, if we could, up to the rim of the Quilotoa Volcano crater. If we were going to spend time in a backwater mountain village, then this was the place to do it. There were only two places to stay and one of them had an appalling reputation.

The main street of Zumbahua was on roughly twenty levels because the weather had been well and truly at it. Great rivulets ran from one side to the other, joining the potholes and the ditches that trucks and buses had made when the conditions were muddy. Since the last rains though, the edges of these different surfaces had become rounded and quite smooth, so riding a bike up and down them wasn't a hassle, just a challenge. It was a little like riding along a riverbed full of rounded boulders.

We managed to snag a room in the good hostal but parking the bikes was a problem. There was absolutely nowhere around the hotel that would be safe, and to add some difficulty to the situation it looked as if there had been a wedding or a festival going on. The road was full of drunken Indian men who were having real problems negotiating the various levels of the road. Some had given up and were sitting, bottle in hand, with their heads nodding gently from side to side as if they were each listening to music that only they could hear. All had their legs splayed out in front of them and it was probably only this that was somehow keeping their rubbery bodies upright. They were completely harmless though – not even a hint of danger about them, but one of them could easily have fallen against the bikes and done some real damage to both themselves and the bikes. The local cottage hospital came to the rescue and allowed us to park inside their compound.

In the morning at 6am, the village Saturday market started up and there wasn't a single thing on display that could be considered touristy. The items for sale had either been produced up in the little farms that dotted the land, or were there to help the farmers do their work. The atmosphere was excellent, especially around the women who cackled and bargained their way through the morning. The men all looked pretty sore headed!

287

To get to the crater we had to ride up a very rough track that would have been an interesting ride even if we hadn't had the bikes loaded up with kit. By the time we got to the crater, and had found a place to stay in the little hamlet just below the rim, we'd had enough. The air was really thin too, but this time, thankfully, Birgit wasn't struggling with the altitude, though she told me later that she was worried about what the road might be doing to my back.

Our lodgings were a really basic mud hut which had the luxury of having a tin roof. It'd do nicely and that night, a pig, a couple of llamas and a handful of chickens kept watch over the bikes for us.

To my surprise, the short walk to the top of the crater took it out of me. I was huffing and puffing like an old steam engine. With all the riding, I hadn't been doing enough walking and as a result I'd got out of shape. As we scrambled around the rim and marvelled at the views down into the crater, which seemed to stretch forever below us, I decided that this walk would be my first on the road back to fitness.

The bottom of the crater was filled with a lake that was a startling shade of deep blue-green. When I stood on the rim and slowly revolved, I could see the snowy tops of other volcanoes in the distance, and the soft almost delicate shades of browns and pale greens of the grasslands below.

I'd now been on the road for well over six years and for the first time since year one, the thought popped into my mind that one day the trip would have to end. I wondered if the trip, now I'd had this thought, would begin to feel as if it were running downhill. That would be grim – downhill can mean going faster, or getting worse. Neither option suited me.

But another downhill option did. Birgit and I headed for the coast again. We wanted to see what it was like to ride through the plantations and forest that run along the coast of Ecuador. It was also a good excuse to get out of the wind and the cold. Altitude may offer some magnificent views and at the right time of year the temperatures could be pretty much perfect – an escape from the heat of the lowlands – but we were running more than four months later than planned by this time, and the weather was not ideal for mountain motorcycling.

The next few days of riding gave us just about every road condition imaginable, other than motorway. Sometimes the changes in road type happened abruptly, within seconds, and that meant that there was no time to get complacent in the muggy warmth. We rode through kilometre after kilometre of jungle, rolling grassy hillsides with battered haciendas clinging to the land, past vast fields of sugar cane and through acres of banana plantation. The names of some of the world's largest growers and exporters of bananas were very much in evidence. The plantations were owned by Dole, Bonita and Del Monte – I'd only ever seen those names on stickers on fruit, or printed onto the sides of cardboard boxes in the greengrocer's at home.

Here, the names related to never-ending rows of lush green, stubby, leaf-rustling banana trees whose bunches of fruit were all clad in what looked like opaque blue condoms. These were for protection against the many bugs that can attack the fruit. Supposedly they also made the perfect homes for the dreaded banana spiders. These fearless and aggressive creatures are supposed to have the most painful sting of all spiders, and in some circumstances their venom is powerful enough to kill a human being. I didn't envy the farmers.

When we weren't battling with the road, we cruised past towns and villages with names such as Santa Lucia, Palestina, Balzar, Santo Domingo de los Colerados, and Rosa Zarate. I wondered who Rosa had been to have a town named after her, but no one could tell me. It was as if her memory lived on in name only in this small town on the road to Esmeraldas.

We weren't interested in going to the city port of Esmeraldas. I'd read about the vicious gang warfare that had been going on there and we understood that it was a large dirty city. But it does have a unique history. It was once known as the 'Republic of the Blacks'. Until relatively recent times the only access to the city was by sea, and as it was so isolated, an unusual population developed there. In the times when African slaves were imported to work in the mines and the sugar plantations, some escaped or swam ashore having survived shipwrecks.

With a combination of violence and breeding with the indigenous people, they eventually took control of the area and the coast became a safe haven for escaping negro slaves from all over South America.

The greater percentage of the population is still of African extraction and it felt really strange to be in a place that had black people, significant poverty, and humid temperatures. It felt like we were riding into a little bit of Africa. So it seemed odd to have the signposts around the edge of the city in Spanish and people talking to each other in Spanish. I rode thinking that life had suddenly turned into a well-dubbed movie.

Nowadays the tourist board has been at work and when the unique jungle environment is combined with white sand beaches to the south, it makes their task of selling the area much easier. Conservation projects are encouraged and that also acts as a draw for the tourist dollar. But we were heading south looking for quiet sandy beaches of our own. This section of coast is well known for its mangroves and these were something neither of us had seen before.

As we headed further south from the city, the El Niño destruction was much in evidence. The shape of the land forms a protective spur for Esmeraldas but here the blast of the storm was very clear to see. There had obviously been quite a loss but the locals were resiliently putting their world back together again. In spite of that, I couldn't help wondering how many people had lost their dreams and their security forever. Most, like those further south, would not have been able to afford insurance.

We found what we were looking for on the coast between the towns of Atacamas and Galera. The tiny camping spot was amongst the mangroves on a river, just metres from a beautiful and sheltered beach with steep headlands at either end. The high water line on the beach was strewn with driftwood, including whole trees, ripped up by the roots and flung into the sea by the storms. They were so inter-twined that they looked like some sort of Tolkien-esque giant nest for mythical ravens.

They also looked as if they had been through an industrial potato peeler; the stems and branches had all been stripped of their leaves and bark. This revealed a beautiful selection of colours ranging from silky creams and starkly white woods, to rich reds and deep dark browns. Nature had formed this extremely bizarre piece of over-sized modern art, but had done so in a way that seemed to be almost spookily unnatural.

The campsite was perfect apart from the plague of mosquitoes under the mangroves, which could even bite through clothes. There were no facilities so we washed ourselves in the strong and muddy flow of the river. As we did so, with the mangroves hanging out above us over the river, I wondered how many chemicals there were in the water. The river had been collecting run-off from the farms and plantations on its way to the sea. I thought perhaps that if the water was full of chemical rubbish then maybe it'd be the right mix to keep the mossies away. It wasn't!

We took a little holiday on this beach. It was the sort of place where time easily stands still. There's plenty of fascination around to keep you occupied and the muggy, mud-scented heat from the mangroves was comfortably kept at bay by salty sea breezes. At night we'd go to sleep with the enormous noise of cicadas and bullfrogs singing as if to compete with each other. With only the tent inner and flysheet between us and them, the noise was both exotic and deafening.

The beach itself was fascinating. Birgit slipped easily into 'collector mode' and spent much of the time strolling the sands with her head down. It was almost as if the beach was a stopping off point on nature's highway. The waterline held a weaving strip of odd-shaped seeds, whitened bones and wonderfully colourful shells. I knew that when the time came to move on she'd be leaving with a few extra grammes of souvenirs.

When we'd first arrived we'd not noticed a rough-and-ready fishermen's camp that had been set up in the branches of the driftwood. Strips of old canvas and plastic had been tied to the weave of wood and underneath were all the accoutrements of beach fishermen. Very fine, red mesh nets were hooked up so they could dry, and large seawater-filled pots sat in the shade. Sun and sea-bleached, fraying clothes hung from knotty stubs on the tree stems. On the ground were circles of stone that had the remains of the last fire lying black and ash grey, and around those fireplaces sat sooty-bottomed cooking utensils. A few empty beer bottles glinted in the sun next to battered thick white plastic water jerrycans, and fish were drying in the breeze. Thin branches had been hooked through their eyes and then hung from one driftwood stem to another.

These fish weren't the fishermen's real prey though. They were after shrimp larvae. In the orangey-red early dawn light we'd see them down in the shallows as crisp-edged silhouettes as they waded in slow motion through the waters, casting their nets with practised, fluid ease. The weather changes and the time of year meant that the larvae were in full swarm. The men would sell them on to the shrimp farms that were dotted along the coast. I knew that the next time I saw 'Ecuador' as country of origin on the label of a packet of shrimps in a supermarket at home they could quite easily have been caught off this very beach. It made for a happy feeling of completeness.

Quito was drawing us on. It was a capital city that I wanted to see. Not only was it supposed to be a city with charm, with a beautiful old colonial sector and a good selection of places to stay, but the airline and shipping offices there were also going to be our first chance to try to find a way to get from Colombia to Panama.

Colombia is separated from Central America by the Darien Gap – a narrow strip of land, roughly 160 kilometres long and 50 kilometres wide. It's full of drug growers and smugglers, Indians who don't like visitors, unmanageable canyons, and rivers. It's also home, reputedly, to the most voracious mosquitoes in the Americas – I doubted that any could be worse than those in Buenos Aires or the site we'd just been camping on, but was happy not to have to conduct a test.

A Norwegian called Helge Pedersen did manage to take a bike through the Darien Gap but he spent a large amount of the time with his bike in a canoe. Loren Upton, a former US marine, took two whole years to drive all the way in a Jeep from 1985-87 but then returned in 1995 and did it in just 49 days on a balloon-tyred, two-wheel drive automatic Rokon motorcycle. I admired both of them tremendously for making it across but knew that this was one adventure that wasn't for us. We had to find a way round it.

We knew there was a ferry from Cartagena on the north coast of Colombia, but then we'd heard that it had stopped running. The rumour was that the ferry company had gone bust after having to replace all the fixtures and fittings that were being constantly nicked by passengers! This sounded a bit far-fetched, but....

We'd heard that some people were putting their bikes on private yachts and sailing across to Panama – they'd have had to be big yachts to get Libby and Henry aboard. One bloke had paid a smuggler to take his bike and another had been lucky enough to persuade a cargo ship's captain to take him and his bike across. We knew that some people had flown their bikes from Cartagena and others had flown them from Bogota, the capital of Colombia.

We'd also heard that some people had reckoned Colombia was far too dangerous to go through, so they had flown their bikes from Quito. When we were talking about this, Birgit always went quiet. I knew that deep in her heart she really didn't want to go to Colombia. She was very wary of the troubles there – it was probably going to be the most unpredictable country on the journey.

She had every right to be worried. If we were to believe the European press, then the only people who lived in Colombia were drug smugglers, blackmailers, the super-corrupt rich, and victims. Not a very pretty picture is it? I wanted to go and see for myself. I wanted to be able to have enough information to form my own opinion. Yes of course we'd pay attention to what the media said, but I preferred to rely on what the people on the ground said, and my own eyes.

I also couldn't get my experience of riding through Ethiopia out of my mind. I'd done it just after the war there and it had been an on-the-edge, phenomenal experience. I wouldn't mind some more of that, but it would be a waste of time and money if Birgit wasn't going to enjoy it. I tried hard not to let my enthusiasm put her under pressure. I knew that, being the person she is, if she thought that I really wanted to go, then she'd give it a try too. In any event, if we couldn't get the bikes out of Colombia then we'd have to think again. Quito would answer some questions for us.

Once clear of Esmeraldas, we hooked off into the hills towards the town of Mindos. The route took us swooping along a road that was in surprisingly good condition, and wound its way following the contours of the hills. We had jumpy moments when one vehicle or another would come heaving round a bend at us, and in one of the villages we were guided off onto a very precarious dirt road along the side of a precipice. The main road had been blocked off for a football match! I loved that, and was sure that even the bus drivers, who were struggling to keep all wheels on the road, could appreciate the logic.

In Mindos we met a couple of characters of the road. Benno and Thekla, from Holland, were riding the Americas on their 350cc Royal Enfield Bullet. I loved this idea as it went completely against the received wisdom of what constituted a suitable machine. Of course it helped that Benno knew the bike inside out, as Enfields are not known for their reliability. And not only were they two-up on a supposedly under-powered bike, but they were towing a trailer behind it too!

One of the quirks of our meeting was that we'd seen their bike parked up in Cusco all those months before, but had never managed to track them down.

They were towing the trailer but didn't use panniers and Benno claimed it was the perfect combination. The trailer itself was aluminium, roughly a metre square and had 2 chunky wheels that looked as if they were no more than 30cm in diameter. I really wasn't sure what I thought of this set-up. I didn't like the idea of towing anything and my instinct was that off road it would have been a complete chore to ride with. It would mean two more tyres' worth of punctures to deal with, and riding with it on roads where ruts had been made by trucks must have been a nightmare. The track of the wheels was nothing like as wide as a car's, let alone that of a bus or truck.

Still, it must have been nice not to have the weight of a fully loaded bike to pick up when dropped, and being able to scoot off without luggage at a moment's notice must have given them a real sense of freedom and lightness.

When we rode on from Mindos together, Birgit and I were staggered at how much the trailer leapt around on the dirt road. I was sure that it must have made the riding complete hell, but both Benno and Thekla assured us that in fact they could hardly feel it at all. Having already ridden the length of Africa and now the Americas with this combination, they obviously knew what they were doing and if it hadn't worked, then they wouldn't have persisted with it – they didn't look like masochists!

It was fun to ride with them on the dirt road as we were only able to manage about 30 kph anyway, but when we hit the tarmac again I began to itch. Uphill, the best they could do was still only 30 kph. That was fine to begin with as it meant that we were taking more time out to enjoy the lush plants at the roadside; they seemed to be strung with flowers as if God had rewarded the landscape with multi coloured necklaces.

But Libby wasn't happy at this speed – with her weight and gearing difference she felt decidedly unstable on the tarmac. It started to get tiring. If we'd been able to ride just 20 kph more then she would have been fine. I really looked forward to going downhill as the Enfield could go as fast as 60 kph. Each downhill section was a mini holiday, though always a bit of a worry as the trailer would take on a motion that was almost dizzying.

By the time we finally made it up to the Pan American Highway, just to the north of Quito, I was happy when Thekla said that they were continuing on north. She said that they'd very much enjoyed our company but their speed of travel was so much slower than ours it meant the partnership didn't gel as well as it could have. We couldn't have put it better, and rather appropriately parted company at the equator marker.

Quito turned out to have the easiest traffic to ride in of any of the South American cities. The roads were mostly wide and relatively well cared for, and the other vehicles obeyed the rules of the road. There was none of the bullish, 'me first', attitude of Lima. Here, it was almost as if the traffic donned its best manners as it reached the outskirts.

We headed for the American Express office. We wanted to pick up our post and to cash some travellers' cheques, but also we hoped that there would be a message from Guy and Marlene. We'd arranged that whoever got set up with a good place to stay in Quito first would leave a message for the others.

Their note had us heading quickly for the Hostal Rincon de Castilla. They couldn't have found a more perfect place and though we'd only been apart for a few weeks, our reunion was more than worth opening a few bottles of beer for. Birgit wasn't so happy with beer, so she and Marlene decided to settle on a Tetrapac of Ecuadorian wine. The wine we'd drunk from these Tetrapacs in Argentina, Chile and Peru had been absolutely fine – even the cheapest ones. So it was a good bet. The girls lost this one though. The wine was one hundred percent disgusting. It tasted as if it was a combination of anti-freeze and paint stripper. You could smell the alcohol but that was the only thing it had going for it! And those first few sips were enough of an intake to repeat in foul anti-freeze belches for several hours!

For the last few days I'd been suffering with horrendous wind of my own. Sometimes it had been quite embarrassing. Once I'd been standing talking to a stranger, trying to understand his Spanish (always harder when crossing into a new country as the accents would change dramatically with each border crossing) and had involuntarily let rip with an enormous blast of methane that equally unhappily smelt as if I'd recently digested a good part of the local sewer system. It was not very gentlemanly…In an enclosed space this was quite a dire happening and I could clear a room in seconds. I wasn't making very many friends and if it was going to continue for much longer then I was probably going to find that Birgit would want a single room! It was time to get myself checked out.

I had amoebas! Foul little beings but at least I hadn't had any vomiting or the squits as a result. Some antibiotics soon had the air smelling fresh again. What had started off as a rather surprised, boyish glee at my new talent, rapidly changed to embarrassment and worry, and then to pure relief at its passing.

Quito turned out to be as good as we'd hoped. It was an attractive place to get things done. Trees and flowering shrubs lined many of the streets and though a large percentage of the buildings could have done with a few layers of paint, the streets themselves were clean and filled with character.

The centre of the city is modern, with tall glass offices sprouting from between the older Spanish buildings like sharp-edged statements of progress. The old part of the city was a pleasure to explore with its stuccoed buildings festooned with wooden shutters, curved terracotta tile roofs, iron railings and narrow, winding, cobbled streets. A pleasure until it rained it rained that is.

This was a time of really heavy rain – it was still an after-effect from El Niño, but at least there was a pattern to it. In the mornings we'd have clear blue skies and we'd duck out to do whatever we had to do. Those mornings were taken up with servicing the bikes, knocking on aviation and shipping company doors, food shopping, and sight-seeing. But by early afternoon the skies would have changed to a weighty grey, and rain and hail would soon sheet down.

This rain was so heavy that the drainage system couldn't cope. Within a half an hour the water in many of the streets would be up to knee level. In the old town, which was perched on the side of a hill, it was like walking through street-width rapids and waterfalls. Loads of fun the first few times we were out in it, but then it was a complete chore. The worst thing was not being able to see where your feet were going down and we'd no idea what was swirling around our legs in the water. We tried not to think too hard about that and always dived for the shower as soon as we were back at the hostal.

Most of the information we were getting about shipping, flying and travel in Colombia was conflicting, or expensive and adventure-killing. The bikes however were looking better than they had for weeks. We'd found a garage, Koshe, that specialised in motocross bikes, and the owner Christian was really helpful. He let us work on the bikes in the shelter of his workshop and disposed of our old engine oil for us.

He and his team refused any payment. Christian even had a new brake part made up for Birgit's bike.

When she'd been cleaning Henry she'd discovered that under the mud and the road dust, part of the mechanism of the front drum brake was disintegrating. It was almost as if the aluminium had developed a cancer or a skin disease. If we'd not stopped to work on the bikes in such a good setting, it was very likely that she would soon have found herself grabbing a non-functioning front brake.

To make life even more interesting, an eruption warning was posted about the volcano that overlooks Quito. It hadn't erupted since the 1600s but there'd recently been earthquakes further down the coast and these, it seemed, had disturbed this sleeping giant's dreams. It was now rumbling and dark grey smoke was floating up into the air over the city. We were told that if Pichincha erupted we wouldn't be in danger of lava flows where we were, so we were tempted to stay a bit longer – the experience could be very interesting. We were told that the worst effect that we'd have to deal with on our side of the city, if we stayed, was a sky filled with dust and pumice. With that in mind we covered the bikes, put our bike scarves in our pockets, and went to church.

Churches are fascinating places in their own right but they are also a superb way to get under the skin of a country. They are intimate places and each adheres to its own mix of Christianity and local customs. In South America the buildings had often been quite spectacular, as in Cusco, and all had been interesting. There was also the chance to connect with people who didn't need the icebreaker of the bikes to start a conversation. In the more remote churches people had initially been a little nervous of us but had soon warmed and everyone we came into contact with treated us with kindness. In Quito that warming welcome happened straight away and after the service we were invited round to the church hall to drink coffee with those of the congregation who weren't dashing off home.

To begin with, a lot of the conversation was about the sudden and damaging devaluation of the Ecuadorian currency that had just occurred. The sucre had just dropped from 5,300 to the US dollar to

6,300. This was going to hurt a lot of people and where we'd seen so many living just off the poverty line, it would surely push thousands more over the edge. There were some very long and worried faces. Some of the people we talked to were from overseas and had their savings safe there. But many had just been dealt a devastating blow.

I was impressed by the strength of their faith that things would work out in the long run. Was this simply because they were Christians and believed that God would provide, or was it that this trust in God was mixed with the experience of generations of inflationary knock-backs and dodgy politics? Perhaps it was also a combination of indigenous Indian stoicism and pioneering spirit. Once again I was glad that I wasn't tied to living an uncertain life in a country such as this.

After hearing some of our story, one of our new acquaintances said, "I have someone I'd like you to meet. He too is from Africa." Michael was a young, very dark-skinned, bespectacled man from Nigeria. Surprised, I asked him what he was doing in Quito. "Ahh," he said. "I work for one of the factories here. They had a big theft problem. I am the security officer – I am very good."

That made sense to us. Sadly, Nigeria has an amazing reputation throughout the world for breeding clever con men and crafty thieves. Perhaps the owners of this factory had set a thief to catch some thieves! Or perhaps it was that Michael had been brought up in an environment where he'd learned all the tricks in the book – he certainly seemed confident.

The Rincon de Castillia was a magnet for overlanders on bikes. During the time we stayed there, Detlef and Esther arrived. We'd last seen them in Chile. They were making preparations for flying their bike back to Germany with Air France. Two Japanese lads turned up on small capacity trail bikes. They'd ridden down from the States to Panama and had then flown their bikes to Quito. Neither of them spoke even a word of English, let alone Spanish! It made me feel quite proud of the level of communication that I'd now reached in Spanish, but also full of admiration for the Japanese. It must have been like travelling with one of their senses turned off.

The next to arrive was a German lad called Stefan, and this turned out to be very important to us. Not only had he just come from Colombia and was full of praise for the country, but he'd kept copies of all the paperwork he'd had to fill in at the borders. He did warn us though that he'd met bikers who'd not been allowed in with their machines, but he didn't know why not.

Stefan's information was the encouragement we needed to get on the move. Birgit now felt happier about going to Colombia and I was chuffed as nuts to be going there. Guy and Marlene decided that they'd like to ride with us, so off we set. We left Pichincha rumbling and complaining behind us. We later heard that things had calmed down and that the volcano hadn't erupted.

In spite of Quito being such an enjoyable city I had my usual feeling as we rode out. It was almost as if we were being spat out. To me, a city is a bubble of unreality in the real world and as always it was a great feeling to get out on the open road again. Adventuring in a city is so totally different from adventuring through the countryside and I was wonderfully happy to be back on the bike again. As I looked towards Birgit I caught her eye in one of her mirrors and she gave me a thumbs up. I knew that behind her helmet she was grinning as much as I was.

The first day's ride was just a hundred kilometres and that was the perfect distance. It allowed plenty of time to get out of Quito and then to relax on the open road, which meandered through land that again looked surprisingly like the Rift Valley in Tanzania or parts of Kenya. Libby purred under me, almost as if she was as excited as I was to be free again.

We were heading for the tiny Indian town of Otavalo. It had the reputation for having one of the best markets in Ecuador. We arrived on a Friday and it was perfect timing as the main market ran on the Saturday. We arrived early enough to get some decent accommodation and then set out to explore on foot. In the meandering streets that house the market, life was bustling. Stallholders were already setting up for the next day and there was an air of concentrated, tense excitement. For once eyes didn't follow us wherever we went – people were far too busy. At times it felt as if the four of us were invisible and that was great.

In many places, when people see tourists, they either consciously or subconsciously change their behaviour and become either more self-conscious or rather predatory. Not this time. Life swirled around us.

The women all wore long, dark blue skirts, shawls and gold jewellery as they carted bundles of rugs, shoes and clothes around. One woman who looked about ninety had a full size Calor gas cylinder strapped to her back in her shawl; another younger woman carried her baby there and another had half a dozen chickens wriggling and squawking from within the folds of her shawl. One of the chickens had managed to pop its head out and was surveying the world with an expression that seemed to combine triumph with fear.

Men were heaving rough wooden poles upright to form frames to carry battered tarpaulins, or to hang rugs and carpets off. Others were busy threading the sleeves of stunningly-coloured handmade sweaters onto poles, and others were heaving sacks of charcoals under trestle tables that the next day would hold cooked meats and breads.

In between this organised and intense chaos, escaped chickens fluttered and squawked, and skinny dogs eased over the cobblestones with eyes ever-watchful for the chance to steal a scrap to eat. For once the dogs didn't look inbred and their colours ranged from tans to wiry-haired brown and piebald. All were being very careful not to catch anyone's eye, though for one young hound, the sight of a tourist was too much. Our eyes met for a second and then he hurriedly looked away, pretending that he hadn't seen me, and therefore I must certainly not have noticed him. He disappeared beneath a stall, only to emerge yelping from the other side with a larger, meaner-looking dog at his heels – he'd been distracted at just the wrong moment.

We were all up very early the next morning. The main attraction was the animal market and this started with the dawn. It was located up on the main road and we had to stride out to get there in time. A chilly mist accompanied us along the dirt roads and up out of the valley until we got to the Pan American Highway. There, hundreds of people had already gathered. All, it seemed, were dressed in their best traditional clothing.

Cattle, sheep and goats were on sale but the pigs were the most memorable. These ranged from suckling pigs skipping around on the end of leashes, to real monster hogs that looked as if they weighed twice as much as their owners. Some of the vendors were having real problems keeping these immaculately presented creatures under control. One poor woman was dragged off down the road by a large porker that had no intention of being anyone's dinner. The last we saw of them was as the pig dragging her over the horizon!

All of the trading was done over the noise of outraged or inconvenienced, squealing and grunting pigs, while the cattle and sheep looked on with disdain. I guessed that this is pretty much how the noise around the Tower of Babel would have been!

We lingered in the town for the rest of the day. In the new morning we would be committing ourselves to something that was either going to be a magnificent adventure, or a complete disaster. It didn't feel as if there was going to be anything in between; for good or ill, life was going to be led to the full. All of us were feeling a combination of excitement and a tinge of fear. The undercurrent to this mood was the fact that we didn't even know if we'd be allowed in. We'd not had that feeling in South America before.

Chapter 16

The gauchos are in town!

'I was recently on a tour of Latin America, and the only regret I have was that
I didn't study Latin harder in school so I could converse with those people'"

Dan Quayle

We stood at the beginning of an extraordinary two months in
Colombia but there was nothing to indicate just how phenomenal the
next eight weeks would be. Eleven months before, we'd climbed down
the gangplank of our ship into South America. We had battled the winds
of Patagonia and made it, by hook and by crook, to Ushuaia,
southernmost town in the world. From there the delights of the Andes,
the beautiful volcanoes of Chile, the harsh beauty of the Atacama
Desert and the Altiplano of Bolivia. We had touched the famous
'Gringo trail' at La Paz, Lake Titicaca, the Inca city of Cusco and at the
awe-inspiring Machu Picchu.

Now we were nervous. The guidebooks and other travellers told
stories of 'refundable' cash deposits being demanded to take our
motorcycles into Colombia. They told of hours of paperwork confusion
and of the good chance that, simply on a whim, we might be refused
entry altogether. We pulled ourselves together and told ourselves not to
worry. They would either let us in or they wouldn't. If they wouldn't,
well, then we would just have to find another way to get up to Panama.
But I wanted to go to Colombia. The desire was strong and I don't like
to feel defeated. I knew that I would feel that way if we didn't make it.
Past adventures had taught us that the world is full of surprises, that
things change and that anything's possible so we approached the border
with a sort of fatalistic calm. Calm is good for borders.

We rode the last kilometres of Ecuador in the grey of the dawn
and were at the line drawn on our map as the officials began their new
day. Leaving Ecuador was a doddle, almost too easy. We crossed the
scruffy, litter-filled no-man's-land, rode carefully round the broken
glass in the car park, took a deep breath and the girls set off towards
the smart new concrete and glass buildings of Colombia. For once,

303

clear signs told them where to go. They were back soon, passports in hand, with the news that we were in. Guy and I just had to show our faces and that was that.

However, Birgit told me that the way my name was written in my passport had caused some real problems. (Yes, in these days of computer-generated documents and machine-readable bar codes it's easy to forget that right up until the end of the 20th century the names and personal details in British passports were still hand-written by bored bureaucrats). So, I cursed the person in the passport office in Wales who'd been too lazy to write my name clearly. It was bad enough dealing with the 'Maricon' sniggers, but it got very tense each time they couldn't read the writing. The officials were perfectly within their rights to refuse me entry. Once again I cursed myself for being lazy when I'd been in a place where I could have had something done about it. I should have gone to the British Embassy in Quito and asked them to write me a letter confirming that Manicom was the English translation of the scrawl in and on my passport. Too late now – again. But we were in.

The bikes still had to go to customs, which for some reason was in Ipiales, the first city down the road. It felt very odd to be actually in Colombia, riding the bikes along a pristine stretch of tarmac (the first for weeks) but, not 'legal'. Many of the borders in South America are a game of 'hide and seek', and we'd really had to 'earn' our permits. This one appeared to be about to cap them all.

One of the most popular Colombian scare stories is that of trainee Grand Prix drivers doing their apprenticeship in anything from an 18-wheeler to a 1930s rust-bucket of North American lineage. But over the ten kilometres to Ipiales, only respect was shown towards our little convoy. A promising start.

At the customs office the ball was really rolling when the girls returned from the chemists. The chemist? Of course, isn't that where you would expect to buy your blank official customs forms? The next step was to show the ladies in the Dirección de Impuestos é Aduanas Nacionales how to fill in their own forms! Then the ball stopped rolling.

So far the clock had ticked round four hours. Another four hours gently eased past while we waited, on the street, in the rain and clouds of carbon monoxide, for a computer to be encouraged to work. For us, it never did. We ended up with slightly suspicious, but impressive-looking typed papers. We listened to the assurances and accepted them nervously. The next morning the computer was still down so we left, deciding to rely on the power of the typewritten page, the rubber stamps and the flourishing signatures.

We were in. Officially in, more or less, and certainly on our way. I had to pinch myself a little. Thankfully the build-up had been far worse than the actual event. Eight hours? A small investment. We rode hard that first day. I think we all had a sort of subconscious need to put kilometres between us and the border.

Just after 4pm our happy world changed. We arrived in the beautiful old colonial town of Popayan, which also happened to be the home town of the President of Colombia. Half a kilometre into the town, all hell let loose. A wave of screaming people came flooding down from a tree-lined square, and through the narrow street towards us. It was a bit like sitting on the bikes in the neck of a giant funnel.

The cars in front of us started reversing. The air was full of panic and we were quickly swamped by it. There's only just enough room to turn a BMW bike round on these tiny cobbled streets, but that was without the screaming people, and without the clouds of tear gas that were now floating down the street towards us.

A few metres in front of us a local biker fell, and in no time the nearest car had reversed over the bike, thankfully missing the rider. A dark canister sailed lazily through the air trailing a stream of gas behind it. It landed almost unnoticed in the chaos. My eyes by this time were stinging and I wondered if I was going to be able to ride with eyes affected by the gas. This was too bizarre a way to start a new country. Being yelled at by riot police doing spooky gas mask impersonations of 'Darth Vader' didn't help much either. Scare stories? Hmmm maybe this time they were true. Welcome to Colombia!

305

The sun shone the next morning, the clean-up crews were out collecting missiles and the paint crews were out covering up the effects of the paint bombs. "The teachers are on strike", we were told, "they are very angry." We gathered as much.

After a day being tourists in the now peaceful town, we headed further inland for the mountains of the Cordillera Central. We rode up past the end of the curving tarmac into a land of low-lying cloud, dripping forest, tiny white chapels and sinister misty moorland. As the flip side to yesterday's coin, the air was wonderfully clean and the world seemed to be completely at peace. It seemed sad to drop down again to warmer air and dusty roads, but none of us felt like camping up in the cold.

When it rains in these latitudes, it really rains. We raced a storm down the valley, occasionally collecting a few warning drops on our visors as a bend in the road would allow the clouds to catch up.

A long loop on a firm surface enabled us to escape from the path of the storm. We could then stand and watch the powerful greys, purples and blacks of the storm sweep on by. I'd lost my wonderful rain trousers that day so I was really glad to have escaped a soaking. Dirt roads can shake loose even the most well-attached items but I was particularly sad to have lost these overtrousers. I suspected that they were irreplaceable in this part of the world.

In the south of Colombia, close to the Amazon, lived an ancient civilisation. Its existence had only relatively recently been discovered, near the town of San Augustin.

San Augustin is a pre-Colombian ceremonial site that's considered, by those in the know, to be one of the most important sites in the whole of South America. It's a collection of burial grounds that spread over nearly four hundred square kilometres on the banks and lower hills of the Rio Magdalena. But little is known about the people who lived and worshiped here. Apart from their large stone statues and carvings, there's little left to help explain who they were or when exactly they lived there, though it's estimated that the people must have started to inhabit the area at around 3300BC. It's quite a strange feeling to be in a place and know that for all those centuries other people's feet had been treading on the same ground that I was now walking across.

We wandered between the extraordinary stone carvings of the ceremonial sites and graveyards. The cicadas were there in the background, singing their now familiar repetitive song in the muggy heat by the river. Some of the statues looked just like abstract people  and each one had a different expression – some of anger, some of pain and some of pure joy. Some looked as if they were deliberately insulting you. Many were animals such as jaguars and frogs and some were great birds. These statues, a few of which are seven metres high, are pretty much all that's left of these forgotten people and the relics had lain hidden for hundreds of years. I had an eerie feeling as we explored, almost as if there was something present but unseen – I couldn't help but wonder what had happened to this civilisation.

The bikes had made it easy for us to get to this place of mysteries and as we stood amongst the stones I knew that we were experiencing a 'high spot'. This was a moment to be savoured and remembered.

It was hard to leave and turn north again but it had to be done. To our delight the main and secondary roads of Colombia were in excellent nick. But they woke us up! The driving style of the locals is completely different from that of the Ecuadorians. There, a slow grind through the never-ending potholes is the norm. Here, we suddenly had to get used to going 50 kph faster and had to grow eyes in the backs of our helmets. The majority of Colombians drive 'foot to the floor'. We could see why warnings had been flying in our direction from bikers going south. Not wise to drive with personal machismo here we decided. Better to have a "You're welcome to go first" attitude. We had time, they obviously didn't.

There were tollbooths a-plenty in Colombia but, as we'd discovered elsewhere, motorcycles don't pay. One saves a lot of beer money on a full day's ride. At each booth a sign directs motocicletas to the right, to the special lane. This country had a surprise for us though.

The builders of these special lanes had never imagined them being used by bikes of our size and load. They are like a cattle run. Once in, there ain't no turning round. We could normally trundle through at the posted 5-10kph. But with some we were almost in trouble. The side walls grew higher the further we got in. I cleared one toll with no more than a centimetre under my panniers! Other bikers had obviously had problems as the toll staff would always stop to watch when they saw us.

Days later, after riding through lush green, gently-rolling countryside, we were below the snowy-topped volcanoes of the Nevado de Ruiz. We were winging it, letting each day happen of its own accord as we rode through the tree-lined back lanes. But this day was growing very long as we hopped from one village to another looking for a place to stay. Our problem was solved by the village policeman who jumped on his moped and took us to a little hostal that was absolutely perfect. I don't think I'll ever forget the sight of him riding hunched down over his handlebars with his 50cc engine whining furiously beneath him. The man had seen that we were tired, and such was his desire to help he didn't consider that he looked quite daft. He wouldn't even let us buy him a beer in thanks but within seconds was buzzing off on his machine, looking a darned sight more macho than he had moments before.

I still hadn't managed to find a replacement for my Hein Gericke waterproofs and some of the kilometres we'd been doing had been very cold in the wet and altitude. I could stand it no longer; I had to have some protection. I might possibly find something suitable in Bogota but that was several days away, so Birgit and I hunted out the local hardware shop. They stocked heavy-duty plastic on the roll so we bought three metres of it and set off back to the hostal . There, using a pair of trousers as a template, I cut out a roughly appropriate shape. We then stuck the 'seams' together with duct tape. The result was a black pair of very crinkly, shiny, clown's trousers, but at least they'd provide laughs and would keep me warmer.

The next day we found the Hotel Los Rios or the River Hotel in the sleepy old colonial town of Ambalema. The streets were cobbled, the thick walls painted brilliant white and the roofs tiled with terracotta. It was a place that time had largely forgotten. Even the vehicles looked as if they were leftovers from another age. Our 'find' had undercover parking for the bikes and clean rooms that reminded me of rooms in old English pubs. To our amazement, tucked out the back in flower gardens was a twelve metre, crystal-clear swimming pool.

This stay also gave me the chance to try to deal with a very irritating slow puncture. I'd been putting off the task but could do so no longer. Guy and I entertained the girls with what we called 'the tyre dance' as we both balanced on the tyre trying to break the bead. We were successful, eventually, but with the tube off and semi-inflated in a bowl of water I couldn't find any trace of the leak. The valve wasn't bubbling either. It was irritating because this was the last of my new inner tubes, but rather than put up with the hassle I put an old tube back in and kept the new, leaking one for emergencies only. Not what one is supposed to do but I was well and truly at the 'Stuff it!' stage.

In the gentle evening warmth we soon learned to promenade like the locals. 'When in Rome...' The tree-lined plaza was the venue for everyone's stroll. At the edge of the square, the majesty of the Catholic Church looked out over the shops, bars and billiard halls that lined the rest of the square. We were surprised at the mania for billiards in Colombia but not by the mania for beer. If you like good German lager then you'll like this stuff.

The Saturday night promenade is when 'everyone' comes to town. Pretty girls on scooters cruise the plaza. Whole families travel three or four-up on well-loved 125cc trail bikes and the rest just stroll. Even the local gauchos (cowboys) are in town. These guys are full of machismo and know how to show off in style. They thunder into town with the full kit on – chaps, Stetson hats and knotted kerchiefs. Their tiny horses are beautifully groomed and are raced up and down the cobbles, sparks flying from their metal shoes. Some of the guys have a real dressage routine worked out and flick their horses through a series of dainty, prancing steps.

Once the whole town knows that the 'boys' are in town, they pile into a bar and get stuck into some serious relaxing. Their steeds aren't neglected either. The horses too seem to have a taste for the amber nectar and are given regular slurps as they wait patiently for their soon-to-be-very-drunk owners to try to climb aboard. Much laughter and loss of face accompanies a failed attempt to hoist aboard, but they always seem to manage it eventually and the 'homing' horses set off with the 'riders' slumped in a very relaxed state.

Stopping in Ambalema for the extra days gave us the chance to do some exploring with the luggage off the bikes — actually we just took the luggage off Libby and went two up on her. It felt really strange to be riding her without the weight of all the kit and she looked almost nude! But it was fun to have Birgit on the back of the bike — for a change we could talk to each other without having to stop.

With no luggage on the bike we were able to head right out into the countryside and get really off the beaten track. The dirt roads were great fun, though at times they were decidedly challenging. The frequent rains may keep the landscape of Colombia lush and green, but it also plays havoc with the roads. Many were washed away and frequently we'd come across sections that looked as if only feet and donkeys had made it through for months. Around us was kilometre after kilometre of coffee plantation. The fields sprawled in very dark green shiny rows across the hillsides. Small villages, with rough-rendered walls and corrugated iron roofs, clustered at road junctions. And at each of these junctions the locals would set up rough-and-ready stalls, from which they were selling second hand odds-'n-sods and fruit. The odds cost little more than buttons and the fruit was the cheapest we'd seen in weeks. A whole stem of bananas cost roughly 20 US cents — very tasty too.

Some of the winding roads were cut into the steeply sloping fields with an apparent randomness that not only challenged logic but made them singularly difficult to ride. Some were across soil that was so black that the beaten wheel tracks had taken on a glossy sheen that made it look as if we were riding on coal. Travelling up and down the hillsides was rather like riding through a health spa. At one moment we'd be down at low level and sweating with the effort of riding through steamy, torpid heat, and the next we'd be up along the side of a mountain and plunged into the cold, particularly when we hit the shadows.

The rain continued on with the pattern that had started in Quito. The mornings were always beautiful and dry, but by siesta time the sun had completely disappeared into brooding inky clouds, and those clouds would open to throw water at us for hours.

If we were caught out in it, the only thing to do was to pull over and find a building overhang to shelter under until the rain stopped. This wasn't so hard because many of the older buildings had been constructed with veranda walkways. We could see now that these provided shade from the sun, and shelter from the rains. If the roofs were corrugated iron then the noise under them would be deafening and there was no point in trying to talk – even shouting at the top of our voices didn't work. Miming was the only way to communicate. As the water literally shot off the iron it would gush out right into the street with amazing force. When I put my hand into the gushing stream one day, the force of it smacked my hand back down to my side.

If we were sheltering under the thick terracotta tiles of an older building then the experience was quieter but even more surreal. The noise of the water hitting the ground took over as being the loudest. This made us feel as if we were standing in a quiet pocket that was surrounded by a noise that was a violent and very persistent collection of slashing and thundering. But, under the overhang we could hear each other talk and sometimes could even hear the conversations going on inside the building.

The longer the rain continued the cooler it got. It was almost as if the rains were sucking out and washing away any of the warmth that had built up in the buildings during the morning. But the cool that had eased in with the rain soon turned into a sticky, sweaty heat as the sun tried to work its way back though the now much paler grey above.

The dirt of the road would always steam in front of us as the sun came through the remaining clouds in laser-like beams. As we rode, these beams of light eased across the landscape like a slow-moving, mirrored disco ball. As they hit the shiny leaves of the coffee bushes they would turn the world from a dank and moody place into one that was alive with brilliant light and dancing shadows.

It was time to move on though. The capital, Bogota, was calling, and the city was madness. How many million people on the road all trying to be first?! There weren't any of the usual South American city speed bumps either. But the potholes were massive and the ever-present threat of missing manhole covers was enough to keep the speed down to a manageable level.

Bogota traffic lights are designed to frustrate drivers and overheat motorcycle engines! Our feet turned into portable swimming pools under the Boxer twins' horizontal cylinders. We had only driven 150 kilometres the day we arrived but were shattered by the time we found somewhere to stay. The few budget hotels all had entrances too narrow to fit the wide handle bars of the BMWs through. Fortunately the old and rather magnificent Youth Hostel building, tucked onto the edge of the city centre, had a large arched double door onto the street. With the help of some chunks of wood we found lying in the gutters, we could get the bikes up through the doors.

Inside, we found a large tiled courtyard lined with plants in big terracotta pots. It was covered with a curved and yellow-stained glass roof. Perfect. The door was locked at night, they had a room that the four of us could share, and we were within easy walking distance of the sights and shops.

The madness that is Bogota continued as we found our way around and continued researching how to get the bikes from Colombia to  Panama. To us, the best option had been less than $US400 to fly the bikes and us across the Darien Gap. As we'd found before, trying to do bike things and bike-related research is a fantastic way to see a city. Yes we could and did go to the things that you are supposed to see, and Bogota has many of those, but the hunt for my rain trousers took us to another world.

The hunt took us into back streets where small businesses survive as punctuation marks nestling between bigger firms. It's a world where large, battered and overloaded trucks lumber through traffic that seems to be mainly made up of pickup trucks, taxis and bicycles. Money never seemed to be spared to paint anything that wasn't advertising something, and most of the unwashed windows were guarded by rusting black bars. Small piles of rubbish had collected against solid objects that sat in the gutters. A trashed and rusting Chevy with no wheels and no glass in the windows had the biggest collection of old newspapers, plastic bags, a broken plastic sandal, water bottles, plastic coke bottles, bits of old string, and silt mashed up against it.

I found some rain trousers, not in a sports shop, nor in a bike shop, but in a workmen's warehouse that was stacked high with tools, small sized work boots, small size overalls and small size fluorescent jackets, all 'Made in China'. It was almost as if we'd stumbled across a store for little people, but then it clicked. Most of the men we'd seen working on the roads, on the building sites and in the fields were of Indian extraction – and they were little people.

Fortunately I managed to find a pair of navy blue waterproof trousers that sort of fitted. The legs were cut for a little person so the crotch of the 'grande' trousers sat at lower thigh level and the waistline was cut so high that it looked as if the trousers had been modelled on a very short, very fat person whose aim was to be able to fasten the elastic over his belly. They made me look like an overgrown toddler. When I tried to walk in the things, it looked as if I were doing so with a filled nappy. Not very elegant... but on the bike, when they'd ridden up over the saddle, at least I'd be dry from the knees upwards!

Another bike-related hunt took us to the posh part of town. We were staggered at the wealth. Majestic houses with manicured gardens and high walls, sat one against the other. We could see large patios, swimming pools and flashy cars lined up inside. We could probably have seen more too, if we'd been nosy and prepared to risk the wrath of the sun-glass wearing brutes that were guarding the gates. Strangely, none of the walls seemed to have the necklaces of razor wire and broken bottles we'd seen in so many other South American cities.

We were in this part of town because we were heading for the Panamanian Embassy. The airlines had told us that we'd be refused entry without a return ticket of some sort, unless we had a permit for single and one-way entry.

Like most things in Latin America, it took us several trips, lots of waiting around and several days to get these permits. At first, the Consul, who was a slim, black-suited, extremely dapper man with jet-black greased hair that sat in place in perfectly spaced furrows on his head, said that such a permit was impossible. We'd have to buy a return air ticket and get a refund from the airline in question. We'd already thought of this option and discovered it was a rip off. We'd get almost nada back.

Then he told us that he'd never done such a permit before, and wasn't sure how to go about it, or if he wanted to accept the responsibility for it. We suggested that he telephone Panamanian Immigration in Panama, but of course the international lines were down, and that meant he couldn't fax either. Days later, he hadn't lost courage; he had managed to contact the Immigration department and managed to get a positive reply. The instructions were that he had to provide a certificate of his own design with the appropriate information and references on it, and had to fax copies of our passports across.

Perfect, and this would also stand us in good stead if we managed to get a boat across. The amazing thing was that even though the Consul had spent hours with us, hours on the phone and had had his secretary active on our behalves too, he wouldn't charge us a cent. He told us that we just had to make sure that we enjoyed his country!

After a week, prices, dates and contacts were in our admin file, as our insurance policy in case we couldn't find another option up on the coast. We headed north again, but slowly – the city's terrible road signs ran us literally round the houses for an hour before suddenly releasing us into the countryside.

Then we were free. Free and heading for the cathedral of Zipaquira. This is a cathedral on a grand scale, but it's underground and carved entirely out of salt. It's the only one of its kind in the world and the salt reserves from which it's built are estimated to be vast enough to last the whole world a hundred years. While Birgit went underground to explore, I stayed with the bikes to work on Libby's carbs. I'd cleaned them in Bogota and still hadn't managed to get them balanced properly. No mercury gauges for us, just sound and vibration. Normally I'd get it right first go but this time I just couldn't get them to level out. She was being a complete pig to ride, and riding in any level of traffic had been quite dangerous; she didn't react as quickly as usual, and I nearly dropped myself in it a couple of times.

As I worked in the peace and quiet of the car park I had time to think about Guy and Marlene. They'd left Bogota a few days in advance of us and I wondered if we'd ever see them again. I suspected not. Through some sections of the country there was only one road that was safe to travel, but in others the choices were wide. I suspected that we would hear about them from other travellers and from the locals but it would be easy to miss them.

With Libby running smoother and Birgit suitably amazed by the cathedral, we set off through an area that could be called the Nottinghamshire of Colombia – rolling lush green fields, the bright yellow of rape and the black and white of Friesian dairy cows. I rode thinking of my mother's home but not for long.

It started to sheet down with rain and the dirt road turned to mud. The village we were heading for was cobbled with riverbed rocks – scary whilst so wet and the streams that flowed out of the side streets didn't help at all. Thankfully, this day, our luck was in. We found a place to stay very quickly. The friendly owner and his wife welcomed us with smiles, clean sheets, hot showers and steaming cups of excellent herb tea.

It didn't rain at all the next day and that was a real blessing. Birgit and I had headed off down out of the Cordillera Occidental towards the Amazon, and the roads had changed from being rough tarmac into long stretches of gravel and dust. It didn't help that there were annoying stretches of roadworks and even on their rough, rutted surface the drivers of the trucks and buses would still be trying to make up time.

If we took it gently through the obstacles then they'd soon be upon us, and without any hesitation would be using their horns and their bulk to bully us out of the way. We'd then be left riding in their dust clouds. As some of these sections were several kilometres long, it was a pressurised and rather scary business.

Things started to go badly wrong for me on one of these sections. My engine cut out when I was right in the middle of a swirling dust cloud. I couldn't see Birgit but I could hear a heavy engine revving as it got closer to me. I couldn't see it though and the dust played games with my sense of distance. All I knew was that if I couldn't see it, the truck or bus wouldn't be able to see me.

Just as the bike jerked to a halt in a rut, the engine started again. Then, with a flash of lights across the instrument panel, Libby cut out all over again. I'd gained no more than a few metres and I could hear the heavy vehicle getting ever closer.

I jumped off the bike, twisting the handlebars as I did so, and the bike leapt to life again. Fortunately I'd taken her out of gear. I rode as fast as I could and cleared the dust cloud to find Birgit waiting for me with an anxious expression on her face. I indicated to her to follow me as fast as she could – I knew the truck was coming, but inside her helmet and over the sounds of two bikes, she'd not have heard it.

Just as I made it to an area of level ground next to the road, which had obviously once been a place for the work crews to store supplies and equipment, Libby completely died on me. At that moment a leaping and jolting articulated truck blasted out of our dust cloud, horn blaring angrily at us as it powered on past.

We stripped the luggage off Libby and while doing so discussed the possibilities. The only clue we had was that it must be electrical and I hated the thought of electrical problems. To me they are the equivalent of black magic.

We got our voltmeter out and started working our way through the wires on the bike. We checked the HT leads. No problem. Finally we made it through the system to the ignition switch casing on Libby's instrument panel. The larger red wire had broken away. It must have

316

connected intermittently when I twisted the handlebars on the dirt – it had been enough to get me out of there.

Thankfully Birgit hadn't thrown out an old set of Henry's points so I could steal some wire and a connector. We cleaned up the tongue that the red wire had been soldered to and pushed the connector on. Success!'

It was Birgit's birthday and as a treat we decided to book ourselves into a posh, (for us) hotel. The old colonial building had stunning and very clean rooms, and balconies from which we could stare out at the surrounding hills from between trailing strands of purple bougainvillea. The shower was a power job and the hot water was endless, but strangely the loo didn't have any water to flush it, and the washbasin didn't have any water in the taps either. The bed was giant, firm and had crisp white, slightly starched sheets on it. The towels in the bathroom were fluffy and white, and there was even a TV in the room. We'd not seen a TV in private for months. Normally the only televisions we saw were those in bars and cafés, though very occasionally a supermarket would have some soap or other blasting away at its customers. We'd learnt that South Americans take their soap operas very seriously indeed.

We bought a feast to picnic on in the peace of our luxury pad, and had just settled down with the TV on when there was a power cut. We lay in the dark laughing helplessly. At least the idea had been good and at least we knew exactly when we'd had our most expensive power cut in South America.

The next day Birgit's bike started to make weird popping noises from the exhausts. We didn't worry too much as so many things could be causing it. Altitude changes, fuel….and we just hoped it would go away…

It didn't. It got worse, much worse. So, we settled down with our Clymer manual (all 2kgs of it) and worked our way through the list of possibilities. We knew the points and condenser were OK as they'd just been renewed and checked. No water in the float bowls, valve clearances correct, all electronic connections cleaned, HT leads swapped between bikes, coils tested, spark plugs gapped, spark plugs changed and so we went on. Nothing, and the popping changed into backfiring. Stumped, we both hoped that it would fix itself. So often our bikes have 'fixed themselves' – suited us very well when it happened. Perhaps now though it was time to accept that both the bikes were beginning to show some signs of their hard lives.

At 27 years old, the R60's exhaust pipes were thin around the ends and it didn't take long for the constant thunderclaps to blast holes through. Birgit was now riding a bike with an early warning system for pedestrians. Range, at least one kilometre.

Usually people stopped what they were doing as we went by. Now they stopped to watch as we came! But that was the least of our worries. Henry was now losing power and was decidedly erratic to ride. We were really puzzled. He died with a massively loud backfire in a dusty, battered old town in northern Colombia.

With real style he chose to die outside a brothel, and with nowhere else within pushing distance that had a yard for parking, the 'Madame' rather uncertainly showed us the way inside. We parked the bikes under the huge tree that dominated her yard. A door in the turquoise wall to the left of us opened, and a weary but satisfied looking couple quietly left.

We were shown to our room. It was damp, with mould on the wall, but had a fan that worked, and had a pipe on the wall of the bathroom that happily threw out a reasonable quantity of water at an angle of almost 90°. Perfect for face washing! We later worked out that if we let the jet of water hit the opposite wall of the shower, the spray that would bounce back at us showered us very nicely. We fell onto the bed, and we lay and contemplated our problems.

Two more days of head-scratching, tweaking this and that and oily dirt under our fingernails got us no closer to the solution. We asked a policeman if there was a mechanic in town who might know about bikes like Henry. He was certain there was not, but very kindly arranged for us to be escorted by a bunch of his colleagues in their police jeep to the local trucking company. As we drove through the streets, more than one person must have wondered what the gringos had been arrested for!

The trucking company said that a wooden box would have to be made before they would handle Henry – they were afraid of damaging him if they were to truck him the 1,200 km down to BMW in Bogota. The whole business would cost $180!

It was time to phone Bob Porecha in London again, but just to tease us a little, the international phones in our edge-of-nowhere town were out of order and had been for some time. They were also out of order in the nearest town. So, we set off through the banana plantations for the north coast and the equally dirty city of Barranquilla, only 120 kilometres of grim roads away. But it was nice to be on the move and at least to be doing something positive.

It's hot in this part of the world; leastways it felt so to us having spent most of the past year either in the cold of the far south or up in the cold of the Andes mountains. We were definitely not used to 30C° and that was on the outside of our leathers! The slow hump and bump grind through the polluted air of Barranquilla was hard work, but we found the Telecom office quite quickly. Sod's law: there was no parking outside, not even for a bike. More hump and bump until we found a pay car park with an armed guard.

Contact was finally made with Bob and helpful as always, he gave us a list of things to look at. He made us feel as if our search for the problem had been quite a good effort considering our circumstances and twenty thumbs. Top of the list was the new points – the one thing we had not checked since breaking down – lesson learned.

The ride back was considerably less tense than the morning's ride, and for that reason we were far more appreciative of the world we were travelling through. The lagoon we rode past no longer looked like a swamp but more like a silver stretch of water that was home to snowy white egrets. We were tickled and impressed by the hitchhikers who jumped on the back of moving trucks and hung off the vertical rear slatted wooden panels for the length of their journeys. They looked like human spiders. The little villages no longer looked quite so much like rubbish dumps and the sun shone all the way home to the brothel.

Of course it was the points. With them set correctly and the holes in the exhaust pipes skilfully welded over, the R60 sounded its usual old self. We said goodbye to 'Madame', who by this time was actually smiling at us, offering us coffee and generally treating us as members of her family. Finally we said goodbye to the working girls and then hit the road with Henry purring from all the attention.

Eighty kilometres further north and just fifteen away from the white sand beaches of the Caribbean coast, my revs stuck high and only sluggishly dropped when the throttle was closed. My mind whirled round all the disasters that might be causing it as we limped towards 'Rosa's House' at the beach. At least this was a class place to break down!

The heavily forested hills were beautiful. Lianas draped down over the road and beard moss tumbled from the tree branches like grey waterfalls. In gaps through the trees we could see the palm-lined coast and the turquoise sea. We knew that it just had to be clear and warm. Fiddling in the roadside shade, it still felt a long way away though. I was really stumped. I'd never had this problem before and I feared it was electrical again. We rode on and the bike got so bad that I had to turn the engine off every few minutes as we negotiated the sandy rutted road down to the house.

A boxer dog, five chickens, three cats, a howler monkey, a parrot and Rosa welcomed us to the house set in the shade of mango, guava and coconut trees. The mossies were quite welcoming too! We settled in to enjoy the peace and beauty of the coast. A stroll down the beach to the fishing village at the mouth of the river loosened the bones and I became quite philosophical. It had been two months since we had last had sand between our toes and yes, the sea was clear and wonderfully warm.

In the cool of the very early morning, covered with mosquito spray, we set to work. Carbs, black box, ignition unit, wiring, valve clearances, trapped cables and then we just sat and stared at her.

As a distraction Birgit took to carving tocuma fruit. These grow as bright green orbs on the tocuma tree and when you scrape out the inedible pulp and seeds inside, you are left with a hard-shelled, gourd-shaped vessel. Though hard-shelled, the skin over the fruit is quite soft, and with a sharp blade, you can carve in all sorts of designs. Once you've finished carving you just boil the gourd for fifteen minutes and then dry it in the sun. The carving is then set and the gourd 'cured' so it doesn't rot. If we'd had more space we'd have carved a bunch of them to sell in the States.

The monkey fell in love with me. At first it was rather cute to see the way it latched onto me and to no one else. It would come and sit with me, would stroke me, would groom me and would curl up in my lap to sleep. I was tickled by this. Yes I am quite hirsute but not as much as a monkey and dammit, I was a hell of a lot bigger. The problem, I suspected, was that she had been around humans since birth and I guessed that she thought of herself as being a small human being. It was therefore quite natural that she should latch onto someone she liked.

The trouble was that Birgit was having a hard time of it. Every time she came close to me, the monkey would bare its teeth and snarl at her. Again, to begin with, this was rather amusing but after a while it became quite irritating. How does one dump a monkey girlfriend? The last straw was when the monkey took major offence at Birgit sitting down to dinner with me. She crept up to us under the table and bit Birgit hard on the leg!

After three days of not finding what was wrong with Libby, I could no longer enjoy the beach. I had to know what the problem was. To my amazement the bike started and went perfectly – for the first three kilometres. We headed for Barranquilla, the phone and Bob again. On the open road the problem wasn't a problem at all, but when we hit the city traffic the nightmare started all over again.

Bob listened to my tale of woe as my thoroughly overheated bike sat trying to cool itself in 30° with no shade to be had. "Has to be the carbs," Bob said, "Could be an air leak." We left the city to find a village hotel with parking – it beat trying the inner city areas with the bike in this state.

I hated to think what damage I was doing with the overheating and having to slip the clutch all the time. I was beginning to really dislike northern Colombian cities with the heat and pollution, and to love the clean open countryside which was filled, it seemed, with friendly people in friendly villages. In fact for us, the friendliest people in South America.

We'd been very pleasantly surprised by Colombians. They seemed to be buzzing with life and good humour, in spite of the terrific problems they faced. An unsettled political system didn't help them, nor did such a wide wealth gap. The drug barons and corruption caused endless selfish, greedy, harm to their countrymen and women. And, in fact, one of the things that constantly struck us was how hard the people worked at trying to make sure that we would carry good news of the country abroad with us.

The message was, "We are not all drug growers, drug users or drug barons. We are mostly ordinary people with the same priorities as most of the rest of the world." Once again, being in a country that one was not supposed to go to had brought dividends. It was already a major high point of the trip and would remains so, provided we made it safely through the country!

We sped on, and took a wrong turning. We didn't realise, but as it started to get dark we began to get worried. We never ride at night if we can avoid it; it's a mad thing to do, particularly in this part of the world. Suddenly there were flashing lights behind us and the police stopped us. The scare stories came back into our minds, in spite of the fact that so far all the Colombian Police had been efficient, polite and extremely helpful; but we'd also been told stories of bandits who would dress in police uniforms and would hold up people at roadblocks. These guys were very edgy towards us.

The forest around us was lit up with regular flashes of blues and reds as the lights on the police vehicle swirled. Beyond the lights, the dark world was silent, even the cicadas seemed to be holding their breath. My senses were working overtime – my ears tingled at the sudden silence. It felt as if there were just the four of us on the planet. I was conscious that the policemen's faces were in shadow as our eyes were being dazzled by the lights as we looked nervously towards the men. It was impossible to read the situation in any way other than, this is very bad news. I tried to look for a way to escape, without giving the game away that this was what I was doing. The darkness around us showed no options and with the heat radiating off my sick bike, I knew that making a dash for it would not succeed – even if I had managed to communicate a plan to Birgit.

"Papers! Open the baggage! Where are you going?!" We carefully ignored the demand to open our panniers but dealt with all the other 'requests' as politely and as friendlily as possible. Then we were told we were on the wrong road, and "Don't you realise how dangerous it is to drive at night?" The first officer said with a tone of voice that combined incredulity with concern. "Would you like an escort to a nearby hotel?" Feeling better about the situation, but still nervous of them, we asked the usual hotel questions: parking etc. They didn't hesitate with a description of the hotel they had in mind. We set off with the cops leading us, lights flashing and well over the speed limit to a perfectly good hotel in a village called Galapa. Phew, and "Gracias, guys".

Mossie repellent out again the next morning, we set to work. Our workshop was the local cock-fighting pit, but it had the advantage of low walls which kept the breeze away from opened engine parts, gave us much-needed shade and boasted a single bare light bulb which provided more than enough light for our purposes. In this bloodthirsty environment, whose battered walls and wire-fronted cockerel cages must have seen endless emotions – excitement, terror and fear, anger and bloodlust - we stripped off and cleaned the carbs once again.

All the settings were checked and as insurance we smeared silicone over the edges of all the joining pipes and seals. She started perfectly, so I set off on a test run. I rode twenty ks at all speeds and it was spot on. Phew... I headed for our hotel, eased over the inevitable speed bump, and the revs began to climb again!

Now I wasn't being so philosophical. What could it be? Then it clicked and I felt really stupid. I'd thoroughly cleaned the carbs inside and out. The elderly idle screw, clean of all the road dirt, was vibrating down on one carb! A dot of Loctite and, ah well, at least it hadn't been an expensive problem.

Now we were free to head for Cartagena. This is a big sprawling city with wide, busy streets that funnel down into the old town. Cartagena old town is a labyrinth of narrow streets and elegantly tall, balconied, old colonial buildings. Pastel tones on walls, terracotta tiles and tubs with flowers meant that every view was packed with colour. Sea breezes slips through the streets cooling the shade that falls from one building or another.

But for some reason Libby was really struggling with the heat. She was pinking that horrible warning 'dit, dit, dit' sound that lets you know you've got an engine that's overheating fast. Usually the way to get round this was to pull over and park up in the shade for half an hour or so, or simply not to ride through a hot city in slow-moving traffic in the middle of the day. This time we'd no choice. It was the time of day we'd arrived and too late I found that there was literally nowhere to pull over and let the bike cool down. The streets were rimmed with steep edged curbs and the pavements were far too narrow to pull a bike off onto, even if it had been possible.

Thankfully, Libby chose to wait until just fifty metres down the road from the 'Holiday Hotel' before she gave a shudder and with a horrible thump, turned herself off. I couldn't start her – there wasn't even a whisper of life. Had I fried the engine? The heat was hammering up at me off it. All sorts of horror thoughts flashed through my mind.

The hotel had a room for us and yes, we could get the bikes in the courtyard. After Birgit had parked Henry inside she came back to give me a hand to push Libby down the road. Behind us, cars honked their horns and their drivers half-heartedly waved their arms out of the windows. At least with it being so hot no one had much energy and most, I felt, were only arm-waving because it was the done thing.

Cartagena's colonial walled city and fortress are set on an enormous bay of 23 square kilometres and both were designated a UNESCO World Heritage Site in 1980. It was founded in 1533 by the Spaniard Don Pedro de Heredia, and named after the port of Cartagena in Spain. The city was a major centre of early Spanish settlement in the Americas and the fame of this prosperous city turned it into a target for plunder for pirates and thieves.

Francis Drake was one of the pirates who attacked Cartagena. He landed during the night and captured the city at dawn. After forcing hundreds of the inhabitants to flee, Drake and his men set about burning and wrecking many of the houses. Then, having shown what he was prepared to do, he forced the authorities to pay him 107, 000 ducats, jewelry and eighty artillery pieces.

After that episode, the city's defences were understandably regarded as inadequate, which is why the kings of Spain decided to approve the construction of castles, forts, and walls. Their construction took 208 years! It finally ended up with some eleven kilometres of walls surrounding the city,

Cartagena was a major trading port, especially for precious metals. Gold and silver from the mines in New Granada and Peru were loaded in Cartagena on the galleons bound for Spain via Havana. The city was also a slave port and in fact, Cartagena and Veracruz (in Mexico) were the only cities authorised to trade in Africans. The first slaves arrived with Pedro de Heredia and they worked as cane cutters, to open roads, and in the construction of buildings and fortresses. The agents of the Portuguese company Cacheu distributed human 'cargos' from Cartagena for mine exploitation in Venezuela, the West Indies, the Nuevo Reino de Granada and the Viceroyalty of Perú.

For more than two hundred and fifty years, Cartagena was part of the Spanish Crown but on November the 11th 1811, the city declared its independence. It then began another chapter in its history that has been anything but easy. It's sometimes known as 'The Heroic City' and from what I could glean this title is well earned and reflects the life of the city. We loved it.

The atmosphere was rich with history, and the colours bright and cheerful. Out of our bike kit the warmth was wonderful, and the people were fun. Though Catagena is Colombia's fifth largest city, it didn't feel that big at all. Based in the old town as we were, it was easy to think that this was all that existed. And after rides out to other parts of the city, we were always glad to return to what we quickly began to think of as home. If we weren't careful we could have got well and truly stuck there. But the one part of the city that didn't interest us at all was the ultra modern area called Bocagrande. Rather aptly, this means 'Big Mouth'. It was modern, brash, had phenomenal wealth and flaunted it, but it had no style or elegance at all compared to the old city.

By the end of the week we'd found nothing wrong with Libby at all. We replaced her front tyre which had suddenly developed a giant blister on one wall, and found Guy and Marlene staying in the hotel opposite ours. By this time we were used to the heat, our legs were shorter from all the exploring, we'd sated ourselves on mail from home and finally we'd accepted that leaving Colombia from the north coast wasn't on. It would have cost $500, (plus agent's fees both sides) to ship each bike to Panama and there were no air cargo planes big enough to take the bikes. It was time to head south, back to Bogota, where all our previous research was now going to bear fruit.

Happily, though potentially more dangerous bandit-wise, we could take totally different roads south. We would have to head towards Medellin, but we had done our homework, asked the right questions and things seemed calm. We were advised that if we stuck to the busier roads we should have no problems with either the drug barons or the bandits. We were comfortable with that, so set off feeling a little as if we were going backwards. After heading north for so long, it felt very strange to be heading back south.

We never saw Guy and Marlene again, but later found out that they had ridden through Africa and settled for a while in Cape Town. There, the trail grew cold.

At one of the regular checkpoints, the police tried to make me understand that I should get off the bike for a weapons and body search. This was the first time for weeks that we'd had this request and at first I didn't understand what they wanted. Then one of the younger soldiers, who was obviously the troop joker, started to mime getting off the bike and having ones body searched, much to the amazement and amusement of all. He was totally and comically 'over the top'. Car and truck drivers sat with bemused expressions on their faces, uncertain whether they should be enjoying what was going on. The rest of us just laughed as I climbed off the bike to be searched. We were always impressed with the courtesy of the soldiers and by the care with which they carried out their searches.

When we passed a sign advertising a natural volcanic mud bath Birgit couldn't resist stopping for a look. The 'bath' was a large open-air pond that was literally full of porridge-like mud. Birgit took the plunge – if that is the right way to describe slopping into dark sludge. She wrote in her diary, 'It was rather like being in a dream. I could swim but it was like swimming through treacle. Slow and exhausting. A very strange, slow-motion sensation.'

When she emerged, she was covered in slime from head to toe. It had moulded itself so closely to her body that she might as well have not been wearing a swimming costume underneath. Surprisingly, all the men were discreetly keeping their eyes off her and the other women who had taken a 'dip'. I couldn't help but laugh. She looked either like the monster from the deep, or a human choc-ice. I knew which description she would prefer!

All went well until day two. We were riding through one of the main road towns at 20kph – it was slow enough to react to just about anything that might happen. My eyes flitted towards the folks standing to the right of the road, was any one going to step out? A pretty girl in a very short skirt caught my eye for one dangerous moment and when I looked forward again I found Birgit right in front of me with her brake light glowing furiously!

I jammed on my brakes and pulled to one side, but I was much too slow. My bash bar and pannier whacked Birgit's right box and bent as they concertinaed her box and threw her bike over. I couldn't hold mine either so within seconds both bikes were on the ground, engines screaming and petrol flowing.

A crowd collected. Neither of us was hurt and we hadn't hit anyone else. Birgit had had to make a split second swerve in front of me to miss a man who had leapt out in front of her to cross the road – she was relying on the fact that I'd be looking where I was going. The man's vacant look led us to suspect that he wasn't all there mentally. We knew that the three of us had just had a very lucky escape. The crowd helped us pick up the bikes and we slipped out of town before the police could arrive to complicate matters.

The rest of the day should have been a dream ride. The everlasting river plain was dotted regularly with elegant haciendas, their fields full of contented-looking creamy-white Brahma cattle. Instead, the day passed in the dream world of those who've been slightly shocked. For Birgit it was worse. She had only just missed the man and this was her first accident on a bike. At this stage she was still too shocked to be angry with me; sooner, or preferably later, I'd have to own up to the cause of my distraction!

The river valley we were following hung a left and our road carried straight on. Straight on and up into the mountains. It got cold and we could see a soaking coming. The mountaintops were ringed by dense grey clouds. Our map told us that shortly we would be right up there in them. The rain waited for us and it fell with cold enthusiasm. It was time to stop, and for once we found a roadside hotel that wasn't an establishment specialising in 'one hour rentals'. It was just what we needed and even had a room that we could squeeze the bikes into.

Next to the hotel was the workshop of a talented man. A good welder was what we needed and a good welder we found. My rack was straightened out and reinforced. Birgit's box was beaten back into a pannier shape and the new holes in her exhaust, from the fall, were sealed. The welder worked very late into the night for us. We went to bed totally shattered, but knew that the day had ended well.

In the morning the rain was still falling with cold enthusiasm. We loaded up and fuelled up at the adjacent petrol station. In Colombia it was never a shock to fill my 43-litre tank. Petrol cost just 12 US cents a litre and was normally OK stuff too. The talkative pump attendant asked where we were heading. Birgit explained our route and we were given some essential information. The guerrillas had just blown up the main bridge on our road: it was impassable. "But," the attendant said, "I know another way and it's very nice". It was too, with unspoilt villages along roads that followed rivers swollen with the recent heavy rains.

The rain had stopped and we were riding through one of the most magnificent dawns I'd ever seen. The sky was wild with colour. Flaming reds and oranges streaked from the rising sun across the sky to soften and reflect off the thin lines of clouds that still floated above us. The hills, trees and buildings between us and this stunning sight were hard-edged and starkly black. It seemed to take an age for the sun to pop above the horizon and for the eclectic collection of colours to start to soften, and for the tones of the sky above us to change into a rich deep blue that had the thin lines of cloud now wispy and gleaming.

We rounded a corner and found a traffic jam! The line went on and on, but at the first hairpin bend the problem became apparent. Much of the traffic from the bigger, faster road was also taking this little country road. If it had been a one-way street it would be no problem but the 153 trucks and buses couldn't pass on these corners in both ways at the same time.

The jam was twelve kilometres long. The air of Latin 'mañana' and patience that lurks beneath the 'me first', hung gently over the queue. Entrepreneurs were selling pies called empanadas, and soft drinks vendors strolled the line. Air conditioners were rumbling softly and groups of truck drivers stood around discussing whatever Colombian truck drivers discuss. We were the lucky ones though.

It only took us three hours to weave our way through the twelve ks. The truck drivers always had a cheery word for us when we too got stuck, and I like to think that we provided a little entertainment in what was a very long day for them. We cleared the jam and cruised. That wonderful feeling of freedom was upon us again when the R60 struggled, backfired, and stopped dead. This time we knew the problem – self-adjusting points. We re-adjusted and carried on through some of the most beautiful land we had seen in South America. The late afternoon sunrays set the world aglow and we relaxed as the scenery rolled by us. I had that wonderful contented feeling of being at total peace with the world.

That feeling carried me through to the next day when we hit the main road to Bogota. One section is dual carriageway and easy to drive. The plan was to stick to the side of the road and let the crazies be crazy, but the road through the mountains was a different story. The crazies were out in force and their blind-corner overtaking was the worst we'd seen. They were constantly putting themselves and other people at significant risk. It was a Saturday and sometimes I had the feeling that small boys had been let out to play in their big and powerful death machines.

A couple of times I felt the mists of rage begin to creep over me. How dare they try to kill us with such stupidity! I worked hard to keep calm; reminding myself that there was really nothing I could do except keep cool, and keep my eyes wide open. All the same, I was glad when we cleared the mountains and I even found Bogota's terrors relaxing as we bumped our way back into the city. Sometimes, going back really is a fine thing to do.

Colombia threw delights and challenges at us till the very end. The twelve-hour marathon day at the airport working through the customs and cargo systems tried our patience. But throughout the day we constantly encountered great kindness, which balanced out some of the system's more bizarre requests. That last night in Colombia we went to sleep knowing that if the system worked and everything went as it should, the next day would be a new start in a new world. Colombia had been a magical final country for us in South America. We'd had to work and sweat to earn the privilege of being able to taste the delights of this beautiful, diverse land and its friendly people, but the effort had been well worthwhile. And now, once again, we were heading north.

Chapter 17

Ice-cold Balboa

'Wandering around our America has changed me more than I thought. I am
not me any more. At least I'm not the same me I was.'

Ernesto 'Che' Guevara de la Serna

The aircraft wheels dropped with a grind and a hollow thump, and moments later the steamy air of Panama welcomed us to the next section of our journey. It felt very strange to be hopping so quickly from one continent to another after a year of two-wheeling through South America. In a way it felt as if the covers of one book had suddenly snapped closed, and that a new one was already open on page one. Over the years this was the first time that we had flown the bikes, but by flying we could do our own paperwork. That was not the case with sea-freighting goods in this part of the world. A shipping agent is a must and of course any agent has fees... and then you have additional payments 'to make things run smoothly' and then... well, it's a mad world!

We'd been lucky enough to find a 6am Bogota to Panama City flight for ourselves, which was perfect timing as the bikes had been flown the two-hour journey during the previous evening. We'd seen them off strapped to an aluminium pallet with nylon net thrown over as insurance. Around them the cargo company had stacked piles of microwave ovens and electric kettles.

The twelve hours of paperwork in Colombia had been a long, drawn-out 'hurry up and wait' exercise which was quite frustrating, but sometimes we were amazed by people's helpfulness and kindness. The busy agents and officials always made time for the two mad gringos who were asking so many silly questions and generally getting in everyone's way. Some of them also seemed to be happy to accept that parts of the system they had to work within were archaic and more of a hindrance than a help. They had no choice, so cheerfully worked on. As part of the process our carefully-packed bikes had been courteously stripped and thoroughly searched for drugs. Then we had waved goodbye to them as they waited under the harsh glare of the hangar security area lights. Next stop Central America.

Our first taste of Panama was an 8am, hot, humid thump to the lungs. Each breath was a bizarre mixture of water, steamy jungle, aircraft exhaust fumes, and a little oxygen. The rainy season was late and of course we'd managed to arrive in the middle of it – El Niño was once again playing knock-on games with us.

The runway asphalt shimmered little mirages behind us as we escaped into the cool of the terminus. It was a peaceful place at that time of the morning and our bags were soon easing their way round the carousel. I was glad that they'd all made it but was not looking forward to carrying them out. The bikes had been charged by weight, so to save a bit of 'beer money', we were carrying every heavy item in our luggage – the X-ray folks must have had a field day with all our spare parts!

The influence of the USA was still strong in Panama and the good old 'greenback' was the local currency. ATMs and bank tellers alike spouted the then mighty US dollar. It made a nice change not to have to do mental currency conversions for a while. By now all our accounting was done in whatever the local currency was, and dollars. European currencies had been relegated to mere numerals that appeared on our bank and Visa statements.

Expensive taxis tempted us as we staggered out of the terminus with our rucksacks, shoulder bags, leather jackets and helmets. No taxis for us though, the 'overlanders' grapevine' had told us that a local bus did the nine-mile journey round the edge of the airfield to the cargo section. Our next taste of Panama rolled thunderously around the corner of the passenger terminal. It was quite a sight, and made a hell of a noise! This was a mosaic of mirrors, rainbow colours, life-size cartoons of pop stars and a declaration of God's ability to keep all four of this bus's wheels on the ground! We climbed aboard this new world with caution, and the fat, perspiring, bald driver greeted us with a maniacal but friendly smile. "Si, you are on the right bus and 30cents is the fee."

The thunderous work of riotous art on wheels took us around the perimeter with enthusiasm that the designers of American schoolbuses never dreamt of (Panamanian buses all being former US schoolbuses). As we travelled I began to realise what a mish-mash of cultures Panama is. Latin Americans, Caribbeans, Chinese, Japanese and North Americans mix with vibrant individualism. Many Panamanians are multi-lingual and a crowd on the street is always multi-coloured.

Our driver dropped us off within a hundred metres of the cargo customs offices. Work for us began, thankfully, in cool but not overly air-conditioned offices. My sweat evaporated and as Birgit's Spanish was still infinitely better than mine she got stuck straight into the red tape. The officials were friendly, and knew their jobs. The next couple of hours of triplicate form-filling passed quickly but we were both impatient. We still hadn't seen our trusty steeds. Had they arrived intact? Had they even arrived at all?

Our next pleasant surprise was that the hangar we needed to get our bikes from was just next door. The bags didn't feel quite as heavy for this walk. Bags and helmets were tucked out of the way and we were straight out there. We found Birgit's bike with a couple of new souvenir scratches and nothing worse, but my bike leaned crazily to one side. We hurried over, extreme thoughts in our minds. On closer inspection, disaster receded. The centre stand was wrecked – it had obviously been hit by something very hard – perhaps the prong from a forklift truck. But the main frame looked OK so, fingers crossed, no worries.

The rest of the day seemed to pass quickly. First a temporary welding job by a crew who just happened to be on hand, and then the rest of the paperwork. Then, just as we were getting ready to leave, the purple grey sky dropped its load on us with total tropical enthusiasm. Were raindrops this big normal in this part of the world? We decided that enough was enough.

The twenty-mile ride into a city of Panama's size, in rain of this monsoon density, did not make sense. We took the bus. This was a wise choice as it rained all the way and it was rush hour. We discovered that the best vehicle to be in during a Panama City rush hour is a bus. The drivers have loud horns and fearsome reputations. We sat back and enjoyed the chaos.

We were heading for the 'Hotel Central', which had once been the best hotel in Central America but now its former class and elegance could only just still be discerned. Our room, Number One, was on the first floor on the corner at the front. Our double balcony afforded us a view of the fine Plaza Catedral and of the cathedral itself. Our bed was a vintage original and felt like it. The cold bathroom tap worked with reliable enthusiasm and we could find no trace of a cockroach anywhere. We had become quite used to these little beasties over the past year.

We were back out at the airport early the next day. This time with a good night's sleep behind us, no rain and of course, no luggage. The final formalities were quickly completed, a couple of gallons of expensive petrol put in the tanks, starter buttons pushed and... nothing, from either of the bikes. Even though we had disconnected the batteries for the flight, somehow both had drained.

We jump-started Birgit's bike from the cargo forklift. With a cough and a wheeze, Henry purred happily into life. But Libby showed no sign of life until I saw that no fuel was getting through. A tweak of the fuel lines and she purred happily too. We were off. Waves from the welders, unloaders and the office staff sent us on our way. At the airport gates Henry died. Not a spark, not even with a jump from my bike and then, it started to rain.

We entertained the locals with a bike striptease as the large wet drops mingled with our sweat. Half an hour of searching led us to the problem: the ignition points, again. This time the bike fired up but erratically so we set off quickly with fingers crossed that we would at least make it to the dry courtyard of the hotel. The indoor courtyard, once the 'Palm Garden', was now the perfect place to work on the bikes. (If only those walls could talk...)

The Palm Garden was going to be doubly handy because as we rode I realised that I had a problem too. The front brakes were binding. Now this was a real pain and I couldn't see what was wrong.

In front of us we had a strange city, a new local driving style, bullying buses, one bike we didn't want to stop and another whose engine was fast overheating with effort and therefore needed 'cool off' stops. And it was still raining, with the humidity fogging our visors, and we only had one map.

As we rode peering through the steamy air inside our helmets, the day got worse! Old Panama town is a rabbit warren of Spanish and Art Deco-lined one-way streets, and half the road signs are missing. Of course, we got lost. By now my bike was really unhappy and so too was Birgit's.

Then the day got better – a kindly traffic cop closed a road, and let us ride up it the wrong way. We were just a hundred metres away from the Plaza Catedral but just had not been able to work out how to get there, legally.

An old brick served as a ramp up into the courtyard of the Central and we pulled off our bike clothes. These were now soaked on the outside by the rain, and on the inside by our sweat. The Chinese supermarket on the corner sold us litre bottles of Balboa beer. Icy cold, they cooled and hydrated us. Then the day looked much better. We had a second bottle. Welcome to Panama!

The days of working on the bikes and tourist rubbernecking settled us into the world through Panamanian eyes. We visited the parks, museums and markets, and strolled the crowded, exhausting streets. We were impressed by the cheerful, noisy people and filled ourselves with cheap tropical fruits. We got stuck into mangoes, bananas, and weird red spiky-skinned fruits with an unpronounceable name and a decidedly odd flavour. We ate in the local people's restaurants for only a dollar a plate and thoroughly enjoyed being surrounded by tables full of characters. The eating styles perhaps were a little less enjoyable but the atmosphere was great.

Then Christmas arrived. At the end of a last day of desperate shopping, which reminded us of how people do things at home, the party clothes were out. We did our best too, clean and wrinkle-free bike clothes, just the job for a knees-up.

335

The streets filled with excited people hell-bent on having a good time. The lights in the plaza's trees twinkled, and the cathedral steps made a stage for carol singers. Carloads of families unloaded for mass and all that was missing from this Christmas card scene was a light dusting of snow. At midnight the Chinese shops and restaurants finally closed. The streets filled with the loud cracking and snapping of red strings of firecrackers. Our balcony was the perfect place to watch Christmas unfold. The fireworks rapidly filled the darkened, cobbled streets with thick, low-lying smoke. Daytime walls of faded, decaying elegance became Christmas walls of mysterious shadows. Each repeated flash of light was gently diffused and dragged out across the streets in horizontal, glowing carpets. The rain stayed away and the city-sized street party rocked on. Armloads of beer and wine soon had people weaving. The mood was good-humoured.

After Christmas we had two key matters to deal with. My back was still causing a few problems and as we were getting closer to the States we were increasingly conscious that at the rate we were able to travel – short riding days only – we'd either have to risk blasting across the country in the three months allowed, which would go against the grain and would potentially cause disc hassles, or we'd have to accept that we just weren't going to see very much of the country and would perhaps have to ship out of somewhere on the West coast. Neither option suited us.

We'd already found out that if we wanted a US visa for longer than the three months they'd automatically give us at the border, then we should be applying in our home countries. Well, that wasn't going to happen – we needed the passports where we were and in some of the countries it would have been extremely dangerous to be without them.

We decided to go to the US embassy in Panama, armed with all the doctors' certificates, the bike papers, a list of what we'd done so far, and a list of things we wanted to do in the States. We hoped that some kindly official could see that we weren't a risk to the USA and that it'd be a sad thing for us to have to wrap up such an amazing adventure in a mad rush.

336

One of Birgit's dreams was to get up into Alaska. I still kept quiet about that option – even after the months of chill in Patagonia and up in the Andes, I still hadn't physically or mentally acclimatised to the thought of riding in the cold. But it was a joint trip and just as I expected her to flex to fit in with my dreams and ambitions, I expected to do the same for her. Besides, there was something rather classic about making it from toe to tip.

No effort was spared to make ourselves look respectable and off we went to the embassy. Luck was with us. After some very respectful fast-talking and fifty-dollar fees, we were told that there was a chance. We should come back in a couple of days. We'd managed to find the right people on the right days and we'd obviously been doing the right things. We picked up our passports with wonderful visas which would allow us to be in the States for six months at a time; they were multiple-entry too. We couldn't have hoped for more. It was only then that I realised we'd both been mentally holding our breath.

The next hassle was that Birgit's bike still had problems with the points. The BMW workshop in Panama could get hold of spares for her, but they couldn't work out why Henry was eating them at such a rate. If anything, in spite of their very well-meaning efforts, Birgit was far more skilled at getting the settings right – we just had to accept that the bike was going to carry on eating them and that from time to time they'd go wrong at a potentially dangerous moment.

Birgit was both niggled and fatalistic about the situation. It was one of the things that I really liked about her, both as a travel buddy and a partner. She'd do everything she could to make something happen and very rarely ever gave up. But, if there wasn't a solution to a hassle available, and she couldn't make one become available, then she just got on with whatever 'it' was, without a hint of a whinge.

Once we had the spares for Henry, we were free to ride and headed straight for the suspension bridge over the famous Panama Canal. The canal itself had been well worth a visit. We'd been to the canal

337

museum in the city first and then, with our minds full of this amazing feat of engineering, we went to see the real thing. As we watched a container ship being nuzzled through the locks by a tug, I couldn't help thinking about the 'league of nations' of workers that had collected to connect the Pacific with the Caribbean. The route through jungle and malaria swamp, plus the inevitable construction accidents had killed many. Others though, became richer than they could ever have been in their own countries. Many of today's Panamanians owe their genes to these hardworking, long-suffering workers from foreign climes.

In the spring of 1999, control of the canal moved into the hands of the Panamanian government. Could it survive the transition? As far as we could see, it was doing very nicely.

Excellent tarmac took us towards the mountainous backbone of Panama. Cool breezes, coffee plantations and fir forests beckoned us into the heights. This was a welcome change from the noise and dirt of the city. The tap water however was still cold and this time, really cold! We eyed the shower worriedly, and both chickened out. A flannel 'bath' would have to do.

Time marched on amidst the cool and the mountain flowers, and as usual for the seasons, we were late. We needed to get a move on or we would end up hitting the wrong weather in too many places. And we had no idea how the recent hurricane and torrential rains in Honduras were going to affect us. We were only hearing horror stories. One biker told us of his battle to solve the problem of the seven main bridges along the Pan American highway being washed away. One scary crossing had cost $40 to have him and his bike rowed across the half mile of raging torrent. He also told us of devastated villages and a greater degree of lawlessness. It sounded as if the coming month's journey across Central America was going to be a different kind of challenge. I reached for another ice cold Balboa.

Chapter 18

A Hard Day's Night

*'Wake up! If you knew for certain you had a terminal illness – if you had
little time left to live – you would waste precious little of it! Well, I'm telling
you...you do have a terminal illness: It's called birth. You don't have more
than a few years left. No one does! So be happy now, without reason – or you
will never be at all.'*

Dan Millman

After a very easy time in Costa Rica and Nicaragua, we were nervous.
In Costa Rica we'd found a country that had strong connections with

 US culture but which still retained a unique
Latin American way of doing things. The main
roads were in good condition, the border
crossing straightforward, the dirt roads fun and
we'd successfully linked up with friends of Joe
and Sarah (the couple we met on the ferry in
Chile). These friends had lent us their country

'cottage' on the north coast of Costa Rica and we'd spent several days
using this as a base to explore the coastline and the small fishing
villages that are dotted along it. Their cottage was one of the most
unique buildings I'd ever seen. Termites and other wood and fabric-
eating bugs are a real problem for constructions along this jungle
coastline. So John and his wife had built their cottage almost
completely of concrete and steel. Even the bed was a steel
construction that hung on chains from the ceiling!

Nicaragua had fast become a favourite for us – mostly because
just about everything to do with the place was how I'd imagined a poor
Latin American country would be. The history of the country is violent,
but the people were amazing and the landscape so beautiful that we
could easily have spent a couple of months meandering along the dusty
country roads where most of life seemed to be lived in a modern-day
Middle Ages. Our time there was a history lesson and, as if we needed
it, another lesson in the fact that those people who have the least are

often the kindest and most generous. In the little coastal town of San Juan del Sur we were given the opportunity to see a series of the most fantastic sunsets. Their power and vibrancy made me feel both insignificant and awe-inspired.

But one of the most difficult border crossings of our adventure faced us this day. You can imagine how we felt after months of hearing scare stories about the Nicaraguan-Honduras frontier. Corrupt officials, crazy customs procedures, thieves, aggressive soldiers and incredible heat. We'd heard of kids whose idea of fun was to throw carefully bent and twisted nails out into the path of oncoming traffic, 'blow outs' being the name of the game. Ten bonus points for foreign bikers? The recent history of wars in Honduras and Nicaragua hadn't eased our minds either.

I knew that one way or another we would deal with the border crossing. So far we'd always won, and had always been able to talk our way out of paying baksheesh or propino as they call 'palm-grease' in this part of the world. This crossing was going to be a major headache; hard but 'do-able'. But even more worrying were the effects of Hurricane Mitch, one of Central America's worst ever.

Honduras had just been hit big time. In front of us were washed-out roads, rivers with bridges blown away, a water system that didn't work anymore, cholera, a wrecked telephone system and whole cities that had been devastated by the storms. We'd also heard tales of severe lawlessness.

Gangs of people, displaced and desperate, were supposed to be on the move within the country. The more I thought about it, the more I felt a target. On our bikes we were going to be pretty obvious. Nerves tingled...

The day didn't turn out as expected at all. It started with a gentle glowing sunrise and feathered alarm clocks yelling their familiar "'cock-a-doodle-do!" The temperature gently increased as we rode through a still-sleepy world to the border. An early start had seemed a good idea.

The crossing started with mild hassles and lots of laughter on the Nicaraguan side. The officials were helpful and no-one even hinted at a bribe. But the photocopy lady was onto a winner. This kindly lady only charged us six times the going rate for the inevitable series of copies – passport, international driving licence, registration card and importation papers. Talk about monopoly, though a little voice said to me "Good for her, why not?"

We'd collected all the rubber stamps, signatures and photocopies within just one hour after kick off – amazing. We said a sad "goodbye" to Nicaragua, and a worried "hello" to Honduras. The Customs and Immigration offices were of the classic decaying type. Peeling paint, crumbling stone and missing plaster hid a soon-to-be-very-surprised policeman. It did not, however, hide a photocopy machine.

We soon discovered that we would have to go back to Nicaragua to get our next set of copies. The border guard grinned a rather embarrassed smile at me as I trudged past waving my passport and muttering "fotocopia" under my breath. At least this no-man's-land was small; some had been several miles wide. The copy lady greeted me with a big smile and suddenly I was glad that I'd not argued with her over the price of the original set of copies!

This time I got a "Welcome back to Honduras" from the guard and six more rubber stamps from the surprisingly amiable officials. What had all the fuss been about? We supposed that perhaps the difference was that we'd decided to ride as much of Central America as possible away from the Pan American Highway. The idea being that perhaps we'd have a little more 'novelty value' at smaller border crossings and perhaps the officials wouldn't have quite so much ingrained corruption. We also liked the idea of being away from the never-ending rush of big trucks, and we felt that in the smaller towns and villages we'd find people who were not so jaded by the constant flow of long distance travellers. So far, so good.

Birgit bargained with the black market moneychangers for a little 'get us to the first big town' money and for enough to pay our bike tax. Somehow, she always got a good deal. Then it was time for the final rubber stamp. The office was like walking onto the set of a gangster movie. It took a moment or two for our eyes to get accustomed to the gloom and I realised why my senses had been tingling.

There, behind a battered metal desk, sat a weasel-like senior policeman. His 'henchmen' seemed to be pretending to do things in the background, but stopped as our eyes focused. "Trouble brewing", I thought, as a hand reached out for our papers. What happened next happened quickly!

An inky rubber stamp hit our passports and a stern demand for payment came our way – we already knew that none was officially required. Birgit said 'No', picked up the passports, and left the office leaving the four of us looking astonished. She'd said "No" with such determination and in such a tone that brooked no argument, even from hardened gangsters.

I regained my wits first and told the policemen that she really meant it, said "Adios", and spun on my heel – still startled at how rapidly she'd flicked into her 'don't mess with me' mode.

It was hard to keep a relaxed look as we climbed on the bikes, started them and rode out of the compound. Around the first corner we stopped and burst into laughter – the official's weasely face had been a picture! He'd not had time to react at all.

Five miles later, the cops pulled us over and aggression was the name of their game. I'd been told that these guys had no radios, so maybe in this part of Honduras the phone system worked. I sensed a weasel at work. The hassle continued. Polite, firm respect was the name of our game in these situations. Certain that we had collected all the required rubber stamps and photocopies, we could portray an air of confidence too. I kept my fingers crossed behind my back though. Suddenly the ordeal was over and it was our turn to look surprised. We were free to go. I had the feeling that we had just been played with.

The villages of Honduras dozed as the first kilometres rolled under our wheels. The heat was oppressive by now, even in the shade, but on the move we kept reasonably cool. Chickens scurried out from under our wheels and fat porkers gave us little-eyed stares as we rumbled past the terracotta-roofed, adobe-walled houses. Inside these squat little houses, it would be nice and cool. Even the dogs were indoors at this time of the day.

As we rode I was surprised at how good the tarmac roads were. No potholes and there were even cats'-eyes. I'd expected far worse from such a poor country. I began to enjoy the mountain roads' swift looping curves with confidence. No traffic, few people and no loose gravel on the corners. I was also beginning to buzz with a high of relief as the kilometres built between us and the border.

But then, a straight section, and half the road was missing! Totally gone, and no warning sign at all. It was the first example of Mitch's damage. A long, hard, sobering look was called for – in the dark we would have been dead.

The next 24 hours left us silent and sad. Bridge after bridge was gone. Great sections of previously perfect tarmac were perfect no longer. Shanty towns of blue aid-agency plastic sheets squatted along the roadsides and very little water was to be seen anywhere. Farmhouses along riverbanks had crumbled and been washed away, forests of trees lay horizontally, all in the same direction, their roots and branches bare to the sky.

The people looked stunned, sad and exhausted. But they also had an air of toughness about them. They seemed to quietly exude their intention to survive, though their dazed eyes implied horrors I hoped I'd never live to see.

Our personal fears about travel in Honduras were pretty much unfounded. Our route took us to the south where the floodwater had quickly disappeared. The new, mile-wide riverbeds often had no more than a few yards of water in them. Heavy trucks had packed the flood plains' sand and gravel hard, and concrete tubes had been put in place to bridge the harmless-looking waters. Gritty dust in the air was the biggest danger to two-wheeling, and as for crime and violence, the oppressive heat and stunned after-shock seemed to have dulled the desire.

Even so, I was glad that having the bikes meant no standing around in bus stations, and no carrying a backpack through a town's dodgy area in search of a hotel. We rode on into El Salvador, very much aware of our wealth and our freedom. We did not feel the need to see and intrude on more of Honduras's pain. I felt like an unwelcome intruder – no country on the trip had made me feel this way before.

An athletic policeman greeted us as we climbed wearily from our bikes at the border. He was dressed in a rather sinister black jumpsuit held in place by webbing and leather straps. He grinned and welcomed us to El Salvador. "Is there any way I can help you?" he asked.

Now this was new. I liked this guy and was sure that he really did only want to help us. Propino? Nah, not with this policeman. We went with the flow, and thanks to Santos, flow it did, from one office to the next to the next. Like all border crossings though, there was a bit of 'hurry up and wait'.

We waited in the shade of the modern concrete buildings. Around us giant White, International and Mack trucks roared their engines. Out in the heat, life was happening at a fast pace. Helpers scurried, vendors hawked, donkeys brayed and the dealers were making deals. Inside, papers were being waved at customs officials who typed furiously, with two smoking fingers. Ancient fans struggled to push hot sticky air from one hotspot to the next.

While we waited, Santos and I got talking – twenty words of English from him, a few more of Spanish from me, and a whole load of sign language from both of us.

"Do you like music?" he asked. "Yes" "What sort of music – do you know any songs?" I'd made a mistake, when I'd answered yes. His face had lit up. "Sing me a song Sam." "Ah, er, um, Ok…Why not?" I replied feeling that actually I had no choice at all. So, there I was, in the middle of organised chaos, singing. I'd never done that at a border before! Soloist and black-suited audience rocked. The audience grew larger, and I can't sing!! Birgit stood to one side with an, 'I'm not with him' expression on her face. Very wise, but I still think that it was my best ever rendition of The Beatles' *A Hard Day's Night.*

The first kilometres of this new country were a lacework of potholes. The old road to San Miguel looked more direct and potentially more interesting so we hung a left. The bikes' suspensions worked hard on a quilt of many generations of asphalt patches, and I found myself wondering if gravel roads would be easier on the spine and the bikes. The countryside was dry and thorny. Black roads and blackened tree trunks stood silhouetted against the faded yellow scrubland. Worn out, rusty pickup trucks loaded with ripe, bright green watermelons were parked in pools of shade. Mangy dogs slunk, heads down, from dark corner to dark corner and I began to feel an air of despair.

They say that there are more people from El Salvador in the USA than from any other Central American country. They also told us that there are few families that do not have a relative in a Latino gang in the States. There were few signs of wealth, but lots of signs of a hard life. The tools were basic, the cars very old, the roads were poor, the buildings were battered and poorly constructed, and all around us were the leftover signs of yet another recent war.

We saw few smiles and a lot of suspicion towards the two gringos on their foreign motorcycles. In other countries, curiosity had been the cause of most of the stares. We'd enjoyed that because curiosity had often been the start of a conversation and usually a fun experience. Here, it seemed not!

Perhaps my discomfort was a leftover feeling from Honduras, but Birgit said that it was just because my ponytail kept attracting wolf whistles! There were more than a few very surprised male faces that changed from lust to horror when I'd turned round and they'd realized that they'd just whistled at a bearded man!

San Miguel is a city of extremes. On one side there's a small section of extremely wealthy housing, complete with security guards, and on the other, a large section of considerable poverty. I could feel an undercurrent of something I couldn't put my finger on, but whatever it was it felt dangerous.

Guatemala was calling. We had both heard and read many wonderful things about it. We were keen to put Honduras and now El Salvador behind us, so headed for yet another border crossing. It hadn't been all bad in El Salvador but we were glad to move on.

The border was fast, easy and once again, friendly. I breathed a large sigh of relief as we rode the first peaceful miles. But before exploring much of Guatemala, we planned a quick visit back into Honduras.

By riding a little north we could get to a dirt road that would take us around the top of El Salvador to a section of Guatemala's border with Honduras. A mountain range and a forest stopped us going a more direct route.

The dirt road was fun after all the tarmac of the past weeks – there was enough gravel and sand to make the adrenaline pop. We sped along leaving cones of dust swirling behind us. Dust that would add itself to the beige layers already coating the roadside trees and bushes. Once again we were glad of decent dual-purpose, trail tyres. We slowed for the few villages, partly so as to leave no dust but also so that we could 'rubberneck' as all good travellers should.

The village women dressed simply and practically in thick, dark skirts topped with brilliant white blouses – their only splashes of colour were the age-old designs of red embroidered flowers. The men wore jeans however, and to my surprise, most had cream-coloured cowboy hats.

Late in the day we pulled into the small town of Jocotan, where we found the rather grim looking Pension Sagastume. Inside, there were simple rooms, a pretty flower-filled courtyard, safe parking for the bikes and a nice cooling shower. The shabby exterior belied the cosiness inside. No more was needed to top off our day than a good feed of tortillas and spicy hot stew at the corner 'café'. Plus a tall cool Gallo beer of course.

The next day we left the bikes locked up in the courtyard under the watchful eye of the hotel owner. Though a powerful-looking woman whom you wouldn't want to mess with, she still had smile lines etched around her eyes, and those eyes held a kindly twinkle. Hers was one of those faces that you just trust; the sort of face that doesn't allow any element of doubt.

The Mayan ruins of Copan were just over the border into Honduras and they had long been on our 'must see' list. The local bus ride to the border was going to be an adventure, goats, chickens, dust and all, and the border itself was going to be quicker, easier and cheaper without the bikes.

The ruins are impressive to say the least. Not long 'discovered', they are still being excavated by archaeologists. A whole city stood here, but once the reign of the Mayans declined the jungle took back its territory. Giant trees worked their roots in, around and over the buildings, causing as much damage as humans caused in their more recent searches for building materials – many of the houses in the nearby village had been made with stone salvaged from the ruins.

The real treasures were discovered deep under the ruined upper buildings. Flat-topped pyramid temples were built on top of previous flat-topped pyramid temples, each new layer a testament to the powers of a new ruler. Each layer also formed a light-proof shroud to the older temple beneath.

To the archaeologists' delight, this dark world had kept much of the original colouring of the buildings intact. In the museum, a whole room is given over to a life-sized replica of what they found. I'd had no idea that these grey rocks, so carefully carved and stacked, had once been painted red, green, yellow and white. A whole city with buildings like these must have been a magnificent sight. I sat on the steps and stared out over the exposed part of the city, and tried to imagine the scenes of hundreds of years ago.

Three days later we said thanks and goodbye to Señora 'Formidable' and headed for the old colonial town of Antigua. It was a longer ride for us, which of course started with the fun of the dirt road. The main road was the busiest we'd been on since Costa Rica but the traffic was very well behaved. To our surprise, the trucks all seemed to be travelling in convoy, with armed guards – heavily armed that is. Later, locals told us that banditry in Guatemala is common. We decided not to ride anywhere near these convoys if it could be helped.

All roads lead to Guatemala City and our route was one of them. With no choice, we soon found ourselves in fast-moving madness. Multi-laned roads were packed with traffic of every

347

description, all of which seemed to be belching black clouds of fumes. My skin soon felt greasy and my eyes began to itch. I hate to think what it was doing to my lungs!

The last section was slow, stop-and-go stuff as we battled our way out of the sprawling suburbs. The combination of crawling in the heat, the higher altitude and low octane fuel soon had my bike pinking again. I hated this sound. Then we were free and were being guided by clearly marked signs onto a long, swooping road which dropped us down from Guatemala City's mantle of mountains into the cobbled streets of Antigua.

Thick-walled houses and shops were roofed with the distinctive Spanish-style terracotta tiles. The walls themselves were painted with pastels of blue, pink, yellow and green, but they were not important to us at that moment. The light was going and not only did we have to find our way through the one way system, but we were also dodging pedestrians and fighting with the effects of the cobblestones. "Give me a dirt road any day" I was thinking, as yet again my front wheel abruptly turned where I didn't want it to go. I was just glad that it wasn't raining!

We found a single storey, court-yarded hostal with a manager called Norma, a little Indian lady who was a gem of good fun and laughter. She had a wild sense of humour and, it turned out later, was a 'wannabe' biker!

Hotel Ruis Dos became our base for two weeks of two-wheeled exploring. The surrounding volcanic mountains were packed with little villages, native Indians and beautiful scenery. This was just what we'd hoped to find. When we'd realized that Norma had a passion for big bikes we lent her Birgit's leather jacket and took pictures of her sitting on Libby – the shots had to be on the biggest bike, of course!

One day, when Birgit was working on her points again, and I was washing clothes, Norma commented to Birgit that we had a very strange way of doing things.

"In Guatemala we do things the right way. The men work on the engines and the women do the washing!" She said. The next day, with

Birgit still working on Henry and me cooking dinner, Norma asked Birgit if she'd like to swap husbands!

This was the right time to be in Antigua. Easter was coming and the weekends in the run-up to it are rich with pageantry. Parades wind their way brightly through the streets. Children's costumes compete for attention with the waving banners. Rose petals are strewn along the way and candles are lit.

Serious faces, proud faces and faces lined with the effort of manhandling the heavy displays, stare back at the crowds. But the town wasn't just a long soak in history and pageantry. It's also one of the few bikers' crossroads in Central America. That should be no surprise with so many good places to stay, its great location, good food and a bike shop that knows what it's doing. Plus, Guatemala City had the cheapest bike tyres between the States and the duty-free port of Iquique in Chile. Word gets around.

We met bikers from Canada, Germany, Israel, the USA and Mexico there. Kawasaki KLRs, Yamaha Ténérés, Suzuki DRs and BMW Boxers like ours were the most popular bikes. Stories, hints, tips and warnings were swapped. Gallo beer was consumed, joint meals were cooked, and Antigua became another of those hard places to leave. But leave we had to.

The fabled beauty of Lake Atitlan and its surrounding villages was on our list. So too were the high mountain towns of Chichicastenango and Chiche, the local markets being the main draw up there. Everything from facemasks to pig's feet, from roofing to tomatoes, from hand-woven blankets to baskets of flowers. This had to be the best of Guatemala's colour riots!

The Indian's traditional clothes, still worn every day with pride, added to the riot. But would you put orange, cerise, red, pea-green and turquoise together, let alone in a wild mixture of stripes, circles and dots? The longer you stay the more you begin to distinguish between the patterns. The inhabitants of each town and village had their own colours and designs. A market day mob is an assault on the eyeballs, but when you see a large group from the same village, it all comes together. These folks were, for me, the most colourful in Central America, and not only in costume. I even splashed out on a pair of the most riotous Indian trousers I could find. Great for the pub back home! (Birgit always wears her 'I'm not with him' face!)

We were also in the mountains for the roads. Humpy-bumpy tarmac and dirt tracks take you through a mountain maze. Our guidebook warned that some were 'a bit rough'. OK with us, but we checked it out with the locals first. There are few signposts on the high roads so you have to keep asking the way. Not always easy as many of the locals don't speak Spanish let alone English or German.

In places it looked as if it had been many years since wheeled traffic had passed that way, but the tracks were still good enough for us so we explored more, enjoying the scenery, the villages, and the cool clean air.

One day a track abruptly turned into washboard on the flat and deep gullies on the slopes. Not so much fun and once or twice, as we were two up, Birgit got off to walk a few dodgy yards. Then I managed to wedge the bike in the bottom of a rain gully four feet deep. An instant of hesitation at the wrong moment literally dropped us in it. Smart move Sam! It took an hour of digging and sweating to get the 245 kilo R80GS out of this hole in the road, a long way from any help. Slow job, digging with a tyre iron…

It was time to head for Mexico. Summer was starting there. We wound our way through the cool shade of strongly-scented Eucalyptus trees and headed for a new continent. In front of us lay the start of North America; and our 'to do' list included Mayan and Aztec ruins, blue mountains, deserts, and jungles a hundred shades of green. We'd heard tales of turquoise waterfalls and knew that there would be white sandy beaches to enjoy. We hoped to link up with Mexican cousins that I'd not seen since I was a child, and then we had all the amazing landscapes and customs of the United States and Canada to explore.

Sitting on our bikes, the sounds of the wind in our helmets and the ticking of our engines were a constant reminder that we were moving through the world, not the dream-like state of the world floating past us. Our exposure to life from the backs of our trusty bikes was full. 'Out there' in the middle of life, we felt the temperature changes of altitude and shade, and we experienced the exotic scents and not-so-charming smells as we passed farms, flower-filled fields and steamy forests.

One type of adventure was just drawing to a close, but in front of us, a new adventure was ready to begin, waiting for the chance to unfold.

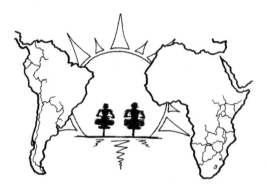

'The perfect journey is never finished; the goal is always just across the next river, round the shoulder of the next mountain. There is always one more track to follow, one more mirage to explore.'

Rosita Forbes

A 3D Jigsaw Puzzle?

'He who would travel happily must travel light.'

St. Exupéry

I'm often asked, "Which is the best bike to go travelling on and what spares, documentation and kit should be used?" My answer is to guide people in the direction of the experts. Chris Scott has written invaluable books such as the Adventure Motorcycle Handbook, and the guys at Horizons Unlimited have built their amazing website and produced DVDs that are packed with 'how to' information. To  date, my books have never had enough space to address these questions with any level of quality or in any depth, so I haven't attempted to do so. But I do have a few thoughts on the subject.

As mentioned in the introduction, my round-the-world travelling was done before the internet became ubiquitous, and before GPS, mobile phones, PDAs (Personal Digital Assistants) and miniature lap-top computers were affordably available. Should you take them? In the end, it all depends on how you want your adventure to be, how much you want to spend and how much you want to carry. I like to be out of contact as much as possible. The Paul Theroux quote on the rear cover of *Distant Suns* says it all for me.

What bike? Actually, just about any bike will do. Quite simply, if it has two wheels, an engine and is reliable, then you can overland on it. You just have to decide what sort of trip you want to do. If your bike is prepared properly then the chances are that nothing major will go wrong.

I chose the BMW because it was designed with off road use in mind, had good ground clearance, simple maintenance and a reputation for reliability. It performed really well and dealt perfectly with every riding condition except very soft sand and very deep mud. The bike was comfortable and the riding position suited my height (6' 1") very well. For 95% of the journey I couldn't have wished for a better bike. Actually, my choice was much influenced by two blokes in the pub when I'd just

352

announced my decision to go adventuring on a bike. Their advice was, 'Go for the R80GS – it's bullet-proof, and idiot-proof!' As I write this, Libby is still my only means of transport, so they were right.

It does make sense to ensure that your bike is in tip top condition before you go, and you should look at basic things such as how good the suspension on your bike is. Will it stand up to weeks of being rattled across corrugations? Are your tyres up for the type of journey you have planned? Dual-purpose trail tyres with a deep tread pattern work well for general overlanding use, though a set of road-legal knobblies can make your ride safer and more fun in trickier going, at the expense of a much shorter life. I prefer to use inner tubes in my tyres as you can inflate them yourself if they come off the rim, which is not usually the case with tubeless tyres. However, provided the tyre bead remains in contact with the rim, small punctures can be mended much more quickly and easily in a tubeless tyre using a BMW-type tubeless repair kit. I carry heavy duty, motocross inner tubes and find that they last really well. Add a couple of large extra patches from a truck puncture kit to your repair kit.

What spares should you carry? The rule for me now is, carry the real basics such as electrical components, filters, and spare cables, and a few of the most important gaskets. Most of the rest of the kit you may need you can get sent out to you if you get stuck, or you can bodge with cable ties, duct tape and silicone. Being innovative is part of the fun isn't it?

I took a voltmeter, full size tyre levers, a torque wrench, and a very small set of jump leads – I don't have a kick-start. I'm not keen on pencil air pressure gauges, they get blocked up with grit and then become unreliable. My gauge gets used a lot as I change my tyre pressures according to terrain. When riding on soft sand or mud, let approx. 50% of the air out of your tyres, for example from 2 bar to 1 bar (30psi to 15psi). This spreads the tyre over a greater road surface area, which gives you a lot more grip. In some deep sand conditions 50% isn't really enough but unless you have tyre clamps (rim-locks) fitted to your rims then you run the risk of tyre slip. This will eventually rip out the valves. Try to time your journeys for the earlier hours of the day. In the desert the low light makes an amazing difference to what you can see of surface texture changes. The sand is also firmer then as overnight dew holds the sand grains together. Besides that, an early start means an early finish and time to explore before dark.

Also look at your fuel range. I think that normally a five hundred kilometre range is more than enough. You can always increase that locally with additional fuel bottles if needed. There is always a big debate about whether to use hard or soft luggage. I prefer aluminium panniers because they suit my style of travelling in just about every way, and they survive the 'two uses' rule. Everything you take should have at least two uses! One of my favourite bits of kit was my sheepskin saddle cover. It was softer and cooler to sit on, and because the surface is never completely smooth it gives your backside a good massage as you ride. Stuff it up the front of your jacket in winter for added warmth, and there you have won the two uses argument, twice. Air seats are also well worth considering – they make great pillows too!

Looking after yourself is just as important as looking after your bike and kit. The keys are sleep well, eat well, drink enough and stay clean. So, get yourself a tent that is big enough to be a comfortable home, but small and light enough to fit on the bike easily. We use a three-person dome tent with two entrances, a porch and mosquito netting on both doors. Do use a groundsheet – there are a lot of thorns and sharp stones out there. Besides that, there are ants which will eat through an ordinary tent ground sheet. I use a thick clear plastic sheet with the idea that if I ever get stuck in the desert, then I can use it to make a solar still to get water. Half a dozen six-inch nails are a good addition to your tent kit. In many places the ground is so hard that ordinary tent pegs just bend. There's a lot of altitude in this world of ours and if you get your planning wrong or life gets in the way, you can end up camping is some very chilly weather. And even the hottest deserts are often freezing at night – literally. I now use a 3-4 season bag with a silk liner. This perfect when it's too hot for the bag, adds warmth when the bag isn't enough and it's much easier to wash regularly than your bag. Not being a macho man, I need a comfortable night's sleep. I use a 3/4 length self-inflating mat. It's very comfortable to lie on, it's light and it packs up very small.

A good cooker improves your quality of life and your flexibility. It also saves you money. I use a petrol stove, that way you always have fuel 'on tap' as it were.

In the desert you'll need to carry at least 10 litres of water but elsewhere, with care, water of sorts can always be found. Mostly I carried five litres and used local plastic bottles when extra was needed. I gave or traded them away when I no longer wanted them. One thing to remember is that you should make a point of drinking, even when you are not thirsty. A nice trick to get a cold drink when you need one is to fix a bottle covered in sacking to one of the front surfaces of your bike. Put a very small hole in the neck of the bottle. As you ride, small quantities of water dribble through the hole, onto the sacking and then the water is whipped away in your slipstream. Result – cold water.

Still on the subject of staying healthy, I carried a mini hospital – far too much! You should talk to your GP. At least take something for diarrhoea, major pain, paracetamol, antiseptic (dry spray is very good), plasters, a crêpe bandage, sterile dressings, a suture needle and thread, talcum powder (feet and your crotch can cause a lot of grief), small container of fungal cream (Canesten), multi-vitamins, anti-malarials, and anti-histamine for insect bites. Don't forget to take along a sufficient supply of any medication you may personally need. Make sure it is in a properly labelled container (stuffed with cotton wool to stop vibration problems). It's also a good idea to take a prescription for this medication so that you don't have problems with customs at any of the borders.

An insect repellent with a large percentage of 'Deet' should do the trick (but don't spill any on your plastic gear, it'll damage it). The golden rule is to cover up at dusk and in the early hours.

I think that a decent travel insurance policy is vital, but hunt carefully, many companies list biking as being a dangerous sport and won't cover you for a long trip. Odd really…

Your national motoring organisation, such as the RAC in the UK, can do your carnet for you. It has been known for travellers to make the length of Africa without the use of a carnet but to do it now would involve considerable hassle and bribery. Quite simply, it's just not worth being without these temporary importation documents. It's also imperative that the forms are filled out correctly, going in and going out. However, at time of writing it is possible to travel through most countries in South and Central America without a carnet.

Make sure you have a set of photocopies of all of your documents at home and another set with you. Getting hold of new documents is always faster if you have copies and if you lose something, then you at least have some proof that will normally keep you travelling. At several borders you are required to hand sets over. It's one less hassle in a potentially fraught situation. The other thing to have is a set of passport photos. You'll need these for visa applications and at some borders.

Nowadays, if you have a yahoo email account it's also worth scanning colour versions of your documents and then saving them as an attachment to a draft in your email. You can then access these or forward them on if that is needed.

I use two cameras - a small 'point and shoot' with a flash, and an SLR. I use a 28-80 and a 210 zoom lens. Take along a polarising filter and a skylight filter for each. There's often haze, dust or heat distortion in the sky and these filters not only help protect your lenses, but they cut out a lot of refracted light distortion too. A lens dust brush helps a lot. Your camera bag should be really over padded, and have the ability to keep water and dust out. If you plan to spend time in damp humid conditions, put some silica gel sachets in your bag.

As for clothes, I try to go for safety and comfort on the bike, plus the minimum for the rest of the time. The balance that's hard is trying to get your selection right for all temperatures and conditions. Things that hand wash and dry easily are ideal. Cotton is the best natural material for both durability and health. Many man-made materials do not deal with sweat well but you'll find that specialist retailers can help you with some very 'trick' fast drying non-cotton clothing. Remember, the more skin you expose the faster you will dehydrate. Bear that in mind in particular when you are riding.

Tough canvas/denim jeans, with removable kneepads and plenty of pockets work well both on and off the bike. Alternatives include jeans lined with Kevlar, or fabric and leather trousers with removable knee and hip armour.

I started with an open face helmet but now use a full face with a flip-up front. You have more protection, and they are in fact cooler as they keep direct heat away. The flip-up front makes asking directions and making friends much easier. White is an excellent colour as it reflects the worst of the heat and makes you more visible. Custom made earplugs are a good idea to protect your hearing on long open road days, but also there are some pretty noisy campsites and hotels. In Islamic countries, the call to prayer is a very early wake up call at 4 am.

Other than that, take a baseball cap (keeping the sun off your head, and your face in the shade can help you stay well, and deal with a day's hassles), and flip-flops (for general wandering and for use in showers and toilets). If you've been sitting with your feet inside hot boots all day it's important to let your feet 'breathe' and at the same time let your boots dry out.

One of the beauties of overlanding is that every bike you meet is loaded and kitted-out in its own individual way. There isn't a 'right' way. You can do it your way according to your own priorities, but in the end common sense rules the day. One of the biggest pre-trip tips is to decide what sort of journey you actually want to make. A personal Paris-Dakar? The idea of trying to go where no biker has ever been before? Or an open, 'see what happens' adventure? You'll need to choose your kit accordingly.

Whatever you do, keep your total weight to a minimum, keep what you do carry as low as possible and make sure that your packing is balanced. A low, even, centre of gravity helps you stay upright. A thought to have in your mind when you are planning your trip is that if you aren't sure that you are going to use it then you probably don't need it. Loading your bike is far more fun than a Rubik's cube. It's an ever-changing 3D jigsaw puzzle!

A final thought. The way you mentally load yourself is just as important as how you deal with your kit and your preparation. Life on the road is full of high points; why else would anybody do it, and keep going back for more? But there are low points where you find parts of yourself, strengths and weaknesses you never knew existed. Paul R. Pratt, the highly experienced motorcycle overlander, said 'The right state of mind allows you to take one thing at a time and cross every bridge when you come to it.' The travellers that seem to enjoy their journeys the most, are the ones who have time, keep an open mind and stay positive whatever they are faced with. The famous round-the-worlder and journalist Ted Simon says 'The interruptions are the journey'.

With each adventure, you can make a set of memories worth having. There's always something good going on, whatever the situation.

Sam's fourth book Tortillas to Totems takes you riding onwards from the Guatemala / Mexico border. The journey takes you on an at times challenging ride across three amazingly different and diverse countries. Mexico, the USA and Canada.

'Any good travel book must involve the reader as well as inspire and Tortillas to Totems does just that with vivid descriptions of the roads, places and people that Sam and his partner Birgit travelled and met. By the end of the book I was definitely itching to get out on the road on an adventure like this — in my opinion, the best compliment one can pay to a story like this. Sam goes way beyond 'we went here and did this...' The Rider's Digest

'Globe-trotting biker Manicom's a natural storyteller. Although this trip may sound like a standard ride through familiar country, be assured, it isn't.' Adventure Bike Rider

'Tortillas to Totems is the story of another epic journey covering the length and breadth of North America. You could be his pillion, so well does he describe the sounds, sights and smells of the road. If you like bikes, riding and people watching, Sam is your man.' Daily Record

ISBN 978-0-9556573-3-7

Sam Manicom's adventure travel books:

You are taken through Africa in a sometimes traumatic but always attention grabbing journey. Once you pick Into Africa up, you won't want to put it down!

'*This is a great adventure and a really enjoyable read.*'
Johnnie Walker – 'BBC Radio Two'
'*The word-pictures that bring a good travel book to life are all here; Sam's perceptions of people, places and predicaments have real depth and texture, their associated sights, smells and sounds are evoked with a natural ease.*'
The Road Magazine
'*Sam has an obvious sensitivity to his surroundings and the people he meets. His joy at simply being out on the road comes through strongly on almost every page.*'
'Motorcycle Sport and Leisure'
'*...you are left with a solid understanding of Sam's experiences thanks to the descriptions of sight, smell, sound and taste, along with an easy narrative of the authors thought provoking questions and learning experiences, making Into Africa a truly excellent read.*' Bikersweb.co.uk

Three years of eye-opening adventures under the skies of Australasia, South East Asia, India and the Middle East.

Under Asian Skies has been called the best overlanding book since 'One Man Caravan'.

'*...a unique and wonderful adventure.*'
Ted Simon
'*...the thing I most enjoyed about this book was the feeling that I was there with him as he went through everything.*'
London Bikers.com
'*What sets this book apart is the detail in the narrative... It's the positive human relationships that make this story, from simple welcomes along the road to meeting life long friends...*'
The Riders Digest
'*While his first book 'Into Africa' was detailed I felt his confidence shine through even more with this second effort.*'
DieselBike.net
'*...a great read.*'
TBM Trail Bike Magazine
'*Accessible and well written, this will prod anyone with a bike license to take off and do something amazing.*'
'Adventure Travel Magazine

ISBN 978-0-9556573-1-3   **ISBN 978-0-9556573-0-6**

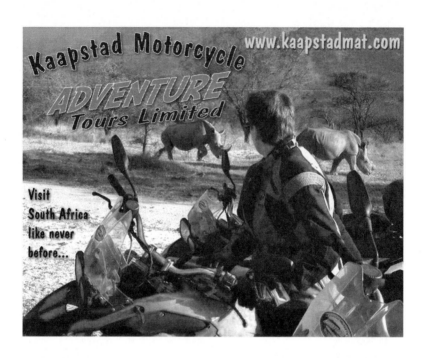

361

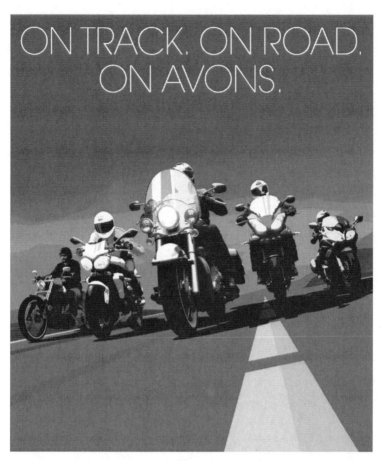

ON TRACK. ON ROAD. ON AVONS.

Winding coastal roads leading to open blue sea vistas. Snow capped mountains rising above oceans of evergreens. Imperious fairytale castles silhouetted against dazzling azure skies. Let the world be your backdrop and the open road your stage. And let Avon performance tyres race with your imagination and take you where you want to go. Avon. The great British tyre that's taking on the world.

Traveldri-Plus
Quality Kit For Serious Fun!

SEALSKINZ
ENDURANCE ACCESSORIES

ORTLIEB WATERPROOF

EXPED

EXPEDITION
EQUIPMENT

ROK straps

Expedition
Kit

PERFORMANCE LAYERING

www.traveldriplus.com
01409 241996